Praise for
HOMECOMING

Named one of the best books of the year by *Kirkus Reviews*

"Fascinating . . . Powerful . . . [A] valuable [contribution] to the understanding of the trends toward regionalization."

    —*Foreign Affairs*

"[Rana] Foroohar's work here is equal parts journalism and visioning, offering a host of case studies of how we might produce and consume differently while simultaneously painting a picture of a more resilient and rooted economy. . . . As [*Homecoming*] spells out in vivid detail, we have our work cut out for us to bring the economy home."

    —*The American Prospect*

"Foroohar has consistently been right on globalization. *Homecoming* explains how local manufacturing is becoming a solution for many communities around the world. The detailed reporting and interviews make for eye-opening and gripping reading."

    —Joseph E. Stiglitz, Nobel Prize laureate in economics

"The way we eat impacts everything in our world, and *Homecoming* is a thorough examination of not just the dire consequences but also the many hopeful possibilities contained in that simple truth."

    —Alice Waters, *New York Times* bestselling author of
    Coming to My Senses

"By asking the fundamental questions of *what matters* and *who matters,* this book comes with some conditioned optimism about the future: Global cooperation is possible (and needed), but can yield positive social outcomes only if built on sound economic thinking that values community, sustainability, and equity. The road to this new form of capitalism is paved with books like *Homecoming*."

—Mariana Mazzucato, author of *Mission Economy*

"In this fascinating book, Rana Foroohar argues that the retreat from hyperglobalization is a fact—and a welcome one at that. *Homecoming* will change how you think of the world to come."

—Dani Rodrik, author of *The Globalization Paradox*

"Foroohar walks us through the fiasco of four decades of devotion to neoliberal economic theory that emerged from the collapse of the Bretton Woods system, leading to the inevitable global and internal imbalances we see today. *Homecoming* offers a truly comprehensive and vivid discussion of the aftermath and what we need to do to belatedly address these errors."

—Daniel Alpert, author of *The Age of Oversupply*

"Rana Foroohar understands what went wrong with America and how to make it right. In *Homecoming* she weaves it all together to show how to build a safer, cleaner, and more peaceful world. A visionary blueprint for a future that works for all of us."

—Barry C. Lynn, author of *Liberty from All Masters*

"In this deeply reported book, Foroohar offers a mix of lively on-the-ground tales and stimulating macroanalysis to explain how globalization and localization are changing business, finance, and our wider society. . . . A must-read."

—Gillian Tett, *New York Times* bestselling author of *Anthro-Vision*

BY RANA FOROOHAR

HOMECOMING

HOMECOMING

The Path to Prosperity
in a Post-Global World

RANA FOROOHAR

CROWN
NEW YORK

2023 Crown Trade Paperback Edition

Copyright © 2022 by Rana Foroohar

All rights reserved.

Published in the United States by Crown, an imprint of the Crown Publishing Group,
a division of Penguin Random House LLC, New York.

CROWN and the Crown colophon are registered trademarks of
Penguin Random House LLC.

Originally published in hardcover in the United States by Crown,
an imprint of the Crown Publishing Group, a division of
Penguin Random House LLC, in 2022.

Library of Congress Cataloging-in-Publication Data
Names: Foroohar, Rana, author.
Title: Homecoming / Rana Foroohar.
Description: First edition. | New York : Crown, [2022] |
Includes bibliographical references and index.
Identifiers: LCCN 2022016180 (print) | LCCN 2022016181 (ebook) |
ISBN 9780593240557 (trade paperback) | ISBN 9780593240540 (ebook)
Subjects: LCSH: Industrial location. | Regionalism. | Nationalism.
Classification: LCC HC79.D5 F67 2022 (print) | LCC HC79.D5 (ebook) |
DDC 338.6/042—dc23/eng/20220414
LC record available at https://lccn.loc.gov/2022016180
LC ebook record available at https://lccn.loc.gov/2022016181

Printed in the United States of America on acid-free paper

crownpublishing.com

2 4 6 8 9 7 5 3 1

Book design by Victoria Wong

For my family

Contents

Author's Note

Economists like to think reality can be captured in mathematical formulas. They plug in numbers about all sorts of complicated things—how we work, what we spend, where we live, when we may die—creating complex models to simulate our world. They then crank the algorithmic engine on these models, and out comes the data that in turn shapes the policies that govern our country, our communities, and ultimately, our lives.

But economics is not a pure science, like physics. It's far more like biology, or sociology, or even anthropology—a messy, complex, all-too-human attempt to make sense of the world around us. It's a world that is ever changing and far from rational.

Since the 2008 financial crisis and, more recently, the Covid-19 pandemic, it has become quite clear that the "invisible hand" that is supposed to guide our markets and our economy as a whole toward a happy and healthy equilibrium isn't always right. We live in the real world—a world of human bias, politics, and institutions that don't always work the way the models say they should. This is the world in which I have spent thirty years reporting as a business journalist.

Reporters, like most people, know that economic "rationality" very often doesn't translate in quite the way experts expect it to. I will never forget, for example, a conversation I had years ago with a labor leader living the harsh on-the-ground reality of America's previous two decades of trade policy. It brought home to me the risks involved when policy makers, while making decisions, think more about math than people.

This aha moment occurred while I was interviewing the late AFL-CIO president Richard Trumka for my first book, *Makers and Takers,* which examines why there is such a glaring divide between the fortunes of Main Street and those of Wall Street. I was interested in learning more about why politicians and business leaders alike, most of whom I knew to be decent, thoughtful people, had made so many decisions that seem to have boosted short-term profits at the expense of longer-term economic well-being. In an economy like the United States', 70 percent of which is based on consumer spending, stagnant wages had to be more important than cheap televisions. So, why were we setting policies that prioritized the latter? How and when had economic globalization, rather than national economic resiliency, become the guiding force in both policy and business?

Trumka shared with me a conversation he had had during the nineties, with a Clinton administration economic policy maker, about the potential fallout of the North American Free Trade Agreement (NAFTA), which the United States was about to cut with Mexico and Canada, and the impact that China might have on the global trading system if it became a member of the World Trade Organization (which it did in 2001). He was concerned about a sudden flood of cheap labor into the global marketplace and the effect this would have on American workers' incomes and lives. "I told [the official] that the deals would kill us, and he agreed," Trumka said. "But he said that, after a while, wages would start to go up again, and things would even out around the world." When Trumka asked the official how long this process of "leveling out" might take, he answered, "About three to five generations."

That's a century in the lives of the communities and the people in question. Is it any wonder, then, that the average American worker is skeptical of technocratic elites from both parties who see people not as human beings, but as mathematical inputs on a spreadsheet? Is it a surprise that we've had, for the last decade or so, the most polarized political environment in the history of the United States? Or an attempted coup in our capital? Or an opioid crisis and an epidemic of "deaths of despair" among people who feel forgotten by the powers that be? Or a generation of young Millennials, now making up the largest voting and working bloc in the country, who are increasingly disenchanted with both capitalism and liberal democracy and inclined to side with more extreme political elements within either party? Or a population at large that feels that globalization itself has failed—a 2019 Pew Research Center study found that many people in the United States and the United Kingdom had negative feelings about it, associating it with loss, longing, and a feeling of being "left behind" or "swept up."[1] It's not just feelings but metrics that tell us that, by some key measures, globalization has failed.

While globalization has made the planet wealthier as a whole, that wealth has been concentrated largely at the very top, among financial and managerial elites who own the most assets, and to a certain extent at the very bottom; wages grew in developing countries, particularly China. *Within* most countries, however, inequality has also grown. Huge areas in many nations, rich and poor, have been hollowed out economically, or environmentally degraded, or left behind politically by globalization. The reaction has been widespread populism, nationalism, and the rise of autocracy in many parts of the world, an indicator that something in the system desperately needs tweaking.

One key part of the problem has been the mainstream economics taught in universities and business schools over the past forty years. It is what supported the "just-in-time" business culture in which redundancy in supply chains was considered a waste of time and money and in which the free flow of capital, goods, and labor across borders to create more economic growth was always considered a good thing, despite any inequality or financial fragility it might create. The idea that there might be human costs to efficiency or that these costs might come with their own snowball cycle of political or economic risks was simply not considered.

Covid-19, of course, ripped the scales from our eyes with regard to such assumptions. Suddenly, it mattered that we sourced the majority of our cheap medical masks or key pharmaceutical ingredients from our biggest geopolitical adversary, China. It mattered that we lived in a country with a bifurcated healthcare system and spotty broadband coverage. It mattered that our economy was built on debt and asset bubbles rather than on income growth from good jobs.

The pandemic and its aftermath have also driven home an important message that policy makers are finally beginning to heed. If we are to solve the world's biggest problems (from pandemics and climate change to the inequities of globalization), then economists must stop tweaking the edges of their models and, instead, think outside the box. Our elected officials and business leaders, too, must begin to think in far more nuanced terms about what, exactly, constitutes economic well-being—not just at a global level, but at a local one, too.

A New Equilibrium

Any economy regularly goes through cycles of expansion and contraction, boom and bust. But the most important of these cycles has little to do with market prices or unemployment rates. It's about a fundamental sense of economic well-being, and that is far less a matter of short-term data than of an underlying political philosophy, one that addresses the three core questions all societies must face. *What* matters? *Who* matters? And how should society reflect those interests?

The exact calibration is never set like some article in the U.S. Constitution; it shifts back and forth with circumstances and the national mood. But whichever perspective such a political philosophy adopts, it ends up being almost a national creed, one that dictates a code of conduct as it favors one interest group over another, be it the state or the private sector, labor or capital, consumers or producers, rich or poor. It establishes the essential hierarchy of society and the economy. It decides who's on top and who's not. For decades now, our capitalist creed has been that laissez-faire globalization is good, full stop.

But the truth is that it hasn't been good for everyone all the time. As the process of globalization has unfolded over most of our lifetimes, there have been winners and losers. Taxes have been slashed. Borders have been opened (though more so for investment and the flow of goods than for people). But labor unions have been squashed, the industrial commons has been outsourced, and the cost of the things that make us middle class (housing, healthcare, and education) has risen dramatically. Corporate monopoly power has grown, and state-run capitalism has, too. Big companies and some emerging markets have benefited hugely from the last forty years. Everyone else, less so. Instead of a world economy in service to domestic policies and the overall welfare of people within a broad range of nation-states, we've gotten a world economy in service to itself.

But the paradigm of globalization is now changing.

Such seismic shifts in the socioeconomic agenda are as rare as earthquakes—and equally transformative. We are going through one now. The world is beginning to reset, not to the "normal" of conventional economic models, but to a new normal. Roughly four decades ago, the United States kicked off the developed world's last major economic paradigm shift: the supply-side revolution. Capital gains taxes were slashed. President Ronald Reagan and U.K. prime minister Margaret Thatcher took on air traffic controllers and coal miners. The power of unions faded, and that of corporations grew. Some people got very rich. The world, as Thomas Friedman later famously told us, "was flat." Place no longer mattered.

In fact, it did. Globalization is generally defined as the free movement of goods, people, and capital. But capital (and the people who have most of it) travels much more freely than either goods or workers. An international elite (of which I, as an educated, coastal knowledge worker who writes for the world's largest business newspaper, am admittedly part) did very well, flying over the problems of the nation-state on a tide of economic globalization. But lots of people on the ground didn't.

I grew up with those people, in a small town in Indiana. In many ways, my family lived the American Dream: my dad is a Turkish immigrant who came to the United States to study engineering, married, and started his own manufacturing business. But my family also lived through the ruinous effects of many of those supposedly "rational" economic policies of the eighties and nineties. They included the death of family farms, the collapse of small businesses as the country traded jobs for the low prices of big-box stores, the outsourcing of manufacturing to China and other parts of the developing world, and the subsequent decline in innovation and growth within the United States in particular.

All this exemplifies a pendulum that has swung too far toward concentration and corruption in markets and the state. Thanks to more than forty years of small changes to everything from tax codes and corporate governance to banking regulation and antitrust law, Anglo-American capitalism has morphed into something Adam Smith (the father of modern capitalism) wouldn't recognize. What we have today is no longer a truly "free"-market system that allows for productive and fair transactions between buyers and sellers who exist on an equal footing, but rather, a system of concentrated power and oligopoly.

In this world, multinational corporations and the people who run them are detached from the needs of the countries that spawned them. In the United States, for example, 75 percent of venture capital goes to just the three coastal American states of California, New York, and Massachusetts. In the decade leading up to 2017, just twenty-five cities accounted for more than two-thirds of job growth.[2] Laissez-faire economics has run way ahead of politics. The same is true, to a greater or lesser extent, in most of the developed world and in many developing countries, too. The result is a Hobbesian paradigm in which countries and individuals are pitted against one another. Globalization, at least the kind we've known for the last several decades, has failed. The free flow of capital and jobs to cheap-labor countries did make most of what you buy in Walmart cheaper, but lower prices didn't make up for the lost jobs and income, particularly as prices rose in everything that makes us middle class: housing, education, and healthcare. Offshoring to multiple countries was supposed to make manufacturing more productive and business more efficient, but many of those supposed "efficiencies" collapsed with any sort of global stress, whether it was pandemics, wars, tsunamis, port backups, or other unforeseen events. And complex supply chains were, well, complex, resulting in any number of production disasters, from poorly made airplanes that crashed to automobile ignition switches that didn't work. Meanwhile, free trade itself, which was supposed to foster peace among nations, became a system to be gamed by mercantilist nations and state-run autocracies, resulting in deep political divides at home and abroad.

It is time for a reset. We need to share the wealth more broadly. We need to understand that economic well-being isn't just about growth at the international or even the national level, but rather about real people, human beings living in specific communities. People matter. Place matters. All places.

So, what now? What's the right vision of shared prosperity for the present moment? How can we remoor wealth and local communities? How can we make sure that economic globalization doesn't again run too far ahead of national policies? And how can we fix things in a way that doesn't result in 1930s-style protectionism, a false fit of nostalgia for a past industrial era, or a high-tech dystopia in which robots take our jobs and Amazon eats everyone's lunch?

This is the question I propose to answer in this book, which aims to tell the story of how we got where we are, not just over the last forty years, but over the last century. It will explain why the choices we've made—some of them in good faith, others not—have led us to an unsustainable place. But it will also illustrate how much of the change we need is already happening. Thanks to a host of shifts—from demographic to geopolitical to technological—the world is already resetting. Regionalization and localization are the future. Countries, cities, and individual communities are increasingly shaping their own futures. Supply chains are shortening. The capital/labor divide is finally, after decades, shrinking. A wave of technological innovation is making it possible to move jobs and wealth to a far greater number of places, including back home. A new generation of (Millennial) workers and voters is pushing politicians and business leaders alike to put the rules of the global economy back in service to the communal well-being.

The voices have become so loud that even economists themselves are beginning to listen. When a prevailing philosophy is no longer sustainable, it falls, yielding to one better suited to the times. We are leaving the era of "Rational Man" and entering a new era, one of a more human-centered, place-based economics. The focus will be on local rather than global, Main Street rather than Wall Street, stakeholders rather than shareholders, and small rather than big. Some people talk about these changes as a negative, something that will reduce growth or create conflict and decrease our ability to work together as a planet on the big issues. They feel that there is nothing else on the spectrum between unfettered nineties-style hyperglobalization and the nationalism, protectionism, and even fascism of the thirties.

I disagree. I think that more focus on the local is actually crucial to saving what is best about globalization—namely, the sense that the world isn't a zero-sum game and that nations can work together to solve humanity's problems and make the world a better place. But that kind of cooperation requires faith in the system itself, a belief that it hasn't been rigged to work mainly for a minority of the world's citizens. Too many people don't have that faith right now. Changing this will mean reintegrating the fortunes of capital and labor, of citizens and corporations, of markets and the state.

Harvard professor Dani Rodrik, one of the rare economists who has been willing to question the received wisdom of his profession in recent years, has argued that "democracy, national sovereignty and global economic integration are mutually incompatible: we can combine any two of the three, but never have all three simultaneously and in full." It's clear that, at this moment, we need to step back from unfettered globalization and work to remoor prosperity to place.

We are entering a new era of localization. This doesn't mean that all things global will fade. Quite the contrary: Ideas and information will still flow across borders, perhaps even faster, as the world economy becomes ever more digital. Capital, too, will be mobile, although it's unlikely to be quite as unfettered as it has been in the past. One of the most pernicious parts of globalization in the last half century has been the ability of global capital to fly far above workers and citizens. There will be more limits to what financial institutions in liberal democracies can do to fund autocratic governments or degrade the economic well-being of citizens in their home countries—as there should be. There will also be a rethink of trade rules, labor rights, and how to figure both the costs and the benefits of economic growth into the data that policy makers use to shape our world. Business won't be just about shareholders, but also about stakeholders. The future won't be about a relatively small number of very fortunate people living in a handful of places, but about reconnecting the fruits of growth to communities everywhere.

All these seismic economic transformations are only getting started. There is no going back—certainly not to the insular national economies of the 1950s and '60s. Nor should we want to go back. If wealth and power are no longer concentrated in a few hands in just a few places, it will make for a better, more stable, and more just world. No one would ever wish for a pandemic or an armed conflict, but events like the coronavirus, or more recently the war in Ukraine, have shed a stark light on issues that had for too long been hiding in plain sight. They have revealed the dangers of our energy systems, risks to our environment, the deficiencies of supply chains, the limitations of our healthcare system, and the challenges to something as essential as our food security. And yet, within these dark stories, there are also brighter ones, stories of companies, countries, and citizens solving complex problems. It's all part of a larger narrative of how we have the power to localize, rather than concentrate, wealth and power.

For all sorts of reasons, from technological to geopolitical to demographic and environmental, the landscape of prosperity will become far more local. It is a new era, one that will come with its own challenges and opportunities. Let us embrace them.

HOMECOMING

CHAPTER 1

One World, Two Systems

Years ago, during a reporting trip to Beijing following the 2008 financial crisis, I interviewed the CEO of a major European clean-energy company that was a market leader in China at the time. I asked the executive how he saw business going forward, and he said he felt optimistic—the company would be in fourth place within the next five years. I was startled. Why was falling from pole position to fourth place good news? And how could he be so precise about the future? Because, as the CEO told me, this is what Communist Party leaders had told him would happen as local competitors moved into the market.

A few years later, in 2013, I was in China again.[1] I happened to be there right as the Edward Snowden story was breaking and as the world was digesting the whistleblower's leaks of National Security Agency material that showed that the United States, the United Kingdom, and various other liberal democracies were regularly gathering surveillance data on citizens, often with the help of private technology and telecom firms. The American public in particular had been shocked—or, as Claude Rains's character says in the movie *Casablanca*, "shocked, *shocked*"—to learn that the U.S. government and the private sector had shared such information.

During one of my interviews in Beijing, I broached the topic with a People's Liberation Army general with whom I was discussing the potential for conflict between the two countries. At the time, the

United States' chief foreign policy problems were still in places like Pakistan, Afghanistan, and the Middle East. But I had been struck on another visit, to the U.S. Navy's Indo-Pacific Command head-quarters in Honolulu, by a heat map showing the locations of past, present, and possible future geopolitical conflicts. The red portions were moving inexorably from the Middle East to South Asia to the South China Sea, which is where the problems of the future seemed to lie. This struck me as a big and very underexplored story, given that most of what you could buy in Walmart had to make its way through the South China Sea to get to American consumers.

I asked the general (a woman, interestingly) what she thought about the Snowden leaks and the role of both the state and the private sector in the global economy and geopolitics. She smiled and said that most Chinese found Americans' naïveté around such things surprising. "In China, there is no line between the country and the company." The two were one and the same, and the latter would always be in service to the former.

These were among the many reporting moments I've had in China over the last two decades that made me wonder why U.S. policy makers and corporate leaders ever thought that China would miraculously take its place in the existing world order and trade system. At the time that I was having these conversations, much of the world—certainly, China—was understandably questioning the wisdom of laissez-faire, Anglo-American-style capitalism and unfet-tered free trade in the wake of the financial crisis. Yet policy makers in the West were still pretending that the world would reset to the mid-nineties. CEOs of large companies were willfully blind to the risks of supply chain problems and market access in China, where a new Great Power conflict with the United States clearly loomed and where the rules of the market game could, in its state-run system, change at any time. There was also a general level of arrogance on the part of the West in relation to China that I found puzzling. Why would such a large nation, with its own long history, rich culture, very different political system, and enormous market, not create its own rules as it retook its historic place on the world stage? Remember that for much of recorded history, China and India, not America, vied for the top spot as the world's largest and most powerful economy. That's important to remember now, because as they rise once again, the decisions that these countries make will be just as influential as anything that might happen in the United States. China's decision, for example, to decouple itself completely from U.S. and Western economic control over the next few years is a crucial part of the story of deglobalization.

China's most recent five-year plan released by the state codified what was already common practice: via the One Belt, One Road infrastructure and lending program, the nation would become independent of Western technology and supply chains by 2025 and would build its own regional trade routes, remaking and expanding the old Silk Road of Marco Polo's time, a pathway that stretched from China to Europe. China would lend to emerging markets, cut its own trade deals in its own currency, buy up farmland and ports, and generally become more self-sufficient and independent of the United States. The Belt and Road Initiative, combined with a host of new trade deals in Europe, Africa, South America, Asia, and the Middle East, would make it easier for China to grow its exports to places other than the United States.[2] Decoupling and regionalization, not a reset of globalization, was the new norm.

The economic decoupling of America and China and, more particularly, the trade war and new cold war between the two nations are sometimes thought of as a result of the misguided policies of the Trump administration. In fact, the conflicts between the two countries and their systems were there long before, hiding in plain sight. The idea that more trade would always be good for the United States has been dogma for the last half century, under both Republican and Democratic administrations. Even if deals were cut with countries that had completely different national goals and political systems, these agreements, we were told by political leaders of all stripes, would inevitably make us safer and richer. But the downsides to globalization—which range from the loss of important jobs and skill sets, to the vulnerabilities of complex and far-flung supply chains and financial networks, to the fact that China wasn't, in fact, becoming freer as it got richer—were papered over for decades.

The only good thing that the Trump administration did economically was to stop pretending that the One World, Two Systems problem, as foreign policy wonks call it, didn't exist. While President Trump had no coherent strategy for countering the rise of China (and was actively supportive of Chinese allies like Russia), and while his vitriolic rhetoric didn't help the United States, the last four years did at least bring an end to the absurd Kabuki act on the part of U.S. policy makers and corporate executives regarding the reality and intractability of the China challenge. No matter how tempting that next quarter of growth in the Chinese market might be, there are no guarantees that the playing field will be fair or that the rules won't change at any time—particularly in the most strategic high-growth sectors.

It was a terrible irony that it took Donald Trump to lift the veil on the hypocrisies of the One World, Two Systems problem, even as his own policies contributed to the challenge. Like the protagonist in Herman Melville's final novel, *The Confidence-Man,* Trump was able to embed a single, visceral truth in a welter of falsehoods. So it was with the U.S. president's anti-free-trade stance. He often couched it in terms that were xenophobic, nationalistic, or just factually wrong, but the criticism that Trump (and, later, President Joe Biden, who has continued much of the trade stance set by the former administration) leveled against China and, to a lesser extent, other nations engaging in unfair trade practices is getting at something profound. Many people simply do not believe that the current system of globalization is working in their favor. As the current U.S. trade representative under President Biden, Katherine Tai, put it in March 2022 at a presentation before the House Ways and Means Committee, "The problem that we are confronted with today—after two years of Covid and also Russia's invasion of Ukraine—is that this version of globalization that we are living in has not taken us to a place where we feel more secure. We are feeling increasing senses of insecurity in terms of our supply chains and our reliance on partners who we aren't comfortable relying on."[3] In fact, even before the events of the last few years, only about one in three people in rich countries believed that trade increased wages. Meanwhile, those in emerging markets are even more dubious about trade's impact on prices; a median of 18 percent believes it lowers them according to a 2018 survey.[4]

These feelings are what drives politics, but there are facts to back them up. Pricing has been driven down by unfettered globalization, but jobs in many places have been lost. This has led, in turn, to a highly bifurcated workforce and economy in hard-hit areas.[5] Think of the wage pressure on labor in many rich countries or of the terrible working conditions for many of those in poor countries as companies use "free" trade to try to raise their own margins at the expense of all else.

Of course, one can't ignore the statistical links between freer trade and economic growth in the postwar period: the two have gone hand in hand at a global level as more countries have entered the capitalist trade system. But given this, how does one account for these negative views of globalization? They are explained in large part by the fact that there can be major losers in free trade. Indeed, the two most consistent winners from the status quo system have been big companies and big countries.

Consider the 2018 annual report from the UN Conference on Trade and Development (UNCTAD), titled "Power, Platforms and the Free Trade Delusion."[6] It likens the past thirty years of unfettered global capital flows and, more recently, the network effects of the digital economy (which encourage the concentration of power) to the nineteenth-century system of colonial control in which great powers (be they sovereign or corporate) prospered at the expense of lesser ones.

The report found that, in the wake of the 2008 financial crisis, the ten largest exporting companies in any given country accounted for, on average, 42 percent of national exports. No wonder corporate profits are at record highs while, for most Americans, average wages have stagnated since the eighties.[7] During that time, corporations spent much of their money buying back their own shares, an artificial sort of price-bolstering wizardry that hasn't changed anything in the real world, where a record corporate debt bubble looms.

Even more interesting is the picture on trade. Looking at the manufacturing sector between 2000 and 2014, the domestic share of total value added and the domestic share of labor income within that declined in most countries, with the significant exception of China. Not only did most rich countries suffer in relation to China, but poor countries that played by the letter of World Trade Organization law did, too. This is a problem, given that opening up to global trade was supposed to have helped these countries move up the value chain.

It turns out that the Chinese tactics of ring-fencing strategic industries and limiting capital flows were necessary to guarantee significant and rapid development. "Cheating" the global system was a smart move, at least for China. As Harvard's Dani Rodrik puts it, "The Chinese used the world economy to advance their own domestic policy agenda." The rest of the world "crafted national policy to serve the global economy."[8] It was a case of the tail wagging the dog.

Ironically, the same U.S. politicians, policy makers, and chief executives who now complain about the unfair competitiveness of those Chinese state-owned businesses warned us for years that Beijing would be less competitive for being less open. "For a long time, developing countries complained that [unfettered free trade] would hurt them," says Richard Kozul-Wright, director of UNCTAD's division on globalization and development strategy. "Now you are seeing rich countries say the same thing."

This bizarre alignment of opinion has many downsides, most notably the overall decline in expectations for global trade growth and the rise of trade-related political risk (all this well before the war in Ukraine and economic isolation of Russia from the West drove the point so painfully home). But it may also have the unexpected upside of creating a consensus around the idea that we really do need a revamp not only of the global trading system but of globalization itself. The global trading system isn't set in stone, but rather has evolved and morphed over hundreds, even thousands, of years. Today, we are still largely in the hyperfinancialized laissez-faire system that characterized the period from the eighties onward. What we need is a paradigm more suitable to the reality of the post-Trump, post-Brexit, post–rising China, post-digital world. The truth is that free trade doesn't work as well when there is no shared political economic value system between partners. It is perhaps a sign of a genuine paradigm shift that even groups as conventional as the Council on Foreign Relations, the International Monetary Fund, and the Business Roundtable have admitted that there are big losers in our One World, Two Systems paradigm. The world—including even some of those who benefit most from the old system—is ready for a reset.[9]

How We Got Here

Whether it is derived from Adam Smith or Karl Marx, no economic movement is purely a matter of numbers. It is instead a manifestation of an underlying political philosophy. It seems obvious to many of us today that nation-states and their citizens should be able to make their own rules and develop global alliances that are in their own best interests. But the system of globalization that has governed our economy and much of our politics for the last several decades was based on an entirely different assumption and on a particular governing philosophy: neoliberalism.

Neoliberalism goes much farther back than the economic history of the last half century. Most of us know about the trickle-down economic policies practiced by Ronald Reagan and Margaret Thatcher, and about the business-friendly Clintonian and Obama-era economic ideas (particularly around financial markets and trade) that so often mirrored them on the political left. These policies had their roots in many things, some of them theoretical and some more practical, such as technological and regulatory shifts in the financial system over the last half century.[10] Globalization never could have gone as far as it has, for example, without the financial deregulation, high-speed communication networks, and faster transportation methods of the last several decades.

But at the theoretical level, the idea of market fundamentalism can be traced to the nineteenth-century European theories of "laissez-faire," which held that individuals should be free from government constraints to do what they wanted and that this would produce the best economic outcome for society. The term *neoliberal,* which is used and misused in complicated ways, actually refers to the way in which these "liberal" ideas from the nineteenth century were picked up and championed in the 1930s by some European economists alarmed by what they viewed as the excessive state control of markets after the Great Depression. For them, neoliberalism became an economic and political philosophy advocating that capital, people, and goods should be able to cross borders freely in search of the most productive and profitable returns. This philosophy held that the interests of the nation-state and democracy itself could be a problem for economic and political stability. The voting public could not be trusted, and thus, national interests needed to be constrained by international laws and institutions so that markets and society could function properly.

The term *neoliberalism* was first used in 1938, at the Walter Lippmann Colloquium in Paris, a gathering of economists, sociologists, journalists, and businessmen who wanted to find a way to protect global capitalism from fascism and socialism.[11] One of the most important of these figures, Friedrich Hayek, went on in the post–World War II period to create the Mont Pelerin Society. Milton Friedman, one of the most famous proponents of the University of Chicago School of Economics thinking that informed the Reagan-Thatcher revolution and "trickle-down" economic theory, was a follower and acolyte of Hayek.[12]

To understand the philosophy of neoliberalism, you have to understand the context in which it originated—from the economically wrecked Europe of the 1930s, in which fascism was rising. It was the kind of historical turning point that, in some ways, mirrors our own. Between 1918 and 1929, the price of assets of all kinds (stocks, bonds, real estate) were going up, both in Europe and in the United States. It was the Roaring Twenties. Central bankers everywhere had opened up the money spigots and were encouraging people to buy things on credit.

But this sense of rising boats and easy money was papering over major political and economic changes.[13] The Industrial Revolution, which took more than a century to play out fully, had led to rising urbanization in many countries and displaced millions of workers, creating political rifts in society. The labor force had gone from one concentrated largely in agriculture to one that worked mostly in factories and industry. This came with big shifts in the family and in class structures. Wages weren't rising as fast as prices, which meant that asset inflation and debt were important for creating a sense of economic well-being. Sound familiar? This is basically where we've been over the last twenty years.

An influenza pandemic and World War I had created a sharp drop in international trade, which fell from 27 percent of global output in 1913 to just 20 percent in 1923–28. Ultimately, the debt bubble exploded in 1929, and the Great Depression caused international trade to collapse to 11 percent of the world economy by 1932. Trade tariffs and punitive taxes on either side of the Atlantic compounded the problems. Cross-border flows of goods and services never made it past 15 percent of the world economy again until after World War II.[14]

Meanwhile, politics was becoming bleaker. Nazi Germany and Mussolini's Italy were rising. European nations were hunkering back down into their colonial stances of resource grabbing from the developing world in order to fuel their war efforts. The world quickly became a Hobbesian one of "all against all"—leading inexorably to the horrors of World War II.

In the wake of the Second World War, the intellectuals and great men of Europe and the United States understandably wanted to prevent a repeat of anarchy and also to address the rising threat of the Soviet Union, which to them was directly related to nationalism and the power of the nation-state. This is important, because as Wellesley academic Quinn Slobodian writes in his history of neoliberalism,[15] the goal of the neoliberal thinkers was "safeguarding capitalism at the scale of the entire world. . . . The neoliberal project focused on designing institutions—not to liberate markets but to encase them, to inoculate capitalism against the threat of democracy, to create a framework to contain often-irrational human behavior."

Fair enough. As we've already learned, human behavior isn't rational, and neither is politics. The architects of neoliberalism believed that if capital markets and global trade were connected via a series of institutions that floated over the laws of any given nation-state, the world would be less likely to descend into anarchy. For a long time, this idea worked, in part because the balance between national interests and the global economy didn't get too far out of whack. Even during the Reagan years, despite the antigovernment rhetoric, there was a sense that global trade needed to serve the national interest rather than merely itself (or, more particularly, the interests of the large multinational companies). Consider the way in which the United States fought back when Japan tried to dominate the entire physical infrastructure of the computer. It was the Reagan administration response—which included putting tariffs and quotas on Japanese exports and subsidizing the development of next-generation computer technology—that kept America in the game. The United States also pushed a lot of manufacturing away from Japan and toward South Korea, Taiwan, Singapore, and Malaysia, which was ultimately a good thing, because it reduced the concentration of power and created both lower prices and more resiliency. That sounds a lot less like "government is the problem" and more like smart industrial policy. "While the Reagan administration embraced free trade, it opposed mercantilism," notes Clyde Prestowitz, a labor economist who worked in the Commerce Department during the Reagan years. The administration strove to maintain American technological leadership by creating an industry-government partnership around research and development. It's worth noting that the deputy trade representative during the second Reagan term was none other than the architect of Trump's trade strategy with China: Robert Lighthizer.[16]

The sense that trade should be a handmaid to domestic job creation and industrial interests began to change quite rapidly during the Clinton administration, when a series of trade deals, culminating with the entry of China into the WTO, took the guardrails off the global economy. While Adam Smith, the father of modern capitalism, held that in order for free markets to function properly, participants needed to have a shared moral framework, the United States and many other liberal democracies were suddenly enmeshed in major trade relationships with countries that had entirely different moral frameworks, not to mention economic ones—from Russia and any number of other petrostates in the Middle East, to numerous Latin American dictatorships, to the biggest and most problematic trading partner of all, China.

It's worth noting—as journalist and activist Barry Lynn did in a prescient *Harper's Magazine* piece in 2002 that eventually became a book on the fragility of global supply chains titled *End of the Line*—that "many of our new partners are not democracies, and their internal workers, long-term goals, and ability to live peacefully in the world we imagine ourselves to be making remain obscure at best."[17] This statement, so crisply true then, is only more so today. While the European nations that came together after World War II to craft trade agreements (like the European Coal and Steel Community, which became the basis for the European Union) had similar cultures and values, the same cannot be said for the WTO nations as a whole today. Liberal democracies, autocracies, surveillance states, and any other number of political and economic systems, transparent and not, have become tied together in deals that were more often than not drafted and approved by global technocrats rather than elected officials.

Ironically, as the neoliberal pendulum shifted too far from national interests to global market interests, it led to new kinds of fascism. In the United States, this was manifest in the form of Donald

Trump. Trump capitalized on the economic disenchantment of so many Americans, diabolically using nationalist rhetoric to forward his own personality cult rather than to put in place any coherent alternative to unfettered economic globalization. While neither he nor his British doppelganger, Boris Johnson, is anticapitalist (quite the opposite), I'd argue that they fit within a larger shift toward more extreme politics on both sides of the political spectrum. From Bernie Sanders to Trump, from Johnson to Jeremy Corbyn, and from the nationalists of continental Europe to a rising breed of autocrats in many emerging markets—it has become clear that neoliberalism is no longer constraining political extremism, but rather enabling it, as rage against our current system builds.

Despite the global market backlash, it would be a mistake to think that neoliberals, who crafted institutions like the IMF, the World Bank, and the beginnings of the WTO, were pure "free"-traders, or entirely in favor of unfettered global capital markets. Like both the famous English economist John Maynard Keynes and Marx, Hayek (perhaps as much as anyone the father of neoliberalism) believed that the markets didn't necessarily revert to equilibrium. They needed to be controlled by a "framework" that would connect capitalists and businesspeople around the world, allowing them to float above the socialist interests of labor or the fascism of the 1930s. As one of Hayek's students put it, "The common starting point of the neoliberal economic theory is the insight that in any well-functioning market economy, the 'invisible hand' of market competition must by necessity be complemented by the 'visible hand' of the law."[18]

This is a key point. Many historical references to neoliberalism tend to start from the Reagan/Thatcher era, in which Milton Friedman's Chicago School thinking led policy makers to deregulate markets and break unions. There's a general narrative that the people who supported neoliberalism were first and only "free-marketers" and that everyone else was a statist or a protectionist. We will come back to much of the history of deregulation and market liberalization from the eighties onward later in this book. But, for now, the point is that neoliberal thinking wasn't so much about unfettered markets as about "constrained democracy."[19]

As Slobodian writes, "For neoliberals, the democratic threat took many forms, from the white working class to the non-European decolonizing world." All these groups threatened, in their view, a well-crafted global economy. From the breakdown of the gold standard after the First World War, which allowed nations to battle one another via currency wars, to the trade wars and hot wars that followed, it was clear to neoliberals that the masses were incapable of governing themselves properly. The world needed to be kept safe from their "demands for social justice and redistributive equality by the guardians of the economic constitution."[20]

The core of that constitution was put down on paper shortly after the Allied landing in Normandy during World War II. In anticipation of victory, Allied powers met in Bretton Woods, New Hampshire, during July 1–22, 1944, to come up with a plan for what the new world economy should look like. Much of what has happened in the world in the last half century was shaped there at Bretton Woods. The conference led to the establishment of the International Monetary Fund, the World Bank, and the General Agreement on Tariffs and Trade (GATT), the precursor to the World Trade Organization. These organizations crafted, but also enforced, the rules of globalization in the post–World War II period. Their goal was in large part to make sure that capital goods could move freely wherever it was most "productive" for them to do so. The IMF's role was to govern global finance. The World Bank would give loans to countries for reconstruction—this was eventually expanded to giving development aid to emerging markets—and the GATT would rule over global trade. This system of global economic governance eventually became known as "the Washington Consensus."

Many of the Bretton Woods delegates, including Keynes, were influenced by neoliberal thinkers like Hayek. Indeed, on his Atlantic crossing to the United States to attend the Bretton Woods conference, Keynes had read a copy of Hayek's famous book *The Road to Serfdom,* which laid out the need to protect the global economy and free markets from fascism, nationalism, and statism—the Soviet threat was by now looming large.[21] One of the key jobs of the delegates to Bretton Woods was to figure out what the new world monetary system would look like. While the United States, which was by now the preeminent global power on the world stage, decreed that the dollar would be the world's new currency, Keynes had been in favor of a different solution. He wanted to create something called a bancor, an international reserve currency made up of a basket of various country's currencies and managed by the IMF. Looking back, one sees this would have been a good idea: it would have prevented some of the imbalances in the global system that have driven up debt levels in rich countries and led to defaults in poorer ones. But, as always, the world wasn't rational; it was political. The dollar became the global reserve, which led to a host of problems with globalization that we shall explore more later in this book.

Shortly after Bretton Woods, in 1947, Hayek convened a group of like-minded thinkers at Mont Pelerin, Switzerland. The ideas developed there spread throughout the world, influencing policy makers and business leaders and shaping the way the markets and companies work today. The time was ripe for the spread of neoliberalism, which presented a simple and stark contrast to the rise of Soviet-led socialism. (China was, at this point, still a poor and relatively unimportant country economically.) A condensed version of Hayek's book was published by *Reader's Digest,* and companies ranging from General Motors to New Jersey Power and Light gave copies of it to their staff.[22] Hayek became an economic celebrity, appearing on television and radio, assuring the West in general and the United States in particular that the connection of global business and global capital markets was the way to peace and prosperity.

One of the people whom Hayek and the Mont Pelerin Society influenced was University of Chicago professor Milton Friedman. To Friedman, neoliberalism decreed that shareholder value was, in effect, the only value a company should honor. Companies existed to make a profit for their owners, full stop. And, for the public companies that made up the bulk of U.S. business, the owners were their shareholders. Seductive in its simplicity and in its implication of American-style liberty, neoliberalism thus found its way into U.S. foreign and economic policy as a core principle. It also paved the way for the loosening of regulations in the eighties that gave Wall Street so much more latitude to maximize profits by any means necessary, which in turn fueled the march toward globalization. Indeed, the Wall Street banks were the first to go global, followed closely by the corporate titans whom they pushed to maximize share price above all things.

Free-market globalism was pushed in large part by the powerful multinational companies best positioned to exploit it (companies that, of course, donated equally to politicians from both parties, to ensure they saw the virtues of neoliberalism). It became a kind of crusade to spread this new American creed around the globe, delivering the thrill of McDonald's franchises and Apple iPhones as it went. Our goods, in effect, would represent our goodness. They would serve to advertise American philosophical values, the liberalism tucked inside neoliberalism. The idea was that other countries, delighted by the fruits of American-style capitalism, would now be moved to become "free" like us.

Like most simple solutions to complicated problems, neoliberalism didn't work out quite as well as intended. Institutions like the International Monetary Fund and the World Bank became less protectors of political liberalism than exporters of what Nobel laureate Joseph E. Stiglitz famously called globalization and its discontents.[23] The WTO, which evolved into being from the GATT in 1995, didn't set enforceable rules so much as pretend to disintermediate disputes between nations over which it had no real control. (It is no surprise, then, that disputes can take years or even decades to resolve, if, indeed, they are resolved at all.)[24] Still, the shifts were inexorable, as was our faith in globalization. The fall of the Berlin Wall, the oil shocks and debt crises of the eighties, and the natural slowing of growth in the European Union and the United States relative to emerging markets all led to a push within rich countries and poor ones to adopt the "free-market" ideas of the Washington Consensus.[25]

Yet, far from making us all "free," the free market changed us from citizens into consumers, increasingly beholden to the increasingly large companies that outsourced our jobs and mined our personal data even as they sold us the increasingly bright and shiny objects of late-stage capitalism (often on credit). As even the ideology's chief international proponents like the IMF and the World Bank (American-sponsored ones at that) have come to acknowledge, the holders of capital may have prospered under the new world order in which capital could move wherever it found the greatest rewards, but workers very often did not. In fact, as we've already learned, research shows that two groups prospered disproportionately under American-style neoliberalism: multinational companies and the Chinese.

China was perfectly positioned to take full advantage of this new global economic environment the United States espoused, leveraging its cheap labor to attract lots of capital—and foreign industrial expertise. To U.S. policy makers, it was a win-win to off-load our low-paying jobs to China. China would do the grunt work of making lightbulbs. The United States would do the brain work of writing software. China would do the bad jobs; we'd keep the good ones. Meanwhile, as China became richer, its citizens would develop into consumers of high-end American products. As they bought iPhones and ate Big Macs, the thinking went, surely they'd absorb the democratic values that lay behind them. American goods would be, in effect, a propaganda weapon, a Voice of America that would challenge China's one-party state and show the Chinese people the attractions of U.S.-style democracy.

It was pretty to think so, but naïve. In my multiple trips to China over twenty years, I have always marveled at the willful blindness that led Western businesspeople and policy makers to think that China would give up on its system of centralized autocracy—one that had been honed under centuries of dynastic rule and that had worked well for the country in many ways—in favor of a foreign economic system that had been around only a few decades. The financial crisis of 2008, which put the hypocrisies of neoliberalism on full display, only confirmed this. The Chinese leadership responded by doubling down on its core party-state principles. Over the last decade, it used the surveillance opportunities posed by digital technology to hone its command-and-control operations. It has also created its own world-beating innovations, very often off the back of intellectual property acquired from the United States by multinationals forced to share trade secrets in order to access the Chinese market. This makes a lot of sense from a Chinese domestic perspective, but it also violates the spirit of the system of globalization and free markets that allowed China to prosper so wildly. This is the great paradox of the last few decades: gaming the neoliberal system often paid higher dividends, at least at a national level, than playing fair did.

Chinese-made Xiaomi phones now sell more than Apple iPhones in China and in other countries, such as India. The Chinese have moved ahead in key technological areas such as digital currency, clean technology, artificial intelligence, and 5G. The U.S.-Chinese trade turned cold war has hurt the Chinese, no doubt, but in the long run, they are positioned to weather it. Like the United States in the post–World War II period, China is a large, single-language country with plenty of room to grow and with a state-run capitalist system that is drawing many other countries into its orbit. Beijing wants to create its own consensus. All this means that the challenges of the One World, Two Systems problem will persist. As the United States, Europe, and China move in separate directions, we will have to live in a bipolar, if not a tripolar, world.

This is often portrayed as a terrible thing—a comedown for the United States and a risk for the world at large. But I would argue that it is just as it should be. Politics takes place at the level of the nation-state. But economics has, for the last forty years, been an increasingly global affair, the rules of which have been dictated by a global technocratic class whose members have more in common with one another than with the majority of the people in their own countries. Too many of the people crafting and/or benefiting from the system mistook free trade for foreign policy and believed that unified global markets would always beget peaceful global politics. The idea that economic interdependence alone would save us from conflict, let alone solve problems at home, is an old mistake, one that authors, economists, and political scholars have been making for decades.

Populism is a natural result of this disconnection between the global economy and national politics. One of the most pernicious neoliberal myths was that unfettered globalization was always a good thing, always the best way forward for everyone everywhere. The truth is that a U.S. economy built increasingly on just two sectors, finance and technology, and with only a handful of major players in those markets, is a vulnerable one. As such concentration has grown, wages have stagnated and technological innovation has sputtered. It turns out that innovation, even twenty-first-century innovation, depends on the same thing it always did: a broad and deep economic ecosystem in which a diverse group of people and companies has a chance to grow, collaborate, and compete.

Efficiency Versus Resiliency

The Covid-19 pandemic and more recently the war in Ukraine have driven home the fact that we are now at a tipping point in our system of globalization. Considering that the political economy cycles in fifty-year intervals and that it has been only forty years since neoliberalism took hold, you might think that it would run for another decade. But Covid-19 came along to reveal the underlying philosophy's shortcomings as only a pandemic can. It showed that unchecked neoliberalism was ill-advised not just economically, but also socially and politically. It has been deadly on a vast scale.

To understand neoliberalism's role in the pandemic, you have to realize that any economy is an operating system like the one that runs a computer, an office, a city, or any other complex network.

Such systems must choose between two mutually exclusive characteristics: efficiency or resilience. Neoliberalism is a system designed almost entirely for efficiency, the kind of efficiency that is measured in corporate profits (or losses). This is the so-called shareholder value that Milton Friedman extolled. And if that is the measure, then neoliberalism has indeed been wonderfully efficient. It has encouraged companies to put factories wherever in the world it was cheapest to do business, no matter how remote, how awful the working conditions, how destructive to the environment, or how devastating to the national economies where these companies were supposedly based. If costs were down and revenues were up, that was all anyone needed to know. What's more, in their search for profits, these companies drew in material resources only as needed following the latest just-in-time manufacturing principles. The result was a system that was far-flung and fine-tuned, but full of unseen risks held by the relatively few corporations capable of handling such mind-boggling complexity long-distance. Over time, those few became fewer still, as the winners deployed their profits to gain an ever-tighter hold over an ever-wider market. In the increasingly globalized economy, winners took all.

But efficiency is not resilience, and it comes with plenty of liabilities that do not show up on the balance sheet. For one thing, it leads to dangerous fragility. As corporations grow more concentrated and their supply chains lengthen, their control attenuates, leaving those systems more vulnerable to the unexpected. And as those few corporations start to interlock—manufacturing depending on technology, power depending on transportation in the phenomenon that systems analysts call "tight coupling"—a failure anywhere becomes a failure everywhere. Imagine a city with just one power plant, one airport, one fire department, one electrical grid, one internet service provider, and one supermarket, all of them linked together into a single network. Highly efficient, but utterly precarious. If any one element goes down, they all go down: the power goes out, screens go dark, planes are grounded, traffic lights go blank, cellphones go dead, and the supermarket closes. This is what happened in too many key sectors of the economy after the Covid-19 pandemic hit: suddenly, the food, medicine, and personal protective equipment essential to survival were in short supply or nowhere to be found.

Such breakdowns have happened many times before—although, perhaps never at this scale. Think of the disruptions after tsunamis or cyber-attacks or collapsed factories or violent conflicts. Because resilience is inherently inefficient, it has been ignored under the tenets of neoliberalism. Resilience involves the redundancy that modern managers mistake for waste: duplication of services, extra supply chains, multiplicity of providers, and better-trained workers. It also requires a shift from a winner-take-all environment, in which a handful of large companies control everything, to a diverse economic ecosystem in which many companies work together to create shared value within a community. Imagine a building made of multiple pieces of wood slotted together like puzzle pieces. Such a structure may seem less sturdy than a concrete block. But when the earthquake comes, these are the buildings that remain standing, because they have the flexibility to move and adapt. Redundancy allows the system to keep running if any one part of it breaks down. Resiliency, in the long run, is actually more efficient than efficiency.

How do we create resiliency? What might a new and better postneoliberal world look like? This is the topic of the rest of this book, which will explore the ways in which change is already occurring, but also lay out what we need to do to ensure that it continues. The starting point is a new economic narrative in which place matters— all places, not just the handful of cities where the wealthiest citizens live, but elsewhere: the places between the coasts, the "flyover" states, and the hollowed-out parts of myriad counties that have lost out in the relentless push toward globalization and concentration. Our economic and political future depends on rebuilding a thriving middle class in those areas. There is, after all, a limit to economic growth in places like the United States, in which 32 percent of total net worth is held by 1 percent of the population and where most people haven't gotten a raise in real terms since the late 1960s. (Even prior to Covid-19, purchasing power based on average inflation-adjusted hourly wages was roughly where it was forty years ago.) In rich countries like the United States and in many parts of Europe, where the economy is typically made up of 70 percent consumer spending and where incomes have been flat or falling since the early nineties, the economic math simply stops working. For Americans, one particularly sad statistic tells the tale. Over the last two decades, the number of jobs lost in U.S. manufacturing has almost exactly equaled the jobs gained in leisure and hospitality (i.e., restaurant work). We have stopped being a nation that makes things and become a nation that eats things.

But middle-income nations and poorer countries must also change their economic model. For them, too, the benefits of laissez-faire globalization are tapped out. These nations used to make the leap to greater prosperity via industrialization and manufacturing. But in a new and more digital world, industrial jobs will increasingly be done by robots, and wealth will be held in intangible assets like software, patents, digital data, and the brains of the "knowledge workers" whom every country must now cultivate. As incomes in China and other parts of the developing world have risen, the wage arbitrage of sending manufacturing jobs from rich countries to employ millions of laborers in poorer ones is largely over. Capital has become cheap and readily available—and businesses in an increasingly digital economy tend to require less of it in any case. What's needed is a greater focus not on *global* economic development, but on development *within* countries and communities. This requires thinking beyond the neoliberal paradigm, something that is already happening via the burgeoning field of "place-based" economics.

Already, for the first time in forty years, policy makers are beginning to think more about the development of Main Street than of Wall Street. The wealth creation of the last half century is giving way to a new era of wealth distribution. Through the stories of the companies and communities that follow, I'll outline how the short-term pressures of the public markets have forced American business to eat its seed corn. Since the eighties in particular, global flows of money and transportation have grown in ways that neoliberal thinkers couldn't have expected. Advances in container shipping and the growth of global capital markets (which are now nearly four times the size of the real economy) took globalization far beyond what they ever imagined. In such excess, these flows of money and goods now distort national economies rather than serve them. As the policy pendulum begins to shift away from neoliberal thinking, supply chains are shortening and "shareholder value" is giving way to "stakeholder" value, shifting the purpose of the corporation itself. The signs of this new, post-neoliberal era are all around us already. Witness the resurgence of unions; the rise of the B Corporations, which balance purpose and profit; and the growth of investing based not merely on share price, but on "ESG," or "environmental, social, and governance" factors.

Change is coming not only in corporate governance, but also via new decentralized technologies, from 3D printing to blockchain, which are being deployed around the world to help communities and even individuals hold on to wealth and create resilience in new ways. In the post-neoliberal world, technology is an opportunity as well as a challenge. The post-Covid-19 shift to a far more digital economy will disrupt labor markets, but also present an opportunity for individuals and small businesses. As they can work more easily from many more places, they will be able to engage more easily in global commerce while keeping the wealth garnered from it at home. Such technologies are also bringing vastly more transparency to the process of governance in some countries, as we will explore toward the end of this book. Leveraged properly, they could start to change the balance of power between capital and labor and perhaps even between corporations and citizens.

Globalization over the last twenty years in particular has been about the hegemony of giants: Big Tech, Big Ag, Big Banks, Big Pharma. Corporate behemoths have been answerable mainly to themselves, writing their own rules, running their own markets, and transcending national borders, some of them to operate virtually tax-free. The largest tech firms have even argued that they deserve special treatment for being self-appointed "national champions" in the new cold war against China. But in our evolving world, decentralization, localization, and redundancy of supply will be the name of the game. Creating resiliency will mean getting more economic participants into the game, not allowing a small number to hold all the power.

In a world of Big States and Big Companies, the advantage for free-market liberal democracies lies in restoring competition to the market economy while also investing in the public commons. Historically, broad, inclusive economic growth comes when the public sector seeds the development of a transformative new technology. Such state investment is often driven by a national mission to boost development or security. Think of the British and American railway booms, fueled by the needs of the military; or the creation of the Interstate Highway System that linked the United States for the automotive age; or the digital economy itself, much of which came out of the U.S. Department of Defense's Defense Advanced Research Projects Agency (DARPA) (which pioneered the internet, handheld GPS, and wireless technology).[26] The digital revolution of the last two decades has created tremendous gains. And yet, we are still only in the first stages of it. Consider that the "killer app" of the railroad boom, the mail-order catalogue business, didn't take off until about fifty years after the railways were created. Some aspects of the digital revolution, such as the "internet of things" (meaning the interconnection of nearly all everyday objects via the internet), could help solve the productivity puzzle and bridge the inequality gaps. Other bets, including the ability of artificial intelligence to displace human thinking, may be oversold. Perhaps the clearest opportunity today around which the public sector could seed a new, more equitable growth boom is climate change. The need to move away from fossil fuels produced by autocratic petrostates like Russia has created yet another tailwind for the shift to clean tech, and in the coming pages, I will lay out the surprising common ground that already exists among the American right and left to support cleaner technologies that will create jobs and investment in left-behind communities.

Globalization isn't going to reset to "normal." We will live in a bipolar, if not a tripolar, world, as different regions go in somewhat different directions. Globalization also isn't going away wholesale. Ideas and data will still flow across borders. So will many goods and services, albeit in far less complicated supply chains. According to a late 2021 McKinsey survey of global supply leaders, 92 percent of respondents said they'd already begun changing their supply chain footprints, to make them more local and regional, and increasing the redundancy of suppliers, to improve resiliency and ensure that companies aren't reliant on a single country for crucial supplies.[27] Likewise, a December 2021 report on the future of global supply chains by the nonprofit the Conference Board noted a growing movement from globalization to regionalization, with government initiatives like the Industrial Policy Bill approved by the U.S. Senate in June 2021 and the European Union's "New Industrial Strategy" communication from October of that year both "focused on restructuring supply chains more locally."[28]

The bottom line is that globalization as we've known it for the last half century is over. But a certain amount of deglobalization is not a retreat or a failure. In fact, it's both necessary and welcome, for economic, social, political, and environmental reasons. We need to understand that globalization is something we shape ourselves, not something that must de facto shape us. We need to understand that it's okay for different countries and communities to have different ways of doing things—ways suited to their own local needs. China should be able to make decisions for the benefit of its own population. So should Europe, the United States, and the rest of the world. The world economy must serve the needs of the people who live within nation-states—not the other way around.

Indeed, if we are to save what is best about globalization and not descend into further trade wars and global conflict, we need much more focus on the local. Economic, technological, and demographic forces are all pushing decentralization and localization. This is to be celebrated. We should not fear the fact that the United States and China will move ahead with fundamentally different political economies. Rather, we should work with allies to craft alternatives to the monopsonies of Silicon Valley or the surveillance state of China. The United States and Europe in particular should come together to craft a new paradigm for digital trade, one that fosters both competition and personal freedom.

If they are to succeed, many of these propositions require active government and private-sector participation across the aisle. In the United States, one might well ask if this is even possible, given a divided Congress and a still-polarized America. I believe that, over time, the answer will be yes. Change is already afoot, particularly at the local level. It's just not getting its due. The seeds of any new epoch are always planted in the previous one. The New Deal did not start with Franklin Roosevelt's inauguration. Woodrow Wilson inspired much of the governmental fervor on which FDR capitalized; the Progressives had long assailed the trusts; and Herbert Hoover began many of the recovery programs that were folded into the New Deal. The distrust of government in the Reagan years was born of the widespread protests over Vietnam and Watergate and of disenchantment with corrupt and inefficient unions; and the privatization that encouraged monopoly power was actually begun under Jimmy Carter, whose "inflation czar," Alfred Kahn, deregulated the airlines well before Reagan's inauguration.

Now, in our time, a better future is already taking shape. The seeds of change are already pushing up shoots in transformative projects and initiatives now quietly but unmistakably under way across the United States and many other parts of the world. The chapters that follow will sketch the outline of the new, post-neoliberal world that is emerging and show what a "homecoming" of economic prosperity could mean.

CHAPTER 2

The Problem with Big Food

Most businesspeople think in terms of efficiency. Military types are trained to think about resilience. On the battlefield, synchronization is what matters. Do all the pieces of the puzzle fit together? Are the troops all marching in the same direction? Is there plenty of redundancy in the system? And if things go wrong (which they always do), is there a plan A, B, C, D, and, if at all possible, E? "That's our training," says Col. John Hoffman, a retired army aviator and food security and infrastructure expert, who could have told you twenty years ago what would happen to America's food system in the event of a global pandemic.

Hoffman, a burly, broad-shouldered thirty-year military veteran with a full head of silver hair and an easy smile, has been thinking about food security since before the fall of the Soviet Union, when he was sent to Europe by the U.S. government, with the mission of protecting food infrastructure in Germany and revamping the military's commissary system. He quickly began to see security vulnerabilities in the system. The local milk going to European consumers and U.S. military families in Europe had different packaging from that sold in stores, for example, which made it all too easy a target for terrorists or other adversaries who might want to disrupt certain supply chains but not others. Hoffman began thinking about the vulnerabilities in highly concentrated global supply chains and wrote doctrine papers for the U.S. military about how to fix them.

As he put it in one of the many Senate testimonies he has given on food security over the last two decades, "Food is the one infrastructure you can't opt out of. You can live without electricity, you can stop flying in planes or riding in trains. You can stop using banks. But you must eat to survive."[1] And yet, since the 1980s, government policies designed to make food prices cheaper have made the system itself far more vulnerable to disruption.

Hoffman, though formally retired, is a senior research fellow with the Food Protection and Defense Institute housed within the University of Minnesota. He is still active as an informal adviser to the U.S. government in times of emergency and is often called in for discussions with the FBI, the Department of Homeland Security, and the intelligence and defense community around emergency events. He saw the looming disaster of the pandemic coming as early as anyone. In December 2019, before Covid-19 had even made the news in the United States, Hoffman was on the phone with a Chinese doctor talking about what was happening in Wuhan. As the news began to break a few weeks later, Hoffman and a group of colleagues, including other retired and active security and military personnel and a number of academics and other infrastructure and systems experts, got on a conference call to discuss their concerns about a global pandemic. The consensus: it was only a matter of time before the novel coronavirus reached the United States and started to disrupt any number of crucial systems, from public health to the economy.

In January, they began speaking to the Department of Homeland Security, recommending that it immediately roll out the National Strategy for Pandemic Influenza. Between 2004 and 2005, Hoffman had helped write this road map for what the government and private sector should do, together, in the event of a biological event like Covid-19, to protect food and other critical systems. The plan outlined the various risks to critical infrastructure should just such a major viral event spread to the United States. One of the many issues Hoffman had raised was the level of consolidation in U.S. food production facilities, many of which were owned by foreign companies.

Among those was the South Dakotan slaughterhouse that became one of the hot spots for Covid-19 contagion, with more than a thousand workers sick and at least four dying from the disease.

Hoffman and his network began calling the White House, the Department of Homeland Security, and their contacts within the intelligence community to urge them to implement steps in the National Strategy for Pandemic Influenza Implementation Plan to protect the country's food-supply system.

They were more or less ignored by the Trump administration, which downplayed the threat of the virus during those first weeks of its spread in the United States. By February 2020, Hoffman and his group had reached out to the U.S. Department of Agriculture, laying out what was going to happen to the meat industry as a result of the crisis—there would be not only shortages, but supply chain disruptions and the possibility of superspreader events in slaughterhouses, many of which were also vulnerable to cyber-attack. "This isn't rocket science," says Hoffman. "It's simply the way these interconnected systems work." The USDA, along with every other government body the group contacted, ignored the risk. "They just said, 'Oh Hoffman—there he goes again.'"

The pandemic plan, which had been updated as recently as 2017 by the Department of Homeland Security and the Federal Emergency Management Agency (FEMA), had been cited by numerous administrations as the key to successfully dealing with something like Covid-19, which everyone knew would arrive eventually. It was the reason many international bodies cited the United States as the nation best prepared to handle such a crisis.[2] And yet, the plan was never implemented. Some of this was due to the dysfunction within the Trump administration. Some of it was due to polarized politics. The pandemic, like nearly everything else, became an opportunity for Democrats and Republicans to line up on different sides of the fence, creating policy paralysis that made it difficult to act quickly and decisively.

But perhaps the largest problem was that no single person in the White House was in charge of thinking about such global systems failures. While the Department of Homeland Security ostensibly plays this role, in practice, it has no power to coordinate all the government bodies—as many as sixteen federal agencies are involved in food safety—let alone get them all rowing in the same direction. "In the wake of the crisis, industry got the brunt of the criticism," says Hoffman, "but at the end of the day, industry follows government policy. Where was the government reaction?" It wasn't there, because policy itself had been built around maximizing efficiency rather than resilience in a globalized system where risks, while growing exponentially, had become more and more opaque.

Pile It High, Sell It Cheap

Of the many vulnerabilities in our economy and society exposed over the last few years, one of most gut-wrenching was the dysfunction at the heart of our food system. Americans are used to their food being inexpensive and plentiful. Our entire system is designed to "pile it high and sell it cheap," as the old grocer saying goes. In 1930, the average American family spent 24.2 percent of its income on food. By 2007, that number had fallen to 9.8 percent.[3] This is directly due to the U.S. food system's becoming, like most of the world's food systems, dramatically more concentrated, industrialized, and globalized over that period.

Three companies now control 70 percent of agrochemicals. Ninety percent of global grain is controlled by four multinational companies. Nine food companies control what is bought and sold in retail outlets. What's more, 60 percent of our food supply comes from just three plants (corn, wheat, and rice), the production of which is controlled by a handful of Big Ag and chemical companies.[4]

Agriculture has become incredibly efficient. U.S. farmers have nearly tripled their production over the past seventy years. But this efficiency has come at great cost to everything, from our health to our food security to working conditions for people in agriculture—not to mention the treatment of animals and, of course, the disastrous consequences of it all for our environment.

These costs were hiding in plain sight, but the pandemic exposed them. We had to face the reality of horrifying labor practices within the highly concentrated meatpacking industry, for example—workers who have to cut animals apart so quickly that they don't have time even to cover their mouths to cough; managers who can't hear the workers speak because the factories are so noisy.[5] The result was that the meat industry came under more heat than it has since Upton Sinclair wrote *The Jungle*. More recently, as the war in Ukraine has led to the first synchronized food and fuel price spike in many years, other highly concentrated parts of the global food supply chain (grains and fertilizer to name two) have come under fire. In the United States, Big Food now rivals Big Tech as a focus of antitrust action, with the Department of Justice investigating big companies, including Tyson Foods, Cargill, National Beef, and JBS S.A., and with Sen. Cory Booker launching a bill to stop agricultural monopolies and place moratoriums on large factory farms.[6] The Federal Trade Administration and other regulatory bodies are also looking into what part corporate price gouging may play in rising inflation.[7]

But while industry is taking the heat, it's only following where government policy has led it since the 1970s. As with everything from trade shifts to financial deregulation, concentration in food supply chains is part of a multi-decade move toward policies that prioritized the global economy over national resilience. Like the complex securitization that blew up the financial system in 2008, highly complex, globalized food supplies are a result of neoliberal thinking and, in particular, the doctrine of shareholder value that became ubiquitous in the eighties. In both cases, the goal was to move the cost and the risk off the balance sheet,[8] put it elsewhere, make it someone else's problem. But risk, like energy, never really goes away. It just takes on a new form.

There wasn't any one silver-bullet regulation that made our food system suddenly more vulnerable. It was more a process of small, steady tweaks throughout the system over many years, tweaks made on the basis of neoliberal policy assumptions. Oftentimes, the changes would start from a legitimate need or a worthy idea, but then, slowly, over time, would morph into something that actually increased fragility and created new problems. Consider, for example, the food stamp program, officially known as SNAP, or the Supplemental Nutrition Assistance Program. SNAP was born from a realization, in the run-up to World War II, that farm surpluses could be used to feed hungry people in cities.[9] But gradually, as the program expanded in the 1960s and '70s, it began to fuel a system that was all about lowering food prices. This sounds like a great idea, but lower prices also mean consolidation, concentration, and "efficiency" over resiliency. The goal of making food cheaper has become the de facto driving force within agencies like the USDA, which makes it very difficult to do anything fundamentally different in agriculture at scale. This is how you get China owning most of the pork supply in America, or five states producing more than half the country's milk.

Meatpacking, for example, wasn't the only food production vulnerability exposed by Covid-19. In the wake of the pandemic, even as lines formed at supermarkets and people hoarded goods in preparation for lockdown, farmers had to destroy crops and dump milk. Why the juxtaposition? Because a system designed to promote "efficiency" had led to two entirely separate supply chains—one supporting supermarkets; the other, restaurants and institutions such as schools and hospitals. When demand in the second supply chain collapsed thanks to pandemic-related shutdowns, grocery prices in the first supply chain surged upon higher demand, even as farmers destroyed crops that could not be easily funneled from restaurants to retail outlets.[10]

As Vanderbilt University academic Ganesh Sitaraman has pointed out in his work on the geography of inequality,[11] the reason that two highly concentrated and separate supply chains with far-flung transport systems (which make very little sense from an energy or security standpoint) can even exist has to do with regulatory shifts in areas like transportation, communications, tax, and antitrust. Why, for example, is there so little warehousing of supply in grocery stores? Because high taxes on inventory lead companies to keep less on hand and to ship more "just-in-time" supply all over the country by planes, trains, and automobiles. This, in turn, favors large suppliers that can afford such systems of scale. Does it make more economic sense to drive large quantities of milk across the country than it does to buy it locally from a farm that can deliver it to your door? If you look at the problem in a 360-degree way, of course it doesn't. But if you are a grocery store CFO looking at your balance sheet, it does. This is how insecurity in the system builds.

Such issues aren't just a matter of economics, but of national security. Food has become a focal point around U.S.-Chinese decoupling challenges and around the broader deglobalization of supply chains. Covid-19 exposed the fact that crucial pharmaceutical supplies and personal protective equipment, or PPE, came from China, but it also illuminated how food could be used as a trade weapon. Why did pork prices spike after the pandemic hit? Because the largest pork producer in the United States, Smithfield, is owned by a Chinese company that takes orders from the Chinese government, which understandably wanted to export from the United States to China what pork was available during a time of scarcity to feed its own people. Likewise, after U.S. and European officials asked for more information on how the novel coronavirus had been spread in China, Beijing threatened to boycott imported salmon, alleging that it could be linked to new cases of Covid-19.

Suddenly, countries everywhere began recalibrating the risks of globalized food systems. European countries, including Italy and France, doubled down on protections for local producers. In the United States, there were calls to support local agriculture and small-scale farmers, not just for health and national security—consider that two of the top beef processors in the United States are based in Brazil,[12] a country whose long-term economic fortunes are linked more to China than to the United States—but also economic and environmental reasons. There was also a sudden uptick in interest in community agricultural co-operatives, farm-to-table supply chains, and locally grown produce boxes delivered to customers' doors.[13]

The war in Ukraine, a global breadbasket, has only added to the desire for more local food security.

The Rise of Big Ag

It's a pendulum shift that tracks the rise and fall of the modern neoliberal era. Roughly a century ago, we were coming out of the Great Depression and entering the period leading up to World War II, during which neoliberal economic thinking was becoming influential. This was around the time policy makers were trying to relocate people from rural areas to cities, so that they could take part in the Industrial Revolution. "Technological efficiency [in agriculture] was important as a part of that, and crop specialization and mechanization (and the subsequent industrialization and concentration that followed) allowed that to happen," notes Dawn Thilmany, former president of the Agricultural and Applied Economics Association and a professor of agriculture at Colorado State University. American farmers rose to the challenge of producing lots of food ever more cheaply and by fewer people in order to fill the stomachs of the hordes of hungry factory workers flooding into cities. By that measure, the U.S. agricultural system was a great success.

But the rise in productivity and the fall in prices came with many side effects, like the loss of biodiversity, extensive habitat losses, increases in dietary health problems, pollution, and climate change. What's more, the entire system was predicated on government support, particularly when it came to mass-commodity crops, which the U.S. Department of Agriculture backstopped by guaranteeing prices for farmers. This, in turn, locked everyone into a system that is no longer suited for farmers, consumers, or the planet. "It used to be that the problem was malnutrition in the form of not enough calories," says Thilmany. "Now we have problems with the mix of calories we are receiving."

Much of the current system comes out of the Agricultural Adjustment Act, the first of which was signed by FDR as part of the New Deal. Since then, there's been a new farm bill roughly every four to seven years, and it usually stipulates that if you grow crops of something the U.S. government wants (like corn or soybeans, which are major exports and key components for livestock feed and processed foods), then the government has your back. But because farmers don't want to try cultivating something new and risk losing those subsidies, this system results in the overproduction of a few highly globalized crops. "It's like health insurance in this country—because it's linked to jobs, people don't leave their job to do a start-up, which then decreases innovation and entrepreneurial vibrancy," says Thilmany. The same perverse incentives are at work in agriculture.

More recent farm bills eventually got rid of price subsidies, but they introduced subsidized insurance for farmers, which adds another layer of distortion to the system. Farm insurance is a private market, but one that is backstopped by the federal government. It has its preferred insurance providers, and those providers want to make loans to farmers who have a history and data showing yields, yearly growth figures, opportunities, and challenges to their business model. But this kind of lending doesn't always align well with innovation and what's best for the agricultural system as a whole. "It's like an investor sticking with a low-yield, stable financial product, but getting no growth," Thilmany says of the perverse incentives in the federally insured farm system. "If you do something new in farming, there may be no way to even insure it . . . and be reimbursed for failure." It doesn't matter whether it's a good idea. It doesn't matter whether your new idea—be it working with fewer chemicals or growing new kinds of crops or producing healthy foods rather than cattle feed—actually improves the system overall. All that matters is whether the farmer can make a strong and stable business case to the bank, which mostly wants to make loans that will be backstopped by federal subsidies, which are in turn given to the biggest cash-crop farmers.

Concentration and vulnerability in the food supply chain increased further during the Reagan years, when the rewriting of antitrust laws led to a massive wave of mergers and acquisitions in many industries, including agriculture. The idea was that as long as a merger lowered prices for consumers, there was no problem. This philosophy was a major shift from 1930s laws that took into account the political power of large companies and how they might distort the market if they had too big a share. The turning point came in 1978, when Robert Bork, a Chicago School acolyte who would go on to become a federal court judge, published an influential book titled *The Antitrust Paradox*. Bork held that the major goal of antitrust policy should be to promote "business efficiency," which from the eighties onward came to be measured in consumer prices. It was a shift that took the United States away from antitrust policy predicated on the welfare of the "citizen" and toward the more laissez-faire politics of the Reagan administration and those who followed.[14]

In the case of the agricultural industry, the economies of scale from mergers, along with an increased use of fertilizers and other chemicals in food production, dramatically increased output and exports. A mere 1 percent of farmers today can produce what 37 percent could sixty years ago. The number of calories available to the average American per capita per day has gone from 3,200 in 1980 to 3,900 today. (Thanks to the rise of cheap food, the same directional increase in calories can be seen in most countries.) But consumers have been encouraged to eat more and more of exactly what isn't good for us: refined carbohydrates, meat, and sugar. "Americans have, quite simply, gotten used to cheap food over fifty years," says Thilmany. "We consider it our right."

Collateral Damage

I witnessed the shift toward Big Food growing up in Indiana from the seventies onward. The state was (and is) a major producer of pork and corn. Crop sprayers were ubiquitous, as were obesity and asthma. I remember how shocked I was when I learned that of the miles and miles of corn that surrounded us, only 1 percent of it was meant to be eaten on the cob, by people. The rest was "dent" corn, used for food oils, corn syrup, and in large part, feed for cattle. Indeed, 67 percent of total calories from food grown in the United States goes to feed factory-farmed animals.

All of it is terrible for our health. The processed Western diet has been directly linked to dramatically rising healthcare costs over the last forty years, not just at home but also abroad. Global companies have exported this system throughout the world, which is why obesity has more than doubled in seventy countries since 1980. Many of the trade deals cut since that time have allowed Big Food to expand its reach. Since NAFTA was signed, for example, Coke has become three times cheaper than water in Mexico. The result? One in ten children there now has type 2 diabetes (something that until quite recently was seen only in adults).[15] You can tell the same story around the world—from Italy, Spain, Greece, and Cyprus to Southeast Asia and China, where diabetes is spreading so rapidly that the country can't build hospitals fast enough to handle the caseload.[16] There are now more overweight people in the world than there are hungry people. Indeed, given that the processed diet is cheaper, many of the world's poor are both overweight and malnourished.

As Thilmany points out, cheap calories are no longer what the country or the world needs in terms of health, the environment, or food security. But thanks to Big Food lobbyists (who regularly rank alongside Wall Street, Big Tech, Big Pharma, and the oil industry in terms of lobbying dollars spent),[17] farmers continue to be paid to grow cash crops like corn, soybeans, and wheat in huge quantities, but are disincentivized from growing fruits and vegetables. (From a calorie perspective, the world grows only a third as much as are needed.) This isn't just an economic issue, but a matter of public safety. For example, decades ago, it was understood by scientists that "finishing" cattle on grass rather than corn as they were prepared for slaughter would greatly reduce problems with *E. coli* contamination in meat. But corn growers pushed back on any new rules around this. Likewise, cattle lobbyists made it more difficult to pass livestock traceability regulations (which allow the government to track farm-raised animals back to their source). There was even an effort within the food regulatory agencies to suppress news about the first episodes of mad cow disease in the United States.[18]

The result is a "commodity treadmill," a system of taxpayer-funded price supports that generate big corporate profits regardless of the consequences of overproduction. "The result is a vicious cycle where farmers, struggling with low prices and high debts, respond by producing more of the commodity to try to recoup their losses," says Molly Jahn, an agronomy professor currently working with DARPA, the innovation arm of the U.S. Department of Defense, on issues of food security. The system works economically on corporate and government balance sheets only if the full costs to health, the environment, and national security aren't tallied.[19]

Unfortunately, money politics has made it tough to tally these costs. Lobbyists make sure that FDA rules and dietary recommendations don't shift the current system too much and that food stamps can't be leveraged to change existing incentive structures. The government bureaucracy—more than a dozen agencies are involved in regulating the U.S. food system—exists to reinforce itself. All this makes cheap and energy-intensive food omnipresent, while healthier choices become scarcer and more and more expensive. The Walmarts of the world, which carry only a handful of top consumer brands, add fuel to this fire. Each year, they pressure suppliers to cut prices more and more, which of course favors only the largest players in the existing model. The results are low prices, low wages, fewer choices, higher energy consumption, and strange extremes within the food system. "Food deserts," places where there are few grocery stores or other venues to find fresh, healthful food, have proliferated around the country. Some of them actually exist nearby the largest industrial farm fields, in places like the San Fernando Valley,[20] where many migrant farmworkers live. This means that the very people helping to harvest food for the rest of the country have little access to it themselves. In short, fresh produce has, for many people, become a luxury good. It's simply impossible to come by at a reasonable price. Meanwhile, "cheap" food raises the price tag of diet-related diseases, which now cost us $3.7 trillion a year to treat.[21]

As bad as globalized, industrialized agriculture is for our health, it's even worse for the planet. Food production is the single-biggest cause of climate change, from the energy and chemicals required to grow the crops to the emissions and methane produced by factory farms and the animals within them.[22] What's more, industrial farming is almost by definition overfarming. Mass meat production requires enormous amounts of corn and soybeans, both of which are heavily subsidized by farm bill provisions, through both direct payments and subsidized crop insurance. These payments made it possible for big companies like Tyson, Smithfield, and JBS (some of the country's largest meat producers) to get even bigger, because their feed costs are so low. But it translated into a decrease in the diversity of crops in the heartland between 1978 and 2012, as farmers couldn't afford to grow anything but industrial-scale corn and soybeans.[23] It has also meant that the United States has begun to import more of what it can no longer grow itself.

Our system of industrial farming takes a toll on the land, in the form of soil erosion and reduced fertility from overuse of chemicals. As it becomes harder and more expensive for companies to create the same yields on land that has become strained by the production of single crops, a vicious circle occurs. Only the biggest, most globally integrated companies have the financial muscle to compete, and they use their capital to buy up more land, which becomes ever more expensive, squeezing out smaller players.

Rain on the Scarecrow

The beleaguered American farmer has been a powerful political icon for decades—think of Dorothea Lange's photographs of Dust Bowl migrants, or of the 1985 Farm Aid concert featuring musical artists Neil Young, Willie Nelson, and my fellow Hoosier John Mellencamp, whose hit song "Rain on the Scarecrow" was inspired by the worst rural economic conditions since the Great Depression: "The crops we grew last summer weren't enough to pay the loans / Couldn't buy the seed to plant this spring, and the farmer's bank foreclosed."[24] That song, a staple of midwestern drive radio, came out in 1985, around the time large-scale farm consolidation in the United States began. In just twenty-five years, from 1987 to 2012, the share of farms of fewer than a thousand acres—meaning most family farms—fell from 57 percent of cropland acres to 36 percent.[25] According to an academic report commissioned by the Family Farm Action Alliance, this disproportionately affected poorer regions of the country and communities of color.[26] "Consolidation started in the eighties, but you really saw a lot of changes with Clinton, and later with Obama, too—you had the globalization folks controlling economics, and various pieces of legislation supported the feed/fuel/ meat complex," says Joe Maxwell, a Missouri-based family farmer, former lieutenant governor of Missouri, and head of the Family Farm Action Alliance. "Farmers today are on a treadmill. They have to take on debt to make their businesses work or end up being in the real estate business instead of farming," thanks to additional government subsidies that will pay for building improvements, but not for the changes that are actually needed to create a healthier farm system overall.

The numbers bear this out. In 2018, farmers whose primary occupation was farming but who had sales of less than $350,000 had a median net income of *negative* $1,524. The upshot is that it's nearly impossible to make a decent living as a farmer in the United States today without being big, which means being part of the existing dysfunctional agricultural system. The depopulation of rural areas has contributed to the collapse in communities that has fueled much of the populism in politics we've struggled with over the last decade. It has frayed social relationships, contributed to "deaths of despair" among the white working class, and compromised the physical health of people within communities of color, who bear a disproportionate burden of exposure to excessive pesticide use or large-scale animal operations.[27]

But the cycle isn't over yet. Between now and 2035, some 40 percent of the mainland United States' 991 million farm and ranch acres will change hands, and most of them will be purchased by Big

Ag. Indeed, as Democrats campaigning in heartland states in recent midterm and presidential elections have pointed out, the concentration of power in agribusiness has been a bigger and certainly a longer-term problem for U.S. farmers than China has been. Although, to be fair, the two are sometimes one and the same, as Beijing has prioritized the purchase of agricultural resources in the United States and many other countries as part of its own food security plans. As a few companies gained control of key areas of the food supply chain, spending on research and development fell, input costs rose, and margins for individual farms went down. Large multinational corporate lobbyists have created a system in which small farms can be forced into opaque contracts and held up by ridiculous rules, such as those forbidding them to repair their own machinery without permission from John Deere or other large manufacturers.[28] Those who try to organize unions have faced retaliation.[29]

The Financialization of Food

Amazingly, many of those acres changing hands will be bought not to farm food, but as a financial investment.[30] This brings up a final pernicious problem in our food system that is linked to neoliberal economic thinking: the financialization of food. Commodities like food, oil, and gas are natural resources, raw materials that are literally the stuff of life. But they are also financial assets and have been so for literally thousands of years. They are inexorably tied to one of the most crucial and yet most volatile and problematic financial markets: the derivatives market. Derivatives are a financial tool that has been used for millennia as an insurance policy for farmers who own things like wheat, corn, or (in the case of the ancient Greeks, who may have invented the concept of derivatives) olive groves. By purchasing a derivative like a futures contract, a farmer can lock in a future price for their crop, lest prices drop before the crop is harvested. Airlines or trucking companies can also "hedge" oil prices with commodity derivatives to protect their business in case of sudden price increases. These are all necessary and useful functions for derivatives.

But over the last forty years, the market for food (and for commodities of all sorts, from oil to aluminum) has increasingly been about trading it as a financial instrument rather than using it as a raw material. It's all part of the process of prioritizing the free flow of capital over anything else. While the needs of farmers and goods producers on the ground are local, the commodities markets in which they hedge are global. The capital within them flows to investors everywhere around the planet. This process of financialization has allowed Wall Street to grow many times the size of Main Street and to become the tail that wags the dog of the real economy. Global financial assets are now roughly four times the size of the real economy. And commodities are a particularly financialized area of the economy—since 2000, there has been a fiftyfold increase in dollars invested in commodities-linked index funds.[31]

In the run-up to the 2008 financial crisis, commodities derivatives boomed. The industry has been a particular target for this sort of "financialization," in part because, in the past, commodities tended to move counter to the price of other assets, making them a good "hedge" for traders. But all this trading has created much more financial volatility in food and fuel. It's a boom-and-bust cycle that is, quite literally, a life-or-death matter for the world's most vulnerable populations. In 2008, for example, the world faced a serious and unusually synchronized surge in inflation, the bulk of it due to a precipitous rise in the price of food and energy commodities. Some of that was due to people in emerging markets eating more food and driving more cars. But this was the period of the Great Recession, which should have driven prices down. Instead, even as the world plunged into a downturn, oil hit a record high of $150 a barrel. The price of many foodstuffs skyrocketed, too. The year 2008 became the first one on record in which more than one billion people in the world went hungry. There were food riots in twenty-two countries.[32]

"What we are experiencing is a demand shock coming from a

new category of participant in the commodities futures markets . . . corporate and government pension funds, sovereign wealth funds, university endowments, and other institutional investors," said hedge fund portfolio manager Michael Masters in Senate hearings on the topic at the time,[33] noting that such investors held the largest share of outstanding commodities futures contracts. They still do, and have more recently been joined by average Joe retail traders, as became evident during the Covid-19 pandemic, when day trading boomed.

There are many differences between the Covid-19 pandemic and the 2008 financial crisis. Yet both illustrate the way that market speculation and an economy built on asset bubbles supported by unfettered global capital flows can exacerbate dangerous price swings, particularly in tumultuous times. Consider a case from the end of May 2020, when the pandemic was in full swing. A big sell-off of West Texas Intermediate futures contracts by the country's largest oil exchange-traded fund (ETF), the United States Oil Fund (USO), resulted in a plunge in U.S. crude prices. There were many reasons for oil prices to crash, from the massive drop in demand due to the coronavirus lockdown to the petropolitics of Russia and Saudi Arabia. But another reason was the level of speculation in oil markets. The CME Group, a derivatives exchange, "became concerned" about USO, an ETF that deals in oil futures, its having amassed a quarter of the WTI futures contract due to be delivered in June. The CME felt this was a dangerously large position and ordered USO to scale back. At this point, furious trading ensued, and June futures prices plunged, wreaking havoc with energy and food commodity markets.

This reminds me very much of 2008. Then, as now, there were some real supply-and-demand dynamics at work, but increased use of commodities as a financial instrument also played a role. This is particularly worrisome at a time when geopolitical events such as Russia's invasion of Ukraine have caused another spike in global food and fuel prices, one that may have further destabilizing ripple effects. The financialization of commodities simply adds kerosene to any existing problem in the market.

The rise of ETFs like USO, for example, means that plenty of retail investors are dabbling in oil derivatives. It's hard to understand why anyone would have wanted to be in USO, given that the fund had a -94 percent return from its start in 2006 through to mid-April 2020. But retail investors aren't commodities experts—very often, they are teenagers playing with trading apps. According to Robintrack, which follows the number of users holding each asset on the online trading platform Robinhood, a record 220,905 user accounts held the USO fund at the end of April 2020, almost thirty times more than two months before. It's part of a long-term trend toward retail investors using low-cost vehicles like ETFs to take part in a specific investing trend that was hitherto available only to professionals—for example, using oil or corn or any other commodity as a financial asset class to hedge against inflation and geopolitical events.

But it is also part of something bigger—the forty-year neoliberal shift to what President George W. Bush dubbed "the ownership society," an economy based on asset price growth rather than income or job growth. From the eighties onward, both Democrats and Republicans have supported "market knows best" policies, whether it was the end of fixed-benefit pensions and support for the 401(k) system (which covers only half of Americans); shifts in the tax code that made it easier for companies to pay corporate executives in share options (creating incentives for them to bolster short-term stock prices rather than long-term business); or low interest rates that encouraged stock markets to rise and pushed more Americans to hold wealth in markets that have become increasingly volatile. In 1989, 32 percent of U.S. families held stock. Today, it's over half.[34] This itself creates a certain policy inertia, because changing things would mean risking the economy itself, given that personal consumption (nearly 70 percent of the U.S. economy) is tightly linked to asset inflation. Consider that net capital gains plus taxable distributions from individual retirement accounts are equal to 200 percent of year-on-year growth in consumption. If the market crashes, the economy literally cannot grow.[35]

In some ways, commodity ETFs are just the latest iteration of a trend that began with index funds and has extended to low-cost brokerages, e-trading platforms, and even fintech robo-advising (more on fintech in chapter 7). It's all part of the same trend: an economy based on "efficiency" rather than resiliency, on Wall Street rather than Main Street. The financialization of food is simply one of the most colorful examples of how far this trend has gone. Given that technology platforms such as Robinhood (which added three million users between January and May 2020 alone, half of them first-time investors) allow novices to make such bets in the blink of an eye, teenagers were suddenly able to gamble on the prices of grain and oil. This created tremendous new volatility in the markets. "I'd wager that 90 percent of investors in USO couldn't explain what contango is," says Masters, referring to the difference between the current market price and the futures price traders must try to navigate. Indeed. After oil ETFs eventually imploded in 2020 and USO's own broker refused to place more orders, plenty of average Joe investors lost their shirts.[36] Meanwhile, small farmers and consumers had to cope with increased fuel price volatility and food price spikes.

Given the myriad risks that go along with the highly globalized, financialized, and concentrated food system, many business leaders and policy makers are looking for a solution—something that will encourage resilience rather than efficiency. "You aren't going to be able to change the system overnight—in fact, with as big and diverse a population as we have [in the United States], you are going to need to keep some of the system in place. You can't get completely away from technical efficiency and mass manufacturing and production," says Thilmany. "But it's about the mix. It's about the portfolio of projects. And it's about whether cheaper really is cheaper when you factor in all the different costs."[37] Clearly, it's not, for either the planet or its population. The question now is: How to fix things?

CHAPTER 3

Systems Failure

The term *food security* wasn't used anywhere outside emerging markets until quite recently. But these days, you'll hear it bandied about in Washington, London, and Brussels, very often by defense and intelligence experts who are thinking about how to create more local resiliency in a polarized world.

People like Col. John Hoffman, for example, have traditionally gotten very little attention outside defense and intelligence circles. But after 9/11, in early 2002, a friend of Hoffman's at the country's National Infrastructure Protection Center, part of the Federal Bureau of Investigation, asked Hoffman to come immediately to Washington to help the newly formed Department of Homeland Security understand critical infrastructure issues. It is amazing to think that, at that point, the food and agriculture infrastructure itself was not considered "critical."

Hoffman, who was retired by then, was called back to government to work with DHS. Between 2003 and 2005, he began to understand that cybersecurity—or, more particularly, the lack of it—was a huge vulnerability in the nation's food and agriculture systems. "The DHS began to take on more responsibility for thinking about food security, but there were sixteen agencies at that time involved in food, and everyone had their own technology standards, working in their own silos," he says. Different agencies had entirely different operating systems, many of them outdated.

Smart devices at the "edge" of networks (things like cameras on grain combines) were completely unprotected. The staff who ran processor operations in most food production facilities were monitoring system operations and corresponding about sensitive matters from home with no virtual private networks (VPNs) on their computers. Meanwhile, there was little to no coordination between the public and the private sector on much of anything. The whole thing reminded Hoffman of the standard failures he'd long seen in critical systems. "When I was in Vietnam, as an aviator," thanks to a lack of tech standards coordination, "the army radios couldn't talk to those on the navy aircraft carriers," he says. Needless to say, this added a measure of complexity for pilots figuring out where and when to land on a navy aircraft carrier or, more dangerously, when and where to fly under or around naval gunfire targeting enemy positions on land.[1]

Systems failures created by such organizational silos have been with us for ages. "Napoléon wanted to create a military without silos," says Ranjay Gulati, a Harvard Business School professor who has spent twenty years studying silos. "Adam Smith spoke about the problem of labor silos. Events like 9/11 might have been prevented if there had been more sharing of information across organizational divisions." Globalization has, of course, increased the complexity of systems, particularly in business, which has in turn created more opportunity for such communication gaps.

Numerous corporate debacles in recent years have been linked to information silos. Consider the disaster caused by the California energy utility Pacific Gas and Electric, where some employees knew for years that hundreds of miles of the company's power lines needed upgrading, lest they fail and spark fire—which of course they eventually did, killing eighty-five people and costing the company $30 billion in potential legal claims.[2] Less tragic examples of silos in blue-chip firms abound: Sony once had two separate divisions working on creating the same electrical plug without anyone realizing it. The company spent millions of dollars building the same equipment, within the same organization, twice.[3] Despite such well-publicized business disasters, executives still tend not to focus on global complexity as a risk. The Covid-19 pandemic has changed things—but slowly, as the neoliberal "efficiency" paradigm dies hard.

Military people, for their part, tend to be great systems thinkers because they are laser-focused on resiliency and have little room for error in their jobs. And Hoffman was no exception. As he worked with DHS in the wake of 9/11, he became convinced that the only way to cut through the bureaucracy of Washington and the economic capture of Big Ag was to create a White House–level body that could integrate all food systems within both the physical and the digital worlds. In 2004, he met with then-DHS secretary Tom Ridge and presented a paper arguing for a policy coordinating committee on the issue, which would be run by a resiliency czar in the White House who could dictate terms and guarantee cooperation among agencies on technology and supply chains and other infrastructure-related issues. The idea was to get all the government ships sailing in the same direction. "After that, the private sector has to follow," he says.

It didn't happen—in part because the DHS didn't have enough clout to push through the plan. But the department did fund two centers of excellence to study the issues, one at Texas A&M and another at the University of Minnesota. This led to Hoffman's connecting with Molly Jahn, a genomic scientist born into a famous family of Canadian plant breeders. Jahn had landed at the University of Wisconsin–Madison after stints at MIT and Cornell during which she was funded by the National Science Foundation and the USDA to do plant biology research. Like Hoffman, she is extremely mission driven. Mistakenly diagnosed with a terminal illness as a child, she became, in her own words, "extremely focused, but also a bit reckless with regard to certain considerations in my career." Translation: she cared about ideas, not politics. As Jahn studied plant genetics, she became extremely focused on the damage that humans were doing to the environment and also convinced that the problems within the food system were about more than food. "It was all about energy," she says. "Climate change was about humans using fossil fuels to support practices like conventional agriculture that were releasing too much energy into the system. Obesity was about too much caloric energy in the biological system."

Her day job was coming up with new plant varieties—"You can't walk down a supermarket aisle in the United States today without seeing my varietals," she says proudly, which include Delicata squash and Hannah's Choice melons, named after her daughter— but she was also thinking about how dysfunctional the globalized food system itself had become. "I was becoming more and more convinced that humans were driving the planet way, way outside historical bounds," she says. "And agriculture turned out to be one of the primary ways that human beings acted thermodynamically on the planet." The problem, according to Jahn, was that we had viewed abundance as a risk management strategy. While that may have been true earlier in human history, with the rise of industrial, globalized, highly concentrated agriculture, this reflex carried its own perils: billions of people on a planet under acute stress. And not just climate risk, but food safety risks, supply chains risks, labor risks, and national security risks. All this meant that, ironically, food was now front and center as one of the chief potential vulnerabilities for the nation. In order to guarantee our safety in any potential conflict with China (which had begun hoarding land, ports, water supplies, and seed banks), make any clean-energy transition, and ensure our own health and livelihood, the United States' food system needed to change.

When Jahn was dean of the agriculture school at the University of Wisconsin–Madison, she won a multimillion-dollar grant from the Department of Energy to come up with ways to reduce carbon emissions at the "food, water, energy nexus." In 2009, she was appointed by the first Obama administration to work as a deputy and acting undersecretary within the USDA to turn its internal and university-based research toward twenty-first-century challenges.[4] It was there that she began to see how the problems within the system were being reinforced by the government agencies themselves. For starters, because of its budget structure, the USDA was a basket of siloed agencies, each with tightly prescribed responsibilities, staffs, and budgets. As the acting undersecretary for research, education, and economics, Jahn had two federal statistical agencies in her portfolio, along with the USDA's internal and external research agencies. And yet, her budget was less than 1 percent of the department's total. "That's because SNAP, the food stamps program, is such a large share of the USDA's budget." The goal of that program was to align these benefits with incentives for healthful diets and more profitable and stable agricultural production. But SNAP is the proverbial battleship among USDA programs, and turning it in an entirely different direction isn't an easy proposition. Jahn's concerns lay even deeper. "Actions that do not address the underlying thermodynamic imbalances, mining all that fossil energy to support humanity's massive binge on the planet's stored energy, are more like a game of whack-a-mole," she says. She needed to find people who could help her "steer our planet back into a safe, or at least safer, space," where human demands on the planet fell within the boundaries needed to maintain stability of our resource base and environment.

John Hoffman was thinking about all these issues in the same way around that time, watching with concern the growing concentration in the milk and meat industries. "When I was a kid, we had milk delivered from local farmers," he notes. "Now there's one company, Milkco, that produces most of the milk supply in major parts of six states. If one plant goes down, there is no milk." In 2010, he advocated for using the newly inked Food Safety Modernization Act to put common cybersecurity standards in place across the country's critical food infrastructure. The FDA refused, and over time, both the FDA and the USDA pushed back on the food security conversation as a whole. They argued that food security in America had never been a problem; food was cheap and plentiful. Nobody was yet thinking about the vulnerabilities of massive industrial consolidation of the global food industry hiding in plain sight.

In 2012, Hoffman crafted a paper on the evolution of food safety and how it had driven decision making in the private sector, which had become increasingly concentrated, globalized, and vulnerable. In 2013, he testified to the Senate agriculture committee that the United States should not, under any circumstances, allow a $7.1 billion Chinese purchase of Smithfield, the country's largest pork producer, to go through. It did. "I told them this was crazy," said Hoffman. "Government policy creates these conglomerates within critical, strategic industries, then it allows them to be foreign owned," in this case, by the country's number one strategic adversary. "What does that mean for our food supply?"

It meant that there were significant risks in crucial areas. Most of the country's pork, for example, was processed at the Smithfield plant in Tar Heel, North Carolina. Some thirty thousand hogs were churned through the system each day, creating not only huge energy, water, and environmental issues, but also significant price and security challenges. These "risk hubs," as Molly Jahn calls them, were common throughout the U.S. food chain. Most of the country's fruit and vegetable supply, for example, flows through five counties, including two adjacent counties in California that are subject to earthquakes and wildfires and have relatively low socioeconomic profiles, all of which can exacerbate risk to stability from even medium-size or small events.

Risk hubs tend to attract risks of all kinds. California's Inland Empire isn't just America's center of produce production; it's also one of the most financially vulnerable regions of the country. The two adjacent counties were among the hardest-hit places in the subprime mortgage crisis and have higher-than-average unemployment, tent cities of homeless people who were evicted following the 2008 financial crisis, and immigration problems. California itself is ground zero for wildfires, earthquakes, floods, and drought. "One of the things that you look for, if you are interested in the functioning of a network, is where is the embedded risk hub?" says Jahn. "Where is the intersection of food poverty, financial insecurity, health, and national security?" All these pointed to just a handful of places.

Market Power

The doctrine of shareholder "value" had driven this vulnerability, so it was perhaps no surprise that Jahn came to the conclusion that the people who could change things fast were in finance, not government. The USDA tended to block actions with longer-term benefits that could be construed as threatening already-stressed bottom lines. Meanwhile, agricultural companies within the private sector were simply geared up to do exactly what neoliberal regulators and the market system itself encouraged, which was to get bigger, cheaper, and riskier.

Enter Trevor Maynard, the head of emerging risk at the insurance giant Lloyd's of London. Maynard had heard of Jahn's work and requested a meeting. In 2014, Jahn got on a plane to London and, as she puts it, "came in with all my stacks of research papers," ready to launch into a lengthy presentation about the risks inherent in the world's food, energy, and water nexus. Maynard, a crisp British actuary, told her that what he needed was a "two-page, extreme and plausible scenario for systemic risk in food systems with the potential to cascade to other sectors." If she supplied this, he could perhaps convince his board that the insurance industry needed to rethink how it covered the food industry and, indeed, a host of other industries affected by climate change. If food companies were at risk of losing their coverage, things might just begin to change. Jahn went back to Wisconsin, sat down at her kitchen table, and began thinking up a scenario that was risky enough to disrupt the global food supply and cause all sorts of ancillary damage. The idea was to present Lloyd's not with something that *might* happen, but with something that, given a bit of time, surely *would* happen.

She didn't have to look too far back in history for something to plug into her model. She realized that if she used an El Niño year (a year in which changes in air and tidal flows led to strange weather patterns) and "threw in a couple of other one-off events, nothing extreme, just another major flood or fire, then suddenly you have a scenario in which production of all the major commodity crops—corn, rice, soybeans—are being slashed by five to ten percent." After that, the theoretical dominoes begin to fall fast, with plunging stock markets and global famines leading to political instability and geopolitical conflict.

Jahn went back to Maynard to discuss her findings. In 2015, Lloyd's commissioned Jahn and a colleague, Aled Jones, to do a study on food insecurity and finance and produce a follow-up report in 2019. These garnered much attention within the underwriting and insurance communities, which began pushing companies for more information on their supply chains, their exposure to climate change, and their general preparedness for extreme events.

Meanwhile, security types from the United States, Europe, Australia, New Zealand, and other countries were becoming interested in Jahn's work. Talking to them, she became convinced that defense departments, rather than government agricultural departments, might be another major lever for change. "There's a relationship between the DoD, food security, and humanitarian crises around the world," she says, and notes that in about 80 percent of those crises, the U.S. military is deployed in some capacity.

Since 2016, Jahn has met regularly with a number of military officials and politicians who are concerned that food could become a weapon in any future conflict. What might have sounded mildly hyperbolic in 2019 now sounds prescient in 2022. Food has become a focal point around U.S.-Chinese decoupling and the broader deglobalization of supply chains. And like any critical system, it has become central to defense types as part of the changing nature of war, which may be less about missiles and more about the resilience of highly technical, connected systems like agriculture.

Reengineering Food

Jahn's quest led her to DARPA. The acronym stands for "Defense Advanced Research Projects Agency," and what this most innovative of U.S. government agencies does is truly the stuff of science fiction. DARPA scientists invented the internet, the computer mouse, unmanned deep-sea vehicles, stealth aircraft, robotic prosthetics, and hundreds of other groundbreaking things. Many of the people who've worked there since its founding (by President Dwight Eisenhower in 1958 to counter the Russian launch of Sputnik) look to be straight out of Cold War central casting, complete with either thick glasses, white shirts, and pocket protectors or camo, lace-up boots, and buzz cuts. But there are also plenty of twentysomethings in hoodies wielding laptops, perhaps part of the agency's cyber-ops; several women; and a host of characters you wouldn't expect to be working in the Defense Department.

Jahn—now one of twelve program managers in DARPA's Defense Sciences Office, each of whom heads up a key area of technology development—is one of them. She's the one with the rather broad goal of reinventing the entire process by which food gets made. If that sounds ambitious, it's only because you don't work for the agency. As one staffer put it to me during a reporting trip there in 2021, "If you come to DARPA and don't invent the internet, you get a B." People who leave their already-lofty regular lives to come work there for a few years tend to be A students. They also tend to dream big.

Jahn is now leading a broad and deep conversation among farmers, agricultural academics, defense leaders, and politicians about how to change the system. The challenge of her four-year DARPA project, dubbed Cornucopia, is to create a new global food system that more closely matches human needs than the one we currently have. "Could we shift our entire food paradigm in ways that could ensure national security, reduce energy usage, and produce a healthier system?" she asks rhetorically. (Jahn, in that visionary professor way, is a fan of rhetorical questions.) "Could the relatively unexplored universe of microbes, bacteria, and fungi produce nutrients in hours or days—far more quickly than it takes to grow crops in a field?" The answer? Yes. In fact, some of this is already being done in labs around the world.

But what if you could take the concept of making food not from animals, or even plants, but from microbes and use it to decentralize food production itself? "What if everyone could produce basic ingredients for household needs?" Jahn continues. "What if food was more like air, so no one could easily control it and everyone could be a farmer in a pinch? If we really want to make the world better, then giving individuals more agency over their food is not only safer but also empowering. Maybe everyone should have a gizmo that can turn air and water into a basic substance, or at least back up food systems when they fail."

A "gizmo" that makes food from nothing is exactly how the crew of the starship *Enterprise* fed itself, and even by the standard of sixties sci-fi, it sounds improbable. Except that companies in different parts of the world are already working on it, with prototype programs that use minimal energy to turn microbes into food. Microbes are, after all, all around us. We ingest trillions of them every day as part of everything else in our food. Existing private-sector efforts are small-scale, because they are almost exclusively focused on using microbes to create complex proteins and thus must rely on industrial equipment that isn't mobile. But the aim of Cornucopia is to sketch out the necessary technology and science to make it possible, say, for U.S. troops to feed themselves in extreme circumstances in which they can count on nothing but air, water, and their own power generator. As a 2021 press release about the program puts it, "carbon, nitrogen, hydrogen, and oxygen from air and water" would be transmuted, using mobile power sources, into more microbes, which would then be used to produce food molecules, including proteins, fats, carbohydrates, and dietary fiber—all in the form of safe, palatable foodstuffs.

To do this, Jahn is bringing together some of the existing commercial efforts with other public- and private-sector research, academic, and defense personnel. Using the techniques of chemical engineering and synthetic biology, she and her team are splitting water and air into their component elements and then splicing them into new types of microbes. These could ultimately be used to generate different types of food, replacing the standard-issue ready-to-eat meals for troops.

If this is starting to sound like pie in the sky, just remember: so did mRNA research when DARPA invested in it years ago. "We want to be able to create different flavors, textures, and types of food," Jahn says. In order to get the project off the ground, she didn't have to prove a food-from-nothing device was producible. But she did have to show it was mathematically possible. "I push a lot of boundaries," she says. "But I live within the realm of the laws of thermodynamics." Her team has already devised a raw solution of nutrients that could be crucial. That lab work isn't done at DARPA facilities, but rather among the project's numerous corporate and academic partners. Jahn will coordinate their efforts from her office in Arlington. Because she's at DARPA, she has to think about innovations that involve national defense and resiliency. But Cornucopia has tremendous commercial potential. It's also very disruptive. It is, in essence, attempting to reengineer the last ten thousand years of evolution in food systems.[5]

For Jahn, the first step toward changing how we think about agriculture and food systems has been to convince people in government, defense, and the private sector that change is possible. Her inspiration is a nineteenth-century British schoolteacher, Elizabeth Heyrick, who was a pivotal force in helping the British see slavery as abhorrent. Heyrick, whose story is told in the 2005 book *Bury the Chains,* found a blueprint for the hold of a slave ship—the block print picture that became ubiquitous in textbooks around the world, showing slaves packed tightly, lying foot to head, and left to vomit, defecate, and often die.[6] "It's one thing to know something as an idea, another to make a bunch of British women see that picture every time they look into their sugar bowl," Jahn notes, referring to the role of sugar in the slave trade. As a result of Heyrick's efforts, Britain ended slavery decades before America did. Jahn's mission now is to get the global public to see their dinner plates as they really are today and, slowly, to help us make food healthier, less energy intensive, more local, and ultimately, a source of resilience.

The Reason for Iceberg Lettuce

One of the easiest ways to do this is simply to lay out for people the journey that a typical food product takes to their plate. The emissions involved in getting a strawberry or a piece of asparagus flown off season from one country to another are enormous. But often, the bigger problems come from long-haul shipping at home. Consider, for example, the life of the country's most popular lettuce, the humble iceberg. Efficiency is responsible for the very existence of this produce, one of the most ubiquitous (and tasteless) vegetables ever created. Nobody really wants to eat it, except as a vehicle for scooping up blue cheese in a wedge salad. But it has been a major cash crop in the United States for most of the last fifty years because, although lettuce is among the most perishable commercial vegetables, iceberg travels well and can survive in supply chains for weeks. Yet lettuce is mostly water, and this variety has few nutrients. As much as 60 percent of its weight can evaporate as the lettuce travels from farm to grocery store to your table. This means that we are spending large sums of money on fuel and transport for something that is literally getting smaller en route and is contributing almost nothing to our health or well-being (not to mention taste buds) once it arrives.

This is clearly a ridiculous way to grow and eat food. This sort of senseless long-haul industrial farming is why the European Union has for years now promoted a popular but globally contentious "farm-to-fork strategy" that seeks to make agriculture more sustainable and to protect a diverse group of producers. Americans are constantly attacking Europeans in trade negotiations for their protections of local agriculture. But more recently, as the dangers of globalized food systems have become better understood, they've also begun to copy things like the "Slow Food" movement. Years ago, I visited the Northern Italian town of Bra, the birthplace of the movement. Though not far from the bustle and industrial stench of Turin, Bra smelled of lilacs and boasted a clock that ran behind by a half hour. It is one of dozens of Italian municipalities that have joined a sister cause, Cittaslow, or "Slow Cities." By local decree, these cities have declared themselves havens from the accelerating pace of life in the global economy. Shops are closed every Thursday and Sunday. Cars are limited on the grounds that traffic is "a precursor to stress." All fruits and vegetables served in schools must be organic and locally grown. The city offers cut-rate mortgages to homeowners who renovate using a local butter-colored stucco, and it reserves choice commercial real estate for family shops selling handmade chocolates or specialty cheeses.

The movement, which has now spread across Europe and the United States, was a reaction to the proliferation of McDonald's outlets, but it became a way also to mobilize to protect local products from being driven into extinction by global brands. Eventually, for some cities, it became a way to revitalize local economies by promoting regional goods and tourism. Slow Cities now has a waiting list of places hoping to copy the success of its member municipalities, many of which have lower-than-average unemployment rates and relatively high growth. "This is our answer to globalization," said Paolo Saturnini, the founder of Cittaslow and the mayor of Greve from 1990 to 2004.[7]

Food is primal in this way. It's no accident that the French farmer, agricultural unionist, and former member of the European Parliament José Bové, the man who sprang to fame after organizing the dismantling of a McDonald's in a village in 1999, was one of the first antiglobalization activists. In the United States, chef and restaurateur Alice Waters has for years led an "eat local" movement; her Edible Schoolyard Project has put thousands of gardens and local produce into communities around the country. All too often, "local" food simply means something that's precious and expensive. Waters's effort has been to turn it into something mainstream, an entirely new way of feeding ourselves. By starting with schools, which feed 30 million students each day, and then moving out into other areas of a community, Waters has seen her "eat local" mantra gathering steam. Nearly 5,700 schools in 48 states and 14 countries have launched Edible Schoolyard programs since the project started in 1995. "Local is simpler, and therefore more direct and responsible," Waters says. "Small farms are better able to satisfy the specific needs of their communities, and vice versa. It's a ground-up, self-sustaining approach to agriculture that avoids globalization and overreliance on corporations headquartered in another part of the world." As she correctly notes, "Our country was founded, in part, on the ideal that the values springing from small farms and economies would best inform the values of a representative government."[8]

In South Los Angeles, farmers are now teaching people how to plant organic edible gardens in unused strips of dirt between the street and the sidewalk. Groups like City Slicker Farms and the People's Grocery are bringing healthful, affordable food to urban residents. In colder climates, like Maine, new technologies are allowing indoor organic produce to reach customers year-round at cheaper prices.[9] One such greenhouse in Milwaukee uses composted by-products from local breweries to supply regional markets with carrots, salad, and herbs even when it's snowing.[10] In Waters's view, American agriculture would ultimately be more affordable, more resilient, and healthier if we "decentralized and localized, supporting as many different small and medium sized organic farms and ranches as we can."[11]

Of course, many consumers have no choice but to select their food based entirely on price. However, strong research shows that when consumers have a bit more disposable income, even as little as a few hundred dollars a year, they'll spend it on healthier, more local food. "Consumers are leading this shift," says Thilmany. "Food isn't just about economics. It's about culture and society." Her bet is that the United States will continue to become more like Europe in terms of support for regional growers. "Just witness the double-digit growth, year on year, for organic products. This has been going on for two decades, and it's not something that is going away, but is actually getting bigger."

People who care about organic food tend to care about food miles—that is, the hours and distance that produce has to travel to get to market. But there's another burgeoning group of middle- and even working-class consumers who are particularly interested in "local," meaning not necessarily something certified organic, but rather something grown in their communities. "Covid-19 really brought this forward," says Thilmany, as shoppers actively wanted to support neighboring farmers, restaurants, and markets as a way of keeping their communities afloat.[12]

Research has shown that, from an economic point of view, the dominant model of agribusiness is most destructive to small business owners, labor, and communities of color. Black and Native American farmers in particular are vulnerable to displacement as big business buys up more land and many are locked out of traditional rural farm co-operatives that can help small harvesters unite to create economies of scale.[13] All this attention to rural areas and corporate concentration fits into the larger Democratic Party reset from trickle-down economics and a technocratic approach to public policy to one that acknowledges that markets aren't perfect, that power exists in politics, and that, ultimately, that power must be curbed by appropriate regulation.

Still, in the face of Covid-19, ensuring resiliency and localization in agriculture has become a bipartisan issue, one that crosses class and political boundaries. Increasingly, Republicans, too, are concerned about Big Food, for security reasons, but also because red states are disproportionately affected by the fallout from it. A survey of fifty-one studies found that 82 percent of participants reported negative effects on communities exposed to industrial farming, including growth in income inequality, higher poverty, reduced retail trade, and depopulation. Of the 70 percent of nonmetro counties that lost population since 2010, most were concentrated in the Great Plains and the Midwest, the heartland region that provides most of the country's corn and soy crops. As migrant labor and, increasingly, robotic harvesters do the work of farming, entire swaths of the country (like Western Kansas and parts of Missouri) have experienced large population declines and the accompanying collapse of social relationships and, ultimately, entire communities.[14] These are among the communities that voted for Donald Trump in 2016 and 2020.

It's all part of the focus on efficiency versus resilience. And as we've seen, it's not really working for anyone but executives at the largest agricultural companies. So, how to move away from the current system to something more sustainable? The big question there revolves around how to make more localized agriculture affordable and scalable without re-creating the problems of Big Ag. Smaller producers who supply high-end restaurants and groceries in big cities with premium goods are largely boutique businesses, as anyone who has bought a twenty-dollar wedge of cheese on a weekend jaunt to the country knows. Much of the United States' fruits and vegetables come from places like California and Florida, where it is easier to grow them year-round. The rest of the country's inability to fill winter demand is a big reason food imports have risen sharply in recent years. But many of those imports are more expensive than what can be grown locally, and as we've already learned, as food security becomes a more pressing issue globally, it will be important for the United States and many other countries to bolster home-grown supply. And yet, this supply can't be just for an affluent few. It must feed, and economically support, communities everywhere, across all socioeconomic lines.

The Next-Generation Farm

There is no silver bullet. Radical reinvention of the system, à la what DARPA is doing, is possible, but it takes time. In the short term, simply making some key tweaks to the existing corporate model of farming is a good thing. On that score, co-operatives, rather than limited liability companies, provide one possible answer. This type of business, with roots in the nineteenth century, is already widespread in the U.S. agricultural industry. Big brands such as Ocean Spray, Welch's, Land O'Lakes, and Sunkist are owned by individual farmers who can team up to secure prices above market average for their products. There is any number of advantages to this approach. For starters, it allows farmers to leverage economies of scale without having to go public, as a Big Food firm must. This, in turn, allows the people who run co-operatives to spend their time on things besides squeezing margins and jacking up share prices.

A few years back, I interviewed Randy Papadellis, then the CEO of the ninety-one-year-old Massachusetts-based cranberry co-operative Ocean Spray, a collection of seven hundred growers, most of whom are small, independent farmers. He told me he spent most of his day on calls not with Wall Street analysts, but with the growers themselves, given that *they* are management. "I often say my title should be chief alignment officer, because most of my job is to make sure the interests of the growers are aligned with those of our suppliers, customers, and consumers," Papadellis told me.

Already, there are thirty thousand co-operative businesses in the United States collectively generating revenues of $650 billion. There are also high-profile examples outside agriculture—REI, the outdoor gear retailer, is the country's largest consumer co-operative. In Europe, particularly in southern countries like Spain, the co-operative model is used widely in retail, manufacturing, and services.

The model is becoming more popular as the U.S. economy becomes increasingly "Uberized," with more workers operating as independent contractors rather than traditional full-time employees. The trend got a major push amid the pandemic, when many people who lost their jobs or who were in industries decimated by Covid-19 banded together to start co-operatives. These have grown in number by 36 percent since 2013 and look likely to double that growth if the many co-ops that began amid the pandemic take root.[15] Indeed, a range of new co-ops is showing the potential for restoring the balance of power between companies and small contractors and workers in services. The Bronx-based Cooperative Home Care Associates, for example, employs two thousand workers in jobs with higher-than-average wages and better scheduling standards and benefits. Swift, a new Uber-like taxi app, is run and owned by drivers. In 2015, New York City launched a $1 million fund to help develop co-ops for neighborhood businesses like print shops and cafés. It was so successful that the city doubled the fund to $2 million the following year.

Ultimately, co-operatives are a way of increasing the labor share of the pie, building economies of scale that independent contractors can't achieve alone, and in the process, rebuilding wealth locally. At Ocean Spray, Papadellis told me, farmers can get three times the average price per barrel of cranberries paid on the open market because workers, rather than Wall Street, get to make strategic decisions. He says he has been similarly liberated as CEO, able to make investment decisions for the long haul rather than the quarter, allowing Ocean Spray to create economies of scale and grab market share from large competitors under more pressure to keep share prices and margins high. That's a key competitive factor, as research has shown that a concentration in Big Food, as in most areas where monopoly power exists, has led to a decrease in research and development capital and, thus, innovation and, ultimately, incomes.[16]

In an era in which returns on corporate investments vastly outpace income gains by employees (partly because of pressure from Wall Street to keep profit margins and stock prices up), few large public companies can focus on workers' long-term success. "Since the 1980s, business success has been measured by a firm's ability to extract value and store it in its share price," says Douglas Rushkoff, author of *Throwing Rocks at the Google Bus: How Growth Became the Enemy of Prosperity.* As a result, "firms have become holding companies for capital. They are much better at extracting it than releasing it." The co-op model lets workers become owners of capital rather than being dependent on a set wage. Or, as Rushkoff puts it, "workers, suppliers and customers become rich enough to sustain the marketplace" rather than having individual firms (and the people who run them) take such a disproportionate share of wealth. Some economists see the potential in co-ops like Ocean Spray to help decrease the nation's gnawing inequality. "To the extent that co-operatives can help move us from a large employer/employee model to a more entrepreneurial system that empowers labor," we could see more robust economic growth, says New York University professor Arun Sundararajan, author of *The Sharing Economy*.[17]

Co-operatives have downsides, of course. Given legal and regulatory hurdles, it can be challenging to raise capital and difficult to scale up to *Fortune* 500 size.[18] And as they become more successful, co-operatives can sometimes become too big and begin to resemble the very agricultural giants they were set up to compete with. Some large co-ops use the very same industrial farming techniques that create environmental damage.[19] Problems tend to come more often when management becomes too geographically remote from farmers. A company like Ocean Spray works in part because most of the cranberry farmers are in New England, rather than being spread out across the country. Place, after all, matters. This is true not only when it comes to agricultural co-operatives, but in areas like real estate, where rents tend to rise and standards of property care decrease as landlords become more remote (a topic we will explore in more depth later).

This argues for encouraging economic development that enriches a broader variety of small and middle-size local enterprises, rather than focusing so much on luring big multinational firms to nab deadline job numbers in a single go, to which many politicians aspire. (Remember the national bake-off among cities to host Amazon's second headquarters?) Research by the Upjohn Institute[20] has shown that communities that offer subsidies to lure big headquarters may see positive headlines and short-term gains, but the result is often negative. One recent study found that 70 percent of such subsidies fell into the category of property tax breaks and job creation tax credits. The big companies pay less for their real estate, but human capital is undermined, because property taxes often fund schools in the United States. State and city business subsidies have tripled since the nineties, which leads to a snowball effect: employers that demand skilled workers and good infrastructure are degrading the very tax base that creates them.[21]

Clearly, fighting Big Ag and creating a more resilient and secure agricultural base is a complex challenge. Doing so will require finding a middle ground between more localized nineteenth-century agriculture and modern industrial farming, between efficient and resilient. As we have learned, there are many ways to improve upon the model of Big Food without fundamentally disrupting it. But there is also a variety of more innovative solutions already rolling out in the real world. Venture capital investment in agriculture is booming—in fact, technology investors poured a record $22 billion into food and ag start-ups in 2020.[22] Many of these ventures will fail, but some will transform the industry, ushering in entirely new ways of thinking about food and farming. In the next chapter, we will follow a few of the agricultural entrepreneurs who are already changing the globalized model of farming by using cutting-edge technology to decentralize food production.

CHAPTER 4

Move Fast and Grow Things

As we've learned, agribusiness doesn't grow food so much as manufacture it along an assembly line that starts in vast industrial farms like the ones in my hometown and stretches all across the country, traveling potentially thousands of miles at enormous trucking costs for the food to reach the dinner table. Whatever the final product, whether animal or vegetable, nothing about the process is especially appetizing—the chemicals, the bioengineering, the industrial scale, the distance, the packaging. To say nothing of the taste, which is hardly farm fresh.

But imagine if you could grow crops not horizontally, on farmland that stretches out to the horizon, but vertically, hanging *down* off high indoor walls in a space-age version of the Hanging Gardens of Babylon. In fact, you can, via a process called vertical farming. Using the virtual sunshine of tiny, patented LED bulbs, finely calibrated water infusion, and a host of other innovations, vertical farmers are growing luscious leafy green vegetables and farm-fresh fruits—succulent kale, crisp lettuce, strawberries that taste like candy—all tumbling down from walls that reach twenty feet high.

Vertical farms are the very definition of local in that they can be placed anywhere, as the light and water are controlled by technology. These high-tech farms almost eliminate transportation costs and the need for preservatives, fertilizers, chemicals, packaging, and all the carbon loading that goes with these things. High-tech farms save the environment in other ways, too. Operating with technical precision indoors, vertical and modular farms require only 5 percent of the water needed by conventional farms and just 1 percent of the land, a remarkable savings in two precious resources.[1] They also change the nature of the labor force in agriculture. Typically, harvesting is a low-paying menial job often done by migrant labor (which, like it or not, will face increasing restrictions in a more regional world). Vertical farming involves high-pay, high-tech jobs that add more value to the economy. In Asia, political leaders are counting on homegrown versions of such companies to help feed the billions of people who will move from rural areas to cities over the next decade. Vertical farms and other such agricultural innovations won't eliminate all traditional farming; nor should they. But they are one of many ways in which the desire for local resilience and control of something as essential as the food supply is changing an industry that was once global.

One of the most dramatic of the many vertical farms springing up around the United States and the world is located in South San Francisco, California, and it is an amazing thing to see: literally a million plants growing off high walls that rise up like library shelves in an airy space the size of a basketball court, their shaggy leaves hanging down, all the plants feasting off feeding tubes while electronic arms attend to them. Green everywhere, floor to ceiling. What agribusiness did genetically to modify food for industrial production, Plenty has done technologically to bring forth all-natural food in the sustainable and nutritious fashion of the locally grown. For now, the company has restricted itself to producing a handful of leafy greens, including kale, arugula, and a luscious lettuce that is the polar opposite of the dreaded iceberg. But there is no limit to the fruits and vegetables (strawberries, broccoli, green beans, radishes, and many more) the company expects to farm vertically. Plenty's vertical farms are in three locations across the West, including in the former food desert of Compton, part of South Los Angeles. One of its first farms adjoined the cafeteria of the Googleplex in Cupertino, California, where Google incubated the company as an early hands-off investor. It is now partnering with companies like Walmart and Driscolls to bring them to many other communities. As Plenty's founder, Matt Barnard, put it to me, "We make farms like Intel makes chips."[2]

In fact, Barnard has experience with both. Before turning his energies to farming innovation, the forty-nine-year-old midwesterner worked for more than a decade in wireless telecom and technology for electric, water, and gas utilities. Agriculture is in his blood, and the failures of the conventional farm model were the impetus for Plenty. Barnard is actually a ninth-generation farmer, born and raised on the family's orchards in Door County, Wisconsin. "My family was granted the land," he says, referring to the historic U.S. government incentives to push white settlers from the East Coast toward the Pacific Ocean over the last two hundred years by offering cheap or even free farmland to those with the gumption to go west. "I grew up on it, farming apples and cherries" and whatever else the family could coax from the soil.

By his father's generation, the farm had proven unable to compete with California agribusiness, and he was forced to start a financial services business, too. The Barnard family pulled up stakes and decamped to North Carolina in the mid-eighties, when Matt was thirteen. After college at Northwestern, he went on to get a master's degree from Stanford's business school and worked as a telecom executive, eventually becoming the CEO of a company that designed and built the networks for wireless telecom giants. But always, in the back of his mind, was a desire to see if there was a better business model for farming. Barnard became preoccupied with water, which struck him as the key to the whole food conundrum. Industrial farms need a flood of water. Their plants and animals gorge on it. But then, fattened up, they have to be shipped vast distances at great expense to reach their market. Was there not a better way? "Seventy percent of agriculture is figuring out water usage," says Barnard, who began researching water rights and water technology. It was clear to him that as cheap as water was now, it would ultimately become more expensive—as would farming.

In 2013, as Matt Barnard was contemplating the next phase of his career, Rich Kelly, an investor from his Silicon Valley network, reached out to him. Kelly knew that Barnard had been thinking about water. The venture capitalist was looking to match problems with people, and he asked Barnard if he might be able to apply what he'd learned to the area of agriculture and food, which was a hot industry for investors. Climate change was a reality, big companies were pricing in a future of constrained carbon emissions and limits on natural resource use, and California farming in particular seemed more and more vulnerable, with fires, droughts, mudslides, and other climate-related natural disasters increasing.

Kelly, whose firm specialized in small and midsize businesses, introduced Barnard to the vertical farming industry. Barnard dove deep into the subject and eventually crossed paths with another burgeoning talent in the field, Nate Storey. Like Barnard, Storey came to agriculture honestly, the descendant of a Montana ranching family. Barnard was obsessed with the hard numbers of making healthier, more sustainable agriculture work. But Storey, now the chief science officer of Plenty, was caught up in the romance of farming. "My family had these long-term ties to the land, but I always grew up with the sense that something had been lost," he says, referring to the structural changes in the agricultural industry over the last several decades. "My grandfather's generation had already been affected by these. By the time my father was born, my grandfather had left the ranching business, but he still had strong ties." Storey's father joined the air force, and the family started moving every two years. It was during those years—years filled with settling and resettling, making new friends and losing old ones—that Storey turned to reading as a solace. "I read a lot of Victorian novels, which are really all about the relationship between rural and urban worlds, the divide between rich and poor, and the consequences of industrialization." Storey laughs: "I guess I had a romantic notion that, someday, I could get back to the land."

It was a notion that only deepened after he spent a year as a nonprofit worker in China between 2001 and 2002, teaching rural farmers and urban immigrants better business practices. (The private sector in China had by that time grown quite large, but it was still relatively unsophisticated, particularly as you moved farther inland.) "I saw women in China threshing grain and drying garlic. . . . It was really dreary manual labor." It seemed to Storey not only that there was much room for improvement, but also that this was an area in which the Chinese might value Western help. "Producing food and feeding people seemed like a really noncontroversial way to get involved."

Once back in the United States, Storey realized (much as Barnard had) that his family had no immediate future in agriculture. He decided to get a PhD from the University of Wyoming and set out to find a smarter way to farm. To him, the issue wasn't so much water as space, although the two were interconnected. Did farming really need those endless crop fields? Not just all that water, but all that land? Perhaps family farms and community co-ops could stay in business and compete with the bigger players if they figured out a different way to do things—a more productive way, something that eventually helped them together reach the same economies of scale as the big farms with hundreds of thousands of acres. (Note: vertical farming itself is predicted to triple in value between 2019 and 2025.)[3] The eureka moment came when Storey was in a greenhouse. He saw all the flowerpots hanging off the windows, one above the next, each one bearing a tiny seedling, and it hit him: Food did not have to grow *up*. It could grow down, hanging off walls that were like the array of flowerpots before him. Such an arrangement would not just cut down on acreage, but also, with some advanced technology, use far less water and drastically shorten supply chains.

He began experimenting with building the system himself, ultimately starting a company, Bright Agrotech, to create the physical platform on which plants could grow. "When I started Bright, I was broke," says Storey. "I was dumpster-diving for food so that I could use whatever money I had to buy tools." He spent a lot of time sourcing the right type of plastic to make his new vertical system work and found a company in Arizona, Homestead Fence, that agreed to build what he needed. Eventually, Storey met Barnard at an agtech conference. And from there, Plenty grew.

As the company evolved, it did what start-ups do best: it innovated. When it couldn't find the right kind of lighting and sensor technology to power the vertical farms, it sought out help from local suppliers. While such small businesses don't have the scale that multinationals do, they have a nimbleness that lends itself to innovation and community prosperity. "As the company grew," says Storey, "it became both more complex and also more local." Plenty wants to grow in areas where there is a need for agricultural innovation, but also a local supply chain that can support growth. The solution to that problem led not only to California—the state is the country's top innovation hub in large part because of its communities of designers, producers, and laborers within close proximity to one another—but also to industrial hubs in the Midwest.

Plenty sources some of the equipment needed to create the vertical farms from other small "makers" in states like Ohio and Michigan, which have traditionally been filled with small and medium-size enterprises (SMEs) that contribute to the automobile component supply chain for Detroit. As those supply chains moved overseas, many of those businesses went under. But the innovation legacy of the area is great enough that Michigan is still the number one state in the nation for industrial designers, boasting a higher concentration of engineers and materials experts than California. In recent years, some of these SMEs have reinvented themselves as industrial workshops in which companies can experiment with new ideas on a small scale before rolling them out en masse. While it would be impossible for Plenty to get a company like Dow Chemical to create a new plastic for it, any number of smaller firms would be happy to take on this sort of small batch work.

I'm personally familiar with this model, as it's exactly what my own father, an industrial and electrical engineer who started a machine tool company, does for a living. After many years spent working for large multinational companies, both American and Japanese, he started a machine shop that now churns out prototypes and small-run orders of specialized items (anything from a bespoke tool bit to a custom dental chair) for local and global customers. Interestingly, many of his clients are in Mexico, which, as it has grown wealthier, has become both a consumer of higher-end products and a producer of lower-end ones. His small business is one of many that are part of a growing network of hub-and-spoke systems of regionalization in which one or two large anchor businesses support a robust network of small and midsize supplier firms in a given area. Those smaller businesses can then grow faster and expand at both the local and the global levels, all while supporting one another and the community at large.

A number of big manufacturing firms like Caterpillar and large technology companies like IBM have used this more regionalized model for years as a way of better understanding the needs of local markets and responding to them more quickly, but also as a natural hedge against currency and energy costs. Caterpillar nurtures a network of about two thousand local suppliers in the Illinois area alone, many of whom make a good living designing and producing customized goods for the firm—items destined for particular U.S. markets or specialized needs. Where things can be sourced locally, they are, in every Caterpillar territory internationally. This is a pattern many multinational firms, in the wake of the last several years of supply chain disruptions, are starting to copy as they look to reduce complexity and source and produce closer to their customers.[4]

Companies are also starting to realize that localnomics can help support their revenue growth in ways that conventional globalization cannot. Suppliers can also buy things from their customers, and customers can be suppliers, too. Companies like IBM have used this model for years, explicitly sourcing locally and regionally to build up a base of smaller and middle-size companies that would eventually buy IBM's own products and services. For the large firms, it's just smart business.[5] For communities, it's an economic boost, as it takes a mix of businesses of all sizes to support healthy and diverse local employment, which ultimately relocates wealth from global business back into local communities.

Localnomics has been happening for some time. Indeed, as the process of internationalization of production that really took off in the nineties reached its apex, the decade leading up to the Covid-19 pandemic was sometimes referred to in business circles as a period of "slowbalization." By the 2008 financial crisis, there was a growing awareness that too much globalization in supply chains had become, well, too much. Localization gathered steam from 2011 onward, when, as a 2021 Conference Board report noted, "foreign content in manufacturing production reached a peak."[6] This was especially true when it came to the sourcing of finished and semifinished goods and to energy in Europe. Chinese policy also encouraged a shift toward regionalization of supply to account for growing demand from a wealthier local population. Since the pandemic, this trend toward regionalization of supply chains has grown, and multinational companies have begun talking about "local-for-local" supply chains, in which production and consumption are hubbed as much as possible. As colleagues of mine noted in a full-page *Financial Times* article on the topic in December 2021, logistics problems and energy inflation have simply shifted the calculation of far-flung supply chains, which are increasingly being seen as costly, time-consuming, and too carbon intensive. "It now takes anywhere from 28 to 52 days to ship a pair of shoes produced in China from Shanghai to Los Angeles," they noted, "up from between 17 and 28 days before the pandemic." And the total cost has gone up by nearly two dollars, which squeezes already-tight profit margins.[7]

For many countries, there is opportunity in the shift toward regionalization. In the United States, the Midwest, one of the areas most hollowed out by globalization in recent years, is especially well positioned to take advantage of this pendulum swing toward place-based economics and regional innovation hubs. It's an area rich in design and engineering talent, with plenty of universities and a diverse mix of industries that can, with the right leadership, be retooled to function as innovation hubs and drivers of local prosperity. One of the most successful examples of this is Columbus, Ohio. The city has long been an economic and political bellwether for the country. Politicians come there to take the preelection temperature of the nation, and companies test-drive new products there. After the global financial crisis, Columbus was one of the U.S. cities that suffered most. In 2009, it was faced with chopping $100 million in municipal spending, more than 15 percent of its total operating budget. The city did all the usual back-end trimming of public services. But then, rather than become Detroit, which, for a period, literally couldn't keep the lights or water on, Columbus did something else: it thought ahead. The Democratic mayor went to the Republican city fathers and persuaded them to support a tax rise, the first in nearly four decades. They agreed, on the condition that a chunk of that money go into a public-private economic development partnership that focused on how to cultivate human capital for an era in which all value would reside in intellectual property, data, and ideas. They connected community colleges with local companies, domestic and global (L Brands, JPMorgan, Worthington Industries, Honda) to train a digitally savvy technical workforce. They renovated the crumbling downtown and created new housing stock to appeal to the Millennials who had been leaving the city for greener pastures after their studies.

Columbus is now one of the top ten areas that young workers are pouring into. (It ranks number three, after Los Angeles and New York, as a city of choice for fashion designers.) In an effort to move from making bumpers and hubcaps to being part of the internet of things, Columbus bid for and won a $40 million Department of Transportation grant to become a "smart city" focused on electric vehicles. About $500 million in additional investment has followed. "This isn't a five-year plan for economic development; it's a one-hundred-year plan," says Alex Fischer, head of the chief executives group the Columbus Partnership. The city is part of Elon Musk's "hyper-loop" plan to create a train that can connect Chicago, Columbus, and Pittsburgh in minutes. Ohio State and Columbus State Community College have started some of the first degree programs in data analytics. Tesla, AWS, and Apple have moved into town. Accenture now has an innovation lab on what used to be the site of a large buggy manufacturer. (It is hard to imagine a greater symbol of change.) Since 2010, the Columbus region has created roughly half of all new jobs in Ohio, and Harvard Business School wrote a case study about the city's accomplishments.[8]

This is exactly the type of model Plenty wants to help build in the places where it sets up its vertical farms. "Food resiliency, food sovereignty, and the local production and distribution of products are all connected," says Storey. In the beginning, the company had to build or source from scratch nearly everything it needed—materials, architectural ideas, lights, and so on. But this created opportunity. For example, Plenty has built its own LED lights, which are as efficient as anything else on the market in the same category today. "That's a moat," says Storey, referring to the barriers to entry that will make Plenty more and more competitive in the agricultural marketplace. By creating a kind of spin-off ecosystem of innovation, a new, fast-growing company may start with one dazzling new idea that can, in turn, spawn an array of new technologies that, in turn, produce a host of new products and businesses to deliver them. Such innovation yields real economic growth—growth based on providing things that people actually want to buy, not just the asset bubbles that inflate the stock portfolios of the privileged class. This is how Silicon Valley was born and why Austin, Texas; Cambridge, Massachusetts; and other hubs have grown—because industrious, inspired people clustered together to develop ideas that sparked many more ideas. Place matters. The communities that keep jobs close by fare much better than those that don't. The income they generate stays in place to make the community better—more prosperous, more equal, and stabler.

This sort of innovation hubbing is increasingly attracting big-name investors and big money. Steve Case, the co-founder of AOL, has famously championed the cause of midwestern and rural innovation hubs through his Revolution venture capital firm, which every year hosts a road trip across heartland states, looking for new businesses to fund and regional innovation hubs to plug them into. (It's helping turn Chattanooga, Tennessee, into a digital logistics center and St. Louis into a hot space for agriculture technology firms.) As Plenty has grown, it has attracted investors like Eric Schmidt, the former CEO of Google and founding partner of Innovation Endeavors, who believes that decentralized technologies like Plenty's will be the "big disruptors" of the twenty-first century. The world's richest man, Jeff Bezos, is also an investor, as is the giant Japanese private equity firm SoftBank.

These types of investors want to buy not only a business, but a pool of talent and ideas. That's what Plenty is offering as it moves into areas like 3D climate and thermal modeling, robotics, plant science, sensors, and energy-efficiency light development. Unlike with most agricultural firms, Plenty's workers, thanks to the company's training program, are mainly highly skilled technicians. This means they are highly productive workers, exactly the type whom rich countries like the United States need to cultivate. The plant science team, for example, has figured out a way to increase yields fivefold, growing pesticide-free crops that are not genetically modified. The results are similar to the best of what a shopper might find at a local farmers' market. "Our shipments since Covid-19 have tripled," chief executive Matt Barnard told me. "The pandemic has really changed the conversation about where and how people get their food."[9] Thanks in large part to the supply chain and economic resiliency concerns that followed in the wake of Covid-19, the U.S.-Chinese trade conflicts, and the war in Ukraine, Plenty is about to pop. It made a breakthrough deal with Albertsons, a Whole Foods–like chain of 430 grocery stores, to sell its vertical food (starting with kale and lettuce) throughout California. It's also working with Walmart to grow vertical stacked fresh produce on location at stores in California.[10]

The key impetus for such deals is not just the dangerous concentration of food production, but also climate change, which is of course making hyperconcentration in agriculture increasingly untenable. The average share of the continental United States experiencing drought rose from a little less than 24 percent in 2019 to over 40 percent in 2020. Drought affects not only farmers and agribusinesses, but also the banks and insurance firms that lend to these companies, the people who invest in them, and of course the communities in which the farmers and businesses reside. Losses from the 2012 drought in the Midwest totaled $35 billion, and California's 2014 drought cost the state $4 billion.[11] Drought leads to all sorts of other climate issues, like the fires that raged through the Golden State in 2020. Big Ag needs that land. But what if it were simply unavailable for traditional farming?

That eventuality has led to another major deal for Plenty—with Driscoll's, the world's largest distributor of berries. As our planet warms, it is running out of places to grow berries. Right now, the best cropland for berries is in California, Chile, and the foothills of the Alps. But as temperatures rise, all these areas are now suffering from climate-related disruptions, which means Driscoll's has a big problem. Vertical farms are one solution, as they are immune to issues like the wildfires that spread throughout the West Coast in 2020, upsetting traditional farms. "For us, it didn't matter if there was ash in the air; our people could still work safely," says Barnard, who increased his company's market share during that period. As Driscoll's president, Soren Bjorn, told me, "Rather than moving up a mountain, we can move into vertical farms."[12]

The idea is to begin growing in the United States and spread to localized growing in any number of global territories, particularly places in the Middle East and Asia that either can't grow such produce locally or are suffering from disproportionate global warming–related climate shifts. That's a huge investment, running into the tens of millions of dollars, but vertical farms can produce far more berries per acre than anywhere else, with far less water and no transportation costs.

It must be said that vertical farming is not, as of yet, creating the cheapest produce. Plenty is able to churn out lettuce that is more or less on par in terms of cost and quality with what you might find in, say, a Whole Foods, but it is thus far a relatively upscale product. Still, growth eventually creates economies of scale that bring down prices. And hubbing production and consumption locally allows Plenty to adjust its model and grow more quickly. This is the model that some of the most innovative companies, like Tesla, have followed in recent years. As author Ashlee Vance noted in a biography of Tesla founder Elon Musk, the company discovered that it was much harder to innovate and more expensive to work with cutting-edge technology in real time when its supply chain was far away. Ultimately, Tesla became committed to sourcing and innovating as much as it could around its battery and powertrain technologies locally.[13]

The idea is that just as a company like Tesla started with a one-hundred-thousand-dollar car and then moved into making models costing half that much as it grew, Plenty will be able to move from six-dollar heads of lettuce to lettuce and other produce that is as cheap as anything industrially grown, but of a much higher quality. Barnard argues that such price metrics are, in any case, a "false choice," because the old model of farming is quickly becoming obsolete. "You can't even buy the land to increase production in traditional farming anymore," he points out.

It's also becoming harder to find the labor to support traditional farming. Political tensions over immigrant labor have grown, not only in the United States, but globally, for all sorts of reasons over the last decade. Already, since Covid-19, global migration has slowed, and governments of all stripes have become more reluctant to accept low-skilled workers in particular. But most agricultural production everywhere in the world involves migrant farming. California, Washington, and Florida, the places that produce most of America's fruits and vegetables, have the highest levels of undocumented immigrant labor, creating another pressure point for traditional, globalized food production. These positions are, as Covid-19 showed us so clearly, low-paid and often dangerous.

This reflects an uncomfortable truth about the effects of globalization on labor markets. Companies have been able to move investment, profits, and jobs to where it is cheapest for them to do so.

Immigration at the lower end of the socioeconomic spectrum has filled cheap labor gaps in many rich countries. But higher-end immigration has been declining as a proportion of overall immigration—in 2019, for example, 33 percent of immigrants to the United States had a college degree, as opposed to 48 percent of those coming between 2014 and 2019.[14] This is partly due to skilled immigrants' being turned off by the xenophobic rhetoric of Donald Trump and the Trump administration, which ironically had the effect of shifting the overall immigrant population toward the lower end of the educational spectrum. Why would, say, a Chinese engineer or an African doctor want to come to the United States when the president himself has denigrated people from their country?

But this is also about what author Fareed Zakaria has dubbed "the rise of the rest." As the fortunes of emerging markets have improved, there is simply more global competition for what economists call "human capital." For all former President Trump's rhetoric, there was hardly any need to "build a wall" between the United States and Mexico. Despite the high-profile stories of Mexican migrants pouring into the United States, the overall data tells a different story: the flow of migrants from Mexico to the United States has been decreasing since the mid-2000s.[15] Increased border patrols and tougher U.S. laws have clearly played a part, but a more important reason is that the economic calculus of migration has changed. The 2008 financial crisis and subsequent recession hurt prospects in the United States.

Meanwhile, a strong Mexican economy and better educational and job opportunities in Mexico have led many Mexican immigrants (who make up 25 percent of the foreign-born population of the United States) to go home. (The Pew Hispanic Center estimates that between 65 percent and 95 percent of immigrants who return to Mexico do so voluntarily.) "We've been so overwhelmed by a very emotional discussion about enforcement and security that the economic component of migration has gotten lost," says Janet Murguía, president of UnidosUS, the nation's largest Hispanic civil rights and advocacy group. That's a pity, as the facts show that we should be courting, rather than turning away, new immigrants all along the economic spectrum.

Creating a path to legal immigration would put an end to immigrants' being oppressed and used to keep wages down. Immigration reform is something that both labor and many big businesses support (as it also helps ensure a supply of needed workers). Research shows that legalizing immigration would shore up wages (much needed in the U.S. economy, 70 percent of which is based on consumer spending), but is unlikely to result in the offshoring of jobs. Most sectors in which those migrants work (hospitality, construction, tourism, and agriculture) simply aren't offshorable. (More on this later.)

Meanwhile, immigration reform would bolster public finances, increasing Social Security revenue by $300 billion over ten years. The Congressional Budget Office forecasts that it would also reduce the federal deficit by $685 billion over the same period. And the liberal think tank Center for American Progress estimates that legalizing the eleven million undocumented workers living in the United States would add $1.7 trillion to the economy over ten years.

Plus, immigrants punch above their weight in growth creation. They are more than twice as likely to start businesses as their native-born counterparts. They are responsible for over a quarter of all new business formation—and new businesses have been the only source of net job creation in this country for the past thirty years. They have founded a disproportionate number of export businesses, which tend to create more and higher-paying jobs, and they often locate their firms in economically beleaguered areas, where new jobs are needed the most.[16]

I would argue that the goal for the post-neoliberal era should be not to unleash capital, but to unleash people. We should aspire to be laser-focused on creating high-quality jobs *for all* here at home. With appropriate policy, the most talented immigrants will then naturally follow. While new high-tech industries like vertical farming will create fewer jobs than traditional agriculture, they will be better jobs. Because the technology must be placed locally, close to the consumer, economic resiliency will be bolstered and sustainability increased. It's the very opposite of the current model of agriculture, which is highly concentrated, fragile, and monopolistic.

Decentralized technologies have the potential to be a big part of the post-neoliberal move from efficiency to resiliency. And they are by their very nature localized. Up until now, the rise of the digital economy has been about the growth of superstar companies (giant platforms like Google and Facebook) and the extraction of wealth from consumers to companies. But what if new technologies could actually remoor wealth in communities? Steve Blitz, the chief U.S. economist of financial research firm TS Lombard, believes that "technology will increasingly reset where firms can be located, which will be mostly closer to consumers." In the past, says Blitz, "technology moved production away from the center, toward far-flung supply chains. Now decentralized technologies will bring it back." He's referring not only to things like vertical farming, but also to additive manufacturing, in which component parts of everything from engines to furniture can be "printed," layer by layer, via small machines that can fit into a single room, rather than in a huge factory. "Consumer tastes are changing more quickly, Millennials are moving to suburbs and rural areas (thanks to rising housing costs), emissions curbs are coming, and automation is increasing," all of which will make it easier to localize the production of all sorts of goods and services.[17]

Decentralization, like localization, is a movement for our time, and it will only grow. Decentralized financial technologies are beginning to break the hold of the world's largest banks on financial intermediation. (More on this in the next two chapters.) Assuming that antitrust efforts prevent power from being concentrated in the hands of other large industries (like Big Tech), it's possible that decentralized finance could be a cheaper way for individuals and small businesses to engage with one another across borders in ways that actually spread wealth. Data unions and trusts are another possible way to reconnect wealth and place. Countries like France and states like California are considering ways they might reimburse people for the use of their personal data via digital sovereign wealth funds. Just as such funds make it possible for Alaskans or Norwegians to reap the benefits of their mineral resources, citizens in any country might be compensated for their data (something we will explore in more detail later in the book). Whether given as a check or put into a public development fund, this entirely new kind of "digital dividend" will locate economic value not just in companies, but in all of us. This is how you bring about a homecoming at a micro level.

The Future of Food

In the case of farming, decentralization is also part of a narrative of how an old-line industry is, for the first time in decades, doing something truly innovative. "In 1837, John Deere invented the steel plow, and productivity went up," says Barnard. "In the 1890s, it was the tractor. In the 1940s, you got chemical fertilizers; and in the eighties, genetically modified crops." But, as he points out, all these things were part of solving a problem of calories—creating more food, more cheaply. The planet (and certainly our country) has more than enough calories and yet only a third of the available nutritious food needed. We now have a different problem: how to shift to a system that is healthier, more sustainable, and more local.

Like vertical farming, decentralized technology is helping to solve the problem, not just in the United States, but in any number of countries where such farms are springing up, from Germany and France, to Canada, Singapore, and the United Arab Emirates. Indeed, in many of these countries, the government is part of the solution, funding high-tech farming, offering tax incentives for research into clean tech, and helping to bolster training for a twenty-first-century workforce to do these higher-skilled jobs.

The changes are happening even in bastions of agricultural tradition like France. There, on the outskirts of Paris, thirty-four-year-old Guillaume Fourdinier, a tech entrepreneur and tenth-generation farmer from the tiny Northern French commune of Verton, has figured out a way to grow fruits, vegetables, and herbs inside abandoned shipping containers. His company, Agricool, buys up the rectangular boxes that might have been crushed and piled into landfills and seeds them with the garden-fresh produce that are the base materials for good French chefs. Like Barnard, Fourdinier had to create his own lights, plus a cooling system and heat shields, to make his modular farms work. Now they are stacked like giant Legos in Paris, Lille, Cannes, and numerous other French cities, where three supermarkets now grow their own produce in Agricool's mini-farms. "Food resilience in Paris is three days," Fourdinier says. That means the city has only enough fresh food to last seventy-two hours should supplies be cut off. Fourdinier has expanded this to a matter of months, saving himself weekend trips back to his village for his own regular stock-ups on fresh produce. His technology also allows small local French farmers who can't afford huge storage facilities to expand production cycles, preserve food for longer periods, and better compete with the Big Ag producers that have made inroads into France.

Just as Agricool creates the building blocks of farms, so farming may become a building block for communities. Ag expert Dawn Thilmany notes that food and urban planning are becoming inexorably intertwined as part of smart building design. "In the future, it will become common to have a building with a rooftop garden or a hyperlocal vertical farm on a wall," she says. This will offer the benefit not only of more localized food production, but also of building insulation and energy conservation. This is already happening at both the residential and the commercial levels, à la the trial farm at Google that launched Plenty. (The vertical farm at the Googleplex was able to supply all the produce needed to serve five hundred meals a day.)[18] Indeed, many cities (e.g., New York, Amsterdam, London, and Milan) are offering tax credits to businesses and residents who opt into this sort of urban farming, just as they offer subsidies for clean energy. "You'll start to see planned communities in the suburbs that might have once been designed around a golf course now organized around a farm, or an orchard, or even a pasture with livestock," says Thilmany. In this way, smart agriculture becomes something interlinked with smart design, smart living, smart cities.[19]

The innovations in agriculture we've just learned about will play their role in that transformation. They will take time to come into being, and they won't come in the form of a silver bullet. All the transformations in agriculture—from the work of innovators like Barnard, Storey, and Jahn, to the new corporate structures of farming, to antitrust efforts and technological innovations—will together ultimately add up to a sea change. Disruption will mean lost jobs and adjustments to old-line industries. (Just witness how online shopping has changed the way we get our groceries within the last few years.) It will require regulatory shifts and reskilling, but it will also create entirely new jobs and industries, perhaps ones we can't even guess at yet. History tells us that technology-driven change is, over time, always a net job creator.

To come into being, Plenty relied largely on the ingenuity of its founders. But remaking the economy at a deeper, broader level across more industries and communities will take both private efforts and a fundamental shift in neoliberal economic policy, particularly when it comes to trade. The next two chapters will look at how this is playing out today in the corridors of power and the halls of academia as well as on Main Street.

CHAPTER 5

Trade and Its Discontents

I f there is a single organization today that exemplifies the last half century of globalization, it must surely be the Council on Foreign Relations. The Council, as it is known to insiders, sits on a grand block on New York's Upper East Side, at Sixty-eighth and Park Avenue. It is housed in an elegant, double-fronted limestone townhouse filled with Persian carpets, oil paintings, and wood paneling. There, members come to hear world leaders, CEOs, diplomats, and other dignitaries talk about the geopolitical events of the day. Want to hear what's on the mind of Nancy Pelosi, Mahmoud Ahmadinejad, Angela Merkel, Jamie Dimon, António Guterres, or Christine Lagarde? Interested in the details of cybersecurity in Israel or corporate governance in Latin America? Want to network for your next job on Wall Street or in the White House? The Council is your place.

Many of the meetings are off the record, and the members, comprising a who's who of influential Americans, are often as important or in the know as the people speaking. In recent years, the group has even let in a few journalists like me, who get access to the corridors of power through our work. We are, in the words of the *Financial Times*'s former U.S. editor Chrystia Freeland (now deputy Canadian prime minister and CFR regular), the "intellectual geishas" of the place, moderating panels and providing entertainment value—and, to a certain extent, diversity; many of the media types are women—in exchange for access.

The Council was founded in 1921 by a group of scholars and policy makers who were tasked with briefing President Woodrow Wilson on options for handling international affairs and U.S. foreign policy once Germany was defeated in World War I. The group had an internationalist bent from the beginning, being associated with the London-based Royal Institute of International Affairs (also known as Chatham House). Its members shaped Wilson's thinking around "the effect that the war and the treaty of peace might have on postwar business." A former dean of the Harvard Business School and director of planning and statistics at the U.S. Shipping Board during World War I, Edwin F. Gay, set up the Council's magazine, *Foreign Affairs,* which is still the most prestigious policy journal in America. From 1945 to 1972, more than half of a group of 502 key government officials were Council members. The CFR helped birth NATO and the Marshall Plan, set U.S. policy around Vietnam and the opening of China, and is today filled with titans of industry turned diplomats and, in particular, the Wall Street–based financiers who exported American-style globalization and laissez-faire economics to the world from the eighties onward. Former treasury secretary Robert Rubin is chairman emeritus. Larry Summers, another former treasury secretary and the architect of Clinton-era financial deregulation, is also a regular.

My point here is that when the American policy establishment wants to say something important, the CFR is where it's done. So, it was quite telling that, at the end of 2020, as President Donald Trump was leaving office and Joe Biden was taking over, I was asked to preside over a CFR meeting with former U.S. trade representative Robert E. Lighthizer, the architect of the United States' shift in trade policy with China (and, to a lesser extent, the world) under Trump. His policies were, in my view, one of the only bright spots in the Trump presidency, perhaps because Lighthizer had been honing them for years under much more serious leaders than Trump. During the Reagan administration, for example, he pushed for national security as a consideration in trade talks and used tariffs and other trade weapons to push back against Japanese efforts to monopolize supply chains in computers. As early as 2010, in testimony before Congress, he noted the arrogance of U.S. policy makers who believed triumphantly that history was over and that liberal democracy and free markets had won. Hardly. By 2017, Lighthizer was calling Chinese state capitalism "a threat to the world trading system that is unprecedented."[1] By openly acknowledging the problems and hypocrisies of the One World, Two Systems paradigm and neoliberal economics in general, Lighthizer broke with forty years of establishment policy. His North Star for trade was not efficiency or even geopolitics, but rather the idea that the "right policy is one that makes it possible for most citizens, including those without college educations, to access the middle class through stable, well-paying jobs."[2]

In this sense, there is quite a lot of overlap between right-wing security hawks and the old labor left (with which I identify somewhat politically). As the former trade rep pointed out in a pivotal piece in *Foreign Affairs,* the idea that trade liberalization fosters peace between nations is not only untrue today (as exemplified by the U.S.-Chinese conflict), but has historically not always held true, contrary to the neoliberal narrative. In the United States, economic ties between North and South did not prevent the Civil War. The rise of Germany as a major exporter in the nineteenth century did not pacify that country in the twentieth. Japan's dependence on the United States for raw materials during the 1930s was part of the motivation for the attack on Pearl Harbor. "More recently, China's accession to the WTO in 2001—which was supposed to make the country a model global citizen—was followed by massive investments in its military capabilities and territorial expansion in the South China Sea," wrote Lighthizer.[3]

In short, the world isn't flat and never really has been. I'm referring here of course to the title of *New York Times* foreign affairs columnist Thomas Friedman's 2005 book,[4] which lays out a vision for an ever-more-connected world, an idea that is now being challenged. Friedman's earlier book, *The Lexus and the Olive Tree,* in fact, makes for more interesting historical reading. Its hypothesis—

that globalization had inexorably replaced the Cold War system—is often summed up by Friedman's pithy Golden Arches theory, which holds that no two countries with McDonald's franchises have ever fought a war against each other. But there are more than three thousand McDonald's in China. This has hardly stopped China and the United States from starting a new cold war (or Russia from invading Ukraine). The truth is that the whole idea that countries with a McDonald's never go to war with one another stopped working around the time that Yugoslavia fell apart and NATO bombed Serbia.

Would that more people had read Barry Lynn's book *End of the Line,* which came out the same year Friedman's *The World Is Flat* was published and, yet, took an entirely different message from no-holds-barred globalization among countries with differing economic systems and values: that it would eventually end in tears. The subtitle of that book, *The Rise and Coming Fall of the Global Corporation,* pointed to the fact that hyper-"efficient" global supply chains were not only far more fragile than we could have imagined, but that free trade with no concern for national interests would eventually increase corporate monopoly power and be exploited by state-run capitalist systems for their own interest. Lynn was one of the first to see that China would eventually use the economic benefits garnered by taking advantage of the neoliberal system to export its own brand of autocracy to any number of countries. He also pointed out that far from being the American norm, the type of trade agreements struck from the nineties onward represented a "radical reversal" in U.S. policy. "During the Cold War," he writes, "America promoted extensive trade and cross-border investment as a sort of cement to cohere an alliance of democratic nations against a common enemy."[5] But the deals struck under Bill Clinton in particular represented not the spread of liberalism, but "a sort of policy coup by American corporations, a takeover of U.S. trade strategy by firms intent on keeping their hard-won beachheads [in China]."[6]

If the Trump administration did anything good, it was in exposing the mythology and flaws of this kind of "free" trade. His administration did so unproductively, in the sense that they started a trade war with China but had no real plan for how to make the U.S. economy itself more competitive. The Biden administration is attempting to develop a post-neoliberal view of how to build national competitiveness in a world in which multinationals and state-run economies have as much power as many liberal democracies. The Biden administration's long-term economic growth plan is in many ways akin to the industrial policy of the sixties; this time, not in the form of public underwriting of the computer industry as part of the Cold War, but rather in the form of a Green New Deal that would reenergize the U.S. industrial base, encouraging production of things like wind turbines and solar panels (which could be installed by former coal miners or steelworkers), in an effort to transition the country to clean, local energy sources. That's a very progressive goal. Still, both the Trump and the Biden administrations were on the same page in acknowledging that trade is never totally free. It always reflects the needs of one interest group or another.

That's a massive shift. Until quite recently, it was impossible to question the neoliberal economic theory of free trade in polite circles. And yet, as Lighthizer writes, academic theory could not "hide the basic fact that if a country imports goods it could produce domestically, then domestic spending is employing people abroad rather than at home." When former president Bill Clinton normalized trade relations with China in 2000, he predicted that the move would allow the United States to "export products without exporting jobs." In fact, the opposite occurred. The U.S. trade deficit with China rose to more than $400 billion at its peak, and at least two million U.S. jobs were lost between 1999 and 2011, in large part because of the shifts in trade policy.[7] At the same time, U.S. companies doing business in China were forced to hand over intellectual property and trade secrets for the privilege of entry into a supposedly "free" market. All this has helped China become the world's top exporter of high-tech products. Over the last few years in particular, the Chinese have moved far ahead of other nations in key areas like clean-tech manufacturing, electronic components, green batteries, and 5G technology.[8]

Plenty of business and policy elites would have us believe that this kind of globalization is the best thing for everyone—the United States keeps the "good" jobs, like software engineering, and China gets the lesser ones. But what we've learned over hundreds of years of industrial development is that doing the "lesser" jobs can, with the right policies, help countries move up the economic food chain. It's widely understood that since it opened up to global markets over forty years ago, China has become the factory to the world. But it's in large part the knowledge gained by forty years of making things for other countries that enabled China to become a leader in the manufacture of high-value technologies, from lithium batteries to quantum computing. Manufacturing is an iterative process, and practice makes perfect. China, like Germany, focused on creating regional economic ecosystems rather than outsourcing everything but the highest-end service jobs. In an increasingly regional world, that strategy is now paying dividends.

As Chinese venture capitalist Kai-Fu Lee put it to me in an interview a couple of years ago, China's massive consumer market and its continued growth potential are already making it possible to develop a digital ecosystem that exists quite profitably and independently from the West, with homegrown brands like Xiaomi and Huawei already connecting the dots up through the digital supply chain to the consumer. It is, after all, far easier to control large swaths of your own supply chain and then slap a consumer brand onto a product than to reverse-engineer that process (as Americans and Europeans discovered in the wake of Covid-19-related supply chain shortages). "The question in the future will be why buy a Western brand?" said Lee. "I think you'll see China owning the digital ecosystem not only at home, but also in ASEAN [Association of Southeast Asian Nations] and many Middle Eastern countries."[9]

History Rhymes

This is exactly how America leapt ahead of Britain in global trade over a hundred years ago. The neoliberal thinking that has defined

globalization in the West since the eighties decrees that state involvement in the economy is verboten. But that's actually antithetical to
America's origins. Until very recently, the United States itself did
exactly what China today does—funnel capital to the most productive places, connect the dots between job creators and educators,
and link the public and private sectors to pursue goals in the national economic interest. That's industrial policy—which has been a
dirty word in the United States for decades now, but it wasn't always. As Cornell professor and legal scholar Robert Hockett, who
has advised several presidential hopefuls, puts it, "In our very own
Hamiltonian development model, the public sector played a crucial
coordinating role, empowering the private sector, and enabling its
efforts not to be scattered, haphazard or wasted."[10]

Alexander Hamilton, one of the founding fathers and the first
U.S. treasury secretary, supported the creation of a national bank,
which he viewed correctly as a "political machine of the greatest
importance to the state."[11] He also started a public-private partnership to provide cheap water power and financial capital to investors
in the early republic. Subsequent administrations—from Lincoln to
Roosevelt, Eisenhower, and Kennedy—took pages from his book.[12]
The U.S. auto industry, for example, was a crucial part of the ramp-
up for World War II. Public- and private-sector actors worked together on economic strategy geared toward preparing for battle. Bill
Knudsen, chairman of General Motors, was tapped by Franklin
Roosevelt to lead the retooling of civilian industry for wartime production. The production lines that were created not only helped win
the war, but also increased productivity and bolstered growth and
competitiveness in the postwar period.[13]

You can draw an invisible line directly from this strategy back to
Hamilton's own *Report on the Subject of Manufactures,* published
at the end of 1791, which outlined why manufacturing had an importance to the nation that went far beyond security: it would not
only protect citizens, but help them diversify their own industrial
efforts, raise productivity and wages as a result, and bolster invest-

ment. Hamilton expected that as American manufacturing grew, "parts of Europe, which have more Capital, than profitable domestic objects of employment," would invest and import U.S. goods, making the country richer and stronger.[14] He was right. The United States under Hamilton (and, in fact, until the postwar period of the 1960s) protected its industrial base, using tariffs and state subsidies to help bolster it. Hamilton strengthened patent protections in order to lure entrepreneurs and inventors to the United States.[15] The nation used its growing prosperity to help push westward expansion, which in turn fueled more growth and prosperity. That's exactly what China does so successfully today, using industrial policy and state subsidies to protect industries, investors, and workers and moving people and infrastructure where it makes the most sense.

This strategy has always made sense for the United States, which is a large economy with plenty of food, fuel, and consumer demand. It makes sense for China, too (which doesn't have access to as much of an agricultural base as the United States, but which has bought farmland and ports in other countries to ensure its own security). It makes less sense for smaller nations like the United Kingdom, birthplace of Adam Smith and David Ricardo, the father of today's neoliberal trade theory. Ricardian economics has shaped today's trading system. But it's arguably not the best formula for a bigger, more self-sufficient nation like the United States or China (or even a region like the European Union, which can essentially act as a large self-sufficient bloc). In a world that is more regionalized, there are inherent tensions within the Ricardian model, and cracks that are only just now beginning to show.

Ricardo, a financier who made a fortune betting correctly on the Battle of Waterloo and subsequently bought himself a seat in Parliament, was a fan of Adam Smith's *Wealth of Nations,* which outlined, among other things, how productivity could be increased when nations specialized in certain tasks. Smith's oft-cited example was of a pin factory in which different workers performed different tasks, each becoming faster and more productive.

Ricardo took the idea farther, arguing that free trade could make two countries richer and better off, even when one country was more productive than the other in every way. His 1817 book, *The Principles of Political Economy and Taxation,* put forward a case against mercantilism and economic planning, arguing that open markets and national specialization was the way to grow the pie globally. Ricardo famously compared Portugal and Britain: The former could make both wine and cloth more cheaply, but it would benefit greatly by being able to sell wine in particular (where it had a huge cost advantage) over Britons. Great Britain, for its part, would be better off using its industrial skill to produce more cloth, because its relative disadvantage in wine making was so great. Ricardo's idea, which is really the basis of laissez-faire trade, took off. The British became the low-cost producers and manufacturers to the world, importing relatively cheap raw materials and churning out finished goods. Britain in 1860 was the "factory of the world," with virtually no trade barriers.

But as Peking University professor Michael Pettis has explained in his co-written book *Trade Wars Are Class Wars,* economic specialization was a win-win only when capital and goods were far less mobile than they are today:

> Neither Smith nor Ricardo thought it would make sense to divide the stages of pin-making or textile manufacturing across national borders. Rather they were thinking of the world as it was then—two hundred years ago. In those days, people happily traded raw materials and finished goods with each other across long distances, but would not trade intermediate goods or services. The communications technologies available at the time—carrier pigeons and couriers on horseback or sailing ship—would not have been adequate for coordinating the various stages of production across disparate locations. Travel was dangerous, and wars were common . . . what many forget today is that Ricardo's argument made sense only under these primitive conditions.[16]

The laissez-faire case for free trade made more sense when entire supply chains couldn't be outsourced to myriad countries and when international capital was far less mobile. Ricardo thought that all the risks outlined on the previous page would prevent British financiers from simply outsourcing the entire industrial supply chain to Portugal (or whichever country could produce pins or cloth most cheaply). He also suspected that national patriotism would be a limiting factor in the outsourcing of entire production systems. As he put it, "Most men of property [will be] satisfied with a low rate of profits in their own country, rather than seek[ing] a more advantageous employment for their wealth in foreign nations."[17] This is a crucial point—Ricardo himself realized that if capital were entirely mobile, his own theory wouldn't hold up, and excess offshoring would lead to job loss and economic decline.

For a long time, the "laissez-faire" approach held. But with the invention of the telegraph, the steamship, the limited liability company, and global banking, his theory began to break down. Between 1870 and 1900, the United States surged ahead of Britain in nearly every sector.[18]

Ricardo's case for free trade worked for Britain in the preindustrial age. But the financier's theories "depended on persistent differences in rates of return across countries, which in turn depended on investors' unwillingness to move money abroad," as Pettis quite rightly sums it up. "Those assumptions broke down as technology improved, communication costs collapsed, and global politics changed."[19] While the risks of investing in a faraway place (not to mention a sense of national pride in the industrial commons) were limiting factors in 1817, they were far less so by the twentieth century.

The age of hyperglobalized capitalism from the 1980s onward was enabled by technologies that Ricardo never imagined. Consider that today we live in a world in which the production of *both goods and services* can be spliced, diced, and located anywhere and that the software that tracks and enables it all can be endlessly reproduced for near-zero cost.

Add into that the realities of this level of interdependence with nations that have entirely different political economies, and the fact that there has been a huge shift in authority over who negotiates trade deals (it used to be Congress, but now it's the White House that appoints the U.S. trade representative), we've moved well beyond the nineteenth century. It's one thing to trade Portuguese wine for English wool. It's another thing to give up your entire industrial base to Asia and then not be able to, say, put masks on your citizens in the beginning of a pandemic because the country that supplies 70 percent of your masks, China, has an entirely different economic and political model and decides to nationalize its personal protective equipment industry and (quite understandably) cover the mouths and noses of its own people first.

And that's just the most extreme example of how fragmented global production systems have changed the world. As Israeli entrepreneur, academic, and author Dan Breznitz puts it in his 2021 book, *Innovation in Real Places,* which looks at why keeping a broad range of industries and skill sets at home is important to economic competitiveness and national well-being, "Great innovations and entrepreneurship always translate to growth and job creation. However, in the current global economy, growth and job creation do not necessarily occur at the place of innovation."[20] U.S. taxpayers funded plenty of basic research that is making the middle classes in Denmark, Ireland, and Switzerland wealthy, just as software created in Silicon Valley actually results in more job creation in Asia, which is where most of the actual work of putting together electronic gadgets happens. It's not all bad, but you can't make good economic policy if you don't acknowledge these basic facts.

None of this should have come as a surprise. Indeed, we've understood the risks of this sort of globalization for decades. Consider the Barry Lynn essay in *Harper's Magazine* in June 2002, titled "Unmade in America," which formed the basis for his later book on supply chains. As Lynn wrote in *Harper's,* "even as the corporations celebrate" the rise of the globalized industrial network, "almost no one asks what would happen if just one of the still very sovereign nations that underlie this web was to grab hold of a few of the strands and start yanking." Lynn also points out that while the first wave of post–World War II globalization involved European nations with quite similar values, each successive wave involved trade between nations with more and more political divergence, culminating of course with China's World Trade Organization entry.[21] As Adam Smith could have told us, trade gets tougher when the partners don't have a shared moral framework.

Why This Time Is Different

Globalization has always existed to some degree, and it has usually gone in waves, back and forth, like the tides of the sea on which migrants have traveled. Goods and people have always crossed national and cultural borders both with huge benefits to society and with pressures. When the pressures became too much, there would be a backlash and a retrenchment while geopolitical and economic systems were recalibrated. In modern times, there have been two distinct eras of globalization. The first, from 1860 to 1914, came off the back of the Industrial Revolution. It brought higher trade, migration from rural areas to cities, and higher population growth, but also new pressures on workers, monopoly power, and a run-up in asset prices that increased inequality. (The Gilded Age, at the end of the nineteenth century, has much in common with today in that sense.) That first period of globalization ended with the beginning of World War I, which was followed by a depression and yet another world war before the Bretton Woods system was born.[22]

The Bretton Woods institutions created a framework for modern globalization, but it was one still largely bound by local politics. Postwar America had strong labor unions that protected worker rights, and the banking and capital market regulations put in place following the Great Depression were largely untouched. Capital was far more tethered to national interests. For this reason, the second era of globalization didn't really take off in full until the eighties. Until then, relatively tight financial market regulations curbed the power of Wall Street to set the terms under which business should operate to maximize profits. The fortunes of the country and of companies generally rose and fell together.

This started to shift under Reagan, who began the process of market deregulation. One of the most pernicious changes during that period was the legalization of share buybacks. Consider that until 1982, stock buybacks, the shell game by which companies re-purchase their own shares in order to artificially raise their prices, was considered market manipulation. After Reagan legalized this, such financial maneuvers, which bolstered share prices but didn't fundamentally alter the reality of what was happening in a com-pany, simply became the cost of being a public company. Today, they are one of the reasons that asset markets are at near-record highs even as the country struggles with the tail end of a pandemic and conflict abroad.

As Wall Street gained more power, capital became freer, and the ethos of share maximization took hold, companies became far more global, and their fortunes became disconnected from those of the countries in which they were based. Outsourcing and profit maximi-zation were demanded by financiers and encouraged by politicians, who made small but steady tweaks to everything from tax codes to accounting standards, tweaks that pushed companies to favor share price increases above any other metric of success. As part of this shift, "the global manufacturing system" began to increasingly "act independently of national considerations," as Lynn puts it. And yet, right under the surface of it all was a system still made up of nation-states and voters who hadn't explicitly agreed to any of this. Eco-nomics was global, but politics, as always, was still local.

As Wall Street was unleashed through deregulation under both Republican and Democratic administrations, the trade landscape changed, too. This process continued throughout the nineties and didn't really end until the financial crisis of 2008. NAFTA went into effect in 1994 and fundamentally shifted the incentives for business, making it far easier for companies to move assets and jobs abroad. It quickened a process already under way in areas like the technology industry. Semiconductors, the crucial hardware for any smart device, were invented in the United States. But in the 1970s, the Japanese got into the market, as did the Singaporeans and Koreans. All of these countries subsidized production in various ways, and American companies like Texas Instruments began testing, fabricating, and ultimately producing chips in Asia. Ultimately, Taiwan got into the game, with the creation of Taiwan Semiconductor Manufacturing Company (TSMC), which now produces the majority of the world's high-end chips. In Asia, all the infrastructure and capital needed to create testing, packaging, and fabrication facilities for such a crucial industry was provided by governments. In the United States, this was not the case, and so companies kept a few good design jobs at home and outsourced the rest.[23] It was the classic "cheap labor for investment" bargain struck between Asia and America. By placing manufacturing in places like Taiwan, Americans would get cheaper products, the Chinese could tap into Taiwanese chip-making know-how, and peace in the South China Sea would be maintained. And yet, none of this was explicitly acknowledged by political leaders, at least in the West. Rather, the process was driven by Asian governments and U.S. companies, from Intel to Cisco to Qualcomm and Apple.

The mid-nineties in particular are considered by some to be the high watermark of this type of neoliberal globalization. "That's really when you saw a reversal of the means and the ends of economic policy," says Dani Rodrik. "The world economy used to be a means to an end, but after the nineties, there was a growing belief that nations had to do whatever they had to do to compete in the world economy, and domestic politics had to come second to that." Rodrik notes that finance in particular started to become the tail wagging the dog of the real Main Street economy (a topic we will come to in the next chapter). This was presented by political leaders—people like President Clinton and Prime Minister Tony Blair—as an inevitable process, something with which it was impossible to argue. "The question is not whether globalization will proceed, but how?" President Clinton said during a speech in 2000.[24]

But the truth is that neither Clinton nor his British counterpart, Blair, did much to shape how global trade would impact local populations.

This is an important difference between the modern generation of neoliberals and the new conservatism represented by Ronald Reagan. Reagan was big on deregulation and "trickle-down" theory and was able to run up government budgets in part because of the flood of global capital that came into the United States from abroad from the eighties onward. He resisted imposing restrictions on apartheid-era South Africa and lifted sanctions against Pinochet's Chile because he believed (incorrectly) that free trade would democratize such nations.[25] But when it came to supporting domestic industry, Reagan was arguably more interventionist than those who succeeded him. He was a supporter of U.S. industrial policy, even green-lighting a secret project, called Socrates, through the U.S. Defense Intelligence Agency, to study which high-growth industries of the future the United States should try to bolster at home. (The project was eventually killed by Bush the Elder.)[26] Reagan also put important restrictions on Japan in the eighties, when that country began to take the lead in areas like automotive manufacturing. It's amazing but true that when it came to trade, Democrats in the nineties were far less protectionist than the Republicans who came before them. Indeed, Democrats supported the WTO rules that, by 2000, made it nearly impossible for countries to craft their own trade policies by using things like voluntary export restraints to protect themselves from a flood of cheaper imported goods.[27]

It was the growth in power of the World Trade Organization that, according to Rodrik, marked the real shift toward a new kind of trade globalization. The General Agreement on Tariffs and Trade, or GATT, which came before the development of the WTO (which was founded at the height of neoliberal optimism, in 1995), "was far less ambitious and was limited to manufacturers," notes Rodrik. "The WTO demanded universal commitments to everything from manufacturing to agriculture, services, intellectual property, labor standards, and the environment." The idea that all this could be unified across the globe seems incredibly fanciful in retrospect. And yet, since the mid-nineties, every trade agreement has followed this logic of one seamless, globalized world in which local politics don't exist.

Not surprisingly, the country that did the very best from the system, China, was the one that didn't pretend we'd somehow reached "the end of history," as Francis Fukuyama put it in his book of the same title in 1992, which argued that Western liberal democracy had triumphed and that the world's political economy had reached its final stage of unfettered, free-market globalization.[28] How anyone thought that was possible when, just three years before, the Chinese military had massacred ten thousand of its own people in Tiananmen Square during a protest in favor of democracy and human rights, defies understanding. In fact, Western leaders at the time pursued what Bill Clinton called "a pragmatic policy of engagement." In a 1997 speech, Clinton acknowledged that China was stifling dissent in ways incompatible with liberal democracy, but he argued that the forces of history and U.S. technology like TV and the internet would ensure exposure to "people, ideas, and the world beyond China's borders." The idea was to keep quiet and pour as much money into China as possible. Starting with Clinton's first year in office and continuing over the next decade, investment from the United States to China would increase by fifty times.[29]

And yet, "none of our elected officials or civil servants ever really examined in detail the risks of joining hands with one of the least stable and least transparent states on earth, China, and with that state's number one potential target, Taiwan," noted Barry Lynn in his *Harper's* essay. Business leaders likely did—how could they not?—but they ignored the risks in favor of short-term profits. Is it any wonder, then, that instead of a convergence of economic models, we've gotten just the opposite? While everyone else played by the new rules of globalization, China continued to play by the old rules and use the world economy for domestic purposes. China did well using this approach—not only in comparison to rich nations but also to poorer ones. Mexico, for example, did everything that the wizards at the IMF would have told an emerging market to do from the eighties onward. It liberalized trade, completely opened capital markets, and sat as an inexpensive labor country right on the border of the world's biggest consuming nation. But unlike China, Mexico didn't manage its exchange rate or prioritize and protect its most productive sectors. And so, it remains a laggard compared to China and other Asian tiger economies that took a more self-interested, realpolitik approach to the neoliberal world paradigm.[30]

Neoliberalism on Steroids

Even as nations were drinking the political Kool-Aid of neoliberalism and laissez-faire capitalism from the eighties onward, there were other technological shifts under way that allowed globalization to grow to a depth and breadth that couldn't have been imagined before. The computer revolution had begun, but there were also brick-and-mortar shifts. In particular, giant container ships like the kind that blocked the Suez Canal and wreaked havoc with supply chains in March 2021 became ubiquitous. Before that, extremely far-flung supply chains in which multinational companies sourced thousands, even tens of thousands, of different component parts for products from different suppliers in multiple countries, made no sense. But as Council on Foreign Relations fellow Marc Levinson outlines in his 2020 book, *Outside the Box*,[31] a combination of cheaper container shipping, lower communications costs, and higher computing power made it possible for companies to start globalizing their suppliers in ways that were unimaginable when conventional trade theory was being crafted.

This came with all sorts of risks, of course.[32] Executives who were under pressure from Wall Street to boost profits saw a way to cut costs by using cheaper labor in developing countries. Suppliers sprang up across Asia to fill global demand for specific kinds of component parts. Unlike workers at home, they didn't have to be paid right away. (Billing was done in months rather than every two weeks.) They didn't need health benefits, and they didn't have unions. No wonder the world's biggest companies (GE, Boeing,

Apple, and the like) typically use thousands of suppliers in places with the laxest labor and tax laws.

Metric-driven management has become a corporate touchstone, particularly in big multinational public companies that, for years, have been using cost-cutting measures to slice the fat off their profit-and-loss sheets. But I have long wondered if management by numbers, popularized in the late nineteenth century in the United States by Frederick Winslow Taylor (a mechanical engineer who used to stand over factory workers with a stopwatch to make sure they were doing each task as efficiently as possible), wasn't the ultimate in penny-wise, pound-foolish thinking. Well before the Covid-19 pandemic and the U.S.-Chinese trade wars pulled the scales from our eyes with regard to the risks of unfettered free trade, there were plenty of high-profile disasters that showed how costly short-term profit taking might ultimately be. Consider the Rana Plaza factory disaster, in which eleven hundred people were killed when a shoddily made garment complex in Dhaka, Bangladesh, collapsed. The factory was a supplier to Walmart and other high-profile brands—few of whom even knew this: the outsourcing had simply existed as a decision on a balance sheet.

Boeing is a good example of a company that has repeatedly struggled with the hidden costs of globalization. Back in 2001, four years after a merger with McDonnell Douglas, Boeing moved its headquarters from Seattle to Chicago, to be closer to the financial markets. Despite protests from engineers, a much-hyped new aircraft, the Dreamliner, was taken out of the hands of the more expensive team of U.S. engineers and outsourced to multiple, cheaper overseas suppliers. Seventy percent of the aircraft was made in dozens of countries, often by people who weren't talking to one another. The result? Multiple systems failures, cost overruns, safety issues, and a strike by disgruntled employees—all of which meant the company spent billions more than it expected to and took multiple years to make a profit.[33]

This didn't seem to change things at Boeing, though, because, by 2019, it was in crisis again. One of the company's flagship aircrafts, the Boeing 737 Max, was grounded after two separate crashes involving that model of plane. There were many factors behind the disasters, but an important one was risk taking at Boeing in order to maximize profits. The plane maker outsourced work to Indian software engineers who were paid just nine dollars an hour.[34] It charged extra for certain safety features and rushed the aircraft to market sooner than might have been wise, in order to try to nab business that might otherwise have gone to Airbus. Because of Boeing's disasters, Airbus ended up overtaking Boeing as the world's most successful airline. The entire fiasco illustrates a kind of "management by numbers" approach to business that simply never adds up.[35]

What's Old Is New Again

Before the 1980s, most large companies didn't have hyperglobalized supply chains, but were, rather, "vertically" integrated, meaning they kept control over most of the key things they needed for their products, from raw materials to component parts. This model was pioneered by steel magnate Andrew Carnegie, who built mills and then purchased coke and iron ore and the ships and railroads needed to transport them. It was a model well suited to large, rich companies operating in industries with huge scale and demand, like big automakers in Detroit. Until the eighties, these automakers typically worked with a choice group of suppliers located close by, which could quickly provide them with most of what they needed. At the height of the U.S. automobile industry, Ford's River Rouge plant was the perfect model of this type of manufacturing, which was all about close-knit teams working in tandem—R&D happened steps away from production, and salespeople were a stone's throw away from line workers and management. As my former *Time* colleague and longtime business correspondent Bill Saporito once put it poetically, River Rouge "inhaled iron ore, coking coal and other raw ingredients at the front end and exhaled finished automobiles at the other."[36]

Now, post-Covid-19, vertical integration is once more in vogue as a way of increasing productivity, resilience, and sustainability. Tesla, as we've already learned, produces most of its products completely in-house. Many more companies are moving in this direction, particularly following the pandemic. After problems with its Covid-19 vaccine rollout, Johnson & Johnson took over subcontracting at the Baltimore plant that had spoiled sixty million doses and said it would be "assuming full responsibility" for the factory and adding in-house specialists to oversee things. According to a McKinsey survey, over 50 percent of global supply chain leaders have implemented dual sourcing of raw materials since the pandemic in order to create more redundancy and closer proximity to manufacturing centers. Forty percent have "near-shored" more production, localizing and regionalizing operations. The reasons for this are driven not only by the disruptions of the pandemic—McKinsey found that 73 percent of major companies encountered supply chain problems during this time—but also by the sense that U.S.-Chinese decoupling is here to stay and by the reality that rising wages in emerging markets and increasing energy inflation have made it more costly and less productive to ship products all over the world. Add in governments everywhere moving to put a price on carbon, which will make global shipping much more expensive, and new global tax deals reducing the advantage of putting operations in formerly low-tax jurisdictions, and you have a number of tailwinds to the trend of hubbing more production locally and even keeping more of the entire supply chain within individual companies.[37] As I finish writing this book, in December 2021, the companies that are having the easiest time overcoming holiday supply chain disruption, including Walmart, Costco, Home Depot, and Target, are those that are taking increasing control of their own logistics and transportation businesses, even going so far as to charter their own ships for supply.[38]

Vertical integration is, by its very nature, somewhat deglobalizing. A vertically integrated company might still sell globally, but it will produce more locally or regionally. The political decoupling of the United States and China will lead to more of this, particularly in the most-high-value, strategic sectors of the economy (as we will explore later, in the chapters on technology). But in many countries, like Germany and Japan, vertical integration never really died. On the contrary, it was part of an industrial culture that led to competitiveness. Consider, for example, the Japanese process of continuous, incremental improvement called *kaizen,* which relies heavily on good relations between management and labor. The idea is that when everyone shares information and is part of a larger mission, rather than existing in a silo, risks and mistakes, as well as opportunities, can come to the fore more quickly.[39] Germans consider the process of "co-determination," in which labor union members sit on corporate boards and are part of high-level decision making, a major competitive advantage and one of the secret weapons of their export success.

Unfortunately, Anglo-American companies tend to have just the opposite view: workers and managers are set up as natural adversaries. Part of this is due to the fact that in the United States, Britain, Australia, and Canada, unions negotiate with individual companies rather than with entire industries. The German system, as well as some Asian systems, put unions on one side and industry as a whole on the other, which creates the potential for more of a win-win type of dynamic. Viewed through that lens, the U.S. system is both odd and unproductive. I remember back in 2014, covering the story of the German automaker VW's expansion into Tennessee with a new factory in Chattanooga. The VW management assumed that the plant would have a works council—that is, a group of employees representing the workforce in discussion with management. But under American labor law, you can't have a works council without a union. The very idea was anathema to Republican legislators and conservatives like Grover Norquist and the Koch brothers. Conservatives proceeded to wage a campaign to keep unions out. Chattanooga was blanketed with billboards bearing messages like "Detroit: Brought to You by the UAW," intimating that the last thing Chattanooga wanted to be was a failing Rust Belt city. (Although, it's worth noting that Detroit has since rebounded and is rising off the back of

Biden's electric vehicle initiatives.) On the second day of the National Labor Relations Board vote on the union, U.S. senator Bob Corker (a former Chattanooga mayor and a Republican) raced into the city claiming he'd received a tip from VW that if the union were rejected, a new SUV would be scheduled for production there. (The factory, which opened in 2011, currently makes Atlases.) VW quickly announced that this was false, but no matter—right-wing talk radio grabbed Corker's comments and fanned the anti-union flames. The vote was 712–626 against the UAW.

It was a bitter defeat, and yet, according to labor professor Harley Shaiken of the University of California, Berkeley, the fact that the union got 47 percent of the vote made it by far the most successful organizing effort ever at a foreign automaker in the South. The vote also made Chattanooga one of the rare VW plants worldwide that doesn't have a works council. (Others can be found in China.) Bernd Osterloh, until recently the head of VW's main works council in Germany, issued an ominous statement about the future of the company's expansion in the United States: "I can imagine fairly well that another VW factory in the United States, provided that one more should still be set up there, does not necessarily have to be assigned to the South again."[40]

It's really quite amazing to ponder a company that *wanted* to give workers a voice was prevented from doing so by politicians. But over the last few years, the worm has turned. Union movements are gathering steam in many countries, and for the first time in a half century, the labor–capital balance is shifting. In the United States, the Biden administration's "Buy American" initiatives explicitly support union labor and higher worker standards in general. The $1.2 trillion infrastructure program that passed through Congress in November 2021 includes support for not only organized manufacturing labor, but also service workers like home healthcare aides and nurses. The Biden administration's supply chain report, issued in June 2021, also put forward proposals to support domestic labor in the areas most crucial to national productivity and economic growth. Among these were semiconductors, medical devices, communications equipment, electronics, autos and auto parts, and precision tools. If these sectors decline, so does good employment.

Clearly, we are at a pivot point. After forty years of the globalization of manufacturing supply chains, we are about to see a shift back to more regionalization. And this time around, it won't be rhetoric, but reality. Despite all the headlines about trade wars during the Trump years, according to a McKinsey Global Institute analysis of UN Comtrade data, between 2014 and 2017, only around 7 percent of global trade routes shifted. But now, the change is truly here. Thanks to myriad risks—from fractious politics to climate change and pandemics, or the growing number of cyber-attacks and financial crises—shocks to global trade are becoming more frequent. The wedging in March 2021 of the container ship the *Ever Given* in the Suez Canal, a major global trading route, which resulted in $9.6 billion worth of losses per day in goods unable to get from port to port, is one dramatic visual indicator of the shift.[41] The supply chain disruptions from the war in Ukraine, which shut down factories in Europe and created food and fuel shortages globally, are another. Companies can now expect month-long disruptions to supply chains every 3.7 years. That means that over the course of a decade, they can expect to lose the equivalent of 45 percent of a year's profits.

The McKinsey Global Institute, a think tank associated with the consulting giant McKinsey, estimates that up to 26 percent of global goods exports, worth some $4.6 trillion, could move to new countries over the next five years as companies realize they need to diversify suppliers, cut emissions in far-flung supply chains, and be closer to end consumers. And that is a conservative estimate, based on what is economically feasible right now. Politics may, of course, force changes that are not in a country's economic interest, but that instead represent the desires of electorates or autocrats. One recent example of the latter would be China's decision to force Western apparel brands who have complained about forced labor in Xinjiang and refused to use cotton produced there (which represents about 20 percent of global supply) to stop doing business in China.

This is a major hit for a brand like Nike, which relies on China for nearly 20 percent of its sales.[42]

The bottom line is that supply chains are shifting, both geographically and economically, faster than many globalists thought possible. One of the most telling examples of this was BlackRock CEO Larry Fink's admission in his annual shareholder letter in early 2022 that "the Russian invasion of Ukraine has put an end to the globalization we have experienced over the last three decades." Fink admitted that the neoliberal world order was over, and that localization and regionalization of production was the future.[43] I would argue, of course, that this was obvious long before the war. The 2008 financial crisis made plain the vulnerabilities of highly integrated capital markets. The pandemic was the point at which Western countries decided they didn't want to continue to rely on China, or even India, to produce the bulk of crucial inputs to, say, the world's pharmaceutical ingredients. Indeed, countries don't want to be reliant on a single supplier for much of anything anymore. That means a lot of change. The McKinsey report finds 180 key tradable products for which a single country accounts for more than 70 percent of exports. Concentration is highest in mobile and communications equipment, one of the most politically contentious areas right now. It is also common in lower-profile industries such as textiles and apparel.

This underscores a truly seismic development: we are now living in a world in which two superpowers with very different political and economic systems, the United States and China, are both major producers and major global consumers. Previously, it was mainly the United States consuming and China producing. The existence of two major producing and consuming countries shifts the entire global manufacturing paradigm. Rising wages in China have, for example, increased the buying power of Chinese consumers, but they have also made it much more likely that production of lower-value goods such as furniture or clothing will move to other countries. At the same time, the rise of China and its ring fencing of strategically important areas, including the technology sector, have contributed to the inherent friction of One World, Two Systems.

The supply chains of those systems will continue to decouple. The only question is: How fast and in which industries? Over the past twenty years, China has become a much richer country. It has not only a huge industrial base, but also richer consumers who are increasingly buying homegrown brands—such as Xiaomi phones over Apple. When the United States makes it tough for Chinese sellers to do business in America, they move elsewhere.[44] That is as it should be. Indeed, it's exactly the pattern the United States and Britain followed in the nineteenth century, as America became more politically and economically independent from Europe. The question isn't so much whether trade will decouple; that is already happening. It is whether the world financial system will become more fragmented, too, and what the ramifications of that shift might be.

CHAPTER 6

———

Exorbitant Privilege, Exorbitant Burden

Most economists live in ivory towers, but some live under bridges. Bob Hockett, a professor of law and economics at Cornell University, chose his life's work of trying to create a more equitable financial system and resilient economy during time spent living among the homeless in Kansas City, in a camp under a bridge. It was there that he came up with an entirely new model for bringing banking to people who'd never had it before.

Hockett was taking a bit of time off from Yale, where he had completed the coursework for a PhD in economics. A six-foot-five-inch Birkenstock-wearing Rhodes Scholar and lawyer at the New York Federal Reserve, he is the sort of person who immediately strikes you as a mad scientist, but in the best possible way: crazy hair, huge smile, a far-ranging mind, and an enormous heart. Hockett has mentored many of the era's top law scholars, including Federal Trade Commission chair and antitrust wunderkind Lina Khan. He spends much of his spare time today doing pro bono work for people and organizations that can't afford counsel.

But back in the mid-nineties, Hockett was stuck. He wanted a new topic for his PhD thesis and couldn't come up with anything compelling enough to hold his attention. He left New Haven for Kansas, to spend time with the grandparents who had raised him. (His single mother was a successful advertising executive who traveled a lot.) To keep himself occupied while figuring out his thesis, he started volunteering in homeless shelters and carrying a large back-pack with food around to feed locals in need. That's when he met Chaka, an equally tall, friendly, and brilliant African American man living under a bridge with some friends, all of whom were supporting themselves by detailing cars and washing windows for passing drivers. "The guys had basically formed a homeless camp under the bridge, and I had gone down there to ask if they needed anything," says Hockett.

It turned out that they didn't—at least not food or shelter. "They were making pretty good money and, at the end of each day, would go to the grocery store and buy dinner." Hockett was intrigued. "They were making decent money, enough (at least in theory) to get an apartment together." Instead, the group preferred to live as they were, under the bridge, doing what they could to make a buck and cooking dinner together afterward. Hockett often joined them, and "after eating, we had these various recreations that we would engage in, of a very traditional sort, like dance contests. Somebody would have a boom box, and we'd turn on music and see who could invent the best, wackiest new dance. Another night, we'd sit around telling tall tales, and the competition was to see who could cook up the most ridiculous, crazy-sounding story. It was totally fun. Really, it was just an absolute marvel living with these guys."

Fascinated by what was an impoverished and yet, at the same time, extremely rich life, Hockett became a sort of amateur sociologist, living with the group and helping them as best he could. "There were a lot of reasons that they were living this way," he says. "Some of it was a sense of being alienated by contemporary Western life," with its divisions of work and home, controlling schedules, and technocratic and bureaucratic demands. "It struck me that they had sort of rediscovered a sort of eighteenth- or nineteenth-century-type of village life, a more communal style of living, and it worked in many ways."

But there were challenges, such as the lack of any banking services that would enable the group to create a stabler living situation. Like roughly 25 percent of the American public, the guys in the bridge kibbutz had no access to formal financial services because, in their case, they had no address. This was an impediment to their moving ahead—saving, getting an apartment, or developing more substantial relationships with those outside the group. Chaka, Hockett told me, would say, "My pockets have holes in them," referring to the fact that because he carried all the money he had with him, and was generous, giving it away to whoever asked, he rarely had extra. Hockett had a flat near the camp and began letting the guys come by to shower and borrow clothing for job interviews. He also started an informal banking system he called the Shoebox Bank. Each person had a shoebox with their name and a ledger inside. They could leave the money in it—Chaka was able to start politely telling panhandlers that he'd left his money in a shoebox and didn't have it on hand—make loans, save, and even team up to purchase items for the group, like a new boom box.

By this time, winter was coming. Hockett managed to find the group dorm rooms at a closed parochial school, but he also started wondering if this could be the basis for a business—the guys could perhaps use the parking lot of the school to detail cars more formally, and they could place ads to get new clients. "But there was no way to get a bigger loan without a bank and no way to incorporate a business without an address." The entire legal morass got Hockett thinking about whether he should get a law degree so that he could help create a financial system that worked not for the 75 percent who had banks or, even more particularly, for the Wall Street institutions that Hoovered up the majority of profits from the conventional system, but for people who actually needed basic services—to have a place to put their savings, which lenders would turn into productive investments, thus making money for themselves and for depositors.[1]

Sound familiar? It's the sort of banking system we used to have, until roughly the 1970s. And indeed, it's what Adam Smith, the father of modern capitalism, felt the role of the financial system should be. Smith's worldview was shaped by the eighteenth-century British marketplace system. Back then, people lived in small communities, knew most of their neighbors, and produced much of what was needed locally. Financial lenders were a helpmeet for the real economy, the one that individuals engaged in every day. They were there to turn savings into productive investment, so that businesses could create jobs and employ people who would then spend the money they earned buying things from other businesses. It was a virtuous circle in which supply and demand fueled each other. Smith's theory of finance hinged on a few basic rules. In order for a market to be fair and to function well, there needed to be a clear understanding on both sides about what was being bought and sold and what the price was (in whatever currency or barter was being used). In order for this to happen, each party needed equal access to data. Transparency was crucial, and there had to be a shared moral framework that both buyer and seller bought into.

Needless to say, this is a far cry from today's financial system, which is all too often removed from the needs of not only individuals, but businesses themselves. This is not a new realization; this removal has been building, slowly but surely, since the financial crisis and global recession of 2008. But what groups like Occupy Wall Street and Millennial socialists like Congresswoman Alexandria Ocasio-Cortez, not to mention economic nationalists on the right side of the political aisle (and their counterparts in Europe), have missed in the debate over an inclusive and resilient economy is that in order to have one, you can't simply shift supply chains or even just rejigger trade policy. You have to rethink the entire way the financial system works. This requires understanding how both Wall Street and the global currency system have become a headwind to policy makers' efforts to create a virtuous circle in which things that can be are produced and consumed at home, in countries all over the world.

The World's Currency

Aside from the neoliberal assumptions about trade that turned out to work quite differently in the real world than in theory, there was another reason for the loss of so many middle-class jobs in what economists call the "tradable" sectors of the economy (meaning those most exposed to foreign competition) in the United States over the last several decades: the power of the dollar.

Since that famous post–World War II meeting of the Allied powers in Bretton Woods, New Hampshire, the dollar has been the global reserve currency. For a long time, that position was held by gold, and for a while, when Britain had a global empire, it was held by the British pound. The position held by the dollar over the last half century has been in many ways what former French president Valéry Giscard d'Estaing, when he was finance minister in the 1960s, dubbed "the exorbitant privilege." This privilege allows the United States to run large deficits because the rest of the world has to keep buying our debt and assets to do business in dollars. All that free flow of global capital into the United States causes the dollar to become more expensive than it ordinarily might be. This makes it easier for Americans to buy cheap flat-screen televisions or iPhones, but it also makes it more expensive for countries like the United States to make them. U.S. manufacturers have a tougher time selling to foreign markets (because the flood of overseas capital into dollar assets makes the dollar stronger and U.S. products more expensive), and thus employment in the manufacturing sector is dampened, decreasing productive investment into the real economy and creating debt bubbles. This is all part of the process of financialization, which I explored in my first book, *Makers and Takers*.[2]

To understand why this is such a problem, you need to remember that the chief function of the financial system historically is to act as a helpmeet to the rest of the economy, not an end in and of itself. Traditionally, the role of banks has been to take the savings of households and turn it into loans to real people and businesses. But today, this paradigm has been flipped on its head. The vast majority of money sloshing around the financial system goes to support not new business loans or venture capital investments, but the buying and selling of existing assets—things like stocks and bonds and home mortgages, which are still packaged as securities in just the way they were in the run-up to the subprime mortgage crisis a decade ago. Only about 15 percent of money coming out of financial institutions is used to fund business investment. The rest is used to bid up the price of the financial market assets that are already out there, in a perverse closed loop of "financialization," with the owners of those assets—mainly the top 10 percent of households, which own nearly 70 percent of asset wealth—becoming richer, even as small businesses and many individuals find it difficult to make ends meet on their salaries.

This is why it's possible to have a situation, as we did after Covid-19 struck, in which unemployment is in the high double digits, but stock prices are at all-time highs. With the rise of finance and financially oriented behavior throughout our economy, the tail has truly begun to wag the dog. Executives are manipulating balance sheets to boost their short-term results. Companies are focused more on finance than on their core businesses. Debt is preferred over equity as an instrument of doing business. The trend is ubiquitous. The process of financialization means that Main Street and Wall Street have become fundamentally delinked.[3]

What's more, financialization and globalization have gone hand in hand, each in some ways fueling the other. Because these are complex processes, it's difficult to point to a causal relationship. But understanding the history of the dollar as the global reserve currency gives some insight into how the two processes developed in tandem and how they have become inexorably related.

Part of the original Bretton Woods agreement was that the United States would back the dollar with gold. But as the country grew and spent and produced in the post–World War II period, it became increasingly difficult to do this. Inflation rose, leading to the sort of difficult guns-or-butter debates, in which politicians have to choose from among various voter interests: What to spend on? Defense? Social programs? These pressures grew strongly during the administrations of John Kennedy and Lyndon Johnson, but both these leaders chose to ignore them, preferring instead to act, as author Jeffrey Garten puts it in his book on the breaking of the dollar-to-gold peg, titled *Three Days at Camp David,* "as if there were no limits to America's commitments to peace, prosperity, and stability," either at home or abroad.[4] It was a pleasing fiction, but one that could not be sustained indefinitely. By 1971, inflationary pressures, growing unemployment, and a terrible trade balance that was not helped by an artificially strong dollar led President Richard Nixon to pull away from the gold standard entirely.[5] It was, in some ways, the America First policy of its day, allowing the dollar to weaken, which made U.S. exports more competitive and helped to resolve the country's balance-of-payments problem, as money started flowing back into the country rather than to foreign markets.

But Nixon's solution also gave the United States' central bank, the Federal Reserve, a lot more freedom to print money, and thus, politicians were able to spend more on whatever they liked. Rather than making the tough calls about which public interests to put first or which societal stakeholders would have first dibs on public resources, politicians of both stripes simply passed the buck to central bankers to sort out any problems that might result from profligate spending. Ronald Reagan, in particular, ran up the U.S. deficit with defense spending but also tax cuts. This led to inflation, which former Federal Reserve chair Paul Volcker eventually brought under control by raising interest rates to nosebleed levels.

But because of the dollar's place as the global reserve, along with financial deregulation starting in 1980, this also created an opportunity for further distortion of the U.S. economy. Those higher interest rates attracted lots of foreign investors, who wanted to earn higher returns than they could at home—not so much because they were investing in Main Street America, but because they were investing in higher-interest-yielding dollar-denominated assets. The Japanese and, later, the Chinese and other emerging market investors became huge purchasers of U.S. Treasury Bills. This in turn encouraged American financial institutions to come up with all sorts of new financial "innovations," from complex securities to the sorts of derivatives that exploded the financial system in 2008.

This snowball cycle began to create a money glut that, once

again, made it very difficult for American manufacturers—who were, by that time, the most productive in the world—to make a buck on the global market because the dollar was so strong. As early as 1982, the Business Roundtable, led by Caterpillar Tractor chairman Lee Morgan, was already complaining about this. But the solution—to further deregulate global financial markets to try to push capital away from the United States—didn't work. The flood of cash kept coming into the dollar-denominated assets, and the dollar kept rising. A computer revolution in finance sped the whole process up. The result was that the financial economy became larger than the real economy, something that Nobel Prize–winning economist James Tobin, mentor to current treasury secretary and former Fed chair Janet Yellen, lamented in 1984. "I confess to an uneasy Physiocratic suspicion . . . that we are throwing more and more of our resources, including the cream of our youth, into financial activities remote from the production of goods and services," he said in a speech about the "casino aspect of our financial markets." Tobin fretted that this was an economy all too focused on "activities that generate high private rewards disproportionate to their social productivity."[6]

This is true today by any number of metrics. A large and growing body of research has shown that productivity (that is, the value each worker creates within the economy) tends to decline in markets with rapidly expanding financial sectors. The industries most likely to suffer are those that require a very long-term outlook, like advanced manufacturing. Wall Street wants profits today, not in ten years or even five. And yet, most of the new technologies that require investment today won't pay off for a decade. Financialization encourages public companies in particular to use their ability to raise money in the capital markets not to invest in research and development or worker salaries but to focus on cutting costs (which has, over the last four decades, resulted in offshoring to cheap-labor countries) and engaging in share buybacks (the process by which companies buy back their own shares in order to limit the amount of shares on the market, thus artificially raising their price). Given that most executives are paid anywhere from 30 to 80 percent of their compensation in shares, this works well for the top brass. But it also wastes the corporate seed corn. What's more, the majority of companies have used super-low interest rates over the last several decades to issue cheap debt to pay for those buybacks, hoarding cash in offshore accounts when possible.

Debt, the lifeblood of finance, is well known to be the major cause of economic crises and recession. Financial sector wages have correlated with rising and falling inequality for a century now, rising in the run-up to the 1929 market crash, falling precipitously after banking was reregulated in the 1930s, and then growing wildly from the eighties onward as the financial sector was once again unleashed.[7] Between 1998 (when the Clinton administration further deregulated the banking system and made changes to the tax code to favor stock options) and 2008, foreign governments bought more than $4 trillion in safe assets, and American bankers sold trillions more in riskier assets to the rest of the world. One result was the housing bubble and the 2008 financial crisis (which was only the final and worst of a series of financial crises brewed up since the late eighties, from the savings-and-loan debacle to various emerging market defaults).

Crises on the Continent

Europe wasn't immune to this. Indeed, the globalization of European capital markets, without similar integration of politics, led to the eurozone debt crisis and the populism and nationalism that we can see on the Continent today. Under François Mitterrand, France had been alone in the 1980s practicing Keynesian economics, which are characterized by the belief that fiscal stimulus and the expansion of government in difficult times can help balance the economy if the private sector will not or cannot spend.[8] Keynesian economics had been at the core of the postwar reconstruction of Europe, which was of course done with the help of the United States. Programs like the German Marshall Plan poured public money into "building back better" and created the modern transatlantic alliance. And yet, Keynesians, like most economists of the day, as James K. Galbraith (son of famed economist John Galbraith, who was deeply involved in building the post–World War II order) wrote in a 2021 *Foreign Policy* piece on the failures of neoliberalism, "saw the issues of inflation and unemployment in domestic terms, and focused on the domestic consequences of policy actions."[9] Galbraith says that both he and neoliberal policy makers like Larry Summers, one of the key architects of the economic system of the last forty years, "were raised in an academic worldview that considered the United States to be essentially a closed economy. Global trade and global finance were for specialists in those topics." The idea was that as long as capital could go where it was most productive to do so (and it would do so magically, via the invisible hand), then there was no need to worry about which sectors or jobs or parts of the country might be hollowed out by any side effects of the new policies. Even if such disruption did occur, wages, growth, and opportunity would ultimately even out, even if it took, as the Clinton-era policy maker told the AFL-CIO's Richard Trumka, three to five generations.

In France, in any case, it was clear that the existing barriers within the European Union hadn't worked and that domestic inflation had risen. With the failure of the Mitterrand experiment and the introduction of the euro in 1999, the French became among the most ardent supporters of capital market integration. Capital controls were ended in 1989, and money was able to move around Europe much more freely, in a kind of microcosm of the larger global financialization that would eventually emerge.

Some of this was good—there was suddenly a larger capital market for middle-size European businesses—though as I can attest, as someone who worked in a pan-European venture capital firm in the late nineties, crossing cultural and geographical boundaries to create truly "European" companies was still a big challenge for all sorts of reasons, from language to regulatory systems. This underscores a key point, which is that while Europe got trade and capital integration, it never got cultural or political integration. This goes to the very heart of the issue with neoliberal economics and modern globalization. It's a lot, lot easier to move money and goods around than people.

Europeans have found this out the hard way over the last fifteen years or so, as they have moved in and out of economic and political crises. Consider the 2012 eurozone debt crisis that followed hard on the heels of the 2008 financial crisis. It was about a lot of things, but at core, it was about Europe's having integrated financial markets without having integrated politics. Germany could write checks to save Greece and Italy after the housing crisis, but it couldn't make those countries stick to its own strict Teutonic budget targets—because, at the end of the day, it didn't control their governments. The European Union is, after all, not a government, but an alliance of states. Whenever it passes "laws," they are more ideas or goals, which then have to be taken from Brussels back to national capitals and voted on. There is a shared currency, but there is no integrated fiscal policy, no common tax law, no shared national budget.

This leads to all sorts of imbalances at a European level that one also sees at a global level. Germany, for example, which used to have a very strong currency relative to other exporting nations like Italy and France when it used the Deutsche Mark, now benefits hugely from being able to sell its exports in euros, at cheaper prices than it would ultimately be able to. In this way, Germany is rather like the China of Europe, benefiting at the expense of its neighbors. (Other European countries, which are Germany's top markets, play the role of the United States, being the purchasers of last resort.) German banks shake their finger at Spanish and Greek officials when real estate collapses lead to recession and debt crises. And yet, the banks themselves made many of the loans that are part of the overall European bailouts. Ultimately, the whole dysfunctional cycle masks a willful blindness about the fact that, at some point, Europe will have to decide whether it wants to be a real political union.

Peak Financialization?

Back in 2016, when I wrote my first book, I thought the phenomenon had reached its peak. I was wrong. Looking for the most Kafkaesque example of dysfunction in our financial markets, I wrote about how Apple, a company that hadn't needed to raise money on the public markets since the nineties, was issuing billions of dollars in debt to pay back the richest shareholders while offshoring profits and jobs. But 2016 wasn't the peak of those dividend payments and share "buybacks" for Apple. In fact, we have yet to reach it. By 2019, Apple had issued tens of billions more in debt and even put out its own credit card. The world's first company to reach a trillion-dollar market value had more cash on hand and more global reach than most banks, so the move made sense. It had been coming for years: academic research shows that the share of revenues coming from financial relative to nonfinancial activities in U.S. corporations began to climb in the seventies and then increased sharply from the eighties onward. This was yet another element of financialization: companies (not just banks) that chose to focus more on markets than the real economy. Easy money has become a morphine drip that too many companies and investors can't seem to do without. Low interest rates have papered over myriad political and economic problems not just since the Covid-19 pandemic or the 2008 crisis, but for several decades. Total financial assets are now more than triple the size of the real economy. The corporate bond market is now worth $16 trillion—over twice as much as in 2008.[10] Debt in the corporate sector amounts to 75 percent of the country's gross domestic product (GDP). But the number of "zombie" companies (meaning those that wouldn't be able to pay their operating expenses should interest rates rise) has grown, and they now represent 16 percent of all public companies.[11]

Easy money is a cover for something deeper and more disturbing: the depression of employment and wages (which haven't grown in real terms for the working class since the seventies or for any American since the nineties) and the growth of credit and debt. Credit cards, home and auto loans, and other sorts of consumer borrowing were made easier in order to account for stagnation in incomes. And as those loans were issued, they were securitized by the banking sector in a never-ending cycle of financialized "growth." The business of banking became less and less about productive lending and more and more about helping rich companies and individuals bolster the value of existing wealth through trading and securitization. This is how we can have a financial sector that is larger and richer than it's ever been, even as there are people like Chaka and the rest of the crew under the bridge who have no access to the financial system at all.

These problems happen within the context of the global system, which funnels huge amounts of money into dollars, propping up the value of U.S. assets like stocks and real estate. This can make us feel richer—especially if we own a lot of assets. But it also contributes to a lopsided economy. The eighties and nineties were the period in which American consumers became the "buyers of last resort" in the global economy. We became an "ownership" society in which retirement was privatized, consumer debt was democratized, and personal finance magazines took off, as we all became part of the Faustian bargain that was financialization. Even as our jobs were outsourced, asset prices rose. Our savings rates plummeted, but our options for living beyond our means soared, as did our dependence on rising financial assets versus rising wages. Again, this was due to the power of the United States and, more particularly, the dollar to attract so much foreign investment.

For Americans, it was a sugar high that seemed virtuous but was in fact precarious. Our 401(k)s were growing, but companies (which were becoming just as financialized as the country itself) were cutting investments in productive capacity, reducing headcounts, and giving back most of their spare cash to shareholders. The asset-owning class benefited quite a bit from this strategy, but workers as a whole did not. As University of Michigan academic Gerald Davis put it, "The bonds between employees and firms loosened, while the economic security of individuals was increasingly tied to the overall health of the stock market."[12]

Neoliberal ideas about the free flow of capital always leading to the stablest and most productive outcomes turned out to be just plain wrong. As I covered in *Makers and Takers,* the growth of financial markets and financial engineering within companies is strongly correlated with the decline of business. Over the last forty years, companies have spent far more paying out free cash to their richest shareholders than investing in future innovation. But this is what Wall Street has demanded and what policy has incentivized. Americans suffered because the industrial base was outsourced to cheaper places. Inequality grew, with more and more wealth held by the stock-owning classes, who tend to save more than they spend. Unlike the average American, who saves around 7 percent of their income, rich people save about 40 percent—and yet, there are only so many pairs of jeans, or homes, or cars they can buy. The fact that so much of the country's wealth is held in just a few hands in turn decreases the ability of the United States to consume the goods it can produce.

Part of this is of course alleviated by the process of exporting goods to other countries. But the power of the dollar and the process of financialization also make it harder for other nations to consume our goods, because their governments are too busy buying our financial assets and (in the case of China) suppressing local wages to grab more manufacturing work. This process fuels a dysfunctional marriage between the United States and China in particular, thanks to a financial system that forces one country to buy and spend too much and another to produce too much. This is the very thing that Keynes warned about at Bretton Woods—by giving the dollar too much power in the new financial system, policy makers would ultimately be sowing the seeds of global dysfunction.

CHAPTER 7

The Post-Dollar World

Keynes was right. While the global financial system worked well between the postwar period and the 1970s—when Europe was still rebuilding, the emerging markets had not yet emerged as low-wage labor alternatives, and interest rates in the United States had yet to be deregulated—it was only a matter of time before it began to break down. This process sped up dramatically after the trade agreements of the 1990s and with the accession of China to the WTO in 2001. Many U.S. manufacturers went out of business during this period. About 80 percent of the decline in private-sector employment between 2000 and 2003 can be traced to factory job losses[1] related to what academics have called "the China Shock,"[2] the process by which huge amounts of cheap Chinese labor flooded into markets following that country's entry into the WTO. Jobs went to Asia, and debt came to the United States. The overvaluation of the dollar and the underinvestment in the industrial base meant that American consumers increasingly had no choice but to buy cheap stuff from China sold at Walmart—they didn't make enough to do anything differently.

The parts of the Midwest and the South that were most vulnerable to the China Shock were exactly where individuals took on the most debt. Unemployment rose, as did divorce and deaths of despair, as academics Angus Deaton and Anne Case have outlined.[3]

White middle-aged adults who lacked a college education were particularly hit—in that group, deaths from cirrhosis of the liver increased by 50 percent between 1999 and 2013, suicides went up by 78 percent, and drug and alcohol overdoses increased by a whopping 323 percent. All this meant that between 2014 and 2017, the United States experienced the first decrease in life expectancy over a three-year period since the 1918 flu pandemic.[4]

As University of Chicago economist Raghuram Rajan puts it, when trade-related unemployment rises, "economic opportunity declines, and social disintegration increases. Unemployed workers are unattractive partners; consequently, there are fewer marriages, more divorces, more single-parent families. Broken families, loneliness, and the associated despair often lead to alcoholism, drugs, and sometimes crime."[5] Indeed, some researchers believe that loneliness itself can make individuals more vulnerable to autocratic leaders and even to fascism.[6] Hannah Arendt, one of the great political thinkers of the twentieth century as well as a Jewish survivor of World War II—her family managed to flee with the help of the U.S. State Department—wrote a book on the topic called *The Origins of Totalitarianism*. In it, she identifies the role that loneliness plays in extremism. Isolation is radicalizing, as vulnerable individuals who feel they have no place in existing social structures turn to autocrats, charlatans, and potentially even fascists to give them place and purpose. "The experience of not belonging to the world at all" is "the essence of totalitarian government, . . . preparation of its executioners and victims."[7] Is it any wonder, then, that a displaced white working class in the most-left-behind parts of the country turned to Trump in 2016 and (in all-too-great numbers) 2020? While Trump won a majority of small towns and rural areas, his Democratic challenger, Joe Biden, took communities that represent a whopping 70 percent of the U.S. economy, according to Brookings Institution data. No matter where voters were in the country, if they lived in an economic growth hub, it's likely they voted for Biden.[8]

When Markets Don't Know Best

At this point, it's worth noting that conventional economic thinking wouldn't have predicted any of this. Mainstream economics tells us that people go where the jobs are. If there is a downturn in their city or region, they will simply pull up stakes and move where things are better. This kind of thinking shaped policy decisions in the United States for the last several decades, though much less so in Europe (where centuries of conflict have made it obvious that place matters). I once interviewed an economic aide to a senior Democratic senator from the South who told me with amazement about the sense of certainty within the party that rural areas and low-density locations simply weren't worth considering politically. "I remember back in 2016, I was on the Hill, talking to a friend in the White House who was involved in economic policy making," the aide said. "He'd been traveling and seeing a lot of rural poverty in places like Iowa and Virginia. He told me, 'Don't worry. We've got this figured out. We've done the models, and it turns out that it's cheaper to pay people to move to the top fifty cities than to try to create jobs where they are!'" Can you believe, the aide said to me, "the sense of contempt inherent in that statement?"[9]

I can. I can also imagine that the "models" were only as good as the assumptions of the people crafting them. Economists come with their own biases and predispositions to certain narratives. There is, it must be said, much historical evidence to support the idea that people will move where opportunity is. Immigration is as old as civilization. Immigrants tend to be exactly the sort of people you want to welcome into your country, because they are the type of people with the energy and ability to take a risk to improve their lives in an entirely new place. In the United States, there is a long tradition of westward expansion in search of opportunity. Up until the 1990s or so, there was evidence to suggest that incomes were indeed converging across states and that all policy makers needed to do to fix regional inequalities was to create jobs at a national level, and people would move. If you build it, economists thought, they will come.

These assumptions informed many of the economic policy decisions taken in the nineties around trade and financial markets. Not only was it assumed that, state by state, economic conditions would converge, but that, ultimately, global wages would converge and that, during the decades this took to happen, there would be no negative ramifications—or, at least none that the political system couldn't handle.

But what we know now is that place matters a lot more in terms of labor markets than we once thought it did. Economists have traditionally thought in terms of people, not geography. But from the nineties onward, data showed this convergence across states slowing, as westward expansion itself slowed. It turns out that communities adapt very differently to economic downturns, so a variety of bespoke approaches is needed, rather than just policies designed to create job growth at a national level. Harvard and Berkeley economists have, for example, shown that intergenerational mobility varies quite substantially across the United States. A 2014 study showed that the probability of a child born in the eighties reaching the top quintile of national income distribution when starting from a family in the bottom quintile was 4.4 percent in Charlotte, North Carolina (not a backwater, but a thriving southern financial services hub). By contrast, the probability for the same bottom-quintile group from San Jose, California, was 12.9 percent. Higher-mobility areas like San Jose had some combination of less residential segregation, less income inequality, and better primary schools. They also had greater social capital and family stability.[10]

The point about social capital matters tremendously. Think of the book *Hillbilly Elegy:* when workers without college degrees lose their jobs, they tend not to move, but will cling to what little social capital exists in their home or community. Facts back up this narrative. As "China Shock" authors, economists David Autor, David Dorn, and Gordon Hanson, have found, the classic economic assumptions about labor market adjustment in response to trade- and tech-related job displacement have simply not held true in recent decades.[11] "For reasons economists still don't understand," Hanson wrote in a piece in *Foreign Affairs* in 2021, workers with less education rarely "choose to move elsewhere, even when local market conditions are poor." The result is localized recessions and the dangerous politics that comes with them.[12]

So, what happens when people can't or won't move to where the jobs are? It is a question that U.S. policy makers are finally focusing on in the wake of pandemic-related job destruction. Covid-19 hit different groups of people in very different ways, with virtual knowledge workers doing far better than those in professions that require face-to-face contact. Statistics pointing to declining income inequality during the pandemic are misleading, say some academics, because they reflect short-term government policy responses, such as handing out stimulus checks. Longer term, it's quite clear that the nature of work is going to shift radically, with the possibility of many more jobs being done anywhere—be it Bangalore or Bangor. This may open up a new globalization of white-collar labor markets, which could benefit workers in emerging markets that are moving ahead digitally, while putting pressure on labor in richer countries. On the other hand, American workers unable to afford housing, childcare, and schooling in expensive coastal cities could move to one of the less expensive "Zoom towns" that have grown during the pandemic.

It is impossible to know yet how this arbitrage for jobs, place, and labor will play out. What we do know is that a one-size-fits-all approach to job creation has not worked. When it comes to prosperity, place matters—a lot. Just as particular regions of the country took the biggest hit from the nineties onward, so did certain sectors of the economy, mainly those that were labor intensive and easily outsourced. Because these sectors tended to be grouped in particular areas of the country, the regional recession dynamic was exacerbated. The southern furniture industry was hard hit. So was textile and apparel output, which shrank by 30 percent between 2000 and 2006.[13] Those few companies that survived tended to be small and midsize family-owned operations that became very, very productive, in part because they didn't have to answer to financial markets or shareholders and could hoard cash and invest as they chose.

This is a key point, one that is often overlooked in the debate about American competitiveness. U.S. multinational companies were forced by Wall Street to adopt what University of Massachusetts academic Bill Lazonick has called the "downsize-and-distribute"[14] model of capitalism. They poured money into share buybacks and cut spending on longer-term, more productive types of capital investment (factory upgrades, worker training, and so on). Smaller private companies were at liberty to take a different approach. Research shows that privately owned firms invest more than twice as much in the real economy as public firms of similar size operating in the same sector, a topic we will explore through the lens of some firms in the Carolina Textile District supply chain in the following chapter.[15]

Things would have been easier for business as a whole, not to mention for local communities, if British economist John Maynard Keynes had prevailed back in Bretton Woods. His idea of using a bancor, or an international currency (which would essentially have been a basket of multiple currencies from various countries) was really about preventing the sort of trade and capital imbalances we have today. When a single country has both the privilege and the burden of being the international reserve currency, as the United States has been since the Bretton Woods period until today, only so much can be done to curb economic imbalances. The dollar not only allows, but in some sense *forces*, Americans to become debtors, as investment from around the world naturally flows into the dollar, pushing up its value and encouraging financialization and speculation.

But all this might be about to change. Decentralized technology has made possible what might one day be remembered as a new kind of Bretton Woods–style shift—away from the dollar as the sole global reserve and toward a new system in which countries, cities, and communities of all kinds will be able to take more control of their financial systems, for good and for ill.

The Rise of Digital Currency

Because the dollar is the world's reserve, the United States is flooded with dollars that must be turned into financial assets, which means the financial system must work overtime to make that so, encouraging debt and bubbles. The banking system is no longer primarily about community lending (though it's worth noting that true community banks, which make up a small share of the financial system, do about 60 percent of the Main Street lending that does still happen). Meanwhile, the only thing the Fed can do is give banks money to distribute and hope they push it to the right entities. In recent years, this has fueled enormous bubbles in many different kinds of assets.

But what if the system could be shifted in such a way that it was more balanced? In fact, many financial experts believe there is a way to make this happen, via digital currency.

When most people think of electronic money, they think of something rather speculative and possibly dicey. That's certainly true in the case of some private digital currencies—think of cryptocurrencies like Bitcoin or Ethereum or any number of other virtual coins that have been launched in recent years. In some ways, they represent the apex of financialization—"money" that isn't backed by any sovereign entity and seems to exist only to encourage its own price to grow. The fact that so many small-time retail investors have gotten involved in crypto is yet another reason for concern. The worry is that such currencies could represent a new sort of subprime crisis in which the most vulnerable are hit hard when there is a market crash.[16]

And yet, it isn't only speculators or people like Elon Musk who are experimenting with digital currency today—traditional financial institutions, city planners, and even central bankers in dozens of countries are, too. The idea is to create digital versions of currencies like the dollar, or the euro, or the Swiss franc, that could be used just like the old paper versions, but in ways that are much more flexible, diverse, competitive, and localized.

It should be said early and often that this is very much still the Wild West. Suddenly, any collection of individuals can create their own digital coin, backed by both public and private entities. El Salvador's Bitcoin City, Miami's MiamiCoin, and NYCCoin are all versions of this brave new world in which public entities are encouraging investors to put money into works projects backed by digital coin. Miami mayor Francis Suarez and New York City mayor Eric Adams are embracing "city coins" that lure money into the burgeoning crypto industry in order to fund things their city needs. In late 2021, Los Angeles allowed Crypto.com, a digital currency trading platform, to pay $700 million for the naming rights to the Los Angeles Lakers arena. Wyoming's Decentralized Autonomous Organization (DAO) law will allow new types of companies to start up that are entirely digital.[17]

Much of this is very likely about getting in on the late-stage hype of the most recent tech bubble. We won't really know until the bubble bursts. But some of it is about the way in which cities, countries, and regions are eager to control their own financial destiny. As my *Financial Times* colleague Brendan Greeley has noted, "There is a long history of city-states producing their own money." In medieval Europe, financial skills became a tradable asset, and the places that had the most of them, like Venice and Florence, prospered. "If you think crypto is the future of finance, you want to make sure you invite Fibonaccis and Paciolis to your city."[18] Thus, Miami is trying to lure fintech start-ups and paying salaries in city coin in order to fuel the boom. In some ways, these combined public-private efforts, along with the purely commercial ones, are a bet that, in a postglobalized, post–Bretton Woods world, money is no longer just the purview of states.

Personally, I'm playing it quite cautiously with anything that isn't backed by a legitimate central bank, at least for now. But once these digital currencies catch on—and there is little doubt among experts that they will, especially given that some eighty-seven central banks, accounting for 90 percent of global GDP, are running trials of sovereign-backed digital currency—the entire financial system will change. Commercial banks themselves, which are traditionally the way in which money is distributed from the government to individual consumers and businesses, would no longer be necessary for the settlement of transactions in the same way they are now. Governments could, in theory, simply give consumers digitized tokens inscribed on the computer ledgers of central banks themselves. (Indeed, central banks already do such digital transactions with large financial institutions.) As Jens Weidmann, head of the German central bank, said in 2021, the process will very likely shatter revenues of commercial banks and create a much more decentralized and localized financial system—governments and consumers would be interacting directly with each other in a totally new sort of banking system.

Of course, it's also possible that we'll see many of the same features and risks in digital banking that we do in the current financial system. Some experts believe that the network effects of such platforms will favor monopoly power, while others point out the costs in time and energy consumption required to "mine" digital currencies. Others believe that electronic systems will eventually create their own digital middlemen.[19] While the legal framework and logistical and technological issues have yet to be worked out, it's telling that JPMorgan Chase CEO Jamie Dimon's 2021 investor letter gave a nod to the disruptive possibilities of new financial technologies that could upend the traditional banking business, and international banking agencies like the Bank for International Settlements and the IMF consider it a foregone conclusion that digital currency is the future.[20]

Decoupled Finance

As in so many areas of cutting-edge technology, the Chinese are leading the way. China invented paper money a thousand years ago.

Now Beijing is encouraging more and more business to be done in digital renminbi, a kind of state-backed cryptocurrency that is gathering steam as a trading vehicle, particularly along the One Belt, One Road economic pathway the Chinese are building. Consumers are using digital currency, which provides central bankers in China with data needed to tailor more regionalized monetary and fiscal policies—by tracking the way in which money is flowing at a hyper-individual level, policy makers can decide whether a town or a region needs, say, better infrastructure or tighter lending standards. It's the ultimate in place-based economics—though, in the case of China, it also comes with the assumption of no privacy in a digital surveillance state.

The Chinese increasingly plan to trade with countries in Africa, Latin America, and other parts of the world using the digital renminbi, which also will allow them to start moving away from a dollar-based system. This became a priority for Beijing after the financial crisis of 2008, which was viewed by many in China as a repudiation of both Anglo-American-style financialized capitalism and the Washington Consensus and dollar-based order. In recent years, the Chinese (along with allies like Russia) have moved away slowly but surely from buying U.S. Treasury bonds, which have traditionally been their dollar-based "safe haven" asset. While the shift is still nascent, they've been buying more euros, and even gold, as a hedge against a world in which fewer countries want to hold dollars.

Western sanctions against Russia in the wake of war in Ukraine may speed up the move to a more bipolar or tripolar financial system. The process of financial decoupling between Russia and the West has been going on for some time. But the sanctions announced in 2022 will take that decoupling much further. It will also make Russia much more dependent on China, which wants to create its own Eurasian currency axis.

As we see more regionalization in trade, migration, and even capital flows, there is every reason to believe that different regional currency regimes will emerge. This might seem to be a straw man proposal, given that more than 60 percent of the world's currency reserves is in dollars, which are also used for most of the global commerce. The U.S. Federal Reserve's recent bolstering of dollar markets outside the United States as a response to the coronavirus crisis has given a further boost to global dollar dominance. Some economists argue that "you can't fight the Fed," meaning that the dominance of the U.S. banking system and dollar liquidity, both of which are backstopped by the Fed, will give the U.S. dollar unquestioned supremacy in the global financial system and capital markets indefinitely.

Others argue that "you can't replace something with nothing." By this, they mean that even though China, Russia, and other emerging-market countries (as well as some rich nations such as Germany) would love to move away from dollar dominance, they have no real alternatives at a mass scale (at least not yet). Yet the desire of major trading nations to achieve more financial independence is especially sharp in a world of increasingly weaponized finance. Both Beijing and Washington have been attempting to curb private-sector involvement in each other's capital markets for some time now. Witness the 2021 annual U.S.-China Economic and Security Review Commission report, issued to Congress at the end of each year, which recommended a host of new limits on business between the two countries, not just on goods and labor, but also capital flows.

The commission, whose members are appointed by both minority and majority leaders in Congress, has a good record of predicting legislative and regulatory trends. It was the first to raise Huawei as an issue (in 2004), it highlighted risks within crucial supply chains in areas such as pharmaceuticals as early as 2010, and it put the issue of forced labor in Xinjiang on the political map. As the most recent report put it, not only is the Chinese Communist Party using economic coercion and increasing state control to advance its own political model, but "Chinese policymakers are courting foreign capital and fund managers as they work to make China's capital markets serve as a vehicle to fund the CCP's technology development objectives and other policy goals."

The thirty-two new recommendations for combating this include: limiting investments in variable interest entities (VIEs) linked to Chinese entities; empowering the Securities and Exchange Commission to require companies to disclose whether they are sourcing from or invested in companies that use forced labor in Xinjiang or are on the U.S. Department of Commerce's Entity List (a list of foreign entities that must have a special license to export or transfer items considered a threat to U.S. national security or foreign policy)[21] or Treasury's Chinese Military-Industrial Complex Companies list; and mandating that public U.S. companies report whether there is a Chinese Communist Party committee anywhere in their operations. There are also suggestions on limiting the use of cloud computing and data servicing operations owned by Chinese firms.

Should such rules become law, the potential market implications are myriad. Consider just the idea of forcing "publicly traded U.S. companies with facilities in China" to report on an annual basis "whether there is a Chinese Communist Party (CCP) committee in their operations and summarize the actions and corporate decisions in which such committees may have participated." This may seem an extreme move, but the overlap between nonstate firms and the Communist Party in China has grown tremendously in recent years. Citing figures used by the CCP's own Organization Department (also cited by Western scholars), the report notes that "in 1998, a mere 0.9 percent of non-state firms had CCP committees, a figure that rose to 16 percent by 2008. By 2013, committee presence in nonstate firms expanded to 58 percent, and by 2017 it reached 73 percent, accounting for 1.9 million firms."[22] Assuming these figures are accurate, it's hard to imagine a Western company or financial institution doing business in China that wouldn't have a potential problem. It's also hard to imagine that Western financial institutions purporting to prioritize ESG (environmental, social, and governance) concerns won't come under increasing pressure to justify the hypocrisies of working with an autocratic government.

On the flip side, the commission is also recommending protections for U.S. investors in Chinese assets. In particular, the report flags VIEs, which are used by Chinese companies to get around rules prohibiting them from having foreign investors. Such vehicles include the largest percentage of Chinese issues by value sold on U.S. exchanges. But they are opaque: regulators like the SEC have raised concerns about the risks these vehicles pose for investors, who often don't get the same amount of information as for typical listed firms and who don't have any governing control in any case. Should it come to pass, the combination of regulating VIEs, index providers that have had a huge impact on the flow of funds into China, and approaching U.S.-Chinese capital flows as an ESG issue could be market moving. Indeed, capital has become the next front in U.S.-Chinese economic decoupling.

Some will argue that this will increase geopolitical friction and harm the global economy. That may be true, but while Wall Street understandably wants to exploit the largest pool of new international investors, and while Beijing needs capital to paper over its own homegrown debt problems, it's hard not to see the rush of financial firms into China (at least as this manuscript goes to press) as reflecting a continued willful blindness about the One World, Two Systems paradigm. It's worth noting that the U.S.-China Economic and Security Review Commission itself was formed by Congress in 2000 as a way to monitor the evolution of relations between the two nations, even as China was en route to becoming a member of the World Trade Organization. There were high hopes—but also doubts, even back then—that China would get freer as it got richer. The doubts have, of course, proved well founded.[23]

Regionalization of capital flows may also involve Europe. Look at German concerns about how the U.S. stimulus package and low interest rates have devalued the dollar and made American exports increasingly more competitive. The euro, which represents about 20 percent of global reserves, can't yet compare in terms of liquidity to the dollar, and there are still big questions about the future of the eurozone. But the European Commission's plan to bolster its recovery budget for Covid-19 bailouts by issuing debt that will be repaid by EU-wide taxes could become the basis for a true fiscal union and, ultimately, a United States of Europe. If it does, then I can imagine a lot more people might want to hold more euros (particularly digital ones). This would be one part of a multipolar global currency regime.

I can also imagine a continued weakening of ties between the United States and Saudi Arabia, which might in turn undermine the dollar. Among the many reasons for central banks and global investors to hold U.S. dollars, a key one is that oil is priced in dollars. Continuing Saudi actions to undermine U.S. shale put a rift in the relationship between the administration of former U.S. president Donald Trump and Riyadh. Meanwhile, China has announced a deal to buy $400 billion in oil from Iran, shifting both the economics and the geopolitics of fossil fuels.[24] The war in Ukraine of course threw a curve ball into global energy markets, leading to the United States and Europe to search for spare oil reserves from pretty much any country that could provide them in 2022. But ultimately, the war has also sped up the quest for energy independence, which has become even more strategically important to the United States and Europe post–Russian sanctions. Spare Russian energy has, since the beginning of the war, flowed to China, priced in renminbi. China may very well pick up future spare capacity in the Middle East, with deals done in its own currency.[25]

A decoupling world may be one that requires fewer dollars, and not only because of the rise of China. Investors have questions about the way in which the Fed's unofficial backstopping of U.S. government spending in the wake of the pandemic has politicized the money supply. The issue here is really about trust. Some people will argue that the dollar is a global currency and that its fortunes do not really depend on perceptions of the United States itself. Certainly, events of the past few years would support this view. But there may be a limit to that disconnection. The United States can get away with quite a lot economically as long as it remains politically credible, but less so if it doesn't. As economist and venture capitalist Bill Janeway told me, "The American economy hit bottom in the winter of 1932–33 after [Herbert] Hoover lost all credibility in responding to the Depression and trust in the banks vanished with trust in the government."[26] The Biden administration's global leadership in the wake of the Ukrainian war has gone some way to repairing the trust in the United States lost during the Trump years. But there are still big questions about whether the last forty years of financialization and debt-driven, asset inflation–oriented policies, coupled with the debt that resulted from the pandemic and the large fiscal programs launched to combat it, will eventually undermine global investors' trust in the dollar.

Brave New World

By that light, the rise of something like Bitcoin isn't so much a bubble as what financial analyst Luke Gromen, who has studied the historical similarities between the end of the global gold standard and the current boom in cryptocurrency, describes as "the last functioning fire alarm" warning us of some very big geopolitical changes ahead. Central bankers have over the past ten years (or the last few decades, depending on where you put the marker) quashed price discovery in markets with low interest rates and quantitative easing. Whether you see this as a welcome smoothing of the business cycle or a dysfunctional enabling of debt-ridden businesses, the upshot is that it's now very difficult to get a sense of the health of individual companies or, certainly, the real economy from asset prices.

When there is no more price discovery in markets, investors tend to turn to hard assets—gold has risen on and off in recent years, and the real estate market is as flush as it has ever been. Indeed, two-thirds of global wealth is held in real estate today. But the rise in popularity of highly volatile cryptocurrencies can also be seen as a speculative sign of this central bank–enabled froth. Bitcoin's ascent reflects the belief in some parts of the investor community that the United States will eventually come in some ways to resemble Weimar Germany, as post-2008 financial crisis monetary policy designed to stabilize markets gives way to post-Covid-19 monetization of rising U.S. debt loads. In this scenario, the debasement of the dollar would lead to runaway inflation, and an asset like Bitcoin (the number of which is capped) could have value. It's the same argument that's been used by "gold bugs," typically conservatives who loathe debt.

Personally, I'd rather hold gold as a hedge against inflation than Bitcoin, which financial regulators could eventually squash. I also think that the dollar will continue to be the main reserve currency for some time, with the renminbi and the euro gradually becoming more important stores of value. What's more, all currencies will eventually become digital (the Federal Reserve issued a major report in 2022 about what a central bank–backed digital-dollar system would look like).[27] One of the advantages of government-backed digital currencies is that monetary and fiscal policy could potentially be targeted much more regionally, and even locally, giving authorities the ability to helicopter digital dollars wherever they are needed. As a recent white paper by the European Parliament put it, digital money "can be tailored to almost any shape or usage."

What does this mean in the real world? Advocates of state-backed digital money, like Bob Hockett, say it could mitigate issues like the problem of the Federal Reserve "pushing on a string" by keeping rates low and money cheap and yet being able only to ensure that asset prices go up rather than to target the delivery of money to real people. When spending appeared to be overheating or when inflationary pressures loomed, the Fed could simply raise or lower interest on digital citizen accounts.[28] What's more, it could do this at different times, in different places, depending on how different geographic areas of the country were doing.

Various states and cities have already started experimenting with such a system. In 2019, lawmakers in Albany launched a bill to create a public Venmo system that would allow government payments, such as stimulus checks, to be distributed much faster. By capitalizing on the infrastructure of such a payment system, the hope is that it might ultimately be possible to develop or expand all sorts of productivity and lifestyle-enhancing innovations, like digital health records, better supply chain management, more efficient energy usage, and smart cities in which citizens and government (rather than Big Tech) control the use of public data to improve traffic, housing, and city services.

Of course, this is just the sort of thing the Chinese are already rolling out in their own twenty-first-century digital finance and trade systems. This raises a big question: Is it possible for the government to be involved so deeply in our digital data without worries that the United States will become a surveillance state? On that point, there are two things to say: First, we already have a surveillance system in the United States; it's simply run by private companies. Assuming we want to shift to a system in which data can be used to benefit citizens, rather than to enrich a handful of large platform companies, we will have to find a way for governments and individuals to have more control of it. Part of that may involve shifting to a system of portable data that can be owned by individuals, who can withdraw access to it or anonymize it as they see fit. It might also involve government-controlled data pools that can be accessed by private entities in ways citizens agree to (for example, to conduct health research). Europe is already working on such systems, which might involve neutral, nongovernment data regulators or stewards (potentially, unions or nonprofits) who could oversee the process.

Ideally, a shift toward multiple digital-backed currencies rather than a world dependent only on dollars could help move us away from the trade and financial system imbalances that have been a part of the old system. Hockett, who has been an adviser on some of the digital currency projects just mentioned, hopes to move toward a system of "citizen central banking," in which everyone, whether or not they have access to a traditional bank account, can have a government-administered digital wallet. "Not only would this end the problem of the 'unbanked'—meaning people like Chaka—but it would also make the entire process of monetary policy work better," he says. Instead of the Fed keeping rates low in such a way that allows giant companies to run up debt paying back rich shareholders, central bankers might be able to target the flow of money more specifically to where it is most needed. Essentially, we'd have the national, digital equivalent of a shoebox bank, for all citizens. And different places could have different shoeboxes.

In some ways, it's exactly what John Maynard Keynes always wanted—a much more international system of currency that allows nation-states to do what's in their own best interest, mitigating trade or currency wars. Countries could create their own digital wallets, microtarget policy, fight tax evasion and dark-money flows, and move from a hyperglobalized and financialized system that serves the elites to a much more grounded financial system that reflects what Adam Smith—not to mention Keynes—would have wanted. Of course, there are plenty of pitfalls to overcome, like ensuring that individual systems can interact with one another, regulating privacy issues, and preventing digital currency competition from becoming a zero-sum game. Still, the possibilities of the shift to a digital monetary system are intriguing. "I like to think of Bretton Woods 1.0, and digital currency as being, just maybe, Bretton Woods 2.0," says Hockett, who believes that the political stars may now be aligned in a way that will create the global, and yet local, financial system that will help ease the political tensions that exist over global trade and capitalism today.[29]

A Productive Bubble?

Digital money will be central to the twenty-first-century economy, just as the internet was to the nineties, computers were to the eighties, and semiconductors were to the fifties and sixties.[30] All those innovations, and the productivity that occurred from them, were built on the backs of policies that supported domestic economic innovation. The private sector, of course, came in and built upon those investors in basic infrastructure and science, eventually creating the corporate giants of today. It's a process that is both creative and chaotic, which helps to put the changes in today's currency system in perspective. The shift toward a new and more decentralized "peer-to-peer" financial system, with its many new cryptocurrencies and sovereign-backed digital coins, is a bit like the transition that happened when the automobile was invented. Hundreds of new car companies sprang up. Nobody knew which one would triumph, but it was clear that the era of the horse and buggy was gone forever.

Economist and venture capitalist Bill Janeway refers to periods of disruption as "productive bubbles." That may sound like an oxymoron, in part because bubbles don't seem productive—think of the 2008 U.S. housing bubble, ballooning corporate debt in recent years, and the high-tech "unicorn" bubble of today, in which firms like Tesla have reached nosebleed levels. But not all bubbles are created alike. Unproductive bubbles destroy value, especially when they are created via the banking system. But there are also productive bubbles—like the dot-com bubble of 1998 to 2000. That led to the liquidation of trillions of dollars of value in stocks and junk bonds, but it also spurred the laying of millions of miles of broadband fiber optic cable, which was in large part subsidized and encouraged by public tax incentives to create the network on which a new economy would run.

The 1920s stock bubble, which created even greater pain, also helped fund and fuel the spread of radio, the telephone, aviation, and electricity. Speculation, according to Janeway, is a natural part of the process of innovation. But the seeds of productive bubbles are often sown not by private-market actors, but by the state, which can provide funding that is decoupled from a need for immediate economic results. This point has been made frequently by economists, including Mariana Mazzucato, and historians such as Margaret O'Mara.

Such state investment is often driven by a national mission to boost development or security. Think of the British and American railway booms, fueled by the needs of the military; or the creation of the Interstate Highway System that linked the United States for the automotive age; or the digital economy itself, which came out of basic government research. The digital revolution has created "the most productive collaboration in human history between state investment and financial speculation," as Janeway puts it. And yet, we are still only in the first stages of it.

Some aspects of the digital revolution, such as the internet of things, could help solve the productivity puzzle. Some digital coins may turn out to have value, particularly if they are backed by stable state and commercial entities; many others will go bust. Other bets, including the ability of artificial intelligence to displace human thinking, may be oversold. But the bigger question is whether the state itself—or, at least, liberal democracies in the West—will survive the era of innovation they created. Governments seem to have lost the ability to control the most powerful supranational corporations, such as Alphabet and Meta. These companies are undermining the process of democracy itself, becoming facilitators of political disinformation, influencing the political system, and disrupting labor and capital markets in ways that make it difficult for nation-states to cope. This brings to mind economist Dani Rodrik's "inescapable trilemma of the world economy."[31] According to this theory, it is possible to have only two out of three of the following things: deep economic and financial integration, democratic politics, and autonomous states. Cross-border companies that have more users than the population of the world's largest countries could be incompatible with liberal democracy.

The U.S. state created the most recent productive bubble, the computer era, and the Biden administration clearly hopes to create the next one, via its massive infrastructure program geared toward a carbon-neutral economy. China also aims to create the next one through funding green tech, including solar and wind power and renewable batteries. Autocratic China cannot, by definition, solve the trilemma of the world economy. And the jury is still out on whether top-down control in a digital surveillance state (whether exerted by companies or governments) is incompatible with democratic politics and individual free will. In any case, it may not support innovation. Productive bubbles can be seeded by the state, but they also require smaller companies and individuals acting in a decentralized environment to commercialize new technologies.[32]

It's a tricky balancing act. But what is very clear is that we have left the era of laissez-faire, neoliberal economic thinking and entered a new era in which the public sector itself will play a larger role. The question is whether it will be a productive role. The Biden administration clearly wants to move from an asset bubble–based economy to one that is more about job- and income-led growth. That's the messaging underlying President Biden's "Reward work, not wealth" campaign slogan. After many decades, we are, slowly but surely, beginning to move beyond the notion that everyone in the United States could be a banker or a software designer, or that those who couldn't would be fine with cheaper goods at Walmart. Wages are rising, as are taxes on the multinational corporations that have benefited disproportionately from the last forty years of globalization. But the federal government can't do it all—indeed, given polarization in Washington, it's been difficult for the Biden administration to accomplish even a fraction of its goals. While it is creating a new, post-neoliberal narrative, much of the real change is happening at the local level, in regions and cities.

We are seeing a shift to more locally made products and services,[33] particularly those that are part of the green-energy transition. New clean-tech hubs are springing up in places like South Carolina, Texas, and the Midwest. Conventional wisdom has it that this transition is by its nature politically polarizing, since it pits fossil fuel–producing states (which often vote Republican) against coastal liberals concerned about the environment. But there is more common ground than you might imagine. Localnomics appeals to the type of left-wing voters who support Democratic representative Alexandria Ocasio-Cortez, popularizer of the idea of a "Green New Deal." But they also appeal to security-conscious conservatives worried about the rise of China. Both groups are interested in connecting the dots among sustainable energy, jobs, and economic and geopolitical security. "We look at diplomacy, the military, the economy and information as different elements of national power," says Jeff Kline, a professor at the Naval Postgraduate School in Monterey, California. "You can't separate them." While conservative, such a view reflects the kind of political realism espoused by military theorists such as Carl von Clausewitz rather than the laissez-faire economics of David Ricardo. It also tracks the enthusiasm for industrial policy and stakeholder capitalism increasingly espoused by parts of the pro-labor left and the security-conscious right.

Defense scholars have long been fans of economic resiliency. But the 2008 financial crisis, the Covid-19 pandemic, and several smaller crises have convinced people across the political spectrum that the public and private sectors need to work more closely together. The goals include remooring wealth and prosperity in local communities and solving the most complex, and potentially rewarding, problems of the day. Imagine a national dialogue in which business leaders, security experts, educators, labor advocates, and others came together to find ways to transition to clean energy while also bolstering jobs, security, and relationships with allies. They would want to explore how the public sector could best send signals to private investors to enable funding to flow to the right places. The discussion should encompass how best to connect the needs of job creators and educators of a twenty-first-century workforce. The challenge would be national, but given the size and diversity of the United States, solutions should be local, coming from the ground up and, by necessity, involving people from all over the political spectrum. "The overlap between social priorities and defense priorities is actually quite compelling," says Garth Jensen, director of innovation at the Naval Surface Warfare Center in Carderock, Maryland.

What if there were common ground on how to do so? Having been part of a number of conversations about bridging this gap, I believe there is. In 2020, I participated, for example, in a two-day event with the Naval Postgraduate School, looking at how to build a national resilience strategy.[34] It was amazing how much common ground there was between left and right when it came to creating more agile business processes, a greener economy, and a more capable workforce and citizenry.

The session came on the back of work that had been done by other areas of the defense community. In 2018, there was a two-day event sponsored by the National Defense University, which brought together military and civilian leaders to discuss the topic. Dozens of experts, government officials, and business leaders gathered to talk about the decline in the post–Second World War order, the rise of China, and how the United States could strengthen its manufacturing and defense industries to create both economic and political stability in a post-neoliberal world. The goal: more resilient supply chains that could withstand not just a trade war, but an actual war. Amid the broad and varied discussions, speakers shared a general sense that status quo globalization was over and that this would have serious ramifications for U.S. industry. "If you accept as your starting point that we are in a Great Power struggle [with China and Russia], then you have to think about securing the innovation base, making the industrial base more viable, and scaling it all," said Lt. Gen. John Jansen, the event organizer. This idea has proponents on both the political left and the right.

After years of division, might Americans find some productive common ground around how to structure a new and more inclusive economy?[35] I think the answer is yes. But first, we will need to ask and answer the question: What can, and what should, be done locally rather than globally?

CHAPTER 8

Not Your Grandfather's Factory

As the Covid-19 pandemic began to unfold in the early part of 2020, I reached out to a longtime source of mine, an entrepreneur named Bayard Winthrop, to check in on how his business was doing. His company, American Giant, made sportswear in the Carolinas, sourcing everything (from cotton to construction) within the United States. But with the lockdown and work-from-home protocols, sales had ground to a halt. Winthrop had factories sitting empty, but he also knew that he could quickly shift to filling a growing need for cotton masks. "I've been talking to a bunch of friends in my supply chain," he told me, referring to the collection of mostly private companies that did everything from his yarn spinning to his fabric cutting. "I think we can start making a lot of masks pretty quickly."

And indeed, they did. Within a few weeks of the pandemic, several U.S. factories that usually mass-produced hoodies and T-shirts were retooled to make face masks, as chief executives in the clothing industry came together to try to alleviate shortages of PPE to combat Covid-19. In the midst of the crisis, it quickly became painfully clear that things like masks, humidifiers, crucial vitamins, pharmaceutical supply inputs, hand sanitizer, and even sterile gloves for doctors and nurses were no longer being made in this country. It turned out that most of the planet got these things—most particularly masks—from a handful of global exporters, the largest of which was China.[1] "It was amazing to discover that the things we needed most in the midst of a once-in-a-hundred years pandemic were at the end of a ten-thousand-mile supply chain controlled by our greatest strategic adversary," said Clyde Prestowitz, a labor economist and former U.S. commerce official who has long advocated more manufacturing self-sufficiency.[2]

But that didn't mean that such things *couldn't* be made at home. In a mere seventy-two hours, a group of nine American apparel companies came together to begin producing the masks. Within a month, they had moved from making baseball jerseys and socks to churning out ten million disposable masks per week. It was an effort that belied critics who said that this kind of industrial retooling at scale was no longer possible in the United States because so much of the industrial supply base had been outsourced. It also raised questions about what should be reshored closer to home, not only in the United States but in parts of Europe where industry has been hollowed out as well. It turns out that, thanks to a number of economic, demographic, environmental, and technological shifts that will favor it, there is a place once again for localized manufacturing. But making things in the modern era will look very different from how it was done in the past.

Survival of the Fittest

The mask-making coalition was organized by Parkdale Mills, the country's largest yarn spinner, and it included the large brands Fruit of the Loom and Hanesbrands as well as smaller operations such as Beverly Knits, American Giant, and AST Sportswear. Most of the companies involved were part of a high-density apparel supply chain in North and South Carolina, where the businesses that have survived in the ultracompetitive global clothing market tend to be highly nimble and efficient. Because textiles is a rather low-margin industry, it has gotten very little in the way of support (via subsidies or industrial policy nudges) from the government over the last twenty years, as other industries, like energy and agriculture, have. The textile industry has pretty much been left to go it alone.

This Darwinian phenomenon has yielded some of the most productive textile manufacturing in the world. Over the past two decades, apparel manufacturing in the Carolinas endured major job losses and a spate of factory closures because of technological change, globalization, and China's 2001 entry into the World Trade Organization. But the companies that remain are especially resilient. They all know one another, and although they often compete for work, they also collaborate in teams when big, more complex jobs require it. (Both collaborators and competitors worked closely together on the mask project.) Like the fabled companies of Germany's Mittelstand model of economic success, some of the most productive export firms in the world, many Carolina apparel companies are family-owned, are not subject to public market pressures, and are thus able to reinvest the majority of profits back into their businesses. Parkdale, for example, puts roughly 75 percent of profits per year back into the company.

Most of it goes into technology and worker training, which is one of the reasons the industry can move so quickly. Anderson Warlick, chief executive of Parkdale, a family-owned business (and one of the businesses involved in mask making), told me that the project was launched after he spoke with Peter Navarro, an economic adviser to Donald Trump, in April 2020. The White House official had learned about a shortage of cotton swabs for healthcare workers battling Covid-19, and "Peter wanted to know what we could make," said Warlick. "We don't make swabs usable for testing, but he asked if we could make masks." Warlick quickly organized a conference call with a group of companies and found that several of them were already working individually on mask prototypes of their own. Hanes was farthest along, and its fabric was fast-tracked for approval by the U.S. Department of Health and Human Services for use in medical masks.

There were plenty of challenges to retooling. Warlick quickly discovered, for example, that some of the machines he would need were made in Taiwan and would take six months to import. Many others came from Germany and Switzerland. Those countries had made specific policy decisions over the last several decades to keep crucial industries (high-value machine tooling, pharmaceutical production, and the like) at home. (Germany's manufacturing sector as a percentage of the economy is roughly double that of the United States'.) Had the United States decided to keep such machine tooling at home as part of a larger industrial strategy, Carolina textile makers would have been able to do more much faster.

"We're in uncharted territory here," said Warlick. "We have a lot of inefficiency [in the mask-making process], because we are used to doing T-shirts and sweatshirts. We aren't well prepared right now as a nation, and that's a real issue. Our supply chains have been dismantled for thirty years, and manufacturers in the United States haven't been as respected as they should be. You can't turn back the clock on thirty years overnight. But that doesn't mean you shouldn't start to invest in that capacity now." Despite everyone's best efforts, Warlick felt that the politicians and policy makers he dealt with during Covid-19 were doing crisis management "with their hair on fire."[3] Winthrop, who was prepared to use his own money to rent trucks to drive his masks to where they were needed around the country, says the same: "We have all these incredibly productive companies that want to do the right thing. But nobody was connecting the dots."

That's still true, though it's changing. As this book goes to press, the Biden administration's trade representative, Katherine Tai, has outlined a new direction for U.S.-Chinese trade, one that puts labor and national interests ahead of consumer prices and individual corporate interests. It's a key stake in the heart of the usual neoliberal conventional wisdom. Tai said quite plainly that the United States no longer expects China to make further structural economic reforms and bring its political economy more in line with that of the United States, Europe, or other liberal market economies. Tai didn't explicitly rule out better relations, but she made it quite clear that the United States had left the era of Ricardian fantasy, in which countries happily and successfully pursued competitive advantage without any of the messy subversions of the real political economy.[4]

As she put it in a presentation in March 2022, "We can't just wait for China to change. We need to start doing things on our side [such as] the reshoring and the rebuilding of our manufacturing base."[5]

And yet, as the United States continues to fight Covid-19, we are in danger of going back to business as usual. In late 2021, Tai held a goodwill tour of the Carolinas to support the many domestic textile producers who helped fill the mask shortage (particularly in the first stages of the pandemic, when the Chinese government nationalized its own mask business). But these companies lost some five thousand jobs in 2021 because federal government procurement had slowed and because, while the Defense Department, for example, was bound by Biden's Buy American efforts, individual states, in a major conservative slam to the efficacy of such provisions, could choose to go their own way.

Meanwhile, money politics played its own part in PPE problems. The Biden administration delayed plans to raise tariffs on Chinese medical goods until mid-November 2021, for example, because the American Hospital Association lobbied against it, saying that it would raise costs for them. Whatever the cost, the absurdly distorted system of privatized healthcare in the United States means that hospitals will inevitably charge insurance companies or unlucky patients multiples of it, which makes me feel a lot more sympathetic toward the textile makers, who just want the government to set a price floor under PPE, as promised. If the United States had a broader vision for how such pieces of our economy fit together, as other countries do, perhaps individual industries wouldn't end up fighting one another to the detriment of the country as a whole.

These will be future topics for Tai and others who support the rebuilding of the U.S. industrial ecosystem. But changing the paradigm isn't something the U.S. Trade Representative can do alone. "Buy American" makes no sense if you can't support demand, and demand can't be supported without government incentives or a real shift from shareholder to stakeholder capitalism. The fact that so much supply is controlled by a strategic adversary who doesn't play by WTO rules makes it especially complicated to transition from an economy based on rewarding consumers in the form of lower prices to one based on growing incomes and creating more resilience in crucial industries—including medical equipment, pharmaceuticals, semiconductors, and rare earth minerals.[6]

This underscores something we've long known: a certain amount of self-sufficiency matters and, thus, manufacturing matters. Even though it has become increasingly automated and globalized over the last several decades, manufacturing still holds a special place in the national psyche—not just in the United States, but in many big exporting nations like Germany, China, and Japan. Part of this is due to its disproportionate economic benefits to a national economy. In the United States, for example, although manufacturing represents just 11 percent of GDP and 8 percent of direct employment, according to figures from the McKinsey Global Institute, it drives 20 percent of the country's capital investment, 30 percent of productivity growth, 60 percent of exports, and 70 percent of business R&D. Manufacturing's share of the national economy in most other developed countries is far higher; the destruction of the industrial commons is an Anglo-American phenomenon.

Where and how things get made has always been a highly political topic. This has been brought to the forefront in recent years, not only because of the U.S.-Chinese tech and trade wars and the supply chain shortages from the pandemic and the war between Russia and Ukraine, but also because of human rights. Witness the increasingly difficult position that Western brands like Nike, H&M, and various European luxury producers find themselves in for using cotton produced in Xinjiang, some of which may be harvested and spun by forced Uyghur labor. U.S. and European companies are under tremendous pressure to boycott Xinjiang cotton and use homegrown alternatives instead. Yet, when they do, they risk backlash from the Chinese, who seem to have added the Uyghurs to the list of "no-discussion" areas like Tibet, Taiwan, and Tiananmen.

Which side brands fall out on will depend largely on how important China is to their overall revenue and future growth. But the truth is that the textiles, like a number of other industries, has become less globalized over the last few years. Even before Covid-19 illuminated the fragility of global supply chains and made it a real political issue, reshoring was beginning to happen for all sorts of reasons, from rising developing country wages to concerns about conflict in the South China Sea.[7] Over a decade ago, companies were beginning to move some production from China to Mexico, for example, or from Asia to safer hubs in eastern Europe.

The pandemic sped up this regionalization and localization exponentially. One 2020 survey found that 64 percent of industrial and manufacturing companies surveyed were planning to reshore some production to North America because of fallout from the pandemic.[8] From pharmaceuticals to furniture to clothing and technology, industries are rejiggering their supply chains to make them less dependent on one or two large countries and more resilient to myriad risks, from the geopolitical, to the environmental, to the regulatory and technological.

That's a major shift. In the United States, sectors like textiles and furniture were among the industries hit hardest by the accession of China to the WTO, given that they are both labor intensive and have relatively low profit margins. Offshoring such industries and allowing things to be made far more cheaply in places where wages are a small fraction of what they might be in the United States once made a lot of economic sense (at least for the companies doing it). After technology and furniture, textiles was the most offshored sector between 2000 and 2018.[9]

But now that Chinese wages have risen along with Chinese domestic demand, the entire calculus has shifted. Well before the Xinjiang concerns, apparel supply chains were shifting. Chinese producers exported 71 percent of finished goods in 2005. By 2018, it was just 29 percent. As Chinese consumers have gotten richer, their own domestic demand for apparel has become so large that most manufacturers now focus more on filling that need than in finding new markets abroad.

Some of the cheap clothing and other goods that used to be made in China for Western nations have moved to Bangladesh, Vietnam, and Ethiopia. But those countries are neither large enough nor skilled enough at this point to replace the whole of what was once made in China. Meanwhile, as Chinese salaries have risen, it has made less and less sense for U.S. and European companies to have laborers in Asia sewing T-shirts that they then must pay to ship thousands of miles to other markets. Add in the human rights worries; Millennials' growing concern about the environmental damage from shipping cheap, disposable clothing items across the world; and (on the upside) new technologies that allow for more localization, and you have a recipe for a new business model for textile, apparel, and fashion.

A Retail Youth Quake

It's no accident that "fast fashion" has become a big area of environmental activism. Companies like H&M, Old Navy, and Primark moved a lot of production to China between 1990 and 2018. The result was a 50 percent drop in the price of clothing and footwear. We got cheap stuff; they got cheap jobs. But that was a very linear calculation. If you start to look at the greater cost of fast fashion, it suddenly seems much more expensive. Cheap, disposable clothing meant that people bought a lot more stuff. Retailers, seeing a new opportunity, flooded shops and online stores with new designs every six weeks instead of a couple of times a year. This exponentially increased the number of natural resources (water, energy, and so on) being taken up by the garment business. Next to agriculture, apparel production takes up more resources than any other business globally—some 10 percent of global carbon emissions are produced by the fashion industry. (Just as a comparison, airline flights represent only about 3 percent.) And yet, of the one hundred billion items of clothing produced each year, half are thrown away and are either burned or dumped into a landfill within twelve months.[10]

No wonder teenagers like my daughter are now engaging in street protests decrying fast fashion and increasingly shopping in thrift stores as a way of stopping the cycle of mass consumption.

Like some of her peers, she has plastered her bedroom with signs reading, "Hey, Hey, Ho, Ho, Fast Fashion's Got to Go!" Millennials and Gen Zers are seeking out more sustainable, locally produced goods. A huge body of research shows that younger people have very different consumption patterns than previous generations. They are wildly more concerned about climate change than their elders are; Swedish climate activist Greta Thunberg is their patron saint. They want to shop locally, and from brands that support the same values they do and that are sustainable and held to high environmental and labor standards. They want more experiences and less stuff. They are very smart about tracking how brands are doing in terms of living up to their stated goals and values, and they comparison-shop for items that live up to them.[11] And although they are extremely price-sensitive, given their high levels of debt and the fact that they came of age at a time when unemployment numbers seemed permanently elevated, they would still rather pay a bit more for a product that lasts longer. Some even rent or borrow, rather than buying new items; witness the rise of subscription services that allow consumers to use and return everything from clothing to furniture.[12] All this supports a new business model of making fewer higher-quality goods closer to home.

A Factory in Your House

These shifts in generation consumption patterns and rising concern about the environmental impact of globalized manufacturing are happening at the same time as many other trends supporting the localization of some manufacturing supply chains. Rising wages in Asia are one tailwind to localization of production, but technological shifts at home are another. High-tech manufacturing is beginning to shift the entire process of making things.

In particular, experts are pointing to a technology called additive manufacturing—or, more colloquially, 3D printing. The stocks of 3D printing companies soared amid the pandemic. The industry was able to plug the gap in supply chains by locally manufacturing everything from PPE to medical and testing devices, to personal accessories, visualization aids, and even emergency dwellings. The entire 3D-printing market grew 21 percent from 2019 to 2020 and is predicted to double by 2026.[13] There are now a number of companies, such as Austin-based ICON (which we will learn more about later in the book), that are moving from printing disaster shelters to entire luxury homes. Given the complexity and carbon intensity of home building, with its multiple supply chains, it's a shift that could help curb growing inflation. As a 2020 article in *Nature Reviews Materials* put it, "3D printing of buildings requires shorter building times and lower labour costs, and can use more environmentally friendly raw materials." The resulting homes can be "easily transported and deployed to areas where they are most needed."[14]

When some people talk about 3D printing, they mean fun devices for hobbyists and artisans who can print plastic toys and other objects when those devices are hooked up to a computer. But when they talk about it at places like ExOne, one of the global leaders in 3D technology, based in North Huntingdon, Pennsylvania, they're describing something a lot bigger. Additive manufacturing involves what looks like spray-painting a metal object into existence. These 3D printers lay down a very thin layer of stainless-steel powder or ceramic powder and fuse it with a liquid binder until an item (a torque converter, heat exchanger, or propeller blade, for example) is built, layer by layer. Would-be manufacturing entrepreneurs can buy the 3D printing devices and begin turning out high-tech metal parts for aerospace, automotive, and other industries at a lower cost and of higher quality faster than offshore suppliers. But so can giant companies like Ford, Siemens, BMW, Oak Ridge National Laboratory, and the other large firms ExOne counts as clients.

Such companies are already using 3D printing to cut through long international supply chains so that products can be made much closer to where consumers are located. The pandemic accelerated the shift as countries everywhere grappled with supply shortages. In March 2020, as Covid-19 ravaged Italy, a small local start-up in the Brescia area, Isinnova, responded to the crisis by reverse-engineering

3D-printed versions of much-needed respirator parts. Within two days, the company had delivered one hundred new respirator valves to local hospitals. There are countless examples like this globally, in which cutting-edge technologies are allowing small and midsize businesses to make things more locally. In places like Germany, family-owned export companies that churn out lasers or building tools are placing sensors in their products that can detect when things go wrong, creating entirely new service businesses. Instead of just making equipment, these world-beating manufacturers can now track and trace their products around the planet, observing how they function in different environments and servicing them the way a giant consulting firm might.

The 3D-printing process is attractive because it can produce parts in shapes that would be impossible or unduly expensive through traditional manufacturing methods. I once toured a GE factory in upstate New York where engineers were ink-printing shapes as delicate as snowflakes, in layered metal as strong as steel, to use as components in a new jet engine. The company now makes some ten thousand different parts this way. The nimbleness of the technology helps engineers rethink designs and outdo competitors who might specialize in cheaper, but less precise, ones. S. Kent Rockwell, ExOne's chairman, told me back when he was CEO that one potential client asked him to reproduce a traditional heat exchanger and price it, which the firm did. The customer wasn't that impressed. "Look," Rockwell told him, "give me your optimal design for the heat exchanger." The customer returned with a new design, doubtful that it could actually be manufactured. "We printed it in five days," says Rockwell.

ExOne's 3D-printing machines, like a lot of new technology, displaced some labor. A foundry, for instance, no longer needed workers carting patterns around a warehouse; it could print molds and cores stored on a thumb drive, and no patterns were needed. An ExOne shop with twelve metal-printing machines needs only two employees per shift, supported by a design engineer—though they are higher-skilled workers. Parts will be able to be churned out and delivered within days rather than weeks or months. Overseas competitors will simply not be able to deliver that quickly or at the same level of quality, and will certainly use additive printing for their own purposes in their own markets.[15]

But the nature of the technology means that it will, by default, bring manufacturing home. "I think additive manufacturing is the biggest potential disruptor" for globalization as usual, says Eric Schmidt, former Google CEO, venture capitalist, and the founding chairman of the Defense Innovation Board, a discussion and advisory forum for technologists and security types. "Before this, you could just build the thing in China, wait three months for a slow boat to arrive, and you're fine. Three-D printing on demand really does change the way manufacturing firms can operate technologically. I think you will see the development of more high-tech, localized supply chains as a result of this."[16] In fact, Google itself is getting into the manufacturing business via 3D printing, which grew 21 percent as an overall business last year and is predicted to double in size as a market within the next five.[17] Google's AI division has already designed air-conditioning units via 3D printing that don't require moving parts or even cooling chemicals.

These ventures are built entirely around localized additive manufacturing. But a growing number of traditional manufacturing companies are getting into the technology, too, using some 3D printing in their supply chains to improve efficiency and logistics and to lower costs. Ford, for example, is using 3D printing to make prototype parts more quickly—in days or hours rather than weeks or months. The company even imagines a time when service dealerships will have in-house 3D printers to produce replacement parts. Industrial companies that use 3D printing could reduce the number of spare parts they need to keep in stock by as much as 90 percent—when they need extras, they can simply print them. Indeed, now that the cost of such industrial printers has fallen from around $700,000 to $50,000 over the last decade, it's possible for firms of all sizes to invest. One Wall Street research firm, 13D, which tracks the growth of 3D-printing companies, saw share price gains of 202 percent (compared to 52 percent in the S&P companies overall) from 2011 to the year-end 2019.[18]

According to University of Michigan professor Jerry Davis, those supply chains will go directly into our homes. "Buying furniture is going to become like buying iTunes," he says, pointing to a number of digital start-ups involved in this transition, including a company called ShopBot Tools, which makes computer-controlled routers used for cutting wood and other materials. You can download a blueprint for something you want to create—a small piece of furniture, for example—and then cut it. (The routers can now be purchased for under $20,000.)

This isn't just for home hobbyists. Numerous end-of-the-line "printing" companies are springing up to service the demand for such highly customized items.[19] Invisalign, for example, makes millions of unique dental molds to straighten teeth; the molds are "printed" in a variety of facilities around the country or even in a dentist's office.[20] One 3D design firm, called AtFAB,[21] which began in Kentucky, allows customers to design made-to-order furniture and then connects them with local producers who craft it for them. The idea, as they put it, is to "think globally, manufacture locally." It's an idea that will revolutionize industry and even entire economies, says Davis. "Think about it—Ikea doesn't sell furniture; it sells make-at-home model kits in wood. You don't need to ship those across the world. You can do it completely locally."

There are even a couple of cutting-edge firms, Apis Cor and ICON, that can print an entire small home for $10,000. In 2018, Texas-based ICON secured the first permits for a 3D home built in the United States. It has since rolled out homes for disaster zones and various emerging markets (where they are popular because they are so quick and cheap to build), and in 2021, it announced 3D-printed houses for sale in the United States. The 950- to 1,900-square-foot homes, located in Austin, have the sort of mid-century modern aesthetic beloved of Millennials; they are all concrete and angles, with lots of light and views of the Texas sunrise.

Not only are such homes cheaper and more resilient, but ICON it-self has become an innovation hub, inventing new materials and techniques that are fueling entirely different businesses. The company (which is profiled in more depth in chapter 15) recently built rocket landing pads for NASA.

Such hubs are crucial, because as we've already learned, while more big-company manufacturing jobs are being automated, the sector is still quite labor intensive compared to others, particularly when it comes to small companies and "makers." High-tech manufacturing pays about a 20 percent premium relative to other industries, according to research from McKinsey, and with the advent of digital advances like 3D printing and design, more of it can be done locally, cutting emissions and bolstering local economies. Technologies like additive manufacturing point the way to a future that is more robust, with a greater number of localized "makers" able to produce goods in more places with fewer transport-related carbon emissions. This creates resilience, and security at a local level, while also allowing a greater number of small and midsize businesses to participate in digital trade across borders. It also creates wealth for local businesses that makes its way into the broader service economy—and, suddenly, you have more people who can afford local healthcare, education, housing, and retail services (things that can't be easily outsourced, as we will examine in more depth later). But this kind of "flexible" manufacturing is particularly well suited to countries like the United States, which has plenty of local, in-country consumer demand.

In some ways, this represents an entirely new and better sort of globalization—one in which knowledge can go where it will, but in which jobs and prosperity can be remoored to communities everywhere. It's the opposite of the neoliberal paradigm in which prosperity leaves, creating nationalism and xenophobia that, in turn, result in the rise of populist politics and the closing of minds. If consumers, citizens, and workers can feel that the global economy isn't a zero-sum game, they won't turn to populists who want to use their fears for their own devices. It's a better way to think about markets. By creating more balanced, stabler local economies, you create more balanced and moderate global politics.[22]

The Visible Hand

The entire additive technology industry, it turns out, was developed by MIT, nurtured by grants from the Office of Naval Research and the National Science Foundation before being adapted by private industry. It's the kind of triple play—government, academia, industry—that's held up as an ideal for public-private cooperation, as opposed to, say, the Solyndra debacle (the solar panel company that went bankrupt after getting $535 million in guaranteed federal loans). Traditionally, the United States hasn't been as keen as other nations on this kind of linkage. But states have for years been doing their own versions of an industrial policy. Virginia boasts the Commonwealth Center for Advanced Manufacturing to help companies translate research into high-tech products. To bridge the skills gap, North Carolina links community colleges with specific companies like Siemens.

More industrial strategy has been a long time coming, but it is finally reaching critical mass. President Obama called for such efforts around high-tech manufacturing to go more national. He proposed new manufacturing tax breaks, more robust R&D spending, and vocational training for workers. But those plans were nascent, and the administration was distracted by other issues, like the fight over national healthcare and the cleaning up of the 2008 housing crisis. The Biden administration is attempting to craft a more coherent vision of "industrial policy"—a once-verboten phrase that is still something of a political third rail in certain circles—that would give U.S. manufacturing the kind of competitive advantages held for decades by the German economy, which enjoys a trade surplus when it comes to advanced manufacturing.[23] While the dots are still being connected, the Biden executive order around competition policy issued in July 2021, which included seventy-two provisions touching nearly every area of government, is a good example of how the administration is beginning to articulate its vision of a marketplace run not just for the benefit of a handful of multinationals, but for "consumers, workers, farmers, and small businesses."[24] It's an acknowledgment that while private markets are great at helping individual companies generate profits, they don't always address the broad economic and social downsides to laissez-faire business, from climate change to inequality. Market prices cannot capture the full costs of these problems. Meanwhile, corporations can be just as bureaucratic and dysfunctional as government—if not more so. The economist John Kenneth Galbraith's 1967 book, *The New Industrial State,* explored how large companies are driven more by their need to survive as organizational entities than by supply-and-demand signals. He predicted that, as such organizations rose, innovation and entrepreneurial zeal would decline. This is exactly what happened as the U.S. economy became dominated by superstar companies. Look at any number of troubled behemoths, from Kraft Heinz to Boeing, and it is hard not to see exactly what Galbraith predicted. In an endless search for profits, many companies simply move money around on their balance sheets, creating a short-term financial sugar high without any real innovation.

In such a world, can anyone really argue honestly that the private markets are allocating resources efficiently? It's not that we need centralized planning; it's that we need both the government and the business sector working together more constructively—as is the case in nearly every other major economy in the world. Galbraith once put it well: "I react pragmatically. Where the market works, I'm for that. Where the government is necessary, I'm for that. I'm deeply suspicious of somebody who says, 'I'm in favor of privatization,' or 'I'm deeply in favor of public ownership.' I'm in favor of whatever works in the particular case."

Politicians and policy makers on both sides of the aisle should sear these words onto their brains. Americans don't really do nuance. We like strong, simple statements, such as Reagan's observation: "Government is not the solution to our problem; government is the problem." But the "private good, public bad" argument simply isn't true. How else can we explain the rise of China? It has shown that government planning and economic competitiveness not only can go hand in hand, but that, in the current era of tech-based disruption and inequality, public-sector support may be necessary for the private sector to thrive.[25] As Cornell scholar Robert Hockett, who has advised several Democratic presidential hopefuls, has pointed out, this would actually represent a more traditional American approach.[26]

Think German

One plank of this involves federally funded research centers, including one to promote 3D printing: the National Additive Manufacturing Innovation Institute in Youngstown, Ohio.[27] The institute partners with top universities like Carnegie Mellon and technical experts from the Departments of Defense and Energy and NASA to accelerate innovation in key areas of high-tech manufacturing. It's a system modeled on Germany's Fraunhofer institutes, which have been widely credited with keeping wages and competitiveness high in that country, even in the face of competition from countries like China.

Indeed, the German model is one worth studying in many respects. Germany's manufacturing sector as a share of GDP is roughly double that of the United States, in fact, and has managed to keep wages high because it has never turned its back on vocational training, as the United States did in the 1970s. (Liberals were worried that such training would result in class- or race-based tracking.)[28] As a result, Germany churns out millions of job-ready students per year through vocational high schools and also has a formal process for continuing learning and cutting-edge job training via the Fraunhofer programs. It has a far more co-operative labor culture because of its system of union representation on boards (which helps keep both resources for worker training and wages high), and it offers hefty tax breaks to companies that keep workers on, even part-time, during crises. Export hubs are spread throughout the country, with ecosystems of small and midsize firms serving bigger ones.

It's a model built for resilience, not just efficiency. Indeed, if you were to imagine where the next big competitor to Silicon Valley might be, the sleepy town of Allendorf, Germany, located two hours north of Frankfurt, in the center of the country, probably wouldn't come to mind. Home to fewer than six thousand people, Allendorf is best known as the headquarters of Viessmann, a maker of boilers and heating systems that has been owned and managed by the same family for four generations. The company is a typical Mittelstand firm—one of the many small and midsize German family-owned export companies that churn out top-notch auto components, lasers, high-tech machinery, and healthcare equipment.

Mittelstand firms employ 60 percent of the nation's workers and contribute more than half of Germany's economic output. Instrumental to the country's efforts to produce and distribute the first Covid-19 vaccine, they embody certain key social and moral values, like thrift, conservatism, family orientation, and long-term thinking. "Mittelstand means, 'I don't think about the next quarter—I think about the next generation. I don't try to be cheaper but better,'" said Nils Schmid when he was finance minister for the state of Baden-Württemberg, home to many such companies. "These values stretch out beyond our firms and into our society."[29]

In the Mittelstand ethos, cooperation between the public and private sectors is the norm. Governments, companies, and unions cut deals together, a process aided by the fact that they are all represented on corporate boards. It's a model that is almost unheard of in the United States. By remaining private and largely family-owned, the Mittelstand firms can take the long view rather than be beholden to the short-term-profit pressures of the typical Western public corporation. Back in the financial crisis of 2008, when revenue suddenly dropped by more than 40 percent, Viessmann, unlike many American firms, did not lay off a single worker. Over $100 million of family money was used to keep the business afloat. Management worked with labor to establish flexible schedules that would make it possible for the company to weather the crisis at full employment. "Our employees helped us bear the brunt of things," says Max Viessmann, the thirty-two-year-old scion of the company, who took over from his father following the financial crisis. "We wanted to avoid layoffs at any price—first, because we feel responsible for our long-term employees, but secondly, because we knew that after the recession, things would improve, and we'd need our workers again."

They did improve, and the firm did need those workers. By 2010, the company was back and growing again. Throughout the crisis and recovery, Viessmann continued investing 8 to 10 percent of its annual revenue into research and development. (The average global multinational invests between 2 and 3 percent.) The investment turned out to be worth it, and then some. In 2010, when China began to recover strongly from the financial crisis, Viessmann was ready to start shipping products quickly, picking up market share from U.S. competitors who had laid off workers, shuttered their factories, and now had to spend months retraining and retooling to catch up. The extra profits were shared equally among the Viessmann workforce. "I'm a father," says Max, who, appearing over Zoom in a hoodie and jeans, looked more like a Silicon Valley entrepreneur than a German industrialist. "But I have twelve thousand three hundred people in my family," he said, referring to the number of workers at Viessmann.

Over the last several decades, as wages in the United States and many other parts of Europe have stagnated or fallen, Germany has become singular among rich, non-Asian countries in that it has been able to keep a strong manufacturing sector, one that creates plenty of middle-class jobs. It was the first of the G7 countries to recover following the financial crisis, and it also enjoyed a V-shaped recovery following the first wave of the Covid-19 pandemic for the same reason: its economic model is about resiliency, not efficiency. In Germany, engineers, rather than financiers, are revered. You can hear the disdain for Anglo-American neoliberal capitalism in Max's voice as he talks about his stint working as a consultant at the consulting firm BCG in New York. "I learned a lot—about what I didn't like and what I wanted to prevent in my own family's firm," he says. "Politics, lack of execution, lack of preparation, and lack of transparency." As he sees it, "The soul of a company isn't something you put on a whiteboard. It's about how you live, and how you work, together. It's about a place. It's about a community."

It's hard not to admire the values epitomized by Germany's small and midsize export firms. But can they survive in the digital era? That is Max Viessmann's challenge. "Just because you were successful in your niche doesn't mean you will be successful in the digital world," he says. The fear in Germany is that many of these companies are unprepared for the disruptive force of new technologies like Big Data and AI. "Traditional Mittelstand companies have developed organizational routines over decades," Viessmann tells me. But he admits, "Today, they are no longer a recipe for success."

The solution, according to Viessmann, lies in applying traditional values to the modern world, with innovations like the internet of things, which is where the next major leap in global growth will come from. Since taking over the company from his father, Viessmann has expanded into spheres that are far removed from its original boiler making. Operating from its base in rural Hesse, Viessmann set up venture capital funds in Munich, to invest in promising start-ups, and an incubator in Berlin, to help new technology firms get off the ground. In a converted factory in the German capital's trendy Prenzlauer Berg district, he brings together edgy start-ups and conservative Mittelstand companies to share ideas. Viessmann itself is using sensors to monitor data from its products, which allows the company to anticipate and fix problems before a boiler blows up and gives customers the chance to change the temperature and air quality in their homes from afar. This has created entirely new service businesses and raised revenue by 30 percent in the last couple of years.

One of the people in the Viessmann brain trust is Dr. Jeannette zu Fürstenberg, a third-generation German family business owner.

From her gorgeous lakefront home near Zurich, the startlingly blond, fit, fast-talking thirty-nine-year-old mother of four runs her own venture capital firm, the mission of which is influenced in part by her own family's $600 million industrial sensor business. She also cooks up new ways to embed sensors and analyze data in products like those made by Viessmann, which has put money in her fund focused on the internet of things. The two are determined to make sure that a handful of U.S. and Chinese tech giants don't capture all the value from the industrial internet, as they have from the consumer internet. "What can I control in the digital world?" Fürstenberg says, taking a swig of espresso from a tiny porcelain cup. "That's the question I ask myself all the time." She believes "the answer is that we can control data and information in the industrial realm, across many sectors." She points out that unlike the consumer data that Google or Amazon has feasted on (or that Alibaba or Tencent, for that matter, has monopolized), the manufacturing data of the industrial sphere requires much more particular expertise and a sophisticated understanding of the actual processes involved in a given business. "If you are using sensors and collecting data in, say, a chemical plant, you'd better know exactly what you are doing," she says, or serious accidents could result.

The German government has launched a campaign to support its exporters as they move into the world of Big Data, with a plan to connect Mittelstand companies, start-ups, and research bodies in dozens of cities. The effort will be not just within Germany but in Europe as a whole. The "digital hub initiative" stands in stark contrast to the lack of this sort of connecting the dots in many U.S. industries, which (like textiles) have been left to fend for themselves. This may be why, according to a 2020 McKinsey Global Institute study, more than seventy of Europe's seventy-eight most dynamic high-tech manufacturing hubs are in this part of Germany.[30] Meanwhile, the United States has fewer such centers.

The idea is to create the next great digital hub in the heart of Germany. "How does the country organize itself, so it is prepared for digital disruption?" asked Alexander Kudlich, former managing director of Rocket Internet, the Berlin-based tech-investment fund. "You have the centralized U.S. model, where most activity is concentrated on the West Coast. And you have China, which is quite top down." German industry, however, has traditionally been very dispersed and decentralized. "So, you can't just have one hub in one city. You have to follow this decentralized model."

The Germans are realists. Fürstenberg, for example, estimates that as much as half the value from the internet of things may still be owned by Silicon Valley giants. But that still leaves plenty of the pie. And unlike their small and midsize U.S. counterparts, they are already receiving help from the European Union, which is setting new rules around how digital data of all sorts, from people to machines, must be collected and shared in order to ensure an even playing field. "We know that part of our business will be substituted by digital technologies. But if we get this right, we will be the ones making these new products," says Viessmann with a smile.[31]

The success of this particular company, and of Germany as a whole (as well as other developed countries like Switzerland, Sweden, Japan, South Korea, and Singapore, all of which have held on to their manufacturing sectors), shows that there is a different way for rich countries to structure their economy. The Anglo-American world has made certain choices—to let its industrial base go and to accept a barbell economy made up of mostly lower-level service jobs and high-end, high-skilled positions in areas like technology and finance. We can make other choices. It's not an overnight process. It took forty years to get to where we are, and it will likely take many more to rebuild the industrial base in such a way that the United States can maintain competitiveness in high-growth, high-value manufacturing in the way Germany has. But it's a process that has already begun, and is gathering steam, as both global politics and the global economy are becoming more regionalized.

CHAPTER 9

Why Making Things Matters

The industrial renaissance currently under way in the United States has been brewing for more than a decade. In the wake of the 2008 financial crisis, American manufacturing fell off a cliff, but then rebounded around 2010, creating a half-million new jobs in the three years to follow. This was based on a combination of factors: the American shale revolution, which made homegrown energy and transportation costs cheaper; a desire from consumers for faster production cycles, which necessitated more local production; and cutting-edge technology like 3D printing and robotic production, which made it cheaper to produce at home.[1]

While the United States is still the number two country (after China) in terms of the sheer dollar value of exports, the U.S. industrial base, like most everything else in the country, looks like a barbell. There is a robust auto industry, for example, which employs 3.4 million workers and 75,000 small and midsize suppliers. The United States also has the world's best cutting-edge research and design—it, not Japan or China, invented the iPhone, after all. But many things in the middle have gone. And some of those things, like pharmaceutical inputs, computer equipment, fabricated metals and materials, and semiconductors, are important building blocks of the industries that will matter the most in the future.

What's more, the manufacturing renaissance did not translate into a job boom, for a variety of reasons. One reason for this was that software can now do so much of what people used to do. When I was growing up in Indiana, for example, my father was a plant manager for companies like United Technologies. He supervised hundreds of unionized workers doing gritty hand assembly on noisy production lines. Factory floors today look more like high-tech cleanrooms—they are quiet, and so tidy you could eat off the floor. And even in lower-wage places like Asia, more and more jobs that used to be done by human hands are now being done by robots. The jobs that are left for humans very often require at least a couple of years of post–high school training, if not more.

Much of the national importance of manufacturing has traditionally lain in the number and quality of the jobs it creates. But an arguably bigger part of its impact lies in the fact that the industry enables innovation to occur in entirely new fields. Those two things are intricately connected. Innovation drives national competitiveness and the ability of a country to create entirely new industries and sectors. It isn't just about how many jobs the manufacturing sector creates. It's about how many jobs an entire economy can create and how good those jobs are. Think about the way in which the semiconductor industry drives many other businesses (from automotive to mobile phones), or how biotech innovation builds entire new sorts of healthcare services. If you can't innovate, you really can't succeed in the twenty-first-century economy.

When you look at the impact of the manufacturing sector only through the lens of the number of factory jobs created, you miss the bigger point: manufacturing matters not as some kind of silver-bullet solution to middle-class employment—robots will do more and more factory jobs—but because owning key parts of the industrial commons is crucial for innovation. "The ability to make things is fundamental to the ability to innovate things over the long term," says Willy Shih of Harvard Business School and co-author of *Producing Prosperity: Why America Needs a Manufacturing Renaissance*. The physical process of manufacturing, and the iterative, repetitive, incremental innovation that happens as part of that, is crucial to developing the new new thing. "When you give up making products, you lose a lot of the added value." Shih's work has shown that the outsourcing and downsizing of the manufacturing base have led to decreased innovation not only in manufacturing itself, but in higher-growth areas like clean tech and the internet of things. Basically, when the process of research, development, and production can happen all together, in a hub, new technologies are invented more frequently and more easily.[2] This is, after all, the original formula for success in Silicon Valley—the fact that investors, R&D experts, manufacturers, and labor of all kinds were in one place, working together.

Only by moving up the innovation food chain do economies grow and prosper broadly, creating entirely new industries and new jobs that we perhaps cannot even imagine today. Consider the $170 billion global "app" market, which didn't even exist until smartphones became ubiquitous over the last fifteen years. "While manufacturing may not provide the kind of mass employment it once did, no other sector plays the same role in supporting middle-income jobs across the country, especially outside of the largest cities, both directly and indirectly," says McKinsey Global Institute head James Manyika, who has done some of the most comprehensive research on the manufacturing sector globally.

As Manyika wrote in a 2021 report on the topic, "Although there may be fewer workers on assembly lines, the manufacturing jobs of the future could be more technical in nature, with higher wages than the typical service-industry jobs that the US economy has been adding in great numbers. Modernizing existing plants and building new ones would also draw much-needed investment into local communities, creating geographically broad ripple effects in other industries—like construction, logistics, and sales."[3] In this way, bolstering even lower-value parts of the supply chain (things like agriculture, textiles, and apparel) makes sense. In an ideal world, they become part of a more resilient supply chain that can then feed into higher-value, more strategic industries.

This process is happening in fits and starts all over the country, and there isn't a single magic formula. But success tends to come when a dynamic public or private figure finds a way to leverage the resources of a particular community and bridge the gaps in what is missing. What are the challenges to making things locally again? What is needed from both the private and the public sectors to reinvent the economy in this way? And what is at stake politically in this transformation? To find out, I set out on a two-week road trip across the Carolinas with Bayard Winthrop to examine the opportunities and challenges in the textile industry.

Where the Cotton Is High

Bayard Winthrop, the CEO and founder of American Giant, is the sort of person who has been pulled into policy conversations regularly over the last several years, during both the Trump administration and President Biden's tenure, about the state of manufacturing in America. His company was launched in 2012 with a single product, a high-quality cotton hoodie, and has since become a poster child for the artisanal manufacturing now beloved of both politicians and Millennial consumers, the target customer for American Giant. Millennials not only want to see new trends in stores every few weeks rather than each season, but they are also attracted to goods that are sustainably produced and have an ethical provenance. This is why companies such as Chobani, the yogurt maker that brought jobs back to upstate New York, and Shinola, the watch and leather goods producer that has helped revitalize Detroit, have become so successful. Winthrop started American Giant with the aim of appealing to this very group. Before launching it, he managed a high-end skateboard/snowboard company called Freebord and a boutique accessories maker called Chrome, and he sold an early social media company, WBS, to Disney. "Younger people have lost faith in politics, they're losing faith in the media and in institutions of all kinds," he says. "One of the last areas that they have left to really say something about themselves is how they're spending their money and what they choose to eat, or drive, or put on their bodies."

Winthrop first went to Washington, Jimmy Stewart style, in 2018, hoping to have a deep policy discussion of the kind that could help him connect the dots in the parts of rural North Carolina where he does most of his sourcing—about worker education and skills training, tax credits for investment and infrastructure. Instead, it was a shallow interaction punctuated by backslapping between senators and advisers who "were all vacationing together in the Hamptons," he says. "They wanted me to start a vocational training program for the workers in my area, and I said, 'Sure, that's a great idea, but what are you going to do to help?'"

The question encapsulates much of the economic and political tension in the United States in recent years. Thanks to globalization and rapid technological disruption, manufacturing has shifted dramatically over the past few decades. NAFTA, which created a free-trading bloc among the United States, Mexico, and Canada in 1994, sent jobs in many industries, including apparel, to Mexico. Politicians on both sides of the aisle, advised largely by neoliberal economic policy makers, supported that deal and the 2001 entry of China into the World Trade Organization. This resulted in significant job losses in the Midwest and South as supply chains moved overseas, particularly in lower-margin industries such as clothing. These losses happened at the same time that technology made manufacturing both more productive and less job intensive.

Given that every dollar spent in manufacturing adds $1.89 to local communities in the form of direct spending, but many times more in indirect economic benefits (like innovation, greater tax take, better public services, and education), this was a huge loss. For workers, skilled factory jobs can still represent a path to maintaining middle-class employment in a race-to-the-bottom global economy, as evidenced by the success of rich-country exporters like Germany, which has kept wages and productivity higher than most other developed countries because it has prioritized industry rather than the service sector. Manufacturing is, in short, emotionally and politically charged.

The desire to "make things" is certainly what fires up Winthrop, a fifty-two-year-old serial entrepreneur with the look and energy of someone twenty years younger. Now rarely seen in anything but jeans and one of his own hoodies, the former investment banker remembers "sitting in these meetings where people were all talking about interest and capital markets, and I just thought, 'I'm not at all inspired by this. I'm not in the right place.' I wanted to do something tactile, to interface every day with people who are actually creating real products in the real world."

He ultimately found funding to do just that, from a consortium of angel investors—people like the late Pepsi CEO Donald Kendall— who were interested in seeing if the United States could bring more balance and localism back into its economy, not in an artisanal way, but as a mass-market proposition. As Winthrop puts it, Kendall felt that "we are all so lucky to have been born in America, despite all her flaws. That it was the greatest stroke of luck for us, and that we, while we were here, had a responsibility to take care of her. That we should invest in our towns, our people, our jobs, that we should pay our taxes and support our communities, and by doing that, keep the American project in good shape to pass on to the next generation."

It's a message that resonates with other big-name investors like AOL co-founder Steve Case, who has long been trying to push more capital and opportunity from the coasts to the heartland (his venture firm's "Rise of the Rest" campaign has invested in old-line cities like Chattanooga and St. Louis and in many other parts of the South and Midwest). The idea of investing more broadly in the heartland and in smaller communities in general is also getting quite a boost in the wake of the Covid-19 pandemic, as the entire geography of work changes. Big coastal states like New York and California have been losing population, jobs, and talent, while states like Arizona, Florida, Indiana, and Texas are gaining them. This creates new potential hotbeds for investment in unlikely places.

The cotton fields of America's South are a good place to examine the challenges inherent in making these shifts. In the autumn harvest season, it's a lush country with verdant fields full of white blossoms waiting to be plucked. Thankfully, that backbreaking task is now done not by the hands of slaves or poorly paid sharecroppers, but by reasonably well-compensated drivers who sit in the air-conditioned comfort of $500,000 John Deere mechanized cotton pickers. Just one of these machines can manage an entire field in harvest season.

In late 2018, I visited these fields with Bayard Winthrop, in Enfield, North Carolina, which is where much of the cotton for American Giant hoodies is grown. Cotton is a key cash crop in the United States, the basis for the textile and apparel industry, and a key input for high-value items like the upholstery that goes into automobiles. On a sunny day in late October, I watched a huge Deere picker roll through rows of cotton. I also met the landowner, Jerry Hamill, a seventy-four-year-old, fourth-generation farmer who is worried that his daughters—both of whom have advanced degrees and work in other industries—won't ever want to come back to such a tough, low-margin business.

Hamill admits that the trade wars of the last few years have hit profits. Cotton prices fell in 2018 in part because China, then the second-largest buyer of U.S. cotton, introduced retaliatory tariffs of 25 percent. Still, Hamill (like every producer I spoke with) told me he was willing to take some pain if it brought more manufacturers back to the area. "Growing it is no problem. I want people to wear it," he says. "It's harder to get young farmers into the business. That changed in the nineties, when all the apparel suppliers left and the entire business went elsewhere."

Today, it's coming back, in part due to the backlash against Chinese cotton grown with forced labor, but also because the emerging markets that once supplied these raw materials now need them for their own middle-class consumers, as we've already learned. That's why low-value commodities such as cotton matter. While some policy wonks pooh-pooh the idea that something so pedestrian (cotton, soybeans, bananas, etc.) should be the focus of global trade wars, they are missing the point: the larger fight is really about the higher-value industries these industries supply and the jobs and national wealth they create.

Commodity-dependent industrial and manufacturing firms contribute 20 percent more than average to labor income, employ the most people, and have the widest geographic distribution of value thanks to their supply chains and need for physical space and investment into tangible goods.[4] No wonder they are at the center of the national competitiveness debate. Some countries, such as Japan and Germany (where makers haven't declined at all), have made specific policy decisions to support these firms. Others, like the United States and the United Kingdom, have not to the same extent. Those decisions are now being reexamined in light of the post-pandemic, post-neoliberal era. When countries argue about steel, for example, they are really arguing about industrial power and security. What we eat or wear or use to fuel our cars or heat or build our homes seems mundane, until it's not available. Such items are also the raw materials of higher-end products. The most basic commodity items are also increasingly those that people in places like the Defense Department and national security circles worry about.

Not every industry contributes equally to economic power and security, of course. One 2021 study by McKinsey, which examined thirty of the main manufacturing sectors in the United States, found that sixteen of them stood out for their economic and strategic value as measured by their contribution to national productivity and economic growth, job and income creation, innovation, and national resilience. Top on the list were semiconductors, medical devices, communications equipment, electronics, autos and auto parts, and precision tools.[5] Apparel isn't a sensitive or strategic area, but in a more nationalistic world, the idea of being able to ring-fence food, fuel, and consumer demand at home, preferably for locally made products, has increasing appeal for politicians on both sides of the aisle.

Industrial policy, which is increasingly supported by politicians of both stripes, won't solve all the economic woes of this new world, but it is a politically smart nod to the fact that we are in a new world. Meanwhile, there is a newfound willingness on the part of economists to admit that making things actually matters. This idea is being pushed not just by advisers with an aggressive attitude toward China but by those who believe that a large, diverse economy like that of the United States can't be made up entirely of high-end software developers and low-end gig economy workers. "Comparative advantage only works completely for an economy like Singapore," says Sree Ramaswamy, a partner at the McKinsey Global Institute who studies manufacturing, noting that you need to be fairly exceptional—a very rich, small island nation, for example—in order to focus on only one or two key industries. "It makes sense for countries like the United States, China, or India to keep more economic diversity."

This seems obvious in a world in which trade disputes, higher tariffs, and broader geopolitical uncertainty have become the new normal. According to McKinsey, the share of global trade conducted between the United States and countries ranked in the bottom half of the world for political stability, as assessed by the World Bank, rose from 16 percent in 2000 to 29 percent in 2018. Just as telling, almost 80 percent of trade involves nations with declining political stability scores.

More diversity and more production at home could mean more security, the thinking goes. If companies such as American Giant can help revive economically beleaguered areas, then perhaps other economies of scale might grow. And if people in communities like these start to have more opportunities, perhaps the national conversation could be less polarized. "I want confidence that we aren't going to revert back to the nineties, that the government is going to be pro-labor and pro–small business," says Winthrop, who is often asked about the lessons that can be learned from American Giant's journey.

One lesson is that, in a rich country like the United States, making higher labor costs work by raising productivity is both crucial and tricky. Winthrop decided to base much of the company's supply chain in North Carolina in part because it's a "right-to-work" state, in which unions have little power, and thus, there are very competitive labor rates. To compete with China, suppliers in the United States need workers who are more productive than those overseas; even in areas of the United States where labor is cheap, pay per garment is still roughly three times what it would be in China, if not more.

Those prepared to work for this pay tend to come from immigrant communities. Winthrop and I stopped, for example, in Middlesex, North Carolina, the home of Eagle Sportswear, a company recently bought by American Giant. At the factory, I walked the assembly line with plant manager William Lucas. A fifty-four-year-old local who started working there straight out of high school, he shows me the mainly Latina sewers who multitask in teams rather than doing more traditional batch sewing, in which one worker does a single task again and again. In team sewing, each group has a target, and faster, more skilled workers can help slower ones along. The monitor for the team we are watching reads "110 percent," which means a bonus if the women can keep up the pace.

Together, the workers dynamically speed up or slow down the flow of the line as necessary. "Team sewing makes these workers more valuable because they can learn different skills instead of performing the same thing over and over," says Lucas. In every industry, but particularly in low-value ones such as apparel, the goal is to increase productivity and skill levels to grab more margin. A more skilled labor pool could, in turn, bring higher-value industries to the region. "These ladies have a lot of skill," Lucas says. "I could see them doing, say, boots or fabric or leather upholstery."

If these seamstresses could do leather upholstery, then, suddenly, all kinds of new opportunities open up—like connecting to the thriving auto industry and burgeoning business in electric vehicles in Greenville, South Carolina. "Textiles themselves aren't a big deal for national competitiveness," says McKinsey's James Manyika, "though I'm all for communities like these in North Carolina boosting job creation. But if they can connect to something like the South Carolina automotive business, that's when you start to see a real economic multiplier effect."[6] Indeed, a large body of academic research shows that firms need to be embedded in networks of investors, suppliers, managers, workers, educational institutions, and such in order to maximize innovation. That's why Silicon Valley, for example, exists as it does—it's a hub in which all the raw materials for new companies are situated in one place. Such high-tech hubs can be, and are being, created in other places, particularly those in which there are existing legacy industries on which to build.

Greenville is one such place. Only four hours southwest of Middlesex, Greenville has been one of the stars of the post-Covid-19 era. Jobs in the region have grown far more strongly than in other areas of the country, in part because of a model effort by city leaders to retool what was once a declining textile town into a hub for clean-car technologies. Thirty years ago, Greenville had the look of many southern and midwestern industrial cities in decline: its storefronts were empty, its infrastructure was crumbling, and its tax base had been hollowed out. The mayor of Greenville, who also happens to be a corporate immigrant labor attorney, could see that the apparel business wasn't going to come back at scale anytime soon and that, even if it did, the profit margins would be too low to support a robust economy. And in any case, says Catherine Novelli, a former U.S. trade representative who led free-trade negotiations in Europe, the Middle East, and Africa, "the city didn't want the kind of textile manufacturing they'd had before back; you'd talk to people there who said they could tell what sort of color they'd been dying the cloth because the river would run that color."

The city and county eminences looked at what resources they had locally, which was in large part a workforce that still knew how to make things—how to use industrial machinery and how to work in teams to produce things. They then started marketing these resources to the private sector. The city was able to help lure BMW and then Bosch and GE to set up new factories. Suddenly, the once-forgotten idea of "vertical integration" started to make sense in the twenty-first-century world. Big companies needed small and midsize companies as local suppliers. And those suppliers needed businesses to service both them and the workers they were employing. Eventually, this led the city of Greenville to subsidize the building of better homes, a new downtown sports and entertainment center, and a downtown park complete with walking trails, a footbridge, and waterfalls, around which new offices and apartments sprang up. "It's totally delightful there now," says Novelli. "[The city has] become a hot spot for foodies and designers."[7]

In fact, over the last few years Greenville has become one of the country's fastest-growing large cities. The BMW plant in Greenville County supports more than 100,000 U.S. jobs on its own. But more important for the city itself, the small and midsize suppliers that have grown up around it have thrived, in many cases doubling and even tripling their workforces.[8] Not only has this changed the social fabric of the community, but it is changing the competitiveness profile of the nation, from the ground up. The automotive industry and the metals and machinery businesses that surround it employ 3.4 million workers and involve 75,000 small and midsize suppliers in hundreds of counties. What's more, those suppliers produce goods that could also be used by other industries—like transportation, defense, and public health. Indeed, 80 percent of the automotive supply chain needs overlap with the supply chains of other, more sensitive and strategic industries.[9]

By building up one area, you start to build up another. As we've already learned, the real knock-on benefits of manufacturing come from creating those sorts of higher-value ecosystems. Textiles itself is a relatively low-margin, low-skill business. But if you can train a higher-skilled workforce to do higher-margin products, then, ideally, you create the sort of hub of talent and capital that produces not only higher-value goods, but also services. Kim Glas, the CEO of the National Council of Textile Organizations, notes that some of the Carolina clothing makers in her trade group also make filtration units, heart stents, fabric overlay for wind turbines, and yarns used in certain computer parts.[10] It's a hop, skip, and a jump from there to being part of the huge, federally subsidized electric vehicle and green battery business.

Of course, when you are building such hubs, it helps to have a diverse, upscale industrial base as well as research and service sectors that support it. Think about Columbus, Ohio. That city and many others in the Midwest simply had to be retooled for a new era.

The area of North Carolina in which Bayard Winthrop runs his factories has few such resources. With the lack of decent public transport and a workforce unable to find housing in the places where jobs are, American Giant has had to bus workers between their homes and its factories. Minimal state spending on education means there are clearly limits to how far upskilling can go. When I try to interview some of the Latina workers, their English skills are so poor—and I lack Spanish—that it's difficult for us to communicate.

Why are there so few English speakers here willing to work such jobs, even if—as shown by plant manager William Lucas's personal journey—those jobs could lead to something better? It depends on whom you ask—and I ask everyone we meet in the Carolinas. Some give the standard, conservative answer: "Some people don't want to work." Others say that those who can do so tend to leave the area in search of higher pay. But many feel that there are simply no public resources available to those in the area who'd like to stay, but who also want to bolster their prospects. The chief loss has been the disappearance of the vocational training programs—what we used to call "shop" class in high school, short for "machine shop"—that were once ubiquitous in this area of the country. Such programs often had links to local employers, who would take kids straight from high school into employment. In the 1970s, Democrats pushed for these programs to be defunded. The worry was that they would create a kind of class system in which kids from lower socioeconomic backgrounds (very often people of color) ended up as plumbers and richer, whiter kids ended up in professional jobs.

The Skills Gap

It's a legitimate worry. But, ironically, the fix led to an even bigger problem: a massive college debt bubble and a major middle-market skills gap. While most of the jobs created today require a couple of years of post–high school training, only a minority requires a four-year liberal arts degree. Many of the algorithmic hiring programs that companies use to weed out applicants for jobs are programmed to look for a BA or a BS. But most employers I speak to around the country say that too many of these graduates don't actually have the ability to walk into middle-class jobs without a significant amount of on-the-job training. This is true even at the high end. Plenty of MBAs can read a balance sheet, but have neither operational nor soft skills. Four-year business administration graduates are settling for low-wage gigs, while twenty-dollar-an-hour manufacturing jobs go unfilled because employers can't find anyone with vocational training.

Desperate companies are trying to plug the gap. Telecom group AT&T has set up an internal online course to train the 95 percent of those in its own technology and services unit who have inadequate ability in STEM subjects: science, technology, engineering, and math. Walmart Academy has trained thousands of workers, including in basic skills they should have learned in high school. Myriad factors created this dysfunctional system, but the one that hasn't been talked about enough is the unfair bias toward schools rather than skills. According to a 2017 Harvard Business School report, more than six million good-paying jobs in the United States are at risk of "degree inflation," meaning that skilled labor is locked out of a particular market for lack of a degree, even if one is not needed for the job. For some middle-level positions in 2015, two-thirds of employers were asking for a college degree even though only 16 percent of people working successfully in similar positions had them. This system cuts social mobility, but it also inflates the price of what may be a needless credential and costs employers, who pay more for people with fewer skills and a higher propensity to jump between companies.[11]

Business leaders complain about the lack of middle-market technical skills in particular—in many cases, these include the ability to communicate well, learn, and shift tasks quickly—as too many students graduate with heavy debts and useless degrees, at least in terms of employability. Meanwhile, Harvard academics have attributed as many as one-third of the U.S. jobs lost during the years following the Great Recession not to declining demand but to the skills gap.[12] The result, crushing student debt—the average four-year college graduate has $30,000 of it—prevents young people from buying homes, cars, and other consumer goods.

This presents a major headwind for the economy. Forty-four million people in the United States carry student debt. Eight million of those borrowers are in default—a rate that is still higher than pre–financial crisis levels (unlike the default rate for mortgages, credit cards, or even car loans). A Brookings study found that 40 percent of borrowers are likely to default by 2023.[13] Growing student debt has been linked to everything from decreased rates of first-time home ownership, to higher rental prices, to lower purchases of appliances and furniture and all the other things that people buy to fill their homes.

The majority of debt is held by middle-class and rich Americans who spend a lot to send their children to the best universities. The cost of attendance is itself a sign of how broken the education market is: tuition inflation runs at more than three times the consumer price index. Even the wealthy have trouble putting enough away for their children's tertiary education when four years at a prestigious school costs more than $200,000. But the poorest 25 percent of households hold far more debt as a percentage of their income and wealth. These borrowers are more likely to drop out or default, in part because they often do not receive as much of a payoff from their education and because they also have to juggle part-time work with school, which makes it tougher to graduate. Among those who do graduate, debt loads can actually equal *downward* mobility. A 2013 study by the think tank Demos found the average student debt burden for a married couple with two four-year degrees ($53,000) led to a lifetime wealth loss of nearly $208,000.[14] As a result, there are also worrisome links between high student debt loads and marital failure and health issues like depression. Bottom line: a snowball cycle of downward mobility in the country's most vulnerable populations.

It's both a class and a race issue. That lower quartile of the socio-economic spectrum is disproportionately African American. This raises thorny social issues. Working-class whites without a four-year degree struggle, but they are on average better able than minority peers to get by with vocational training or a high school degree. Poor Black people know that it's up or out—try for college, whatever the cost, or risk falling off the economic ladder. And so, they try for a four-year degree, no matter the cost, and very often, the cost is ruinous not only for them but also for their families, who take on disproportionate amounts of debt in this dysfunctional and, ultimately, failing attempt at upward mobility via higher education.[15]

Clearly, this needs to change. But how? The idea of a national student debt jubilee has gathered steam in recent years. I'm for it, as long as it is targeted to those who need it most (as per the statistics just cited, blanket student debt forgiveness would actually reward rich and middle-class families more than the poor). It's also a one-time approach that doesn't fundamentally change the model of education. As economists ranging from Michael Spence to Joe Stiglitz have shown, a good chunk of the value of a college degree lies in market signaling rather than in the acquisition of skills. Paying $75,000 a year for a private, four-year degree isn't the only way to learn.

President Biden has argued for a fix involving the revamping of community colleges nationally. The idea is that more students could attend such local and regional institutions cheaply rather than paying for four years of college. But the truth is that many of these programs are too dysfunctional to be fixed. I'd argue that the country should do what it did in the period following World War II: revamp the secondary educational system so that kids graduate from high school (something they don't have to pay for) with a degree that will get them a job. Several successful models for this have already sprung up at the local level, each one leveraging unique, community-specific opportunities to connect educators and students with job creators in business. My daughter, for example, graduated from Bard Early College in Manhattan, a public high school associated with Bard College, where, over four years, students earn two years of college credits as well as a high school degree. The idea is not only to graduate students who can work right away, but also, if they so choose, to funnel talented New York high school students into local and regional colleges that accept these credits (like City College, the State University of New York, and Bard), thus sparing families huge sums of money on education. Bard Early College is one of many "six-in-four" schools, which are quietly becoming a local solution to a national problem.[16] In six different cities, local colleges now liaise with high schools to create a more robust curriculum and get around the normal, cookie-cutter national secondary school model.

I've spent quite a lot of time in these schools (there are many variations of them, in many different parts of the country), most particularly the one called P-TECH, or Pathways in Technology Early College High School, which was developed in 2011 by IBM, the New York City Department of Education, and the City University of New York. Most employers believe that skills in science, technology, engineering, and mathematics (STEM subjects) will be crucial for the workforce. But many companies think it is crucial that workers have a strong basic liberal arts education to go alongside the high-tech workplace skills that will be required for the "new-collar" jobs of the future. P-TECH blends the two, offering a strong core curriculum of science and humanities (but few elective classes) along with "workplace learning" classes in which students build their own companies and learn the soft skills required to succeed in the white-shoe corporate world—something that middle- and upper-class children learn by osmosis from their parents, but that many others around the country do not.

Every school connects to a group of local industries—in New York City, it's all about software design and Web creation; in Chicago, the P-TECH schools focus on healthcare. Wherever there is a need to turn out more middle-level workers in a specific sector, the school connects with the businesses in need. They in turn help inform the basic curriculum, ensuring that kids who graduate from the program, with their associate's degrees, can step into a fifty-thousand-dollar-plus job, should they desire. The firms also make a commitment to help support students who become employees and then want to finish their liberal arts or science bachelor's degrees later. It's a win-win for the community, which uses a revamped public education system to plug the skills gap, which may vary widely depending on place.

Two and a half years in, the Brooklyn school that pioneered this approach had been visited by everyone from the American president and Harvard academics to Chinese officials. Within its first two years of operation, about half the juniors—none of whom was screened for ability and many of whom will be the first in their family to graduate from high school—were already taking college-level math. It was an impressive achievement at a time when only 65 percent of kids graduated from New York City high schools. Rashid Davis, the principal there, says the public-private partnership has been invaluable: "It's incredible how much further children can reach when industry is closer to them to help set the context for learning."

In many ways, P-TECH is a white-collar, modernized version of the successful Germanic model in which students are taught curriculums geared toward specific, career-oriented skill sets. (Countries that follow this model, including Germany, Austria, Switzerland, and the Scandinavian nations, have lower-than-average rates of youth unemployment.)[17] The model, which has since spread into more than two hundred schools in eleven states, as well as being launched overseas in twenty-eight countries, including Australia and Morocco, aims to reinvent secondary education by giving graduates not only four years of high school but a two-year associate's degree, plus work experience along the way. "Six is the new four," says Stan Litow, P-TECH's founder, noting that you need at least a two-year college degree to guarantee something more than a fifteen-dollar-an-hour future. P-TECH graduates are first in line for positions at IBM and dozens of other blue-chip partners, like SAP, Cisco, and Global-Foundries, where many may already have done the internships that are part of the curriculum requirements.

If You Build It, Will They Come?

Of course, not every place is New York or Chicago or even Peoria, which, like so many midwestern manufacturing hubs, has a deep labor pool and access to good transportation, community colleges, and vocational training programs. Some places start with much less. There isn't enough population mass in Middlesex, North Carolina, to bring in a specialized high school. Some big companies have launched their own training programs for workers, but for a smaller company such as American Giant, that's tough without major tax credits or subsidies. "What do I want from Washington? I want help with my capital investment," says Winthrop. That could be more tax credits for investment in research and development, but also for human capital and worker training. Currently, companies can depreciate money spent on machines, but not labor.

That's something the Biden administration aims to change. President Biden, who keeps a bust of Cesar Chavez in his office, is probably the most pro-labor U.S. leader since Franklin Roosevelt. In some ways, his administration's plans mirror those of FDR, creating more physical infrastructure—not only roads, trains, and bridges, but also the modern broadband network on which the new economy will run. But in the twenty-first century, it's not only physical capital that matters, but also human talent. That's why hundreds of millions of dollars in federal spending will also be going to education and training programs. There is also legislation in progress to allow companies that invest in workers to reap the tax benefits of that, just as they do for other types of investment.

That takes time. It is a decade-long process, not a quarterly Band-Aid. The next presidential election could change plans, but neoliberal economic policy isn't coming back, on either side of the policy spectrum. Rather, as the era of laissez-faire globalization ends, a new place-based economics is being adopted in the corridors of power.

CHAPTER 10

Two Americas

Where you stand depends on where you sit, as Rufus Miles, aide to three American presidents, aptly put it. Heather Boushey, a member of Joe Biden's Council of Economic Advisers and one of the key architects of the administration's "Reward work, not wealth" approach to economic policy, is the personal embodiment of a new focus in Washington on the parts of the country left behind by globalization for a half century.

"My dad was a machinist at Boeing," Bouchey told me in a 2021 interview about the shift away from neoliberal thinking. "I was very lucky. He was in a union. He had great healthcare. That foundation allowed me to get to college and to graduate school." In fact, Boushey, who is a lot younger, warmer, more casual and curious than most people who have advised the White House on economic policy for the last forty years, was herself in a union in her younger years. "I don't know whether I'm the only person at the CEA who's ever been in a union," she says, laughing. "That was not a googleable fact." But it's a safe bet.

Boushey—who, before joining the CEA, ran the Washington Center for Equitable Growth—lived through a forty-year period in which, for a time, most working people had access to the basics of a middle-class life. The fact that the paradigm no longer exists is one of the things that gets the fifty-one-year-old economist up in the morning. "If you walk into a basic economics class, the professor is likely to say that the economy is a three-legged stool made up of land, labor, and capital." Her mandate is to find a way to fix the big four crises in the United States right now—in healthcare, economic growth, the climate, and racial justice—by rebalancing the stool so that capital is no longer so disproportionately advantaged relative to labor. Her 2019 book, *Unbound: How Inequality Constricts Our Economy and What We Can Do About It,* explains why equality and prosperity not only can but must go hand in hand. Boushey is part of a new cadre of young appointees and Washington insiders who are embracing the "political" part of the political economy. They include the FTC's Lina Khan, the Consumer Financial Protection Bureau head Rohit Chopra, legal scholar and White House adviser Tim Wu, and head of the Open Markets Institute Barry Lynn (a powerful behind-the-scenes advocate for the post-neoliberal world and author of a seminal work on the dangers of complex supply chains, *End of the Line*), all of whom are moving beyond laissez-faire, consumer-oriented thinking to look critically at the power structures that underpin (and all too often undermine) the country and its citizenry.

This new crop of Gen X economists takes inspiration not from the Chicago School, but from people like Janet Yellen and Joseph E. Stiglitz, who, like Boushey, grew up in places where it was all too obvious that markets weren't always efficient. "Economists like to talk about perfect competition; that the market has these optimal outcomes, and we just need to tweak around the edges," says Boushey. She wouldn't agree. "I think that one of the things that has become really apparent, especially since the financial crisis, is that at some point along the way, the guardrails have come off."

By this, she means that, over the past forty years, any sort of government regulation of the global economy was considered verboten. Indeed, one way of thinking about the multiple crises that both the United States and other governments are now handling is that for the past forty or so years, we've collectively placed too much emphasis on making sure that capital has had a lot of freedom and not enough on what that meant for individuals. We didn't think as much about the human side of the equation, from the care economy to dealing with issues of inclusivity to paying attention to what we were doing to the planet.

As Boushey put it to me, this is, "quite frankly, unsustainable, and it's also not competitive to not be thinking about that. So, I think that part of what we're doing is leveling the playing field between land, labor, and capital and saying, 'You all have your proper place and it's not either/or.' Again, it's about balance and pragmatism, but it's also about being very clear what the goal is." For the Biden administration, the goal is to take care of domestic interests and communities first, bringing every American along and worrying about the global economy as a second priority.

Like most of the new crop of progressive economists now making policy in Washington, Boushey also rejects notions like share price as the ultimate measure of value in an economy, or the idea that national GDP is reflective of the felt experience of most Americans. "Since the late seventies, GDP has increasingly not been a good indicator of what's happening to the average American or the average American family," says Boushey. "If you look at the period from the early or even the middle part of the twentieth century up until the late seventies, if GDP grew by three percent, then it was the case that most Americans were seeing their incomes grow by about three percent. So, we were really a country that was growing together, and GDP meant something." But for many Americans, GDP has diverged from income growth since the seventies, she says. "Those in the bottom eighty to ninety percent of the income distribution are experiencing income growth that's less than the average GDP growth. But those at the top may be seeing six percent growth in their income. So, because of inequality, that metric that we still report every quarter doesn't mean what it used to mean, and it's confusing. It's not the experience of the vast majority of Americans."

Boushey and many others believe that one first step would be for the number crunchers in Washington to disaggregate GDP, so that when the numbers come in each quarter, we would see not a single national number, but more of a growth heat map across the income distribution. Such a map would likely reflect some of the political divides in the United States today. As of 2021, roughly 70 percent of asset wealth is held by the top 10 percent of households by income. And most of that wealth is held on the coasts, in blue states and cities.

If we go back seventy years, to the beginning of the system of global capital integration that allowed this level of wealth concentration to be possible, we see that it was done for good reasons: people didn't want autocrats or world wars. But after several decades, and particularly from the late 1980s onward, the system that was set up to fight autocracy ultimately enabled it, given that the global economy and the technocrats who ran it were in many cases divorced from national concerns. Ironically, that's one of the things that gave us a new type of modern fascism—in the form of Donald Trump, who was able to cleverly exploit the frustrations of a left-behind group of voters while continuing to enrich those who had benefited from wealth inequality (which was, it must be said, quite the political trick). We don't yet have a clear or complete articulation of what the new, post-neoliberal world, in which nation-states and the world at large can grow together, will look like. How much production should be done at home? In which industries? How can countries ensure their own economic stability and not end up in a thirties-style trade war? These are the issues that Boushey and this new generation of policy makers think about.

"It's such a tough question," she says. "So much of this really does have its roots in the interwar period in the early part of the twentieth century, where we had to connect the dots about what it means to live in a global economy. We are now back to having these conversations. What is [globalization] going to deliver for people? It's a topic that's really big and broad, but fundamentally, it is tied up in whether or not we can have global systems that allow every country to focus on making sure that they are doing what matters for their home economy, that they are delivering for their people while, at the same time, making sure that we don't end up with the beggar-thy-neighbor policies of years past."

While the answers are still taking shape, the last two U.S. administrations have broken with those of the recent past by explicitly acknowledging that there is such a thing as too much globalization. "We live in a democracy," says Boushey. "The president is ultimately responsible for delivering for communities all across the country and, ideally, not delivering a war. [While] it's always going to be much easier for capital to be global, because it's ethereal," a new focus on all things local is driving economic thinking.

Two Americas

Amazingly, the notion of place was, until quite recently, not really thought about in economics. Theory was important; the particulars of how a theory worked in specific parts of any given nation were not. Sure, development economists would consider how to bring up the fortunes of various countries, but the prescriptions for how to do that were unidimensional: follow the IMF prescriptions for privatizing your economy and opening up to free global trade and liberal financial markets and—presto!—watch the wealth and prosperity rise. I won't rehash the excellent work of the many critics who have debunked these ideas, like economist Joseph E. Stiglitz. But today, even the IMF itself has reconsidered the export of neoliberal globalization; in the summer of 2016, some of its top economists issued a paper[1] saying that its benefits had been "oversold," which was a bit like the pope telling us catechism had been oversold.[2]

There were always, it must be said, certain economists, going as far back as the beginnings of the neoliberal era, who thought differently. Karl Polanyi, an Austro-Hungarian economic historian, was critiquing classical economic views as early as 1944, claiming that totally free markets were a utopian myth, because the things that allowed markets to function properly were underpinned by states.[3] Scholars of the postwar period—including people ranging from Nobel laureate Stiglitz and the University of Chicago's Raghuram Rajan to MIT's Simon Johnson and Daron Acemoglu—understood that place mattered. As Stiglitz, who grew up in working-class Gary,

Indiana, once told me, "It was obvious if you were raised in a place like Gary that markets aren't always efficient" and that, in terms of economic outcomes, location mattered.

But over the last couple of decades, a growing body of research has supported these ideas. From the work of people ranging from Thomas Piketty, to Emmanuel Saez and Gabriel Zucman, to Raj Chetty and Thomas Philippon, there is now a consensus that not only does the invisible hand work imperfectly, but it works differently depending on where and when you were born. Things like the level of public health or the quality of the water where you live actually matter in terms of economic outcomes. So does the stress present for a mother while her child is in utero and the wellness of a baby at birth.[4]

For example, one 2011 study published by academics Janet Currie and Douglas Almond found that "child and family characteristics measured at school entry do as much to explain figure outcomes as factors that labor economists have more traditionally focused on, such as years of education." A raft of literature shows that "poorer children have worse cognitive, social-behavioral and health outcomes in part because they are poorer."[5] And of course, different parts of the country fare better or worse on those measures. The outcomes matter based on not just states or regions but also neighborhoods. In the United States, inequality across neighborhoods explains a great deal of the variation in children's access to good healthcare, education, and public services, which in turn matters for productivity and growth.

As Raj Chetty's Equality of Opportunity Project has shown, children who grow up in communities with less inequality, less residential segregation, better primary schools, and greater family stability tend to be more upwardly mobile. No big surprise there. And yet, the economic models don't typically account for such things.[6] In the classic neoliberal model, outcomes for a child living with, say, a single-parent descendant of a coal-mining family (in which pollution degraded parental health, putting stress on the system) in a part of the country with a low tax base and poor public services wouldn't be adjusted in any way compared to an upper-middle-class child living in the fresh air of Silicon Valley with a stay-at-home mother and a nanny to help. According to traditional economic math, both individuals should be considered as similar inputs to a given model.

Within the United States—until Donald Trump's victory in 2016—relatively little attention was paid to place-based economic development problems, at least among top academics. The idea was that policy makers should simply focus on creating jobs wherever it was easiest to do so, and Americans would move to wherever the jobs were. But from the mid-nineties onward—really, the moment of peak neoliberal optimism—a variety of things began to happen all at once. For starters, mobility began to slow. That's because the widespread middle-class settlement of California, which really began in the seventies, had finished by the end of the nineties, according to Harvard economist Gordon Hanson. "During that decade, incomes were still converging across states," Hanson says, referring to the process of westward expansion that we think of as something from a past century, but that was only really completed in the last couple of decades. "But by the 2000s, regional shocks hit, and we began to see a different world."[7]

It was a world in which some states suffered much more than others as outsourcing to Asia and technology-related job losses due to automation began to hit all at once. In their now-famous 2016 academic paper, "The China Shock," Hanson and his colleagues David H. Autor and David Dorn laid out how the country could be doing well, even as specific regions were being destroyed by neoliberal policy decisions. As the academics wrote in their paper, "If one had to project the impact of China's momentous economic reform for the U.S. labor market with nothing to go on other than a standard undergraduate international economics textbook, one would predict large movements of workers between U.S. tradable industries (say, from apparel and furniture to pharmaceuticals and jet aircraft), limited reallocation of jobs from tradables to non-tradables, and no net impacts on U.S. aggregate employment. The reality of adjustment to the China trade shock has been far different."[8]

One look at a map of geographic inequality shows the sad tale of the hollowing out of the heartland from the China shock.[9] While the coasts prosper, the Midwest, Northeast, and central South suffer from rising unemployment and falling incomes. "China . . . toppled much of the received empirical wisdom about the impact of trade on labor markets," the paper's authors concluded.[10] One world, two systems, and some major economic and political problems were being born.

Suddenly, it seemed, there wasn't a single American Dream, but rather a dream that could be dreamed in Austin that was quite different from one that could be dreamed in, say, Western Pennsylvania. It's telling that even people like Peter Orszag, the former Obama budget director and very much a part of the corporatist wing of the Democratic Party, would say, "The Economics 101 approach, which is place-agnostic, has clearly failed." As he put it to me in a phone call on the topic during the Covid-19 pandemic, "If you ask a normal human being 'Does it matter where you are?' they would start from the presumption that, yes, where you live and where you work and whom you're surrounded by matters a ton. It's like Econ 101 has just gone off the path for the last forty to fifty years, and we're all little islands atomized into perfectly rational calculating machines. And policy has just drifted along with this thinking."[11] As Damon Silvers, the policy director for the country's largest trade union federation, the AFL-CIO, once put it to me, "This idea that people have to live in communities that make sense to them—it's key." Globalization, he acknowledges, has always been there, and the labor movement embraces it. "But this sense of being completely unmoored economically from where you live, from your community as a whole—that's new."

"Somewheres" Versus "Anywheres"

This phenomenon has led to a division of the public into two groups, whom British journalist, author, and policy maker David Goodhart has dubbed "Somewheres" and "Anywheres."[12] The latter are the global cosmocrats, who include not only rich elites we might once have called the "jet set," the sort of people who have homes in many places (often as tax dodges), but also the international class of technocratic policy makers, executives, think tankers, literary types, and all the other "meritocrats" who have climbed up the slippery pole of twenty-first-century success and are now knowledge workers who can live anywhere and be employed most anywhere.

I'm certainly one of them. I grew up among Somewheres, but have spent much of my postgraduate life as a foreign correspondent living Anywhere, both literally and metaphorically. Like many of my class, I probably have more in common with other professionals from Beijing to London, Istanbul to Abu Dhabi, than with "Somewheres" who might live in my own country. This is perhaps the most fundamental political divide of our day. Somewheres are the people for whom globalization has been hard. They are typically (though not always) less educated, more traditional, and far more place-bound, sometimes by choice, but often by force. They are rooted where they live for myriad reasons, some having to do with a lack of nationally or internationally marketable skills or of enough money to move to where better jobs are, but also because of the presence of family communities and clans that have helped support an otherwise precarious life (such as multiple generations caring for elders or children) or simply because they are more committed to their own culture and community than your average upper-middle-class American college graduate who is ready to move wherever the next promotion takes her.

The majority of Somewheres supported Brexit and voted for Donald Trump in 2016 and 2020. The narrative around this often focuses on racism and xenophobia, which certainly exist. Race is a central issue in American political life. But as the last two presidential elections have shown us, class matters just as much. Wealth and power have been concentrated in just a few places. When you look at an electoral map of the United States, it is overwhelmingly red, except on the coasts and a few inland urban areas. According to the McKinsey Global Institute, more than two-thirds of U.S. job growth since 2007 has been concentrated in just twenty-five cities and regional hubs.

Meanwhile, lower-growth areas and rural counties where some 77 million people live have had "flat or falling employment growth," even following the recovery from the last financial crisis. This sort of concentration in a few "superstar cities" is a global trend. It also tends to snowball as the most talented young people are attracted to a handful of urban centers, driving up property prices and making it tougher for anyone who isn't part of the superstar club to get a leg up on the socioeconomic ladder. Those left behind are angry—and vulnerable to demagogues. Is it any wonder that the least-urbanized counties in the United States voted for Trump by a margin of 35 percentage points, up from 32 points in 2016?

One of the reasons Joe Biden carried the election in 2020 was that he was able to convince many former Republicans—people not only like Bayard Winthrop but, more important, like those who might work for Winthrop in a factory or on a farm that grows the cotton that makes the yarn for his goods—that he had their best interests at heart. For example, in states like Wisconsin, Michigan, and Pennsylvania, the percentage of white working-class men voting Democratic increased from 23 percent to 28 percent in 2020, while the white working-class women's vote was up 2 points, to 36 percent.

Very simply, Joe Biden spoke their language and ran on policies aimed at helping the Somewheres. Hillary Clinton made a fatal mistake when she dismissed Trump supporters as "deplorables," and Barack Obama once referred to the Midwest working class as "bitter" people who "cling to guns or religion." But Mr. Biden showed up to these areas with empathy and respect, cleverly recasting his opponent. "I've dealt with guys like Donald Trump my whole life . . . who would look down on us because we didn't have a lot of money or [our] parents didn't go to college," he said at a speech in Manitowoc, Wisconsin. "Guys who inherit everything they've ever gotten in their life and squander it."[13]

Trump proposed to care about the Somewheres, but his political proposals were very much geared toward the Anywheres. His 2017 corporate tax cut was the ultimate in trickle-down economic policy. The Trump administration claimed that the cuts would spur huge investment and growth in the U.S. economy, raising wages and ushering in a new era of bullishness. Not quite. They pushed up the market, but they did so because nearly half the corporate profits that were repatriated went straight into stock price–bolstering share buybacks. Five big U.S. companies (Apple, Alphabet, Cisco, Microsoft, and Oracle) increased capital investment 42 percent year on year to $42.6 billion. But the vast majority of that money went into new software and technology investments, which can obviously increase productivity but don't necessarily create jobs in the same way as new factories and machinery.

The Intangible Economy

Investments in data-processing equipment or software upgrades, which make up the single largest chunk of corporate spending over the last few years, tend to be job killing, at least in the short term. This can change when workers are able to use the technology to increase their own productivity. But a positive outcome is possible only if education and skill levels stay ahead of the pace of technological change. Sadly, in many parts of the United States, education levels have fallen woefully behind the digital revolution. This divide is part of the reason behind the twenty-year disconnect between rising productivity and falling incomes. Companies can do more with less, but the number of workers with the skills to leverage technology to their own advantage isn't keeping pace. (There are other headwinds, too, like the decline of unions and the suppression of collective organizing efforts.)

This problem has become even more pressing post-Covid-19. The number of new business applications actually rose by 20 percent in the United States during the pandemic. But most of the businesses being started were digital, not physical. Investment in "intangibles" such as licenses or patents does represent innovation, and it can enrich the owners of that "intellectual capital." Of all the ways in which companies can have an impact on the economy—from wages and the taxes that they pay, through the consumer surpluses they generate with cheaper prices, to negative externalities such as environmental spillovers—the one that has grown most sharply over the past twenty-five years is investment in intangible assets such as technology, software, and patents. This is up by 200 percent. It makes companies more productive, but it is also associated with jobless recoveries in the short to midterm—a significant political concern.[14] Once again, we see a trend that supports the owners of intellectual capital—that is, the Anywheres as opposed to the Somewheres, the latter of whom tend to pay the price for jobless recoveries.

Consider the period before and after the 2008 financial crisis. Between 2007 and 2009, according to an analysis by the Carlyle Group, the share of intangible assets as a proportion of total fixed investment spending rose by 7.5 percent. Carlyle predicts that spending on intangibles may rise by 11 percent over the next couple of years as the work-from-home revolution erodes the importance of physical assets. So far, so good for knowledge workers or those starting an asset-light business. Not so good for the average laborer.[15]

"If Apple acquires a license to a technology for a phone it manufactures in China, it does not create employment in the U.S., beyond the creator of the licensed technology if they are in the U.S.," says Dan Alpert, a financier and professor at Cornell University. "Apps, Netflix and Amazon movies don't create jobs the way a new plant would." You can see these shifts playing out in the key corporate stories of the day. As manufacturing behemoths such as General Electric scale back and struggle, technology groups have risen and enriched themselves. The largest of them spent a whopping $115 billion buying back their own stock in 2018, making them by far the largest beneficiaries of Donald Trump's tax cuts—a great irony, considering how Trump liked to position himself as being tough on Silicon Valley.[16]

Trump was never about "making America great." He was about

himself and the asset-owning class. Biden, for his part, is actually trying to reboot the U.S. industrial base. So far, a big part of that has been about reshaping the narrative, moving it away from a half century of neoliberal received wisdom—but narrative matters. Before any of the changes of the Reagan-Thatcher revolution took shape in the real world, for example, a new narrative was formed about how the economy worked and for whom. This is what's happening today. In June 2021, the head of the president's National Economic Council, Brian Deese, gave a speech laying out "a vision for a 21st century American industrial strategy—a strategy to strengthen our supply chains and rebuild our industrial base across sectors, technologies and regions of this country." Deese pointed out, quite correctly, that industrial policy isn't new—rather, as we've already learned, it's an essential part of U.S. history. But the need for it is compounded by the fact that we are at a unique economic inflection point today, with the speed of technological, climate, and geopolitical change requiring more public-private coordination.

The Biden administration laid out a plan to build more supply chain "resilience"[17] by using the purchasing power of the federal government (and its allies) to drive private-sector investment into four key areas: semiconductors, large-capacity batteries (like the kind used in electric vehicles), rare earth minerals needed for electronic devices and most tech equipment, and key pharmaceutical ingredients. (Remember the pandemic headlines about 80 percent of key pharma needs passing through China?) It was a truly historic shift, a return to industrial policy in a way we haven't seen for decades—one that, as Deese put it, rests on the fundamental belief that creating more shared and equitable growth is necessary not just for the economy but for saving liberal democracy. "The stakes could not be higher," he says. "In the face of persistent cynicism, skepticism and doubt, we need to show that smart public investment can help unleash innovation, unleash the capacity of our private sector, and deliver strong, resilient, and inclusive growth—and it must show that our democratic system of government can serve working people in this country better than any other form of government."[18]

It's a worthy goal, and a massive one. The United States' success in meeting it will depend on finding a way to bridge the gap between conventional globalization à la the mid-nineties, the sort of ring-fenced fifties economy that no longer exists, and a Hobbesian world of the thirties in which trade wars led to real wars. Selling "Buy American" to Americans is one thing. Selling it to the allies who will be needed to create the alliances and frameworks for the twenty-first century, and more demand for U.S. business, is another.

The Red/Blue Divide

At the same time that they do that, politicians of both stripes will also have to court those at home who've been on the sharp end of globalization. Winning over these people will be crucial for the future of any long-term industrial policy in the United States. During my trip through the Carolinas with Bayard Winthrop, I heard from many of these people, the "Somewheres" who needed jobs where they lived, not where technocrats imagined they should. On one day, I visited a cotton gin in Enfield, North Carolina. There, I met Kathy Sparks, the middle-aged woman who managed the facility. I felt I knew her almost immediately. I had grown up with so many women like her: hardworking, proud, kind people who just wanted a fair shot, the sort of women who might have babysat me when I was a child and who now worked at the checkout counter of the local Walmart while cobbling together one or two other gigs to earn a living.

I watched her work alongside four Latino men on her team, all throwing raw cotton into large metal bins by hand while machinery droned so loudly it was hard to speak. As the cotton was ginned, compressed, and weighed, Sparks used a handheld calculator to measure its value down to the cent. "That's four hundred and two dollars and eleven cents," she said, pointing to a three-by-four-foot chunk representing what seemed to me quite a substantial effort for that money. Sparks and the men on her team seemed close. This underscores another issue that red state Americans feel resentful about:

the idea that they don't understand or want diversity in their communities. The truth of the matter is that white women like Kathy have far more daily contact with people of other races and ethnicities than I do as a high-end knowledge worker at a global business newspaper, where the vast majority of employees are white, male, and extremely well educated. Winthrop chatted with Sparks about the operation and then insisted she send him size information for everyone in the factory, so he could send them free apparel. She nodded, but as he walked away and I caught her eye, she smiled and said, "He knows I won't do it."

This attitude of quiet pride on the part of people who live and work like Kathy Sparks is something those who craft trade policy are often not in touch with. We exist, after all, in a cognitive meritocracy in which IQ is valued much more highly than EQ (emotional intelligence) or most physical abilities. Those who want to succeed are incentivized to use their heads. Neither hearts nor hands get quite as much exercise, and we are all the poorer for it. The coronavirus pandemic has, of course, briefly illuminated how essential other types of workers (nurses, caregivers, delivery drivers) can be. But while we laud these professions on the signs we post in our windows during quarantine, it's clear who society's winners really are: highly educated or, at least, highly credentialed global elites, the sort of people who crunch numbers, trade stocks, program software, write newspaper articles (like me), and speak fluently in the officious and all-too-often emotionally distant patois of their breed.

These elites represent a new ruling class who may be even more toxic than the hereditary upper crust who came before them. Harvard philosopher Michael Sandel's 2020 work, *The Tyranny of Merit,* looks at how meritocratic striving is undermining social cohesion and liberal democracy. According to Sandel, who focuses mainly on the United States, the American Dream of being able to bootstrap your way to success has become a myth. It used to be that you could make it if you studied hard enough. Now it's much more likely that you can make it if your parents can afford thousands of dollars in admissions test prep or hire a counselor to beef up or even fake a CV good enough to secure you admission to an Ivy League college.

It wasn't meant to be like this. Meritocracy was supposed to be better than the restrictive social structures of the past, when family and social ties determined outcomes. Over the past several decades, as traditional class structures in countries such as the United States and the United Kingdom began to break down, they were replaced by a new system of educational and professional advancement based on test scores, grades, and intelligence, at least as narrowly defined by IQ. Suddenly, smart working-class kids from anywhere could become part of a meritocratic elite. Or, at least some of them could, in theory.

But there was a dark side. As British sociologist Michael Young observed when he coined the term in his prescient book of dystopian fiction, *The Rise of the Meritocracy* (1958), for all the flaws of the old class system, its moral arbitrariness prevented both elites and the working class from believing they somehow deserved their position in life. Both Goodhart and Sandel, who blend facts, analysis, and opinion in eminently readable nonfiction, cite Young's work and are clearly inspired by his viewpoint. As Young puts it, "Now that people are classified by ability, the gap between the classes has inevitably become wider. The upper classes are . . . no longer weakened by self-doubt and self-criticism." Meanwhile, members of the working class must judge themselves not by their own standards—in which traits of character, experience, common sense, and grit are often as important as test-based intelligence—but by the standards of the meritocratic elite. And without the appropriate degrees, professional qualifications, or opinions sanctioned by their educated overlords, they are all too often deemed unworthy, and thus feel so, too.

It's this contempt that has led to the politics of our moment. The people who work in the Carolina textile industries may or may not have liked Donald Trump personally—most I spoke to didn't—but they liked the idea that someone was finally challenging the notion that globalization was an unfettered good. They know better because they live in places where it hasn't been. "If you ask me what

President Trump did for us on trade, I say I love it," said Bryan Ashby, fifty-one, who, with his brother, Hunter, forty-eight, runs Carolina Cotton Works, an apparel-finishing company in Gaffney, South Carolina.

CCW employs 188 people who dye and finish the cloth for American Giant's T-shirts and flannel lines. "It's about time that we start putting everyone on an even playing field," added Page Ashby, Bryan and Hunter's father and CCW's founder. "For years, the textile industry has been a pawn item for China, or Vietnam or Africa—'If you let us sell Coke, we'll let you ship clothes over here duty free,'" he said, pithily parodying the bet that neoliberal U.S. policy makers placed long ago. This seemed to make sense at a time when everyone thought China would get freer as it got richer and that there would be enough high-paying service jobs for all Americans. "They [the Trump administration] get the hypocrisy of that."

Despite his previous history of working on Wall Street and in Silicon Valley dot-coms, Bayard Winthrop has plenty of sympathy for this position. Though he lives in a townhouse in San Francisco with his jewelry designer wife and three children, he, too, feels the anger that powers the United States' polarized politics. "The reality is that there is a huge section of this country that feels like D.C. is filled with a bunch of self-serving careerists who've never built anything in their lives, and that Wall Street is filled with people making ungodly amounts of money, and Silicon Valley is just totally disconnected from everyone, and all of them are trying to tell me how to live my life," he says. "If you put aside all the stupid, offensive shit that Trump does and says, the fact is that he is posing some big, important questions about how we are thinking about our labor pool, our trade agreements, NATO, and our international relationships."

Winthrop's views reflect his upbringing, which cut across the blue/red divide in the United States. The patrician name comes from his father, a Connecticut financier who divorced Bayard's working-class Massachusetts mother and paid for his son's high-end education but not much else. As the family struggled financially, the juxtaposition between prep school and hardscrabble home life left Winthrop with a keen awareness of the hypocrisy rife among U.S. elites. "There's this bizarre combination of incredible wealth and total moral clarity. If they spent any time in one of our factories," he says, "they'd understand just how much gray there is."

The Ashbys represent some of that gray. Like the cotton farmer Jerry Hamill, they have been hurt by President Trump's tariffs, which have increased input costs for things such as dyes, fibers, and yarns from China and India. Yet they remain supportive of Trump, focusing on the administration's overall message around trade. They say they are glad Trump pulled the proposed Trans-Pacific Partnership, because increased competition from markets such as Vietnam would have flooded the market with even more low-priced Asian competition.

Proponents of the deal say that this is irrelevant, because the United States should no longer be concentrating on low-end industries like clothing. They also say the TPP would have helped give the United States a leg up in the high-end service industries of the future. But this doesn't change the fact that, over the past few decades, things have been tough for apparel makers in the United States. In 1991, U.S.-made products represented more than half of all clothing bought in the country; today, according to the American Apparel and Footwear Association, it is about 3 percent. CCW has survived by diversifying and picking up business from weaker players, but also by selling the idea that staying closer to its end customers can improve quality and efficiency.

This means engaging in intense problem solving with customers (which include not just American Giant but other U.S. brands, such as Major League Baseball and the fast-food chain Chick-fil-A) in a way that remote suppliers in China or Vietnam are less able to. Over the course of several months, American Giant prototyped rapidly to adjust the variety of cotton and finish to achieve the quality Winthrop desired at an overall cost that allowed him a comfortable margin. When the cost of shipping back and forth to L.A. became too expensive, CCW introduced Winthrop to still more local suppliers

with whom American Giant already had relationships and negoti-
ated further economies of scale. This effort took place in a larger
ecosystem rather than one in which each company was simply mind-
ing its own balance sheet. "I liked that he wasn't looking to just
squeeze a penny, but to make something of quality," said Page Ashby.
"We hadn't heard that before."

Quality over Quantity

This sentiment dovetails with the debate about how shareholder-
versus-stakeholder capitalism is growing in America. While larger
public companies are under pressure from global investors to bolster stock prices with buybacks, private companies can put capital
where they will. And because many of their owners tend to live and
work near their businesses, they are more likely to invest locally.
Private companies such as American Giant and nearly all its suppliers have more leeway to invest locally in things such as factory upgrades and R&D, which are crucial to keeping costs down and
productivity up. Research shows that private companies invest more
than twice as much in such things as public companies of similar
size operating in the same sector.

American Giant doesn't disclose its sales figures, but Winthrop
says the company has had compound annual growth of roughly
50 percent over the past five years and expects that rate to continue
in 2022. This is testament to the fact that at least some of Winthrop's customers are willing to shell out $108 for a hoodie made
entirely in the United States, against less than half that for a similar
Gap product. The items, sold almost entirely online, have a cult following among coastal trendsetters who appreciate the superior
manufacturing quality that adds a touch of luxe to a typically utili-
tarian garment. ("You're going to see American Giant?" said my
New York City teenager when I told her about the trip. "Can you
bring me back one of their black hoodies?")

In November 2019, the company expanded its repertoire by
launching the first mass line of jeans made entirely in the United

States in more than a hundred years. "On a piece basis, it's of course cheaper to make things in China or Vietnam," says Winthrop. "But we can now make our garments just as cost-effectively here, because we're more productive, we are selling directly to customers online, and we are cutting out currency fluctuations, transportation, and the mistakes you have to deal with in a more complex supply chain."

The "selling directly to customers online" part is key. One way to offset higher labor costs is by eschewing brick-and-mortar retail spaces for online sales. Another is to become expert at understanding customer behavior. One of the fastest-growing parts of Winthrop's company is the data analytics department. "We have a very clear understanding of what a customer will do after thirty days, ninety days, a hundred eighty days, and so on." Yet, while American Giant's customers may be loyal, ultimately their numbers will be limited by the $108 price point. This is partly why Winthrop is speaking with some major U.S. clothing brands to explore future economies of scale.

Fewer Workers, More Software

The most successful manufacturing businesses these days, no matter the size, tend to be the most high-tech. Much of Winthrop's investment goes into things such as data analytics, software, and new machines. And his best suppliers are those with the most cutting-edge equipment. Anderson Warlick, the CEO of Parkdale Mills, a second-generation, family-owned business in Gaffney, South Carolina, which gins cotton and spins yarn for American Giant, says he puts roughly 75 percent of the company's profits back into the business. "Almost all of it goes into new technology"—so much so that there are hardly any human workers in his company's factories. The plants are a model of efficiency, cool and clean and full of the latest German equipment. Rows of tiny red buttons on the machines show when they've self-diagnosed that they need maintenance. "We're actually launching a project involving autonomous vehicles to move stuff around the plant," says plant manager Robert Nodine, who's been with the company for seventeen years. "A lot of what we're getting rid of is stuff that people don't want to do anymore anyway—heavy lifting, the real physical labor."

Manufacturing will grow, but it will look very different in the future than it did in the past. In 2021, I caught up again with Bayard Winthrop and found out that, thanks to a major uptick in sales post-lockdown, his company was on track to surpass its pre-Covid-19 sales growth goal of 35 percent this year. This was a big surprise. Aside from tourism and commercial real estate, it's hard to imagine an industry that has been as devastated by Covid-19 as retail. In the United States, malls are empty. Big brand chains, from J.Crew to Brooks Brothers to Lord and Taylor, have filed for bankruptcy. In the work-from-home era, people still buy things—computers, home office equipment, and wine—but apparel isn't top of mind. New York City lost thirty thousand retail salespeople alone. When even Anna Wintour, the editor in chief of *Vogue* magazine, has been at home in her sweatpants, who is thinking of dressing up?

Of course, if you are selling leisure wear, it is a different story. After minimal sales in March and April 2021, American Giant's revenues, according to Winthrop, were up 60 percent in May and a whopping 80 percent in June. Part of it was luck—being in the right category. "If we were selling suits or formal wear, I doubt things would be looking good," he says. But another part was about the kind of shopping people increasingly want to do—not for Fast Fashion, but for Slow. In the wake of the pandemic, there has been a huge uptick in desire for his localized "Made in America" products and for those that can prove their sustainability and document the security and quality of their supply chains (no garments made by slave labor, children, trafficked people, etc.) Like many brands favored by younger shoppers, American Giant and its suppliers take great care with regard to recycling, emissions usage, and other sustainability metrics. In the Parkville plant, for example, "pepper trash" (leftover material from raw cotton) is sold and used as cattle feed. "We know the farmers we work with on that directly," notes the plant manager, who shows me the piles of pepper trash. The need to recycle and combat emissions at a local level will be yet another driver of businesses like this one.

Aside from sustainability, the most important factor in success for any company, no matter how big or small, will be the ability to leverage digital technology. This is a key point as it relates to the debate over what will be global and what might remain local. While an influential report on globalization compiled every year by the logistics company DHL and New York University's Stern School of Business found that the level of overall globalization has been slipping since 2018 and dipped farther following the pandemic, not all categories behaved the same. While money and trade flows were down, flows of data and digital information were sharply up—cross-border internet traffic jumped about 48 percent from mid-2019 to mid-2020, twice the annual rate seen in the previous three years.

That's very good news for anyone investing in those "intangible" digital assets like data, software, telecom capacity, and broadband infrastructure. These are the things that will allow twenty-first-century small businesses to catch up with bigger ones and access global demand while still supporting local jobs and suppliers. "If smaller towns and semi-urban areas have to depend only on local demand, there won't be many new jobs," says University of Chicago economist Raghuram Rajan, who has advocated for the devolution of economic activity away from a few large cities and toward a broader number of communities. "However, if the menu can include national or global demand, there are plenty of possibilities. Technology helps connect the local to bigger markets. Online platforms allow small enterprises to advertise and sell niche products across the world."

At American Giant, technology investment is the core component that has allowed Bayard Winthrop to bridge the gap between his higher U.S. labor costs and a larger, national market of people who want locally made goods at scale. Selling mostly online necessitated top-notch data analytics, which is where much of his capital expenditure goes. This reflects a broader prepandemic trend toward higher earnings, innovation, and enterprise value among the most digital-dependent corporations. It's a shift that has, of course, been put on steroids since Covid-19 struck. "For companies that can leverage the power of intangible assets," says McKinsey author Sven Smit, "it could be a golden age, one in which you can start to see a kind of distributed globalism, in which smaller companies and smaller communities can build a creative class and grow the pie."

This, in a nutshell, is the big challenge and opportunity for the American manufacturing sector. Even if the sector comes back to the United States, many traditional jobs will be done by machines. There will be roles at the top: developing the software and sensors to connect the burgeoning internet of things that will enable plant managers to track the entire life cycles of products in real time. There will be some jobs at the bottom, too—but even there, the skill levels required will be higher as the industry becomes more mechanized. To succeed as a worker in this new world, it will probably be better to make the *equipment* that makes a hoodie, rather than the hoodie itself.

Either way, bringing manufacturing back to the United States will require some things that private business can't do on its own: educational reform, tax reform, and smart industrial policy. By that, I mean not picking winners, but building infrastructure and creating a supportive environment for investment with more than just tax cuts. Top of the list should be using federal budgets (and, ideally, state budgets, too) to create demand. The electric vehicle business provides a useful example of how government demand can shift the shape of an entire industry. A report released in the fall of 2021 by the Economic Policy Institute showed that if government subsidies and procurement were used to increase the share of parts sourced domestically, the automotive industry would add another 150,000 good jobs by the end of the decade. Without such encouragement, it will lose about 75,000 (thanks in part to the fact that China and countries in Europe have done more to encourage the electric vehicle industry domestically and, thus, own more of the supply chain).[19] This is perhaps the biggest lesson from my road trip. While Winthrop has made his own business work, there's only so much any one company, or industry, can do. The public sector has to play a role.

Yet, for the past forty years, we've lived in a world in which business has become global while politics has remained local. Business complains that the government fails to train a twenty-first-century workforce or support industries of the future even as it lobbies for tax cuts that make it harder to do those things. Multinationals can fly thirty-five thousand feet above local concerns, putting capital and jobs where it is cheapest to do so, but, eventually, that becomes a zero-sum game, as the political climate, not only in the United States, but in much of the world, makes quite clear. Business leaders and politicians alike realize that they must do something to buffer the communities hardest hit by globalization. Not everyone can be a coastal knowledge worker. People in the Carolinas scoff at ideas like universal basic income; as numerous studies on unemployment show, work matters. And even in a globalized world, place matters, too. "We've given the world a lot of materialistic things," says cotton farmer Jerry Hamill, referring to the throwaway consumer culture of recent times. "But some good things have gone away."

Jobs for people like him are one of them. While both policy choices and business trends will support more local production in areas like apparel and agriculture, and the slow and steady rebuilding of industrial ecosystems will create their innovations and growth, it's unlikely we will see a return to the number of jobs the manufacturing sector generated in decades past. Where will the extra jobs come from? Most likely from healthcare, childcare, and education, a triumvirate of sectors that has become known as the caring economy.

CHAPTER 11

The Caring Economy

For about ten years, I lived in London, working as a foreign correspondent for an American newsmagazine. During that time, I gave birth to my two children, both of whom were delivered in National Health Service hospitals. While many Britons complain about the NHS, I found the British system of national healthcare to be a small miracle, at least in comparison to the American way of healthcare. For starters, everything began with our local clinic, which was a couple of blocks away from our apartment. Anytime we had a cold or needed a checkup, we simply headed over for a walk-in visit. Visits were prioritized in a collective way, based on the NHS's "cradle-to-grave" mission: babies, the elderly, and the very sick got priority.

My own prenatal care began with a local midwife, a cost-effective way to deal with what is, after all, the very natural and usually uneventful state of pregnancy. All visits were done in the same place, my local hospital (in my case, St Mary's in Paddington), which was particularly convenient when it was discovered that I had a heart murmur that required a cardiologist's check. To get that, I simply walked down the hallway.

When I went into labor, I had a private room, provided by the state, and top-flight care. But about forty-five minutes after delivering a healthy baby, I was shuttled into a shared room with about twelve other new moms and their families, all separated by curtains. It wasn't the easiest place to sleep, but it made tremendous sense from an economic standpoint. The money was being thrown at ensuring healthy deliveries rather than at posh comforts and long post-delivery hospital stays, as is the case in the United States for those lucky enough even to have insurance to pay for a birth.

In Britain, priority was also given to excellent but relatively inexpensive community-based postnatal services, like a nurse who came to my home to check in on me for two weeks after the birth (which helped ensure good nursing, thus saving money for both the mother and the healthcare system itself), and to a neighborhood play-and-parenting group that created a built-in support network that any first-time parent desperately needs.

Most rich countries decided decades ago that it made economic, political, and moral sense to provide a basic level of care for all their citizens, rather than offering everyone the "option" of the most cutting-edge medical treatments, whatever the cost. Yet Americans still hold fast to a myth that "choice" is what makes the U.S. system fair. No matter that fewer and fewer people have any kind of choice at all. Medicare, the United States' version of the NHS for the elderly, provides a basic safety net, but it also subsidizes a variety of costly and questionable treatments, money that could be better deployed by offering more people more basic services. We refuse to have a real debate about the fact that resource-draining end-of-life care constitutes the largest share of medical spending. In short, in U.S. healthcare as in most areas of our society, we prioritize the individual over the collective. It is the American way. But it's no longer sustainable.

Demographics as Destiny

The United States has by far the largest healthcare costs in the world—about twice the level of most other developed nations. Our healthcare system is roughly the size of the entire French economy, but we don't have the outcomes the French do; in fact, when ranked against other rich nations in terms of things like infant mortality, maternal mortality, and health in young people, the United States comes in toward the very bottom of the list. A large chunk of the costs within the system go to end-of-life care rather than anything preventive. (What's more, all the heroic efforts at the end can't offset the fact that the American life span is, for the first time in decades, declining,[1] thanks in large part to lifestyle issues like obesity, alcohol and drug use, and workplace stress.)[2] The title of an Institute of Medicine/National Research Council report on the U.S. healthcare system sums up the problem: "U.S. Health in International Perspective: Shorter Lives, Poorer Health."[3]

And yet, thanks to demographic shifts, we're going to need ever more from our failing system. For decades, the United States has enjoyed the economic and geopolitical fruits of its high birth rate. Between 1990 and 2010, U.S. fertility levels were higher than the average for any developed country except Israel, Iceland, and New Zealand. Now the U.S. birth rate is on track to plunge below the recent trend rate of Europe. In 2007, just before the Great Recession, the U.S. total fertility rate (the number of births a woman is expected to have in her lifetime) was 2.12. By 2019, just before Covid-19 struck, it had fallen to 1.71. Now the latest data from the Centers for Disease Control and Prevention show that the total fertility rate dropped to a record low of 1.64 in 2020, roughly the rate in Europe over the past five years.

So much for what economist Nicholas Eberstadt dubbed America's "demographic exceptionalism." For decades, the U.S. birth rate helped buoy growth, which is a function of people, productivity, and global status. But according to a new report by the Global Aging Institute (GAI) and the Terry Group, all the factors that once propelled U.S. outlier fertility (from immigration and religious faith to long-term economic optimism) are now in decline. What's more, the behavioral patterns of a younger generation are unlikely to shift this. Richard Jackson, head of the GAI and author of the report, notes that the Millennials "are a scared generation," having come of age during the financial crisis of 2008 and the Covid-19 pandemic. "People tend to have children when they feel they are economically secure," he notes. For young people loaded with debt and unable to buy homes or start families on the same timetable as their parents, that feeling is elusive. The decline in birth rates has been particularly steep among Hispanics, which Jackson and some other experts attribute to a feeling of economic and cultural vulnerability, which was certainly heightened during the xenophobic years of Donald Trump's presidency. Net immigration, which bolsters the overall fertility rate, has declined to roughly half of what it was five years ago, even as the cost of having a child and caring for it has increased.[4]

The United States isn't alone here. Birth rates in most countries are falling, Baby Boomers are aging, and the need for care of all sorts (from healthcare to elder care to childcare) is increasing. But in many countries around the world, that shift comes with an unexpected upside: we are at the cusp of a new and extremely localized boom in caring jobs. And unlike the jobs of the past, most of these jobs won't be outsourced or done by robots. Care involves high touch, and that means care jobs could be a key part of connecting wealth and employment in forgotten communities. What's more, some experts estimate that these jobs could become an even bigger driver of wealth than old-line manufacturing jobs were, producing as much as double the wealth for local communities.

As Charles Goodhart and Manoj Pradhan explore in their book, *The Great Demographic Reversal,* the balance of power between labor and capital is all about supply and demand. Over the past four decades, the full entry of Baby Boomers into the workforce, including a growing proportion of women, plus the rise of China and other emerging markets created the largest positive-labor supply shock ever seen. Given this, a weakening of labor relative to capital was inevitable. Jobs went abroad, and the global economy decoupled from national labor markets. More workers came into the market, and pressure on wages increased.

Now all these trends that depressed wages for forty years are largely tapped out. China is becoming not only more insular, creating its own protected domestic economy and its own regional supply chains, but also older. Like the United States, it will be increasingly reliant on its own resources and will have to depend on its own shrinking labor force to supply the care services for an increasingly larger population of elderly people. It's a problem that Japan and parts of Europe have struggled with for some time. But now it's coming to the rest of the world. As Goodhart and Pradhan put it, "The concerns about the world running out of jobs are likely to be unfounded—there will be more than enough jobs looking after the old!"[5]

Technology and the Human Touch

The shift couldn't come at a better time. For the last hundred years or so, manufacturing has been the middle-class job creator, fostering more innovation and productivity than other sectors. But as manufacturing continues to automate, it will never again create as many jobs as it once did, regardless of how supply chains are organized, or if they reshore. Meanwhile, as Goodhart and Pradhan put it, "the process of globalizing the manufacturing supply chain has itself achieved most of its gains, which means there will be fewer tailwinds from globalization just as aging problems mount globally."[6] Coping with the end of laissez-faire globalization and the dramatically aging world population is going to require both more workers *and* more technology. As the authors rightly conclude, rich countries "will need all the automation that we can get in the rest of the economy in order to raise productivity adequately…[and] to compensate for that which will be lost to caring for the aging population."

This future presents both a huge challenge and a tremendous opportunity. Over the next decade or so, automation, artificial intelligence, robotics, and other forms of cutting-edge technology will replace not only many manufacturing jobs, but plenty of white-collar work, too. There are already many examples of machines outsmarting even the smartest humans. Think of AlphaGo, the computer program developed by Alphabet's AI subsidiary DeepMind, which beat the world champion in the ancient Chinese game of Go a few years back. It won not by playing better than the human, but by playing in a way that only a nonhuman could. "Almost as remarkable as its overall victory was a particular move that AlphaGo made—the 37th move in the second game—and the reaction of those watching," writes economist Daniel Susskind in his book *A World Without Work: Technology, Automation, and How We Should Respond.* "Thousands of years of human play had forged a rule of thumb known even to Go beginners: early in the game, avoid placing stones on the fifth line from the edge. And yet, this is exactly what AlphaGo did in that move." One expert watching called the move "beautiful." Another said it made him feel "physically unwell."

These reactions encapsulate the common and diametrically opposed views of a world in which machines will do many of the things human workers do today. Netscape founder and venture capitalist Marc Andreessen has famously quipped that "software is eating the world" and that, in the end, there will be only two types of people left: those who program the machines, and everyone else. This is a serious shift. Just as we've already seen the replacement of many factory jobs by technology, so our generation will experience major technology-related job displacement in middle-class work, from sales to retail to back-office functions, accounting, and so on. Inequality, unhappiness, and social unrest could be a result—that is, unless we redesign our economic and technological systems to focus not so much on commerce, but on care (healthcare, education, and childcare), the need for which will grow exponentially. As MIT economist and globalization expert Daron Acemoglu puts it, "We need technology in service to human labor, not the other way around."[7]

The Care Revolution

First among those areas is healthcare, which is, quite simply, where the jobs of the future are. According to the U.S. labor department, over the next decade, home health and personal care is predicted to grow faster than other job categories. While roles in remote diagnosis (so-called telemedicine) can be outsourced to lower-wage countries such as India, most healthcare positions are close-contact jobs that cannot be sent abroad. No wonder six of the ten jobs that the U.S. Bureau of Labor Statistics expects to grow fastest in the next decade are in nursing, therapy, and care services. Many of those care jobs will be at the bottom end of the socioeconomic spectrum, and workers will need more skills and training to achieve the productivity gains that will ultimately help raise wages.

Raising both the quality of work and the pay of that work has been a key priority for the Biden administration. The president has proposed bolstering not only healthcare for the elderly, but also childcare for families. The White House has pushed investment into skills training for those care workers and has backed the employment of unionized workers, many of whom are women of color. Indeed, with the right policy prompts, the shift to the caring economy would actually help decrease inequality and increase racial justice in the United States.

As CEA economist Heather Boushey put it to me during an interview in 2021, "If you want to address living standards of American workers and families, you have to address the care economy, full stop, and on both sides of the ledger. If you're a working parent, you need childcare. You need early childhood education. You need to make sure that if your aging or disabled loved one needs care, they have those services. All of those are inherently expensive, and it's hard to dial back how much you pay." Indeed, only so many four-year-olds can be watched by one adult. "If you're going to pay that adult a living wage, there's a limit to how much individual families on their own can pay. When you look closely at the math on that in the care economy, it really does speak to an important need for public subsidy of these services, which are actually the backbone of the twenty-first-century economy."[8]

The economics of care is being reconsidered in this context—care isn't so much a cost as an investment, not just in the economy, but in human life itself. For example, research shows that when the unemployment rate falls, people tend to leave jobs in nursing homes because they are so low-paying and difficult. "Workers can find other jobs at the same skill level, and that means that deaths actually go up because you have this increasing turnover [in care facilities]," says Boushey. "That's a real consequence of these low wages."

That's the downside. But there's a huge economic upside to better care. The McKinsey Global Institute estimates that better health outcomes could add $12 trillion to global GDP in 2040—much of that from improving the productivity of existing workers who suffer from health issues or have care responsibilities. The broader social benefits of better health—from greater family stability to less mental stress to improved education outcomes—could be as much as $100 trillion by 2040.[9]

That's a huge economic multiplier effect, particularly when compared to manufacturing, the old economic driver. For every dollar invested in manufacturing, you typically see about two dollars of additional economic benefit in a community. With healthcare, you might see double that—as much as four dollars of additional economic benefit, which would be reaped by everything from transitioning from expensive systems of intervention to a more preventive system (as the United Kingdom and other European countries have), shifting to community-based provision of care (less hospital and ER care and more of the neighborhood clinic system one finds in, say, London or Paris), to increasing healthcare efficiency through new digital technologies and better training of workers.

Take the issue of technology. While telecom and banking industries spend 6 to 8 percent of annual revenue on IT, the healthcare industry allocates a mere 4 percent.[10] While most hospitals and doctor's offices use electronic health records, their systems often aren't compatible. Consider the effect that just the implementation of a national electronic health record system could have economically. During Covid-19, for example, every hospital in the country was required to report daily how much of their resources were tied to Covid-19 (how many patients were in the ICU or on ventilators, for example). And every hospital had to do it by hand, because there is no national reporting system in place.

The United States is woefully behind in this respect. In the United Kingdom, for example, a digital system tracks everyone's medical history (and unlike the information tracked by private healthcare surveillance companies in the United States, the tracking is transparent and totally available to patients and healthcare workers). This means that if someone living in London who was allergic to penicillin were to have an accident and go into the hospital in, say, Manchester, the doctor there would automatically know not to prescribe certain medications. In places like Finland and Estonia and Israel, prescriptions are done completely online, emergency responders have access to medical records in advance of taking patients to the hospital (saving time and lives), and individuals are notified in advance when they need to make appointments for physicals or ob-gyn visits. What's more, individuals own all their own data and can transfer it seamlessly wherever and however they like, to whichever private companies or physicians they wish to use.[11]

It's fair to say that even a small boost in digital productivity could make a huge difference in healthcare provision for Americans. But getting there will require more than just technology. It will mean focusing ever more deeply on the human side of the equation, which, if we aren't careful, may well be lost in the race to improve technology. The "professionalization" of jobs such as nursing, which now require more credentials and computer skills, have improved neither outcomes nor job satisfaction. This is due largely to the way professionalization has decreased the time spent on low-status tasks such as caring (which, it should be said, have traditionally been done by women) and increased the amount of bureaucratic paper-pushing. This burden falls disproportionately on middle- and lower-income workers. While digital technology has allowed high-level knowledge workers increased autonomy in their jobs, those with routine or semi-routine jobs have seen it decrease radically. This increases stress—think about Uber drivers or Starbucks baristas whose lives must be organized around algorithmic scheduling software;[12] or about nurses, teachers, and caregivers who have to spend more time inputting administrative data than actually working with human beings.

Clearly, the secret sauce is in combining IQ and EQ, technology and human touch. Healthcare has already become a hub of higher-end jobs for women and minorities. For women without a college degree, for example, the healthcare sector is more likely to provide good jobs than other areas like retail or food services. For working-class men, that's not yet the case—in part because they are less likely to accept care work as an alternative to manufacturing or construction. (This is a cultural issue and one that is particularly pronounced in more conservative areas of the country.)[13] But assuming that such prejudices eventually give way to the reality of the job market, could healthcare become the new manufacturing, a meaningful source of middle-income jobs and a generator of innovation? Experts such as Harvard economist Gordon Hanson, who studies the interaction between labor markets and their location, say that it could. "The areas of the country that bounce back better from downturns tend to have good universities or healthcare complexes that can function as job engines," he says.

It may seem fanciful to imagine that a nursing home or childcare center could ever be an innovation hub in the same way as a big factory or R&D complex. Yet some already are. A prime example would be the Cleveland Clinic, a nonprofit medical center that integrates clinical and hospital care with research and education. The subject of a Harvard Business School case study, the clinic has become a national and international job creator but also a hub of cutting-edge innovation in areas like drug and device development and medical procedures. This it has achieved in large part by leveraging Big Data, digital platforms, and robotics, but also by working in a cross-disciplinary way inside and outside the clinic, prioritizing personalized care.

Consider programs like Lifestyle 180, which focuses on weight loss. Obesity and its side effects, from joint and back trouble to diabetes and cardiovascular disease, carry huge costs—around $109 billion, roughly 20 percent of the entire country's yearly medical expenses.[14] Treating obesity is expensive, but preventing it is much less so. Using a system of digital tracking and monitoring—

the Cleveland Clinic invested in digital medical records way back in 2001 and, three years later, became the first major hospital to begin compiling an annual health outcomes report—the hospital puts patients through their paces with everything from cooking classes to yoga, all while treating high blood pressure, diabetes, and associated illnesses. All this is done on a local campus, which brings together resources from inside the hospital and draws on local businesses.[15]

This model, known as Cleveland Clinic Integrated Care, puts the patient at the center of care, which necessarily involves de-siloing various departments in the hospital (which typically have their own budgets and fiefdoms). It also gets doctors involved in the business side of healthcare. The clinic shares treatment prices, research, and outcomes with all doctors, who typically wouldn't be aware of the costs of the treatments they prescribe. (In one case, after the hospital circulated a note about how five-dollar silk sutures, rather than four-hundred-dollar staples, could be used to close wounds, the use of staples in operations fell from 91 percent to 10 percent.)[16] This has radically increased cost savings—margins rose from 1 percent in 1999 to 7 percent in 2014—productivity, and job creation. It has also resulted in entirely new innovations for the treatment of problems like back pain, sleep disorders, headaches, and substance abuse and in multiple new business offshoots. Cleveland Clinic Innovations, the clinic's commercial arm, has founded some seventy companies, all of which have bolstered the economy not only of the city but of the entire region. The hospital provides 45 percent of care in its county and 25 percent in the broader Northeast Ohio region. Over the last decade, it has begun exporting the model to places like New York, London, Dubai, and the Caribbean.[17] That's exactly the kind of "innovation hub" that manufacturing operations of large industrial companies used to provide.

This combination of technology and high-touch innovation in the caring professions could not only raise wages and productivity, but also lower prices—something that is desperately needed, given that the only kind of inflation we've seen in the U.S. economy in the last several decades has been in things like healthcare, education, and housing. Indeed, there is a historical connection between healthcare inflation and a lack of wage inflation. Runaway healthcare prices, a result of fragmented, inefficient, and completely opaque and asymmetric markets—is there anything else one must pay for before knowing its cost?—mean that health benefits now make up about 20 percent of total worker compensation (up from 7 percent in the fifties) in our employer-led system. It follows that as healthcare prices go up, wages will go down and inequality will rise, especially given that healthcare costs are a much lower percentage of a top earner's salary than of a lower-income worker's pay. According to research by the Kaiser Family Foundation, this is exactly what has happened since 1999. In a 70 percent consumer economy, this is big news. If individuals and companies alike have to spend more on healthcare, they'll have less for iPhones, new cars, and paying down student debt.[18]

Conversely, if technology-driven productivity gains created lower costs for healthcare delivery, but a higher wage for the workers delivering care, that would be a huge win-win for communities. Instead of a paradigm in which you have industrial jobs going abroad because wages there are cheaper, and where lower-quality disposable goods come back into the country to paper over the fact that the labor share of the pie isn't growing, a well-run caring economy could deliver just the opposite: good jobs *and* cheaper prices.

It would be a benefit not only for workers, but for business, which has to shoulder a huge burden by providing health insurance for a private system. This puts U.S. companies at a disadvantage to competitors in most other countries, in which healthcare is considered a public right and run via a national system. Employer-funded healthcare in the United States isn't even a decided choice; it's an accidental system. It came into being during the Second World War, when wage freezes and 1.9 percent unemployment forced the government to allow companies to offer fringe benefits like healthcare in an attempt to attract workers. In 1943, the Internal Revenue

Service ruled that employer-based healthcare should be tax-free—and we were off to the races. According to economic historian Melissa Thomasson, the percentage of the U.S. population covered by employer-led plans rose from 9 percent in the forties to 70 percent by the sixties. It hovers around two-thirds today. Yet tax advantages do not offset the fact that healthcare benefits, according to consulting firm Mercer, are now the second- or third-highest compensation costs for American employers, right after salaries.[19]

Even if the country's healthcare spending weren't double that of most of the rest of the rich world, with far worse outcomes, this would still be a competitive disadvantage in a global marketplace in which rivals don't have to shoulder that burden. No wonder, then, that business itself is now agitating for a change in healthcare. Healthcare emergencies and the costs that result are the number one reason for personal bankruptcy in the United States. Rising prices mean that health benefits now make up about 20 percent of total worker compensation (up from 7 percent in the fifties), which is a contributor to wage stagnation. This is, in turn, a key reason economic growth in the United States isn't higher. Already, corporate conglomerates such as the Healthcare Transformation Alliance, a group of forty-six large companies, have tried to tackle this.[20] By pooling resources, they've been able to negotiate better deals with drug companies, doctors, and hospitals and to focus care on prevention, much of it done at the local level.

In lieu of a national system that offers care at the local level à la the United Kingdom and other European nations, such efforts may be the best way to improve U.S. healthcare, the costs of which are, as Warren Buffett put it in 2018, a "hungry tapeworm" eating away at our economic growth and prosperity. But they are by no means the only such headwind. As Buffett told me in an interview in 2012, the single-most-important thing that this country could do to improve productivity and growth would be to free up female labor. Happily, the way to do that is to generate more and better local caregiving jobs.

The Childcare Conundrum

Women in the United States are better educated than men, and yet they remain underemployed and underpaid relative to men. Women also took an extra hit during the Covid-19 lockdowns. They generally did a disproportionate share of the extra childcare and household work and were also more likely to be laid off or to drop out of the workforce. This came on the heels of a decade following the Great Recession in which female employment suffered relative to that of males. Budget cuts at the federal, state, and local levels of government resulted in 601,000 lost public-sector jobs between June 2009 and May 2012. Two-thirds of those jobs were held by women. University of California, Berkeley, professor Laura Tyson, a former head of the Council of Economic Advisers under President Bill Clinton, believes that's one big reason women over age forty-five began leaving the workforce in droves. "If you've been a decently paid teacher or a public administrator or a welfare worker your whole life and you see what's available now, that might well make you leave the workforce."

Not necessarily by choice, either. Women are now a greater percentage of the long-term unemployed than they were a couple of years ago, in large part because they are squeezed in between an inadequate system of external care and their own life/work balance issues. They thus have much to gain from greater investment in the care economy. As Jay Powell, the U.S. Federal Reserve chair, said recently, the United States "used to lead the world in female labor force participation, a quarter-century ago, and we no longer do. It may just be that [our childcare] policies have put us behind."[21]

Anyone who has spent time looking for an affordable nanny or had to resort to some of the more extreme daycare options available in our 24/7 society knows what Powell is talking about. In her book *Squeezed: Why Our Families Can't Afford America*, Alissa Quart, the head of the Economic Hardship Reporting Project, wrote about visiting an all-night nursery in New Rochelle, New York. At Dee's Tots Childcare, kids are dropped off and picked up around the clock.

It's a perfectly pleasant place, candy-colored and brimming with cheerful-seeming kids, some of whom will be tucked in by caregivers as Dad starts the night shift as a manager at a local big-box store, or they will eat a group breakfast as Mom scrambles eggs for others during the morning rush at McDonald's. While it's good that Dee's exists to provide flexible care to harried families, it's hard not to wince at the grim self-sufficiency of the children as they help one another put on their pajamas and celebrate two A.M. birthdays with others on the night shift. All this is due to the fact that their parents are trying to cope in the globalized, computerized, "always-on" business world in which 40 percent of Americans work nontraditional schedules driven by algorithmic efficiency.[22]

It's just one of the challenges for a new class of Americans whom Quart dubs the "Middle Precariat." These people, who range from professors to nurses to caregivers to lawyers, aren't destitute—they have some means, hold a degree or two, and have made decent life choices. And yet, they are struggling to stay ahead in an economy in which technology is exerting a deflationary effect on everything (including wages) except the things that create a middle-class life. There are PhDs who are drowning in student debt, journalists plunged into near poverty because of the cost of giving birth in a hospital, and out-of-work middle-aged graphic designers paying thousands of dollars to for-profit universities that won't get them a job. These tales of a falling-down middle class reflect a felt experience of anxiety that is often lost in data-driven tales of recession and recovery. Unemployment in the United States may be at a near-twenty-year low, but Gallup figures show that most Americans work more than forty hours a week (the average is forty-seven), and 18 percent work more than sixty hours. Thanks to a lack of adequate social safety nets, better industrial policy, and/or better connection between the public and private sectors, more and more responsibility for coping with a fast-changing labor market and a more bifurcated economy has been left to the individual.[23]

The Biden administration has pushed, with post-Covid-19 stimulus and various legislative proposals, to shift that dynamic by bolstering the childcare portion of the caring economy. The core economic idea is that by improving childcare, economic growth overall would improve, since more well-educated women might choose to stay in the labor market, and those providing care itself would see their industry professionalized and wages go up. Changing the care market is a slow process, but it helps to have people in power who have firsthand experience with care work. Consider Treasury secretary Janet Yellen, the daughter of a family doctor. Yellen grew up in the working-class neighborhood of Bay Ridge, Brooklyn. There, she saw her dad treat dockworkers and factory laborers from his home office—they paid two dollars or nothing, depending on whether they had a job—something that informed her belief that "economics should be about caring for real people."

Yellen had another very personal experience with the economics of the caring economy after giving birth to her only child. Classical economic models held that because childcare required few formal credentials and there were many available workers, employers would drive down wages for these positions. But after going through the experience of hiring a caregiver for their son, Yellen and her husband, economist George Akerlof, wrote a much-talked-about paper explaining why firms do not always cut wages, even if there is an excess of labor. "When you hire a nanny, the question you ask yourself is, 'What's the best for my precious child?' And do you really want someone who feels that your motive in life is to minimize the amount you spend on your child?" Answer: no. Their paper showed that when human emotions are valued, salaries can be far higher than expected. Rational Mom and Dad, it turns out, may behave quite differently from Rational Man.

This insight will become more and more relevant given the move to all things digital and the way in which that move will dislocate knowledge workers higher up the food chain even as it creates more demand for "essential" workers of heart and hand.[24] Heather Boushey sums up the challenge of the post-Covid-19 care crisis this way: "We have done a lot to make sure that those who are out of work and those who are hit hard by the pandemic have had the economic support they need through the direct payments, the enhanced UI [unemployment insurance] benefits, and the expansion of the child tax credit so that families have what they need." But, she adds, "the bigger question moving forward is, how do we put in place the structures to make sure that we are paying people better, especially at the lower end of the labor market, closing that inequality gap? If we implement the agenda that the president laid out . . . we'll be doing things like subsidizing the cost of childcare and home health-care, expanding the child tax credit, making sure that we have all these things that are focused on the immediate but also built for the long haul. They're not helicopter drops of money. They are investments that will put us on a more wage-oriented growth path. This is not a stimulus package. This is a package to shift our economy onto a saner, more stable path."

Back to School

Part of this will mean rethinking how to train a twenty-first-century workforce. We will need, for example, an education system that is geared to teaching people entirely different skills—empathy, for example, and emotional intelligence. It's a paradigm shift, but the human race has been here before. In ancient Sparta, education was about training for war, not work. Solutions like universal basic income, often offered by Silicon Valley, won't work, as any number of interesting historical scenarios prove. (Neither 1930s factory workers on benefits nor Native Americans who receive government funding have thrived.) Just giving people money isn't a life hack; you have to give them meaning, too.[25]

Even for elites who don't have to worry about costs, life on this hamster wheel is oppressive. One Harvard admissions officer quoted in Michael Sandel's book on the meritocracy worries that those who spend their high school and college years jumping through hoops of high achievement wind up as "dazed survivors of some bewildering life-long boot-camp." Even their fancy STEM degrees are no guarantee that software won't someday do their jobs. I've always believed that this may be part of what motivates the young white elites marching with people of color as part of the Black Lives Matter movement. They are protesting injustice, but they are also protesting against a system that pits all against all and rewards a smaller and smaller group of people at the top. No wonder there are signs that Millennials are starting to eschew credentials and earning power for more personal time. The Great Resignation that followed the Covid-19 epidemic, for example, was about many things, but it was in part about a large group of people reconsidering their priorities and work-life balance.[26]

While there is no silver-bullet solution for how to fix our higher education system and the culture it too often inculcates, I'd argue that we already have a number of excellent new models for this plank of the caring economy. For starters, there is a growing revival of the secondary school vocational programs that liberals unwisely threw away in the seventies over worries that poor kids would end up as welders or nurses and richer ones as, say, opinion columnists. (On this point, I would just note that the master plumber in Brooklyn who recently helped renovate my basement makes more than I do at the *Financial Times,* and nurses are seeing some of the highest wage increases in recent years.) Getting rid of such programs was a huge mistake, given that about two-thirds of the jobs being created in the United States don't require a four-year degree—and yet so many young people are taking on crippling debt to try to obtain one. A study by the think tank Demos found that the average student debt burden for a married couple with two four-year degrees was $53,000 and resulted over their lifetimes in an overall wealth *loss* of $208,000.[27] Meanwhile, a highly trained machinist with two years of college education could easily make a higher starting salary than a four-year political science graduate from a second- or third-tier university.

As we have already learned, there are models for secondary and tertiary education in several states and countries that aim to bridge the gap between high school and college, debt and employability. What's more, with the rise of online education, not every student has to accumulate debt to pursue a four-year degree. Education can and should be sliced and diced to suit the needs of individuals. We can, after all, read Melville on our own, or watch a Harvard professor teach *Moby-Dick* via streamed lectures or mass-participation online courses.

I think this will become more the case in the future, as college credentialism becomes seen for what it is: class signaling. (Research by Nobel laureates like Joe Stiglitz and Michael Spence has proven that most of the value of a high-end degree is in the social capital it provides.)[28] As JPMorgan Chase CEO Jamie Dimon, whose company has made multimillion-dollar investments to boost vocational training and support for community colleges, once put it, "Having gone to a four-year liberal arts college, I know just how worthless a college degree is sometimes." While it's fair to say that going to Tufts and Harvard Business School was probably a leg up for him, it's also true that his company (like others, including Google and IBM) is pushing back against credentialism in certain areas by offering more jobs to those without four-year degrees. It's also very fair to say that there are many paths to a good job. In fact, I can't tell you how many CEOs I speak to who say they'd rather find a bright kid with grit and train them on the job than hire someone with an expensive four-year degree, lots of debt, and no marketable skills.

As secondary and higher education continues to evolve, I suspect the common thread in all the new models will be to graduate students with practical skills, but also with the core liberal arts, math, and science background that takes them beyond a particular "vocation" and into a larger world of Enlightenment values. That's key, given that we don't really know what the jobs of the future will be. We simply know that they'll require both technological skills and emotional intelligence.[29]

They also need to focus on serving local communities and connecting educators and job creators in individual cities, creating robust regional pipelines of talent that serve both business and society. Such connections between public schools and the private sector remain scattered, limited, and haphazard, as illustrated by a 2014 study from the Gates Foundation, BCG, and Harvard Business School. The study interviewed superintendents of the ten thousand largest U.S. school districts about business involvement in their areas. While 95 percent said business was in some way involved, in most cases the involvement was limited to writing checks. Only 12 percent of superintendents saw business as deeply involved in their local communities—a missed opportunity given that this and other research has found hugely improved student outcomes in areas with deep business participation.

Education for the People

It's not only students and employers who need to rethink the twenty-first-century mission of education, but universities, too. In fact, it's a financial necessity for them. Even before the arrival of the novel coronavirus, 30 percent of colleges tracked by rating agency Moody's were running deficits, while 15 percent of public universities had fewer than ninety days of cash on hand. After many campuses shut down due to Covid-19, revenues were further reduced, and endowment investments plunged. Moody's downgraded the entire sector from stable to negative. In one 2020 survey, 57 percent of university presidents said they planned to lay off staff in the coming years. Half said they would merge or eliminate some programs, while 64 percent said that long-term financial viability was their most pressing issue. Of course, while those at the very top, with huge endowments, did just fine, many institutions in the middle (particularly state-run colleges) have been very hard hit, reinforcing existing class structures.

It's very likely we are about to see the hollowing out of America's university system. Top U.S. universities are world class, but the system as a whole is in trouble. Cost is a big part of the problem. Some schools, particularly second-tier private institutions, will go under, as many did in the 1930s Depression.[30] Those that survive will be either affordable or even free public institutions tightly moored to particular neighborhoods, à la the programs just described, or they will be top-flight Ivy League schools and other brand-name universities that churn out degrees for the global elite. Institutions in the middle will have to do some real soul-searching about what the twenty-first-century mission for educators can and should be.

On that score, some of the actions being taken by Carnegie Mellon University, in Pittsburgh, are instructive. "Universities like ours are beginning to look homeward," says Illah Nourbakhsh, the head of the newly founded Center for Shared Prosperity and a professor of robotics at CMU, which like many of the country's most prestigious engineering and liberal arts schools has long been focused more on the global than the local. That's now changing, as both the university leadership and regional businesses realize that if they aren't perceived to be addressing issues of inequality, social justice, and inclusion in their own communities, they'll lose both trust and funding. The new center, underwritten by a grant from Pittsburgh-based Heinz, is dedicated to addressing inequalities and social issues across the Western Pennsylvania region, which has been hard hit by the shift from manufacturing to a digital economy. CMU technologies have made plenty of graduates rich. The plan now is to use university resources to solve community problems, spinning off ideas and even new businesses in which the city itself would have an equity stake. "Around the world, a relative handful of major research universities, Carnegie Mellon among them, are literally inventing the future, with significant global benefits and impacts," says Grant Oliphant, director of the Heinz Endowments. "But too rarely are local communities and complex social needs the real beneficiary or even the focus of the knowledge, creativity and wealth creation flowing from these extraordinary engines of innovation. We wanted to see if Pittsburgh could reinvent that paradigm."[31]

It's starting to. Nourbakhsh's Community Robotics, Education and Technology Empowerment (CREATE) Lab and a group of new community partners have, for example, used Big Data sets and computing power from the university to demonstrate how high rates of mortgage application denials and sharply increasing rental prices were impacting the ability of vulnerable populations to achieve housing stability in Pittsburgh. Nourbakhsh and the center team then partnered with local housing and community nonprofits to build an app, RentHelpPGH, to help locals find legal assistance and equitable mortgage programs, identify and combat "algoracism," and identify and stop mass-eviction events. As the program builds scale and commercializes, the same nonprofits would benefit from its growth—just like venture capitalists do. "I think, at core, we are trying to answer this existential question of 'What is university about?' Are we serving all of society? Are we serving the communities we exist within? Or are we just serving ourselves?"[32] It's a question that many industries and institutions, particularly in the most globalized area, technology, will soon be asking themselves.

CHAPTER 12

Chip Wars

Technology has made the world ever more interconnected. While trade in traditional goods and services has been flat or falling for the last few years, and while migration is becoming harder thanks to politics and pandemics, digital trade and information flows have boomed. Between 2005 and 2016, the use of cross-border bandwidth increased by a factor of forty-five.[1] The shift to all things digital during Covid-19 dramatically sped up the already speedy shift to the digital economy, putting 60 percent of the world economy online by the end of 2021.[2] Internet traffic among countries is now growing at twice the prepandemic rate.[3] In many ways, the virtual world is becoming ever more globalized.

And yet, technology is also ground zero for a coming deglobalization in the physical goods on which the digital world depends: silicon chips. Semiconductors power many of the things we need in our daily lives: our computers, our phones, our televisions, our appliances. But within the next decade, they will power even more. By 2030, electronic components will account for half the value of a car[4] and for much of what makes a smarthome smart. As the world becomes ever more automated, and also more focused on climate change, not only will most of the physical goods around us become "smart," but chips will increasingly power the utilities and industrial services we can't see, but on which our very lives depend—everything, from the electrical grid to our water and energy supplies to what we buy in grocery stores or in the shopping mall, will be controlled by networked systems connected to the internet, all of which will be running on silicon. Already, they are crucial to the running of our financial and healthcare systems and of many parts of our critical infrastructure and national security, like weapons systems, telecommunications, and satellite technology. Semiconductors are what enable us to work and study from home, order our groceries, call a taxi, and keep track of our bank accounts. And yet, supply of them is found mainly in a handful of places in the world, most of them in East Asia. The vast majority of advanced chips are produced in Taiwan. According to a recent Boston Consulting Group report, "About 75 per cent of semiconductor manufacturing capacity, as well as many suppliers of key materials—such as silicon wafers, photoresist, and other specialty chemicals—are concentrated in China and East Asia, a region significantly exposed to high seismic activity and geopolitical tensions. Furthermore, all of the world's most advanced semiconductor manufacturing capacity is currently located in South Korea (8 per cent) and Taiwan (92 per cent). These are single points of failure that could be disrupted by natural disasters, infrastructure shutdowns, or international conflicts, and may cause severe interruptions in the supply of chips."[5]

Taiwan in particular is key. A single company, Taiwan Semiconductor Manufacturing, dominates the physical production of chips globally, accounting for more than half the market. While many U.S. companies (AMD, Broadcom, Nvidia, Qualcomm, and Xilinx) develop software and designs for chips, they operate with a "fabless" business model, meaning they contract out the chips' production. Indeed, 80 percent of production of the final product takes place in Asia,[6] a mere 12 percent is in the United States,[7] and the rest is in Europe. Taiwan Semiconductor Manufacturing Company produces the chips crucial to the production of nearly every electronic device. A company like Apple, for example, could no longer produce its products without TSMC chips.[8] A single company in a single tiny country in one of the most geopolitically contested parts of the world has become the choke point for the digital economy.

Why did this happen? Because the United States largely gave up on chip production over the last few decades as part of the neoliberal outsourcing model in which companies off-loaded factory production (which is expensive and lower margin) abroad and kept the high-value "knowledge work" at home. The only leading pure-play silicon chip foundry in the United States, the GlobalFoundries operation in Malta, New York, is owned by the Emirate of Abu Dhabi, via a sovereign wealth fund.[9] This reflects the pressure of Wall Street on real businesses in the United States, particularly from the nineties onward. The cost of a state-of-the-art chip-fabrication operation is around $12 billion. The ultraviolet lithography tool necessary for making top-line chips can cost $150 million. Once a factory is built, the costs for maintaining it are extremely high—the White House estimates that it could cost $20 billion over the course of a decade to run a foundry operation.[10] What's more, until quite recently, the chip business has been volatile. The need for semiconductors tended to rise and fall based on whatever new Apple or Android gadget was being launched next. This was yet another risk factor in building a physical chip-making business—with demand inconstant, things could boom one year and go south the next.

This meant that semiconductor makers who tried to stay in the physical business were penalized by Wall Street: the more they invested, the more their share prices fell. Meanwhile, the move to fabless production, which was exponentially less costly and seemingly less risky, was rewarded. In lieu of state support for the industry, or any sort of industrial policy to create consistent demand, there was simply very little financial incentive for companies to make real chips instead of only outsourced designs for chips. It's the same sort of financialized thinking that resulted in the outsourcing of the industrial base in the United States and many Western countries. Shareholder value stipulated that as long as a company's stock price was going up, everything was fine—even if its very ability to make crucial goods was being given up to strategic adversaries.

Throughout the last few decades, all this sounded good in theory to financial analysts and policy makers. Why *should* the United

States make cheap chips when we could make the more expensive software that powered them? But reality is different, as we experienced during the Covid-19 crisis, when supply shortages due to disruption of production in Asia because of the pandemic derailed the economy. Suddenly, risks that had been hiding in plain sight became all too evident. The problems began in mid-2020, when automakers warned that chips crucial to the production of cars were in short supply and that vehicles could become scarce. Auto parts suppliers began canceling orders at the same time that a rapid shift to work from home increased the need for computing power and chips, which further squeezed supply. By 2021, things were worsened by a major fire at a Japanese semiconductor plant that accounts for 30 percent of the microcontrollers used in cars and by a drought in Taiwan, which further strained semiconductor production, which requires copious amounts of water.

This domino effect cost the automotive industry $110 billion, but the knock-on effect went far beyond that. The automotive industry is one of the most labor intensive in the country, and it supports jobs and business in many other industries (everything from textiles to energy to electronics and logistics). The disruption in Detroit not only resulted in layoffs in the car business, but had a serious impact on 169 other industries.[11] By the summer of 2021, chip shortages had begun raising the prices of all consumer items, contributing to a spike in inflation that led to market volatility and ultimately forced the Federal Reserve to raise interest rates, setting up a risky economic dynamic that many fear will lead to recession.[12]

One might say that these were accidental factors that couldn't have been predicted—a pandemic, fires, drought—except they could have. Everyone knows about "black swans," extreme, one-off events that are impossible to predict. Think of the assassination of Archduke Franz Ferdinand triggering the First World War; or of the 1987 stock market crash, which set a record for one-day price slides. But what about the risks that are all around us? The sudden shortage of crucial semiconductors was a perfect example of this, and it was by no means the only one within the last few years. Efficiency seemed good on paper, but it led to many, many risks that came with huge financial and, in many cases, human costs. Was anyone really surprised, for example, by the Colonial Pipeline ransomware attacks that happened in 2021, creating a shortage of natural gas that left millions of people in Texas without heat or hot water? Or the Camp Fire in California in 2018, which killed eighty-five people and began because PG&E knowingly failed to replace old and failing parts in its 18,500 miles of power lines because of the cost of doing so?[13] Or Hurricane Katrina, the 2008 financial crisis, the Fukushima nuclear disaster, or the Covid-19 pandemic? These are the types of risks that many people, from policy makers and business executives to activists and journalists, saw coming way in advance. The particulars of these "gray swans" may have been unpredictable, but the events themselves were not.

If there is one thing that the Covid-19 pandemic brought home with crystal clarity, it was that seemingly disparate issues (climate change, supply chain disruption, inflation, financial instability, inequality, and nationalism) are in fact intricately related. Add in increasing digital connectivity, and you have what complexity theorists would refer to as an "infinite" problem rather than a series of finite issues.[14] These types of risks can't be handled alone or even definitively. They require a step change in thinking about the nature of the underlying problem.

When thinking about chip shortages, for example, you need to think about not only our neoliberal assumptions regarding which industries and what kind of work has value but also the details of antitrust policy—why did one supplier become so big?—and about the uneven playing field in trade and government subsidies. Many Asian governments, for example, support chip production and other kinds of strategic technologies in ways that the United States and Europe traditionally have not. Consider, for example, rare earth minerals, which are crucial to the building of everything from engines to airplanes to defense equipment. China controls 55 percent of their supply and 85 percent of processing capacity.[15] The United States used to keep reserves of such materials as part of its National

Defense Stockpile program. But at the end of the Cold War in 1991, sources of supply previously behind the Iron Curtain became available to Western manufacturers, as did more Asian labor. Stockpiles were reduced, and jobs were outsourced. At the time, China's economy was 6 percent the size of the U.S. economy. This kind of "efficiency" model didn't seem high risk, and Western businesses turned a blind eye to environmental and labor violations involved in the mining of rare earth materials and the production of component parts abroad (risks that Wall Street, too, preferred to ignore).

Meanwhile, the Chinese government focused, as a matter of strategic priority, on capturing such markets. While the United States operated under "free-market" principles, the Chinese subsidized the acquisition and production of crucial minerals and the high-end products they depended on while preventing foreign players from entering and controlling its own market in such areas. Between 1992 and 2020, the United States, Japan, and the European Union successfully challenged China's export quota on rare earth materials as a trade violation, through the World Trade Organization. Yet penalties didn't change the fundamental dynamic of free-market capitalism and state capitalism existing in different spheres. During this period, the United States lost at least seven rare earth production facilities, and its reliance on imported materials for the production of strategic materials grew from twenty-one products in 1954 to fifty-eight products currently. These are the items that fuel not only the economy, but national defense. And yet, the United States is almost completely reliant on foreign suppliers for them.[16]

This of course prompts us to pose another question, one regarding national security and supply chains, particularly as they relate to strategic technology and chips. What if Taiwan were annexed by China at some point, as many people in the defense and security community believe it will be? What would the geopolitical and global economic ramifications of this be? Who made the decisions that led to this incredibly vulnerable situation—or did anyone think it through in a 360-degree way? The list of concerns goes on and on. And that's just one part of the technology sector. Bring this kind of analysis to food, water, energy, finance, or the internet at large, and the spaghetti bowl of complexity grows. But one thing becomes crystal clear, at least with regard to semiconductors: the United States and most of the West have become dangerously reliant on a single tiny nation for the most important resource of the twenty-first century.

The Tripolar World

This realization has led to the first serious strategic shift away from laissez-faire globalization in both the United States and China in the last half century. In June 2021, at the same time that the White House released a 250-page report on the U.S. supply chain vulnerabilities, Brian Deese, the head of the president's National Economic Council, gave a speech calling for a "twenty-first-century industrial strategy for America" focused not on efficiency, but resilience—a strategy not about shareholder value, but about rebuilding strategic industries (in particular, semiconductors, green batteries, crucial minerals and materials, and pharmaceuticals), retraining workers, and bolstering the country's manufacturing capacity. The strategy Deese outlined would finally bring the United States in line with what most other developed and many developing countries do as part of normal economic planning: make strategic investments in high-growth technologies and use the power of government procurement to support local workers and businesses.

Beyond that, the plan aims to create more domestic and global economic resilience, in part by creating more geographic redundancy in areas such as semiconductors. And although Deese didn't say it explicitly, his speech was a clear call for an economic decoupling with China. As he put it, "Our private sector and public policy approaches to domestic production" have "prioritized short-term cost savings over security, sustainability, and resilience." Meanwhile, "the approach of our competitors and our allies has changed rapidly. We should be clear-eyed that China and others are playing by a different set of rules. Strategic public investments to support and grow champion industries is a reality of the twenty-first-century economy. We cannot ignore or wish this away."[17]

Deese's speech was a seminal moment. He spoke about citizens rather than consumers. He cited the work not of Milton Friedman, but of economists like Dani Rodrik, who have for years questioned the benefits of unfettered globalization and who have pushed for more public-private coordination of resources. He announced major investments in education and infrastructure. He said that the U.S. government would start to "Buy American" whenever it could. And he made it clear that producing things, not just ideas, was once again a priority for the United States. "We have to rethink the balance between competitiveness and cost versus resilience," he told me in an interview following the speech. "The resilience of a supply chain is more valuable in a world in which we've gone through these shocks and we've seen the destruction of value that can come if you have a very low-cost, just-in-time supply chain that is not resilient [to risks]."[18]

It's not an overstatement to say that making U.S. supply chains resilient in the face of risks, be they climate related, geopolitical, or simply unpredicted, is now the Biden administration's number one economic priority. This will inevitably lead to more reshoring of crucial industries. In an interview in mid-2021, Brian Deese told me that the White House was in multiple conversations with American CEOs about the topic, particularly as it related to workers. "We're starting to see an interesting shift where businesses across the board see having a trained workforce at the ready [in the United States] as something that is a key ingredient for their success." This means rebuilding the most strategic industries to employ them, something that the Biden administration is now pushing via the $250 billion U.S. Innovation and Competition Act, which was passed by the Senate in June 2021 and earmarks $52 billion to support the production of U.S.-made chips.

Both Samsung and TSMC have launched new factory capacity in the United States, and Intel has, for the first time in a decade, decided to go back into the business of actually making all its own chips from scratch, rather than relying in part on a fabless manufacturing model. As Intel CEO Pat Gelsinger put it, "The majority of leading-edge foundry capacity is concentrated in Asia, while the industry needs more geographically balanced capacity," not only for business security but also for national security. This is something the Department of Defense has been stressing for years; in fact, DoD has always required its own supply chains to be filled by domestic and allied suppliers whenever possible, but its demand isn't enough to sustain a chip business. As McKinsey chair James Manyika, who has advised various administrations on supply chain issues, puts it, "Size of demand for domestic production matters, especially in industries where there are scale and learning curve effects"—such as semiconductors, which are made far more cheaply in Asia not only because of labor costs, but because the process of making things over and over again (the learning curve effect) actually improves efficiency.

The United States is indeed trying to create more demand for domestically fabricated chips via guaranteed federal procurement of supplies not only in DoD, but throughout all government functions, just as it did for semiconductors in the 1950s and '60s. Indeed, some within the defense community and on the progressive left (which wants the United States to lead on cutting-edge clean tech, which might also create semiconductor demand) would like the U.S. government to leverage its own procurement processes to force larger chunks of the private sector to Buy American when it comes to chips. The idea would be to ensure that any company that wanted to do business with the government focused on resilience rather than efficiency as the core of its business model. This would necessarily mean much more localized production and consumption of goods. Supply and demand would be closer in order to ensure seamless production and delivery in a more turbulent era. In the past, this might not have been so easy, given the pressures of shareholder capitalism. But as the semiconductor industry fuels not only electronic devices, but every area of the economy, supply-and-demand dynamics are becoming much less volatile. "The shift to the internet of things will make it a lot easier for the industry to justify investment," says Don

Rosenberg, the former chief counsel of Qualcomm (a company crucial to the chip wars, as we will learn in the next chapter) and Apple and a veteran of Silicon Valley for a half century. "We lost our semiconductor industry because of a failure to invest for the long term. Now that may finally be shifting."[19] If different regions have a continuous need for chips, it suddenly makes much more sense for them to create their own chip-making industry.

It's not only the United States, but also Europe that is developing a more localized chip supply, which will ultimately lead to a more localized supply chain for all things digital. The European Union's Digital Compass plan, which is similar to some of the U.S. moves around industrial policy, aims to double chip output by 2030. Europe also wants to double its market share in global semiconductor production to 20 percent in that same period. U.S. officials hope that this will be the beginning of a transatlantic decoupling from China on technology, with the United States starting to work with allies like Japan, South Korea, and even the Netherlands (which, via conglomerate Philips, is an important part of the semiconductor supply chain) to create even more demand for U.S.-made chips. As Deese put it to me, the Biden administration wants to connect the dots between U.S. needs and the needs of allies by "partnering to have a more predictable supply" of crucial goods and services.

Chips are the first prong of a decoupling from Chinese supply chains and a rebuilding of the national industrial and technological innovation base, but they are by no means the only part of that shift. In 2021, the Department of Defense announced a major investment in the expansion of a U.S. rare earth element mining and processing company, the largest outside China.[20] The administration is also pushing investments into crucial pharmaceuticals like antibiotics (most of which have elements produced only in China) and large-capacity batteries, which will be crucial to the growth of electric vehicles.

Electric vehicles may provoke a kind of Sputnik moment for U.S. industrial policy. While demand for their batteries is predicted to be more than triple between 2020 and 2025, U.S. production won't even increase by a third without significant manufacturing shifts. That means shoring up capacity in batteries and securing the mineral inputs to electric vehicles, including lithium, nickel, graphite, cobalt, and other rare earth elements. The automotive industry is perhaps the single-most-crucial industry if looked at in terms of both innovation and employment, according to the McKinsey Global Institute.[21] No surprise, then, that one of the first corporate meetings taken by President Biden was with the CEO of General Motors, Mary Barra, who has committed to selling only electric vehicles by 2035.[22] As the UAW president said of the meeting during an interview in 2021, "He [the president] took a very strong position on electric vehicles. He said we had to keep manufacturing in this country. I was really happy to hear that." As Scott Paul, the president of the Alliance for American Manufacturing put it, "The package that they've put together is the closest thing we've had to a broad industrial policy for generations."[23]

This isn't an overnight process. Building a chip foundry and rewiring supply chains is a decade-long turn, and it could shift if a new administration takes a different view. But at this point, it's hard to find anyone on either side of the political aisle who doesn't think we need more supply chain resiliency at home. One of the most striking indications that even conservatives have moved on from laissez-faire capitalism came in May 2021, when U.S. senator from Florida Marco Rubio gave a speech to a closed-door Republican Study Committee lunch, arguing that the party should challenge both "the orthodoxy that the market's always right" and the assumption that what has been good for Wall Street or large multinationals has also been good for America and adopt what he called "common good capitalism." As he put it, "I'm not against big corporations. I think they're an important part of our economy. But I'm not blind to the fact that their CEOs consider themselves citizens of the world. And for them, it doesn't matter to make a billion dollars employing someone in Indiana or a billion dollars employing someone in India." The challenge for conservatives, as Rubio outlined it, was to cope with the reality that the "market outcome" could sometimes lead to an "efficient" outcome that was not in the national interest. "The market is pretty clear it is more efficient to buy basic pharmaceutical ingredients from China," he said.[24]

It's also pretty clear that making everything from scratch at a national level isn't possible or even desirable. The United States and China may in theory be able to grow their own bespoke technology or pharmaceutical supply chains, even if it is extraordinarily expensive to do so, but it would require not just national but regional demand, from partners in smaller countries. For the United States, this means making sure to loop Europe and other allies into more regionalized production chains. In an ideal world, for example, the United States and the European Union would come up with common industry standards in areas like 5G, biotech, and renewable energy, to create an even larger common market in which incremental innovation can occur, with each side making back-and-forth improvements in the most strategic industries and sharing ideas and even some intellectual property.

Working with allies on transatlantic standards for emerging technologies like 5G and artificial intelligence was actually a key recommendation in the 2019 Council on Foreign Relations task force report titled "Innovation and National Security: Keeping Our Edge."[25] The title indicates that decoupling is no longer a fringe idea, as does the list of co-signers, including private-sector folks from the finance, technology, and consulting sectors (including top brass at Alphabet, Apple, Breyer Capital, Facebook, Greylock, and McKinsey). That the CFR, traditionally the seat of neoliberal economic thinking, is now admitting that we are in a more fragmented world, one that won't reset to the nineties, and is advocating what amounts to a U.S. industrial policy speaks volumes about the sea change taking place.

The point about working with allies is crucial. Regionalism isn't the same thing as nationalism. Not every country can or should have a chip foundry, but the idea that 92 percent of a crucial industry is concentrated in one of the world's most contentious geopolitical regions isn't just bad politics; it's bad economics. Corporate concentration, as we have learned, is a key reason for everything from faltering innovation to the suppression of wages. By creating more resilience and redundancy in global supply chains, making them more regional, national, and even local, we can start to address these issues. Indeed, it's not too much to suggest that the kind of global trade shifts we are beginning to see might also function as antimonopoly policies, reducing the concentration of power in certain companies and countries and, thus, creating a more even playing field for workers and businesses in many nations.[26]

Such joined-up thinking in economic policy and foreign policy was common in the United States up until the neoliberal surge of the 1980s, a topic that journalist and Open Markets Institute founder Barry Lynn explores in his book *Liberty from All Masters,* which charts the history of antimonopoly policy and its roots in the founding of America.[27] The desire to break away from Great Britain's monopolistic trading system was a key factor that drove the American Revolution. Throughout the history of the United States, leaders used antimonopoly policy to advance democracy—it even played a role in the Civil War, as slavery was not only a moral abomination, but an unfair economic position for the South. In the post–World War II period, Washington forced large U.S. companies to share technologies with Europe to help countries like Germany and France get back on their feet. It wasn't until the late seventies and early eighties that Milton Friedman, Robert Bork, and other modern neoliberals pushed the country toward a "market knows best" approach in which there was no place for state intervention.

Of course, in most countries, such market orthodoxy never fully took hold. While consumers were the be-all and end-all in the United States, most other nations continued to prioritize not just consumers, but also workers, the public sector, and society at large. But even in the United States, the narrative is changing. As Biden put it in his July 2021 executive order, Robert Bork's forty-year-old "experiment" had "failed." In considering the harms of concentrated power, be it private or state power, the United States would in the future consider not only consumers, but "workers, businesses, farmers and entrepreneurs." By making the U.S. domestic economy stronger, the country might be better poised to help allies and shape a new system better able to balance global with local. "Our core strength as a country," and our ability to support allies abroad, "is our economic strength at home," says Deese.[28]

The New Silk Road

That's certainly the Chinese worldview, though Beijing has no worries about concentrated power in terms of achieving it. In 2019, the country made a bold move to reshore some semiconductor production from Taiwan, creating new friction with the United States, which has long had a stake in a "free" Taiwan, independent of China, while the Chinese have insisted that Taiwan be considered theirs. This shows the bigger moves afoot, as China is expanding its influence into new markets, rolling out 5G around the world, and pushing emerging-market nations into its orbit through the "Belt and Road Initiative," a re-creation of the old Silk Road route that stretches from Beijing, across Asia, and into southern Europe, North Africa, and even the sub-Saharan region. The idea is to create a new trade route that would serve China's own mercantilist needs while also building new alliances through Chinese loans and infrastructure building. (This includes everything from roads and bridges to the twenty-first-century telecom structures that would run on Chinese equipment and standards.) "Asia wants to be integrated with itself," says Dr. Deborah Elms, a supply chain expert and executive director of the Singapore-based Asian Trade Centre. This will, by necessity, create not global but regional economic blocs.[29]

It's a strategy that runs in tandem with China's 2025 plan, which aims to make the country independent from U.S. technology within the next few years. China calls this strategy its "Dual Circulation" policy, which essentially means creating a more bipolar global economy in which China will still export, but will increasingly focus on building its own domestic economy and cultivating relationships with nations within the Belt and Road orbit. In this world, the

U.S.-Chinese economic relationship would slowly but surely diminish. Already, according to Gavekal Dragonomics/Macrobond data, emerging nations represent a larger export market for China than the United States. Beijing's Belt and Road Initiative and its trade-based diplomacy in places such as Africa and the Middle East, combined with the rise of the digital renminbi, will make it ever easier for China to grow its exports to places other than the United States. China looks to dominate not just chips, but artificial intelligence, telecommunications, and even the standards on which the internet is run, making it more controllable at a national rather than a global level, which would serve the autocratic nature of governance in China.

In 2019, a team of Chinese engineers gave a presentation to the International Telecommunications Union, a UN body that governs the standards underpinning much of the digital economy. The engineers argued that the old internet had reached the limits of its use and that a new architecture should be built, one based on a Huawei network, which would give individual countries much greater control over what citizens could see and do online.[30] The idea is built upon the long-standing "Great Firewall" of China, which, as any visitor to the country knows, makes it difficult for Chinese to access censored content—think articles on the suppression of Uyghurs, or criticism of Xi Jinping, or blogs from Hong Kong protesters. But, according to a 2019 study by Freedom House, the architecture that China wants to make ubiquitous is already being exported to eighteen countries, making it easier for governments in places such as Zambia and Vietnam to crack down on their own citizens.[31]

The Trump administration tried to offset these efforts by denying Chinese firm Huawei the U.S.-made chips and software it requires for its ambitious global 5G rollout. This didn't stop China from executing a longer-term decoupling from the U.S. tech ecosystem; in fact, it only helped create choke points around chips during the Covid-19 crisis. If anything, the restrictions have only sped up China's efforts to develop its own chip industry. Meanwhile, the Chinese have been able to access things such as U.S. patents, scientific papers, and even U.S. corporate innovations. This includes ground-breaking work on artificial intelligence, some of which has been published or developed open-source. This is happening at the same time that China's own legal protections around things like intellectual property and patents have been getting stronger by some measures.[32]

This effort is very much in line with Beijing's commitment to decoupling from the United States' corporate interests and financial system, particularly in strategic areas like technology. In July 2021, for example, Chinese regulators announced an investigation into data security concerns regarding DiDi Chuxing, a Chinese-founded ridesharing company that had a very successful initial public offering in the United States. This was followed by revelations of state investigations into two other Chinese companies that had stock listings in the United States. Companies like Alibaba, which have big operations in the United States, have been targeted as part of the Chinese "anticorruption" campaigns. Beijing also banned three U.S.-listed educational tutoring companies from making a profit, a purging of Western interests in the country that many China watchers feel is only just beginning.

Beijing has, of course, downplayed these issues, insisting that they are part of China's new "Common Prosperity" campaign, which aims to reduce corruption and inequality and create more balanced growth. There is something to be said for these efforts, which have included debt reduction in the country's frothy real estate sector and a broad crackdown on domestic companies and business executives found guilty of wrongdoing. In some ways, I have to admire these efforts, particularly the way in which the government has let troubled, debt-ridden companies (like the Chinese property giant Evergrande) melt down without a bailout. By identifying problematic companies and sectors in advance of a crash and attempting to let the air out of a property bubble, China is doing exactly what the United States failed to do in advance of the subprime crisis of 2008. Likewise, sending executives who've broken securities laws to jail is a good thing. (Again, many in the West would complain that CEOs are too frequently let off the hook while shareholders and the taxpayer foot the bill for corporate malfeasance.)

Decoupling from the United States makes perfect sense for China in many ways. The world's second-largest economy should be thinking about how to create a new economic ecosystem that is purpose-built for its future. Linking local production to rising local demand is, as this book has argued, sensible for a variety of reasons. But while the Common Prosperity campaign has some merits, I'd argue that it is no substitute for liberal democracy and well-functioning, transparent markets. Ultimately, the Chinese Communist Party can and does change the rules of economic and political engagement to suit its own need for survival. Witness the recent changes in law that have cleared the way for Xi Jinping to become a ruler for life, just like Mao. Whatever economic sense the Dual Circulation and Common Prosperity plans might make, there is no obscuring the fact that, in China, the party itself remains the biggest market risk.

Western investors should think very, very carefully about what this will mean for their future and the future of the global economy. China's most recent five-year plan (from 2021 to 2025), from which the country never deviates vectorially once it has announced its goals, specifically targets domestic semiconductor production, which the country aims to make completely domestic within a decade. This will have massive geopolitical consequences. Most people I speak with in the defense and security community feel that China will at some point try to annex Taiwan because of the semiconductor issue. Even if that doesn't happen, it is hard to imagine that Taiwan will be able to operate in both U.S. and Chinese orbits indefinitely. As one telecom analyst put it to me in 2020, "What's happened in Hong Kong is fascinating and disturbing in part because it raises the question: What happens if the same thing occurs in Taiwan?" Certainly, many countries in the region are preparing for what they believe will be the morphing of a cold war into a hot one. Witness Japan's mid-2021 announcement that it would deploy defense missiles and hundreds of military personnel on the Ryukyu Islands, which sit on the southwest of the country and provide a defensive wall against China.

A Coalition of the Willing

Decoupling also presents an existential challenge for Europe. In 2019, the European Union came out with a new ethical framework for artificial intelligence, part of its attempt to carve out a "third-way" system of tech governance that can exist between the surveillance state of China and the dominance of the big technology companies in the United States.[33] But Europe's telecom market is dependent on Huawei equipment, which is cheaper than that of its competitors. As one high-level European Commission official admitted to me, "Using Huawei in 5G is a foregone conclusion." This is in large part because 2G, 3G, and 4G systems in much of Europe have been built upon it. It would be too expensive to retrofit the system to build out 5G without Huawei today.

If using Huawei does present a security risk—and I've been told by any number of Europeans and Americans in both the public and the private sectors that it does—then one has to wonder if Europe actually has control over its tech governance. Does it have the ability to defend its own liberal values over privacy and data rights in a digital world? Decoupling may, for Europe, become similar to the debate over defense in general. Even if the European Union has its own strategy, will it be able to enforce it? No wonder the Continent is trying to build more local supplies of chips.

While the United States and China are clearly heading in different directions when it comes to technology, where Europe ends up is still somewhat unclear. Trade between the European Union and China is crucial for the Continent, particularly Germany, which tends to direct policy within the European Union. Not getting Germany on board with its trade sanctions against China was one of the biggest economic errors of the Trump administration (and that's saying a lot). Both Europe and the United States share many of the same concerns about Chinese mercantilism, which creates human rights issues and an unfair playing field. Europeans are understandably frustrated by the loss of trust and cooperation during the Trump years. But the European Union's 2020 trade deal with China, which was blind to the incompatibilities between state-surveillance capitalism and European-style liberal democracy (and may yet be scuppered), was a bad move. So was French president Emmanuel Macron's embrace of Russia, a position that required backpedaling following the war in Ukraine. Given the historic ties between Europe and Asia, it's easy to imagine closer ties between the two regions (although I think that China's close alliance with Russia makes it much harder to imagine that in the short term). But that will come at a huge cost to Europe's professed values.

The solution may be a new liberal-democratic "coalition of the willing" to develop an alternative strategy for trade, technology, and digital taxation. Australia and Asian countries such as India and Japan could work together with the United States and the European Union to reshape supply chains and minimize Chinese leverage in Taiwan (where the semiconductor industry is already a point of conflict) and the South China Sea. There's already a growing alliance to do just this. In September 2021, for example, the United States and Europe kicked off the first-ever U.S.-EU Trade and Technology Council meeting in Pittsburgh, where leaders pledged to work together to create a new regional alliance around technology and trade that supports liberal democracy, human rights, and common standards on which to build a twenty-first-century economy that is not dependent on supplies (either physical or digital) from countries that don't share the same values.[34]

Perhaps most important, the United States should face the China challenge by bolstering capacity at home—in education, infrastructure, high-growth technologies, and parts of the industrial ecosystem. Manufacturing matters not as some kind of silver-bullet solution to middle-class employment—robots will do more and more factory jobs—but because owning key parts of the industrial commons is crucial for innovation. It's telling that China itself is increasingly focused on maintaining its own strategy in manufacturing even as services play a larger role in its economy. As Biden said in his first foreign policy speech, in February 2021, the United States will "work with Beijing when it's in America's interest to do so," but it will "compete from a position of strength by building back better at home."[35] This is the key difference between the Biden and Trump strategies around how to deal with China—Trump tried, unsuccessfully, to cripple China with tariffs, but he had no post-neoliberal worldview for how to make the United States more competitive. The Biden White House does, via a 360-degree shift of the economy from one driven by consumption, outsourcing, and asset bubbles to one driven far more by income, innovation, and a better sharing of the economic pie among the public, private, and labor sectors. It's the right strategy, but how much of it can be implemented will be down to politics.

China is at a different point in its own economic development; thus, its strategy involves relying much more on domestic consumption from its own citizens, which still has far to grow. The Chinese are known for their ultra-high savings rates (as high as 30 or even 40 percent in some places), the legacy of generational suffering under Mao's Communist Party and any number of previous Chinese empires. Meanwhile, the average Chinese person has become a lot wealthier in the last twenty years. Both of these factors mean that domestic consumption has room to run. In 2000, only 3 percent of the population was middle class. By 2018, that share had grown to 51 percent. China is now a nation that will consume as well as produce. Thus, it makes a lot of sense for the country to think about supplying its own people with goods and services, rather than simply exporting them to richer countries.[36]

The United States is, of course, ring-fencing its own corporate sector to a certain extent, too, vetoing new mergers or foreign investments that present any real or even perceived threats to national security. Consider the scuppering of Singaporean tech firm Broadcom's bid for a merger with chipmaker Qualcomm (the topic of the next chapter); or the seven-year export ban on China's telecom giant ZTE and limits on the use of equipment made by Huawei, a Chinese firm with ties to the People's Liberation Army. The treasury department has new restrictions on all sorts of Chinese investment in the United States and has expanded the remit of the Committee on Foreign Investment in the United States, giving it broader powers to veto not only more kinds of such investment, but even outbound investment by U.S. firms.

Assuming that the two countries go their own ways, this invites the question: Which country is best poised to win the industries of the future? The answer depends on whether you believe that a centralized or a decentralized economic model benefits innovation. China has bet on the former. While its largest tech firms (Baidu, Alibaba, and Tencent) are not officially state-run, they are heavily influenced by the Communist Party regime, which can use their technologies for surveillance and data gathering at will. The fact that privacy simply isn't an issue in China may be an advantage in the race to build artificial intelligence, which is dependent on how much data you can stuff into an algorithm. China's roughly seven hundred million smartphone users generate huge amounts of it daily.

Meanwhile, the Communist Party can, to a certain extent, direct the resources of such firms toward its own industrial policy aims, pushing companies like Alibaba to build out rural broadband, for example. The state provides support for strategic industries such as robotics, semiconductors, and electric cars. One recent study found that China has moved ahead of the United States in 5G wireless technology, which underpins the industrial internet and machine-to-machine communication that every company in every industry will depend on for growth in the next decade.

You could argue that this centralized control will be a short-term advantage, as it will help China speed the growth of its digital economy and make sure the benefits of technology are shared (via infrastructure expansion, but also through the ability of the central government to mitigate some tech-related job disruption). But you can also question whether all this will pay off in the long term. "In the next three to four years, centralization will be beneficial, but in five to ten years, you may get the problems of the brittleness of centralized control," says Arthur Kroeber, the managing director of consultancy Gavekal Dragonomics. Think of the disasters of central planning under Mao, or even the recent inability of China to dominate the automotive industry.

Despite the rising power of China, it has yet to become a center of innovation to rival the West—all but five of the world's most valuable companies are in the West (mostly the United States), as are the top five technology firms. The size of the U.S. venture capital industry is more than double that of China's. Half the world's top twenty universities are American; one is Chinese. What's more, centralized control of education and business is becoming tighter in China, which doesn't bode well for innovation.[37] As historian Niall Ferguson points out in his book *The Square and the Tower,* rigid hierarchical structures tend to be undermined by disruptive technologies. Authoritarian capitalism and the internet may not be suited to one another.

The Battle Against Big

That's certainly what Silicon Valley's hippie old guard would have argued. Yet it is important to acknowledge that the U.S. technology industry these days looks a lot more top-heavy than the garage startups of old. While some tech industry figures now argue that bigger is better, I'd point to research that shows that not only does most innovation happen in tech firms when they are smaller, but that younger companies across the board are more innovative, in part because they don't come under as much of the financially driven "efficiency" pressure as bigger public firms do.[38] No wonder fewer and fewer companies are going public. A June 2021 Organisation for Economic Co-operation and Development (OECD) report looking at the capital markets found that since 2005, more than thirty thousand companies have delisted (that is, removed their stock from a stock exchange). That's equivalent to three-quarters of today's total of globally listed firms. The number of new listings hasn't come close to matching this. Unfortunately, this means that a shrinking number of companies is using public equity markets and that the money raised there goes to fewer, bigger firms.[39] That fuels a superstar effect, increasing the concentration of wealth, but decreasing innovation.

Monopoly power threatens the benefits of a decentralized system, which is why bipartisan antitrust efforts are so important. In any case, the United States cannot compete with China on top-down approaches to competitiveness—nobody does big and centralized better than Beijing. But it could reassert the merits of a more decentralized system by curbing the so-called FAANGs: Facebook, Apple, Amazon, Netflix, and Google. Sustainable growth is about enriching the technology ecosystem as a whole, not a handful of firms. The Biden administration has shown a willingness to be more aggressive than its predecessors on antitrust. It could be that the best thing for U.S. competitiveness isn't to fight China, but to fight the FAANGs.

Like the Reagan-Thatcher revolution, which took power from unions and unleashed markets and corporations, the antitrust push around Big Tech (a push that has support on both sides of the political aisle) and the nascent but growing power of workers relative to companies may well be remembered as a major economic turning point—this time away from neoliberalism, with its focus on consumers, and toward workers, communities, and companies of all sizes (not just big multinationals) as the primary interest groups in the U.S. economy.

It will, inevitably, take us away from the Bork era by focusing on the connection between market power and wages. "When there are only a few employers in town, workers have less opportunity to bargain for a higher wage," the White House announced when Biden signed his executive order on competition in 2021. The announcement noted that, in more than 75 percent of U.S. industries, a smaller number of large companies now controlled more business than they did twenty years ago. Solutions included everything from cutting burdensome licensing requirements across half the private sector to banning and/or limiting noncompete agreements. Firms in many industries have used such agreements to hinder top employees from working for competitors and to make it tougher for employees to share wage and benefit information with one another.

This gets to the heart of the American myth that employees and employers stand on an equal footing, a falsehood that is reflected in such Orwellian labor market terms as the "right to work." In the United States, "right to work" refers not to any sort of workplace equality, but rather to the ability of certain states to prevent unions from representing all workers in a given company. But beyond the explicitly labor-related measures, the president's order also gets to the bigger connection between not just monopoly power and prices, but corporate concentration and the labor share. As economist Jan Eeckhout has shown in his work *The Profit Paradox*,[40] rapid technological change since the eighties has improved business efficiency and dramatically increased corporate profitability, but it has also led to an increase in market power. As his research shows, firms in the 1980s made average profits that were a tenth of payroll costs. By the mid-2000s, that ratio had jumped to 30 percent, and it went as high as 43 percent in 2012.

Meanwhile, "mark-ups" in profit margins due to market power have also risen dramatically (though it can be difficult to see this in parts of the digital economy that run not on dollars but on barter transactions of personal data). While technology can ultimately lower prices and thus benefit everyone, this "only works well if markets are competitive. That is the profit paradox," says Eeckhout. He argues that when firms have market power, they can keep out competitors that might offer better products and services. They can also pay workers less than they can afford to, given that fewer and fewer employers are hiring. The latter issue is called monopsony power, and it is something the White House is paying particularly close attention to. "What's happening to workers with the rise in [corporate] concentration, and what that means in an era without as much union power, is something that I think we need to hear more about," says Heather Boushey.

The key challenge is that of shifting the balance of power between capital and labor. This accounts for the emerging ideas on how to tackle competition policy. Many regard the move away from consumer interests as the focus of antitrust policy as dangerously socialist; they see it as a reflection of the Marxian contention that demand shortages are inevitable when the power of labor falls. But one might equally look at the approach as a return to the origins of modern capitalism. As Adam Smith observed two centuries ago, "Labor was the first price, the original purchase-money that was paid for all things. It was not by gold or by silver, but by labor, that all wealth of the world was originally purchased." Reprioritizing it is a good thing.

Reconnecting wealth with place requires more than simple policy and executive orders. It requires an entire shift in the nature of the global company. For a half century, corporations, particularly large multinational corporations, have been run solely for their own benefit. Their leadership has focused on share price as the measure of success, all while more and more neoliberal policy tweaks incentivized debt over equity, dividends over investment, and outsourcing over innovation at home. The United States invented the digital age. Its government and its companies have led it for several decades now. But in order for the country—any country, really—to succeed in the post-neoliberal age, it will need companies with business models that can support domestic prosperity and economic security. This will involve some very difficult choices, as we will see in the next chapter.

CHAPTER 13

Companies Versus Countries

In the United States, corporations capture the state. In China, the state rules corporations. It's a One World, Two Systems paradigm that has changed and will continue to fundamentally change the global economy. It will also change the way businesses everywhere must operate in the twenty-first century. There is no longer a single global paradigm for capitalism, but rather a collection of local and regional paradigms to which companies will have to adjust.

Both the United States and China have, in different ways, benefited tremendously from the last forty years of globalization, financialization, and neoliberal economic policy. While Chinese wages have risen dramatically and innovation has increased, the United States and many other rich developed nations have seen corporate wealth grow to unprecedented levels, even as investment into basic research and productive capital expenditures have declined across the board.

The past two and a half decades have been good for big business if looked at in terms of the sheer amount of corporate wealth created. While the size of the private sector as a percentage of OECD economies has held relatively steady since the mid-nineties, the share of companies with more than a billion dollars in annual revenue has grown by 60 percent since 1995. The big have gotten bigger, and the rich have gotten richer. But behind that headline trend, there is a great deal of geographic and socioeconomic nuance. While productivity in rich countries grew by roughly 25 percent in real terms since the nineties, wages grew only 11 percent. Meanwhile, capital income increased by two-thirds. Globalization increased growth. But in rich countries, most of the gains went to large companies themselves.

These corporate "superstars," particularly in the technology sector, have driven prices lower for consumers—think of falling prices for cellphones or flat-screen televisions. But what economists call the "consumer surplus," driven by lower prices on the products and services created by technologists, isn't fully compensating for job losses due to automation and outsourcing.[1] Tech companies are the largest and most profitable corporations in existence, but they employ far fewer people than the industrial behemoths of old. The intangible nature of their businesses—they traffic not so much in hardware as in software, data, and ideas—makes it very easy for them to offshore profits to favorable tax locales and pay less of their enormous wealth to governments as a percentage of revenue than other businesses. They also employ legions of lobbyists and lawyers to push the tech companies' own narrow interests, and they crush those who get in their way. What's good for Apple, it turns out, isn't necessarily good for the United States or any other individual country, for that matter. Corporate interests and national interests are not always the same.

Great Expectations

It wasn't supposed to be this way. Between 1972 and 1989, following the normalization of U.S.-Chinese relations by the Nixon administration, the United States and China slowly but surely began deepening their engagement with each other. For China, this was a major win—it was emerging from the horrors of the Cultural Revolution, had millions of starving peasants to feed, and needed to trade with the West in order for the Communist regime to survive. Under Deng Xiaoping, the country made ambitious market-oriented reforms and began to integrate into the global economy. The U.S.-China

Business Council, formed a year after Nixon's trip, pushed hard for closer economic relations between the two countries. Business leaders were eager to tap both cheap Chinese labor and help to develop the Chinese consumer market—both were gold dust to companies, who could reduce their costs by sending jobs to China and, ultimately, selling their products to the world's largest population.

By 1979, tariffs on Chinese imports to the United States had been reduced dramatically, and the country was granted "most favored nation" status, resulting in a surge in Chinese-made goods into the United States. The bloodbath in Tiananmen Square in 1989, in which the Chinese military mowed down some ten thousand people engaged in peaceful protests for democracy, put a fly in the ointment, forcing thoughtful people to question the conventional wisdom that China would become freer as it became richer. The country's GDP per capita had doubled, and there was a booming class of millionaires as well as a nascent middle class—and yet, there were no signs that the nation's political system was becoming any less autocratic. Indeed, the Tiananmen Square Massacre proved just the opposite. But greed created a certain willful blindness among business and political elites in the West, who argued that there would be tremendous opportunity costs for business should the United States take action against the regime for not only its human rights violations, but also its increasing theft of intellectual property, opaque industrial subsidies, and currency manipulation.

In the spring of 2000, U.S. trade representative Charlene Barshefsky argued in congressional testimony that not only would continued engagement with Beijing "advance the rule of law in China" and set a precedent for the country to "accept international standards of behavior," but it would also enrich the U.S. economy. Her view was backed by most of the heads of U.S. multinationals, who argued that the United States could not afford to be shut out of the Chinese market and should allow China entry into the World Trade Organization. China did indeed join the WTO, on December 11, 2001. And as a condition of membership, Beijing agreed to more far-reaching domestic reforms that would liberalize the economy—tariff reductions, cuts in industrial subsidies for strategic industries, and market-based governance for state-owned enterprises. The implicit bargain made with the international community was that China could indeed become richer, much richer—but only if it also became freer.

Riches certainly came to China. Between 2000 and 2017, the country's share of global trade increased from 1.9 percent to 11.4 percent. By 2013, it was the world's single largest trading nation. In 2000, the country was the thirtieth-largest source of foreign direct investment. By 2017, it was third.[2] Both in terms of labor and sales, China became a vital market for global multinationals. By 2003, 70 percent of U.S. firms said that the economic shifts in regard to China had improved their business climate "to a great extent" or a "very great extent."[3] Today, there are 626 billionaires in China, a total second only to that of the United States, which has 724.[4] Nearly all this was due to China's ability to trade freely with the world thanks to its WTO membership.

In the first few years following the entry of China into the WTO, the country appeared to be living up to its commitments. State-owned enterprises were curbed, the private sector grew, certain markets (in nonstrategic areas like consumer goods in particular) liberalized. But by 2003, centralized power began growing again, with authorities meddling in markets—between 2005 and 2008, Beijing made significant interventions in currency markets to undermine the value of the renminbi relative to the dollar, which made Chinese imports even more competitive. (These WTO violations went unpunished.) As state control grew, so did corruption and local political fiefdoms, undermining trust in the party. By 2012, revelations of state corruption and kickbacks at the highest level were making world headlines. *The New York Times* reported that Chinese Premier Wen Jiabao's family alone controlled some $2.7 billion in wealth, much of it garnered through political connections.[5]

This was happening at the same time that trust in free-market capitalism itself was faltering. Reformers were dealt a blow when the WTO failed to agree to more trade liberalization in the contentious "Doha Round" of trade talks, which were also the subject of much protest in the West, where people were beginning to understand that globalization had costs, not just benefits—serious costs, such as the loss of jobs, the decimation of communities, and degradation of the environment. Landmark research from economists Daron Acemoglu, David Autor, David Dorn, Gordon Hanson, and Brendan Price showed that "job losses from rising Chinese import competition" between 1999 and 2011 were "in the range of 2 to 2.4 million."[6] What was good for Apple wasn't necessarily good for workers in the rich world or, indeed, anyone worried about the climate impact of extremely long supply chains.

Certainly, the Chinese themselves were beginning to question neoliberal economic wisdom. Even before the 2008 financial crisis, China was beginning to hedge its bets on reform. The country's five-year plan emphasized domestic innovation and reducing the country's reliance on foreign technology. (By this time, many multinational firms were beginning to grumble about IP theft and an uneven playing field, though few of them would complain openly for fear of losing access to the Chinese market.) A U.S. Trade Representative report in 2006 concluded that "over the past 12 months we have seen an upsurge in industrial planning measures as tools of economic development by central government authorities." The time line for implementing WTO commitments had come and gone. China had failed to do what it had promised and become freer as it became richer. Barshefsky and the CEOs had been wrong.

It was a fact that became harder to ignore after the 2008 financial crisis marked a major strategic turning point and was arguably the true beginning of decoupling between the United States and China.[7] Literally the day after Lehman Brothers fell, Chinese authorities began implementing a $580 billion fiscal stimulus package channeled largely through state-owned enterprises.[8] Private investment began to weaken. While most economists agree that Beijing did a strong job of solving the short-term problem, which was how to keep growth high enough to offset massive unemployment and subsequent political unrest, there is growing unease about how the massive stimulus distorted its economy in the long term. China had become an economy driven almost entirely by state investment. In the first half of 2009, state investment accounted for 88 percent of GDP growth—a share for which it is hard to find any parallel, in any country, at any time.[9] Conservatives in Beijing, who had long been understandably wary of the excesses of U.S.-style financialized capitalism, were emboldened. Assets managed by the state more than doubled between 2008 and 2012.[10]

With the ascension of Xi Jinping to power in 2012 following the Wen family corruption scandals, the die was cast. For the first time in decades, state investment grew faster than private investment. China continued to push for trade deals with other nations, but any appetite for domestic reforms was gone. In fact, the state-owned enterprises consolidated power, and the largest players grew bigger; in 2003, only six Chinese state-owned enterprises made the *Fortune Global 500* list. By 2017, it was forty-eight.[11] Private companies were allowed to grow—by this time, China had its own Big Tech giants (Alibaba, Tencent, and so on)—but Western firms saw their market access diminished. Meanwhile, the power of Beijing was always bigger than the firms' own power, even when it came to home-grown firms. And whenever that balance seemed to tip, the party would reassert its own strength. Most recently, Beijing has taken action against the tech sector, which it views as too powerful, tightening control on Chinese internet giants like Alibaba and Tencent and putting new rules around what sorts of digital services can be offered. (The party has been particularly tough about online gaming, which it calls "spiritual opium.") Under the auspices of an anti-corruption campaign, Beijing has struck back at tech titans like Alibaba's founder, Jack Ma, who was forced to pay a $2.6 billion fine to the state.

Some would say this is warranted, particularly when you look at the power of the private sector and, in particular, technology companies in the West to secretly monitor and control much of what we do every day (the topic of my previous book).[12] Indeed, some software allows companies like Google to see not only what you're typing or searching, but where your eyes linger on the text, via the camera embedded in the computer. This data can be put together to create a kind of digital voodoo doll of me, which is then sold to the highest bidder by Big Tech firms who've grown to rival the power of individual countries in terms of wealth and users. (For example, twice as many people use Facebook's platform than India has citizens.)

Plenty of people would like to see more public-sector crack-downs on the private sector à la China.[13] But whatever your opinion on that topic, the key point here is that China and the West no longer operate in the same market system. Indeed, they never really did. Companies that operate in China and in many other state-run systems simply must play by different rules. Now, suddenly, with the supply chain fiascoes prompted by the novel coronavirus and the new cold war between the United States and China, the scrim has been lifted, and multinational businesses are finding themselves stuck in between two systems.

Stuck in the Middle

Perhaps no company represents the quandaries of the post-neoliberal political economy better than Qualcomm, the U.S. multinational that designs the wireless chips that are the smartest thing in your cellphone. It has for decades been one of the most important American firms pushing the development of the internet communications network that is set to culminate in the 5G network that will connect the much-heralded internet of things by which all electronic devices, from dishwashers to basketball shoes, will be able to record and transmit valuable user data. Companies you've already encountered in this book—Plenty, Agricool, American Giant, Viessmann, and pretty much all others—are counting on 5G to compete in this new digital world.

But Qualcomm's hands have been tied in recent years by two entities that represent the pinnacle of both private- and public-sector power: Apple and China. For the last four years, Apple battled Qualcomm on three continents in an effort to reduce the licensing fees it charges for the designs that power the chips Apple needs for all its iPhones. Qualcomm has depended on that income, which amounts to fully half its global profits, to support its research to win the global 5G competition. Meanwhile, it has in recent years gotten roughly half its revenue from China. But thanks to the tech and trade war between the United States and China, it's become harder to grow there. Indeed, the future of any U.S. tech company doing business in China is precarious, as economic decoupling between the two countries plays out.

All in all, the Qualcomm story reveals the staggering complexities of a new world in which Big Tech collides with the largest sovereign interests. Apple's wealth and power equal those of all but the largest national governments. The United States is now in a new cold war with China, and companies like Qualcomm are stuck in the middle of it. Multinational firms that have always freely done business anywhere they like are now increasingly being asked to choose between economic systems.

Goliath Versus Goliath

If computer power is measured by the megabytes of computer chips that have been increasing exponentially in accordance with Moore's Law (which holds that the number of transistors in an integrated circuit doubles about every two years), wireless capability is measured in G, whose evolution has been no less dramatic and is now set to be even more impactful as the world reaches 5G, a telecommunications power that was previously inconceivable. While robotics and AI are likely to be revolutionary on their own, the capabilities of 5G in enhancing data flows are expected to dramatically accelerate and enhance their impact. They are also likely to bring in the sweeping changes of the much-anticipated internet of things, by which every functional element of modern life will be capable of storing and transmitting vast quantities of data about its use and its users. Five-G is being heralded as a fourth industrial revolution that could boost U.S. GDP by a half trillion a year, just to start, with returns only to boom from there.[14]

It's not an exaggeration to say that none of this would have happened without Qualcomm, which, over the last several decades, has been a spectacularly innovative company, the Bell Labs of the current generation of tech firms. The Qualcomm of today is a rather faceless corporate behemoth, but it had a hero in its founder, the brilliant, self-effacing Irwin Jacobs, a professor of computer science and electrical engineering at UC San Diego. Back in 1968, Jacobs joined with some fellow MIT alums to start Linkabit, a technology company designed to deliver satellite communication services, but that instead became known as a fount of bright ideas that ended up seeding an extraordinary number of other tech firms.[15] One of them was Jacobs's own, Qualcomm, an abbreviation of "Quality Communications," a Jacobsesque touch that showed what he was all about. He started it out of intellectual curiosity as much as anything. When he got Qualcomm going with a few Linkabit colleagues in 1985, as he told a reporter later, he had no product, no business plan, no spreadsheet. Well along in his career, he just wanted to keep his hand in. "I just figured something would come that would keep me interested," he said. That something proved to be CDMA, or "code division multiple access," a patented coding system that proved key to the proliferation of cellphones, for it allows myriad cellphone users to share the relatively narrow bandwidth of any single provider's network as trillions of bits and bytes fly through the air.

Qualcomm hearkens back to the old days, when investment in innovation was a mainstay of elite firms—the company pours at least 20 percent of its revenues back into research and development of new technologies. Its portfolio of 140,000 patents, one of the most valuable in the world, was the result of all that reinvestment.[16]

Although Qualcomm largely created the world of wireless communication, that world has now come to grow on its own, leaving Qualcomm at the mercy of forces beyond its control. One problem is that as a fabless chip company, one that designs rather than makes its own chips, Qualcomm may find itself at a disadvantage in a world in which companies and countries increasingly want to control more of their own supply chain. China is spending lots of money to make sure that Chinese chip producers and designers ultimately displace Western competitors. Meanwhile, the largest U.S. companies can often use their market power to set their own terms. Qualcomm is a huge company—it had revenues of $33.6 billion in 2021—but it is dwarfed by the biggest of the big, in particular, Apple, which made $365.8 billion that same year. That size eventually enabled Apple to take on Qualcomm in a battle to lower the price it had to pay for the wireless technology that makes the smartphone smart.

Once CDMA emerged as one winner of the holy wars to make its way into millions of cellphones in the United States (and around the world, for that matter), it was deemed by the U.S. Patent Office an "essential" technology.[17] This was a high honor, but also a tremendous burden. For it meant that Qualcomm was obliged to provide CDMA chips to any U.S. communications company that asked for it. But that very obligation to sell capped the price: set it too high, and the cell manufacturer would complain to the Patent Office that Qualcomm was denying it an essential component. In effect, Qualcomm was being penalized for its core product's very indispensability.

This became glaringly true in 2017, when Qualcomm's legal troubles began. For years leading up to the litigation, Apple had a deal with Qualcomm to sell its iPhones using only Qualcomm chip designs. In addition to paying for the chips, Apple had to pay a licensing fee for the intellectual property that enabled the phones to connect to the internet through the core processor. Qualcomm gave Apple some special discounts in exchange for exclusivity, but it made quite a lot of money from the patent licensing—too much, according to Apple, although not enough according to Qualcomm. The cost of an iPhone XS in 2020 was $999. Apple paid $7.50 per device to Qualcomm, but it wanted to pay only $1.50.[18] For years, the tech giant didn't have the muscle to wage a legal war with Qualcomm and risk losing access to the technology that allowed its phones any value at all. But as it got bigger and bigger, Apple decided to start working with another chipmaker, Intel (which in the beginning of 2022 announced its first new manufacturing site in forty years, in Ohio, to produce its own chips,[19] in a move away from the fabless model, back toward more vertical integration within the chip sector). Apple also started to cooperate with regulators all over the world to push back on Qualcomm's royalty policies.[20]

First, Qualcomm was hit with a Federal Trade Commission suit charging anticompetitive tactics in its supply and licensing terms.[21] Three days later, it was hit again when Apple sued for a billion dollars, claiming unpaid licensing rebates and excessive fees. Almost immediately, both Apple and Qualcomm began suing each other for billions of dollars on three different continents, over royalty rates and access to crucial technology. The details are complex, but they boil down to this: Whose innovations mattered most? Who should get what portion of the value of the world's most-sought-after device?

To Qualcomm, Apple was the queen of marketers, taking cheap Toyota parts and packaging the final product as a Porsche. If Apple could sell its iPhones for a small fortune just because they were beautiful, why wasn't Qualcomm allowed to reap its fair share of those profits? Given that its technology was, indeed, an essential component, Qualcomm based its licensing fee on a percentage of the iPhone's final, exorbitant selling price. To charge every one of the users of its chips exactly the same price ignored the distinct value Qualcomm brought to each individual customer. To the wireless giant, that value should determine the price.

Big as Qualcomm was, though, Apple was far bigger, and for more than two years, the latter company deployed its position to drive a hard bargain with Qualcomm, fighting to cut licensing fees and, thus, forcing Qualcomm to spend less on innovation and far more on legal fees. Once Apple pressed its suit, it simply stopped paying Qualcomm any licensing fees at all, even as it continued to install Qualcomm chips in its iPhones, slashing Qualcomm's worldwide profits nearly in half.[22]

Stymied by Apple, Qualcomm relied more and more on its profits in China. But because the Defense Department had deemed China the chief strategic adversary of the United States, this posed new security concerns, particularly as the Trump trade war heated up. Think about a defense contractor like Raytheon: if it were doing this amount of business in such sensitive areas as China, it would certainly raise eyebrows at the Pentagon. Qualcomm's wireless chips were arguably as important to the United States' national defense as the software behind some rocket launchers. Qualcomm was a crucial source for next-generation technologies that would be essential to America's future. Should China have access to these technologies, increasing the risk that it could hack into the United States' critical infrastructure, or even to the chips made by one of the United States' top telecom innovators (which powered any number of devices, which could in turn be compromised)? Suddenly, policy makers on both sides of the aisle were beginning to ask these questions.

To neoliberals, this was of no concern; multinational companies should be able to do business wherever they liked. (Although these same policy makers turned a blind eye to the fact that, as China's size and status in the global economy had changed, the playing field for that business had become increasingly unlevel.) But as China grew ever more threatening to the United States' global competitiveness, Washington began to reconsider. Perhaps the government should step in. But, of course, to think that way was to admit what it had long denied: that the government did indeed have a role to play in directing the national economy in the national interest. There was, as it turns out, a place for industrial policy.

Like him or not, Trump (guided by U.S. trade representative Robert Lighthizer) was right to call the Chinese out and slap new export restrictions on crucial U.S. technology equipment, including some made by Qualcomm, which could no longer be sold to companies like Huawei, the Chinese telecom giant founded by a former

People's Liberation Army officer. As National Security Advisor Robert C. O'Brien made clear in 2020, Huawei has the ability to retrieve sensitive information in the next-generation wireless services it is building for countries in Asia, Europe, and elsewhere. The concern was that such "back doors" could present security risks for U.S. allies. (Huawei has already been banned from use by U.S. government agencies and contractors for many years.)[23]

This left American companies like Qualcomm doing business in China in a terrible bind. They were under pressure from U.S. shareholders over quarterly losses, while facing down a one-party state that, playing the long game, thought in terms of decades, if not centuries. Locked into a legal battle with Apple, Qualcomm was suddenly subjected to new restrictions on its operations in China. Its two profit centers were getting walled off by government edicts on both sides.

Desperate to find a new revenue stream in China, Qualcomm moved to acquire a Chinese semiconductor firm, NXP. But this required Chinese approval. Now, as the Chinese considered Qualcomm's bid for NXP, they decided the offer price was insufficient, although it was well above market rate. Qualcomm duly raised it. No again. Submitted it again. No again. Repeat. The U.S. government, cognizant of the importance of Qualcomm, pushed to get the deal through by removing some of its own tech export bans, including one on U.S. tech companies selling components to ZTE, a big Chinese telecom firm. Still no dice. Xi Jinping pocketed the tariff removal left over from the Trump administration while continuing to block the Qualcomm NXP deal.[24] In doing so, China revealed—as plenty of American CEOs have over the last few years discovered, much to their sorrow—that it had not become more American in the American-inspired globalist era, but rather more Chinese.[25]

Meanwhile, Qualcomm found itself caught not only between Apple and China, but between Trump and Xi. Its share price weakened from years of battling Big Tech and Beijing, Broadcom, a massive Singaporean-owned player in the chip space, saw its chance to acquire the company on the cheap. Broadcom had an unsavory reputation for acting like a private equity firm during its acquisitions,[26] picking targets clean for their IP and patents and then leaving them to die. First, it swooped in to make an unsolicited bid to acquire Qualcomm for $103 billion, before turning to a hostile takeover for $121 billion. But the president decided it was too great a security risk to let Qualcomm fall to another company if it could result in the former's essential technology reaching Chinese hands. Trump vetoed the Broadcom acquisition. At this, coincidentally or not, China rejected Qualcomm's twenty-ninth and, as it proved, final bid for NXP.

The fact that Qualcomm in 2018 poured a whopping 25 percent of revenue into research and development was cited by the Committee on Foreign Investment in the United States, which supported the Trump pushback against efforts by Broadcom. The move followed pressure from Texas senator John Cornyn and California representative Duncan Hunter, who, it must be said, received more than $15,000 in donations from Qualcomm's political action committee, according to Federal Election Commission records. Many of the arguments against the deal—which ranged from worries that Broadcom would shrink Qualcomm's investment in crucial areas such as 5G, to fears that the United States could not remain digitally competitive and secure if a Singaporean company owned Qualcomm—were legitimate. Government officials fretted that Broadcom, which lined up $106 billion in debt financing from private equity groups Silver Lake, KKR, and CVC for the deal, would indeed take a short-term-profit approach and cut Qualcomm's rich R&D budget. If Qualcomm were to be starved of investment, the United States would lose a "national champion" in the technology race against China. But their arguments failed to take into account the looming elephant in the room: the neoliberal model of trade itself and how it is fundamentally at odds with the new realities of state capitalism.

China has made quite clear its aims to be independent of Western technology. The West must now focus on building its own digital ecosystem. That means investing in production capacity in strategic industries like semiconductors, green batteries, and the like. It means making sure that large U.S. incumbents don't crush innovation. It means providing the educational reform that is desperately needed to train workers for jobs where they will not be displaced by robots. And it means thinking more carefully about how to balance foreign and domestic concerns when thinking about trade policy. We can best bolster growth by investing in our own industrial commons and creating a twenty-first-century digital ecosystem that supports, rather than degrades, liberal values and democracy. Addressing those issues is the right way to protect national security.

Patriotic Capitalism

The technology industry goes well beyond even Big Ag in terms of capturing the full complexity of globalization over the last half century. The industry involves geopolitics, national security, and ultimately, even national sovereignty. We have the Washington Consensus and the Beijing Consensus, but we also have what some might call the Silicon Valley Consensus, in which digital giants in both the United States and China operate in the same sphere, and on the same terms, as nation-states themselves. Big Tech firms can locate their trillions of dollars of asset wealth anywhere, which is why they typically pay a far lower percentage of revenue in tax than other types of multinational companies. They are the most global of businesses. And yet, in our new tripolar world, they also like to pretend that they are national "champions" of innovation in need of protection from the U.S. government, even as they try to do as much business in China as possible. This inevitably leads to hypocrisy. Witness the way corporate leaders like Apple's Tim Cook have been obliged to agree to all sorts of censorship and user privacy violations in China that never would have been accepted at home.[27]

The truth is that both Big Tech and China are monopolies—it's just that the former exists in the private sector, and the latter operates under the guise of a state. Unfortunately, politicians and business leaders operating within the neoliberal paradigm now find themselves at a crucial disadvantage. While Chinese companies have the protection and support of the state, U.S. and, to a lesser extent, European firms are left to their own devices. This works if you are Apple, but not so well if you are Qualcomm, which has been caught up in the heavy geopolitics of the new world order. It eventually settled its patent disputes with Apple, but while the FTC's antitrust charges were dropped (helped in part by the Department of Justice, which made it clear that the company had crucial value to national security),[28] Qualcomm faces continuing restrictions on how it does business in both the East and the West. In the post-neoliberal world, companies can no longer fly completely above the concerns of the nation-states in which they operate.

Multinationals like Qualcomm sit uncomfortably in the middle of this new world. And its story raises the key questions for the next era of capitalism: Where do the responsibilities of companies lie? With shareholders in the traditional neoliberal paradigm or with stakeholders in a new paradigm that is just now starting to form? Does a business owe anything to its home country? Or does it float above any one nation to be part of some stateless global community? If business has benefited from the taxpayer-funded commons, how can any one government ensure the country itself benefits from corporate success? In short, can the fruits of a global corporation like Qualcomm be harvested at home? Is it possible to be both global and local? I believe the answer is yes. But, in a world that will have at least two, if not three, separate tech/trade and digital tax paradigms, it will require a new social compact for business.

On this point, the West should not kid itself. While the usual suspects in policy circles are talking up a reset in relations with China, and while business interests complain that economic decoupling with the United States is impossible, the truth is that China is very much going its own way. Xi Jinping has committed himself to "the great rejuvenation of the Chinese race." In speech after speech (in Chinese, and not translated into English by state media, which instead publishes bland statements about win-win cooperation with the West), he says that the current world order is not fit for China and that China intends to change it. The country will, he says, use its military to defend its interests all over the world. He claims to be building "a community of common destiny for all mankind" and wants Chinese-style techno authoritarianism to be copied by countries around the world. Xi has called on people with Chinese heritage anywhere on earth, no matter their citizenship, to join together as "sons and daughters of the Yellow Emperor" who are obliged to work for the "great rejuvenation" in whatever way the party deems fit.[29]

Some of this may be the sort of nationalistic rhetoric that many political leaders use to try to drum up support for their regimes. But whatever interpretation one might give to the details, it's clear what the vectorial direction of China today is—toward more, not less, top-down control of what is already the world's largest surveillance state. The United States, Europe, and all other nations now have two choices: be looped into the Chinese orbit or forge a new model for a post-neoliberal world.

Assuming the choice is the latter, both businesses and governments will have to change the way they operate. Paradigm shifts are challenging, but already Covid-19 has presented some very interesting new opportunities for reinvention. Start with what's happening in the business sector itself. If there is a silver lining to the Covid-19 crisis, it is the remarkable creativity shown by the many businesses that thrived by transforming themselves in unexpected ways during the pandemic. The examples I've come across are numerous. There is the airport security company that made plans to launch a vaccine-tracking app after the travel business tanked. Or the mall and store owners renting out empty retail areas to schools that needed more space for students to social-distance during lessons. Or the in-person event companies that quickly transitioned to digital businesses. More new business applications were filed in 2020 in the United States than in any year on record—applications were up 24 percent from 2019.[30] But 2021 was even better: Applications rose 42 percent in the first nine months compared to the same period in 2019. Yes, brick-and-mortar retail is still lagging, and the travel and tourism industry may never be what it once was, but areas like e-commerce, fintech, and healthcare are positively booming. This kind of Schumpeterian creative destruction is just what you want at a time like this. But the rise of entirely new kinds of businesses also creates new challenges for both capital and labor. I'd point to three particularly pressing issues that will require more attention from policy makers.

First is the question of how to value and protect intangible assets, which after the pandemic will probably double as a percentage of corporate investment. Most big business battles today are over who owns what slice of the digital pie. Consider the case in U.S. federal court between Epic Games and Apple over App Store commissions. Or the fight over pandemic exemptions to World Trade Organization rules around intellectual property to bolster vaccine production. Or Google and Apple battling it out with SAP, Siemens, and BASF over patent protection in Germany. As a greater percentage of corporate wealth is held in intangible assets, these types of conflicts will only increase. This underscores the desperate need for a twenty-first-century transatlantic alliance around technology regulation and digital trade rules. China is going its own way on many of these matters, but Europe and the United States must not. Regional unity can, and should, replace laissez-faire globalization that denies the incongruities of the One World, Two Systems paradigm.

The second big issue is that the expansion of intangible assets will probably mean fewer jobs in the short term even as it creates new businesses and entirely different industries over the longer term. Neither the public nor the private sector in the United States is grappling fully with this problem. In the United States, for example, with the exception of groups like the Freelancers Union or the National Domestic Workers Alliance, the labor movement is focused largely on protecting traditional forty-hour-a-week work that comes with benefits. Companies are meanwhile trying to push more and more people into gig work and to replace as many jobs as possible with technology. There are ways to bridge the gap. Portable benefits have long been proposed by politicians such as Sen. Mark Warner, a Virginia Democrat.[31] They would allow independent contractors to carry health and pensions coverage with them from job to job, rather than having them tied to employment with a single company. I'm also a fan of the idea of taxing and redistributing some of the massive wealth captured by corporate data collectors. This includes not just the big platform giants, but many other types of companies, from online retailers to consumer goods brands. California governor Gavin Newsom has already proposed a digital dividend for consumers, a version of which could be implemented in both the United States and Europe.[32] The proceeds could go to workforce training or to improve public education. Both would act as a buffer against looming digital labor shocks.

Third, while antitrust action is desperately needed to ensure a level playing field in the age of platform monopolies, we need to stop looking for a silver-bullet solution on competition. I suspect there are going to be a lot of different solutions for different companies. A company like Amazon could easily be broken up into a retail platform and a logistics provider. Others, like Google, might be turned into tightly regulated public utilities, which would mirror the way corporate behemoths of the past, from railroads to telecom, were put in check when they became too large and powerful. Real-world rules and regulations must be made to apply to the online world as well. Otherwise, digital players can easily use regulatory arbitrage to jump around even the largest incumbents in the most powerful industries. Even too-big-to-fail bank executives, like Jamie Dimon, chief executive of JPMorgan, have warned in recent years about commercial banking being replaced by fintech.[33] Change is good. However, if we don't acknowledge the full extent of the transformation we are going through, we'll end up with all the problems of the prepandemic economy, but on steroids.[34]

This process is going to require some coordination of public and private resources by the state. That's not about picking winners or losers, and it's certainly not about becoming a top-down Big Tech–run version of the Chinese surveillance state. It's simply about bringing a smidgen of strategic and long-term foresight to the way the

U.S. economy is run. In a world in which we have to compete with state-run giants like in China, which think on fifty-year time horizons, quarterly capitalism simply doesn't cut it anymore (not that it ever really did). Most countries today have some form of national industrial strategy to ensure the well-being of citizens rather than just shareholders, and the United States needs one, too. Indeed, it did successfully implement a mini-industrial policy with its Covid-19 vaccine effort. The federal government supplied about $14 billion worth of subsidies to pharmaceutical companies to produce a vaccine as quickly as possible. By guaranteeing massive orders up front and covering other costs (retrofitting manufacturing plants, for example), Washington eliminated most private-sector risk. This enabled corporations to throw everything at finding a rapid solution. The National Institutes of Health also supplied companies with much of the sequencing work and access to its vast databases. As a result, the country went from sequencing the virus in January 2020 to phase three trials by October of that year. In the history of medicine, nothing like this had been achieved. "This is a historic, unprecedented achievement," Dr. Anthony Fauci told a think tank webinar in December 2020.[35]

And yet, the United States has a long way to go to regain its muscle memory about how to achieve broader goals for industrial policy. As we've already learned, industrial policy has its roots in America, but over the past forty years, the United States has moved completely away from any kind of state involvement in the economy. Research shows that U.S. multinational corporations and the Chinese benefited from this approach, but most workers in the developed world did not. The Deese speech in 2021 outlined several ways the Biden administration plans to address this, most specifically by rebuilding the United States' semiconductor supply chains. This should involve allies who will help bolster demand and also innovation across a newly revamped ecosystem that will make everyone less reliant on Taiwan. If anything, the U.S. plan isn't radical enough—yet. We could do more to help build back better, stronger, and faster; one way to cut through the bureaucracy would be to appoint a resiliency czar who would answer to the president. Such a person could bring together all the various departments across government faster, addressing things like the most-needed critical infrastructure, connections between the public and private sectors, and areas where there is low-hanging fruit to be plucked to create more resiliency. Industrial policy by its very nature requires action at the top, but the process shouldn't become too cumbersome or involve too many different budget line sheets or vested interests, lest it drag along too slowly to do any good.

Wanted: A Resiliency Czar

A valuable guide to this approach can be found in a lengthy paper entitled "Anticipatory Governance," which proposed ways to help the executive branch cope with "the increasing speed and complexity of major challenges." The paper was written in October 2012 by Leon Fuerth, a veteran Foreign Service Officer who was national security advisor to Vice President Al Gore. As Fuerth puts it, "If we are to remain a well-functioning republic and a prosperous nation, the U.S. government cannot rely indefinitely on crisis management, no matter how adroit. We must get out ahead of events or we risk being overtaken by them. . . . Our 19th-century government is simply not built for the nature of the 21st-century challenges."[36]

A resiliency czar, perhaps someone with a defense background—military types tend to focus on the synchronization of complex systems, from infrastructure and logistics to technology and people, as everyday business[37]—could work to create a kind of 3D picture of all the resources available to meet the White House goals (e.g., world-beating private-sector businesses, top vocational schools or industrial programs, areas with too much or too little skilled labor). Simply creating this kind of knowledge hub and then allowing anyone who wanted to do so to tap into it would go a long way. Think how it might have helped those private-sector textile companies trying to retool themselves to create masks amid the pandemic without much help from the Trump White House or anyone else. If there were a place these companies could go to quickly find out the best way to source demand from the public or private sector, get tax incentives for retooling, find workers, and so on, they could have done what they did even more quickly and efficiently. A resource database might also help build regional resiliency—again, I'm thinking of those highly productive textile supply chains in North Carolina, which could deploy in some more productive way the Darwinian skills learned over the past twenty years of battling the outsourcing of their businesses to China. Instead of leaving them on their own to make low-margin T-shirts, the government might offer contracts for the creation of fabric interiors for electric vehicles, or cloth covers for wind turbines. It might also connect such makers with a broader range of businesses with higher-margin, strategic government subsidies in areas like lithium batteries and clean energy. This could be done in any number of regional hubs around the country, with any number of products and industries. Again, this isn't about picking winners or any kind of heavy top-down planning; it's just about connecting the dots. Nothing protectionist about that.

On that note, the United States will of course need to coordinate such systems with allies. Regionalization can be the new globalization. That will require some hard diplomatic work. The relationship between the European Union and the United States in recent years reminds me of troubled celebrity couples on the red carpet—they smile for the camera and act as though everything were fine, but in private, we all know, they are anything but content. At the first G7 summit following Biden's election, there were happy photo ops and even some progress around trade conflicts, such as the Airbus-Boeing truce. But at bottom, Europeans remain deeply skeptical about whether the current U.S. administration is just a way station en route to another bout of toxic populism. Meanwhile, Americans are frustrated with Europeans for hedging their bets between a tighter transatlantic alliance or a closer relationship with China. It doesn't have to be this way. In fact, it must not be. If the European Union really wants to protect liberal values in the age of surveillance capitalism, it needs the United States. And if the United States truly wants to decouple from China economically in strategic areas such as semiconductors, green batteries, and electric vehicles, it needs demand from more than just the domestic market. There is low-hanging fruit to be plucked here, but doing so requires some real empathy and understanding on both sides. In this, the European Union and the United States should "focus on common answers to existing challenges within their democracies," rather than on China, says Renaud Lassus, minister counselor for economic affairs at the French embassy in Washington and author of *The Revival of Democracy in America and the Better Angels of Your Nature,* a Tocquevillian call for optimism about the future both of the United States and of the transatlantic alliance. The key challenge will be shaping a new, post-neoliberal framework for how market capitalism works in the twenty-first century, something that ensures that neither Big Tech nor the Big State will dominate.

Start with tech regulation. Already, there is a virtuous circle of ideas sharing between the United States and the European Union in areas such as digital privacy, with Europe's General Data Protection Regulation (GDPR) inspiring even more aggressive California privacy laws that may one day be adopted nationally in the United States. Antitrust is another such area, where both sides have informed each other's efforts to curb platform monopoly power. One could imagine more cooperation on issues such as press freedom, the ways and means of creating a digital bill of rights, and principles for regulating artificial intelligence and genomic research. This would go some way toward creating a new basis for the transatlantic relationship, one focused more on fixing domestic weaknesses and bolstering regional strengths than on bashing China. Indeed, the two regions have already created a new Trade and Technology Council with the goal of doing just that. According to a statement given by National Security Advisor Jake Sullivan in mid-2021, Biden and his EU counterparts "will focus on aligning our approaches to trade and technology so that democracies and not anyone else, not China or other autocracies, are writing the rules for trade and technology for the 21st century."[38]

That should involve a shared set of standards for 5G and the internet of things, innovations that will massively increase the depth and breadth of digital data over the next few years using home-grown equipment from companies such as Qualcomm, Nokia, and Ericsson, as well as any number of smaller players and start-ups. It's essential that the next phase of digital innovation allow for a broader group of countries and companies to profit than the last phase did. As we move from the commercialization of the consumer internet to the development of the even bigger and potentially more profitable industrial internet, Europe, as a huge producer of potentially "smart" devices such as white goods and automobiles, has much to gain— but also to lose. For example, it is easy to imagine Google Nest own-ing much of the data generated by a German washing machine or a French refrigerator without the data sharing and portability that are a core element of the new EU proposals.[39] That's why the current U.S. and EU regulatory discussion is key. I would also love to see any future digital competition solutions include public data banks in which anonymized personal and industrial data can be shared be-tween platforms and individuals, with independent oversight. It would be a way to ensure that companies of all sizes, as well as citi-zens, consumers, researchers, and academics, had equal access to data.

It's a question of values, really. China has been incredibly smart about building standards and structures for the twenty-first-century digital economy that support *its* values, which prioritize state con-trol over privacy, freedom, or the private sector. And yet, people in most places still gravitate toward freedom, equality, rule of law, and democracy. The United States, Europe, and all liberal democracies must better articulate their values for this new, post-neoliberal era. What does a values-based technology and trade policy look like? How can the needs of the nation, and the companies that have prof-ited from any given nation's economic commons, be balanced with those of other countries and regions? Articulating this will be crucial to finding a new balance between national politics and the global economy in the post-neoliberal era. Ironically, digital technology itself is already providing part of the answer, in the form of decentralized markets in which individuals are pushing back against both Big Tech and the Big State.

CHAPTER 14

Digital Power to the People

Big Tech's power to squash competition and degrade liberal democracy is one of the most well-rehearsed story lines of our time. Likewise, the surveillance technology used by the Big State to control its citizens presents the deepest existential threat to democracy the world has ever known. Between these two powers, there is a danger that human beings lose not only freedom, but free will itself. But there is a counterexample: the power of decentralized technology to support individuals and liberal democracies all over the world, even as surveillance states threaten it. And the best real-world example of this so far can be found at the very heart of the U.S.-Chinese cold war: Taiwan.

The backlash against both Big Tech and the Big State is being led by that country's digital minister, Audrey Tang, a free-software programmer and self-described "conservative anarchist" who first came to prominence during the 2014 "Sunflower Student Movement" protesting the growing power of Beijing in the country's politics and economy. Tang was one of the "civic hackers" who helped mobilize people online. She's now using distributed ledgers, quadratic voting, and various open-source, decentralized online platforms to enable greater participatory democracy in Taiwan, turning the country into the world's most fertile petri dish for experiments in decentralized governance and markets.

In some ways, Tang is herself the best emblem of the possibilities for liberal democracy in the digital world. A self-proclaimed "post-gendered" person—she began transitioning in her twenties and says she doesn't care what pronoun people use to describe her—Tang was a child prodigy born to Taiwanese intellectuals. She read classical literature at age five, did advanced math at six, and began programming code at eight, ultimately dropping out of school in junior high—she couldn't adapt to student life—and spending much of her teens online as a way of coping with her gender dysphoria. "My principals and all the teachers actually blessed me," she told me during an interview in 2020, citing how her school validated her decision by telling her parents she was working beyond their levels of teaching anyway. "They covered for me, which is why I've believed that career bureaucrats are the most innovative people since." She worked in the public sector on internet governance issues for five years before she even had the right to vote, and she ultimately moved to Silicon Valley. By the age of nineteen, she had worked in a number of major software companies and started her own firm to create open-source software for countries without access to such technology.[1]

Tang calls herself a "conservative anarchist," but the decentralization and localization of power has always been central to her mission. In the wake of the Sunflower movement, the president of Taiwan invited her to become digital minister, with the goal of using decentralized technologies to build trust in governance and greater resiliency in the public sector. After occupying the parliament for three weeks and demonstrating, the students showed that, in a country in which such protests were unusual, "this was actually a viable way to listen to half a million people on the street," Tang says, and that one could listen to "many more online." One of the first things she did as digital minister was implement a policy called "radical transparency": every meeting she takes is recorded, transcribed, and uploaded to a public site. She also shifted the underlying structure of the government's technology to make it more open and accessible to the public and began encouraging citizens to weigh in on nearly every aspect of governance via digital petitions. The idea was to do exactly the opposite of what Facebook and other Big Tech companies were doing in the United States (polarizing politics by pushing individuals into their own limited "silo bubbles" of news), but also to buck the state-backed surveillance of the People's Republic of China. Rather, Tang aimed to create "a shared reality when it comes to technology. When we all have the same facts, backed by open government data but also open citizen data," she says, "there really is no way for moral panic to happen, because people really know what is happening."[2]

Roughly half the country now participates in digital governance via an online platform that allows the public to weigh in on everything, from whether Uber should be allowed to operate in Taiwan (yes) to whether it should be allowed to undercut traditional taxi fares (no) to whether a ban should be levied on plastic straws in takeaway drinks (yes).[3] Around ten million people are now active on the platform, helping not only to craft law, but also to fact-check politicians via a Wiki-like blockchain system that can be corrected in real time. All the citizen involvement has made the government itself more efficient. Taiwan's government now requires state agencies to rebut within two hours any false claims made online or on social media relating to its areas of responsibility. Users also engage in "presidential hackathons," which aim to generate innovative solutions to public problems. They learn, as part of the public school curriculum, how to be "data stewards" rather than simply data consumers. As Tang puts it, "In Taiwan, what we're saying is that instead of a large IoT [internet of things] platform or multinational company collecting, say, environmental data, humanitarian data, or health data for the government" and then distributing it to the very citizens from whom it has been taken "through charity," Taiwan is pushing citizens themselves to take responsibility for the process—and reap the resulting rewards (better public services, more connectivity and inclusion, and a rich and robust democracy).[4]

The building of trust in the country's system of governance has happened amid tremendous digital headwinds. A report by a Swedish research group called V-Dem found that Taiwan has, over the last few years, been subject to more disinformation than nearly any other country, much of it coming from mainland China. Yet the popularity of pro-independence politicians is growing there, something Tang views as a circular phenomenon. When politicians enable more direct participation, the public begins to have more trust in government. Rather than social media creating "a false sense of 'us versus them,'" she notes, decentralized technologies have "enabled a sense of shared reality" in Taiwan. The result is that rather than becoming more polarized in recent years, like many other liberal democracies, Taiwan has become less so, and its politics have a level of nuance unheard of in most of the West. "Liberal democracies amplified social media, which meant that you didn't get useful signals anymore," Tang says. "Without useful signals democracy can't function."[5]

A number of other countries are now using decentralized technologies in the public sector to try to capture a more nuanced and inclusive political debate, including Israel, where Green Party leader and former Occupy activist Stav Shaffir crowdsourced technology expertise to develop a bespoke data analysis app that allowed her to make previously opaque treasury data transparent. She also headed an OECD transparency group to teach other politicians how to do the same.

Part of the power of decentralized technologies is that they allow, at scale, the sort of public input on a wide range of complex issues that would have been impossible in the analog era. Consider "quadratic voting," a concept popularized by economist Glen Weyl, coauthor of *Radical Markets: Uprooting Capitalism and Democracy for a Just Society*. Weyl, who teaches at Harvard and also works as an adviser to the CTO of Microsoft, is the founder of the RadicalxChange movement (of which Tang is a part), which aims to empower a more participatory democracy. Unlike a binary yes-or-no vote for or against one thing, quadratic voting allows a large group of people to use a digital platform to express the strength of their desire on a variety of issues. Voters are given digital tokens, which they can put on various issues to represent those issues' level of importance to them.[6] Quadratic voting has already been used by dozens of state, local, and national governments to gauge public priorities around contentious issues, such as gun rights in Japan. The former head of Colorado's House of Representatives appropriations committee Chris Hansen used quadratic voting to help his party quickly sort through how much of its $4 million budget should be allocated to more than one hundred proposals. "We got to yes so much more quickly," said Hansen, who is now a state senator and plans to use the system in senate appropriations decisions. (Many other state governments are now following suit.) Canadian conservatives are considering using quadratic techniques to help allocate public funding to the media. The Christian Democratic Union in Germany is also experimenting with the procedure.[7]

From Top Down to Bottom Up

The concept of decentralization overlaps with localization in many ways. Decentralized technology relies on the dissemination of information flows across distributed networks in a variety of locations. Security is not about building a wall, but rather building a network of users who, together, help achieve resiliency within the system, each by fact-checking the others.

One of the key building blocks for decentralized technology is blockchain, a system of distributed computing in which users create a shared ledger of information or transactions involving almost any asset—a currency, a document, a piece of property, a patent, anything. Approved users within the network all have access to a shared understanding of the information and/or transaction at all times because the data is stored and processed within the network, in multiple nodes. Already, blockchain technology is used to process hundreds of billions of dollars' worth of transactions, and the technology research firm Gartner estimates that it will generate $3.1 trillion in business value by 2030.[8] It will very likely allow for the decentralization, localization, and individualization of data and commerce at a scale we can't imagine today.

One can look at many other types of technologies and network structures developing now and see the trend toward decentralization building. Consider the digital currencies we've covered, or 3D printing, which we will revisit later in this book and which is a core part of building decentralized resilience in supply chains. Also consider the rise of telehealth, which received a huge boost during Covid-19. It hearkens back to an earlier era, before giant hospital conglomerates, in which medical care itself was largely decentralized. (House calls accounted for more than 40 percent of doctor–patient interactions in the 1940s; by the end of the '80s, it was less than 1 percent.)[9] The volume of telehealth claims grew by an almost unbelievable 4,132 percent in the United States from June 2019, before the pandemic, to June 2020,[10] while hospital admissions via emergency rooms fell by 32 percent.[11] While some of this will reset, analysts believe that decentralized medical treatment is here to stay, as it allows more flexibility and affordability for both doctor and patient.

Alternative energy is yet another area ripe for decentralization. Over the last few decades, the risks of centralized utilities and networks that can be taken down with the failure of a single server or node have become all too clear—think of PG&E or the Colonial Pipeline debacles as two recent examples. While fossil fuel energy systems are built in a centralized way, with a handful of extractors funneling raw materials to another handful of utility firms that serve large swaths of the country, the proliferation of both renewable energy and smart grids is changing all this. Traditional energy grids are mature, large, and extremely interconnected—a failure in one place can trigger a failure throughout the grid, as we've seen in cases like the hurricane that destroyed much of Puerto Rico's power system in 2017 and the ongoing California wildfires that regularly result in large-scale power outages.

Smart grids, which are being developed around the world as countries modernize their energy systems,[12] allow the grid system itself to operate in a blockchain sort of fashion, sharing information but also sharing unused energy, or even selling it back to the grid for use by others. If my home, for example, were on a smart grid and equipped with, say, solar panels on the roof, I could not only pull energy from a shared electricity service, but also give back whatever extra energy I wasn't using and receive a credit for it. In fact, many of my neighbors already do this. Localized wind and solar power are increasingly cost-effective compared to fossil fuels and will become more so as government subsidies are shifted from polluting industries to renewables (a key policy goal in both the United States and Europe at the moment). Now imagine the possibilities as electric vehicles take the place of gas-guzzling cars. Suddenly, the extra power from the grid might fuel an entire neighborhood's automobiles.[13]

Such localism makes sense not only as an economic prospect, but as a political one, too. In his 1996 book, *Democracy's Discontent*, political philosopher and Harvard professor Michael Sandel sharply outlines why decentralization is crucial for democracy. Encapsulating Woodrow Wilson's 1912 argument against centralized monopoly powers of all kinds, one of the many precursors to the massive trust busting of the 1930s, Sandel writes, "Restoring liberty meant restoring a decentralized economy that bred independent citizens and enabled local communities to be masters of their destiny, rather than victims of economic forces beyond their control." This sums up not only the founding principle of the country, but the core challenge of the post-neoliberal era: how to reconnect global markets and the value created within them to nation-states.

Here, decentralized technology might play a role in helping people profit from the means of production, as Marx might have put it, which is increasingly their own data. This is the notion behind the "data-as-labor" movement, in which everyone from poets to politicians to scientists and economists are working to help people around the world find ways to own and make use of their own data. In some ways, it's the ultimate in localization. If data is the new oil, it can't be owned by a handful of large companies and state entities alone. It must be shared, so that the fruits of global capitalism can accrue to the population at large, rather than to multinational companies and China.

Data unions are potentially one of the most powerful ways of leveraging technology for the greater good. While the individual bits of data collected from us while we are shopping, working, reading, or playing have little value in and of themselves, when together, they have tremendous value. Think about the fact that Google or Facebook can charge more than double the rate for customized online advertising. Now imagine huge pools of data collected. These pools are what gives platform companies such a granular understanding of political decisions within a state or a country. (Google, Facebook, and other platforms are now major players in the political strategy arena as a result.) Imagine also the way in which being able to see what billions of people are trolling for on Amazon has made Jeff Bezos the world's richest man many times over. Data is valuable, particularly when it's pooled.

Until quite recently, this pooling has been done mainly by big corporations. But blockchain and other decentralized technologies can allow individuals to pool data and use it for their own advantage. The British tech co-operative known as Streamr, for example, helps groups of individuals with access to unique data find ways to pool it, sell it, and value it properly so that they, not Google or Facebook, can reap the rewards. One of their clients is a community of fishers in the Philippines who've found a way to monetize not just their catch of seafood, but the information garnered from it. They take pictures of their daily haul, upload it to a common data bank, and get paid for it by international nonprofits, like the World Wildlife Fund, looking to see which species are endangered or overfished—information that governments typically try to keep secret. The fishers, rather than some Big Tech company, own their data. If WWF lobbies for new fishing restrictions based on that data, it subsidizes the fishers for any lost income. But the data has a second use: the fishers now have proof of their work and value in a way that allows them to secure bank loans and build their businesses. They have gone from being part of an undocumented, informal economy to having new power and status.

"It's all about breaking down silos," said Shiv Malik, a blockchain and crypto expert (and former *Guardian* journalist) who worked in communications and strategy for Streamr until 2021.[14] "The antidote to neoliberalism is mutualism, which is really about getting back to a notion of capitalism that is rooted in community." As he put it, "A data union is really like a collection of nineteenth-century laborers. We all produce this data, it's work, and so we need to be paid for it." The goal is for such data sharing for profit to be as "boring as insurance," something that is simply done as a matter of course. Along with other technologists and activists from the old-line labor union, Streamr is working on shifting collective bargaining rights into the digital realm (allowing employees of, say, Amazon to own and use data) and changing privacy laws to allow for more pooling and for the transfer of data to allow users themselves, rather than giant states or conglomerates, to profit from it.

This localization of wealth will be crucial if predictions about the rise of artificial intelligence—which is almost entirely dependent on huge pools of data that allow machines to learn and act more like humans—holds true. Already, the share of income that goes to labor in the largest technology companies is only between 5 and 15 percent, which is lower than any industry aside from extractive ones like oil (which employ few people but use lots of machines). If increasing dependency on artificial intelligence leads more and more companies in nearly every industry to depend more on data and less on labor, then finding a way to allow individuals to recapture the value of their own data will be crucial to a stable political economy.[15]

The democratization of the data economy will require disrupting both the public and the private sectors. But, as the American baseball great Yogi Berra once put it, "When you come to a fork in the road, take it!" We are at one now in the twenty-first-century digital economy. Liberal democracies everywhere are playing regulatory whack-a-mole with platform monopolies, trying to enforce new privacy, tax, and antitrust rules. All the while, the value of intangible assets such as technology, software, and patents is expanding as the power of labor decreases. Covid-19 has only sped up this trend.

Markets are supposed to enrich society. But in the age of surveillance capitalism, they are debasing it by concentrating all the gains in the hands of the very few who can ring-fence the most data and intellectual property.

Nation-states should certainly push ahead with things such as a minimum global corporate tax, antitrust action, and a framework for digital trade. But in the meantime, we need to rebalance the market system itself, so that players on both sides of any given transaction have equal access to information, a shared understanding of what is being bought and sold, and a common set of rules. This is true for buyers and sellers on Amazon, drivers and riders on Uber, and advertisers and the sites they wish to reach via Google. Right now, we have none of that. Uber, for example, can charge you and me different prices for a ride even as the drivers themselves are unable to leverage their own data in ways that might be beneficial to them. As it is, ridesharing companies like Uber can charge consumers different prices for the same ride based on their willingness to pay and can then pocket any upside themselves without offering it to the drivers. This is what is so nefarious about the rise of an intangible economy based on networks. It leads to an asymmetry of power that offsets the usual benefits of capitalism.

Modernizing Markets

This is not new. Every time there has been a transformative new technology, from railways to telephony, we've seen growth in the concentration of economic power. And in each case, the state itself had to take transformative action to ensure that such periods of disruption didn't lead to a Hobbesian world. In the most successful historical cases, rather than taking on individual companies one at a time, governments simply set new ground rules for how markets must operate. Think of the era of "wildcat" banking, from 1816 to 1863, during which individual financial institutions in the United States issued their own currency; eventually, the U.S. government made everyone deal in dollars. The public sector also stipulated which side of the road people should drive on when highways expanded, how reservoirs would be coordinated to supply clean water, how the telecommunications system should work, and so on.

Now think about ridesharing today. Uber has its own set of standards, fees, and policies, as do Lyft and any number of smaller providers. (And that's just rideshares; every area of gig work is the same.) Consumers are largely subject to individualized pricing, and workers have no ability to bid up their own value by offering their work in real time to different employers across the same platform. But imagine if the government simply set the rules for platform "concessions" in areas such as ridesharing, or bike rental, or home sharing—or any kind of gig work—and then let the private sector compete on an even playing field in a bid to operate particular ones. You might have various private-sector companies involved at a national level. Cisco, Microsoft, Google, or Amazon could compete to run the technological backbone of such a system. But retailers, city governments, or even local entrepreneurs could be the storefront providers. Everyone would have access to the same data and algorithms, getting rid of information asymmetry, which is antithetical to truly efficient and fair markets. It's Adam Smith 101.

Various technologists and policy makers have pushed aspects of this idea for some time. But it has perhaps been best articulated by British policy entrepreneur Wingham Rowan, head of the nonprofit group Modern Markets for All (another fan of Weyl's radical market ideas), who wants to turn gig work into a public utility. His goal is that rather than having individual companies maximizing profits in silos, the public sector could simply set a floor under gig work (how it should run, how much companies should pay) and then let the private sector do its thing.

Gig work is especially ripe for this, as an increasing number of Americans—between a third and a half, by some accounts[16]—are either involved in gig work or work on some kind of variable swing shift in which companies have far more power than workers. If the state itself were to mandate decentralization of power by turning the platforms on which gig work operated (Fiverr, Uber, and any number of other sites) into franchise players in a larger public orbit, rather than monopoly powers that dominated and distorted various areas of work all by themselves, labor markets would function better for individual communities.

"About once in a generation, a technology comes along that's so potent, the private sector alone cannot unlock its potential," says Rowan.[17] The internet is that technology. So far, a handful of private-sector companies has reaped most of its commercial gains. But by tweaking the model of how digital markets work, profits from data extraction could be remoored within individual communities, and more of them could go to workers themselves—the ultimate in localization. Rowan, Weyl, and others working in the digital policy space want to see the rules that govern markets in the physical world moved into that space.

Modern Markets for All's ideas, which won the group the U.S. Conference of Mayors' prize for Best Economic Development Initiative in 2018, got an important test run during the Covid-19 pandemic, when the California city of Long Beach used them to cope with a labor mismatch. Suddenly, there were too many home health-care workers and not enough child minders. "The pandemic killed some labor markets, but suddenly there were all these unemployed people who had skills that could be deployed in other areas that were booming," says Nick Schultz, director of Pacific Gateway Workforce Innovation Network for the City of Long Beach.

Using a bespoke gig workforce platform designed to serve "the economy as a whole, rather than a single company," he notes, Schultz and his team were able to bring ten different companies to help plug the gap, while raising wages in the process. Businesses would post jobs, and the public sector helped vet skills and qualifications, ensuring that both labor and employers understood what they were getting in the bargain: a transparent transaction à la Adam Smith rather than a one-sided market in which the company (be it Uber or Fiverr) held all the key data (wages, scheduling information, etc.). City officials made sure employers were abiding by basic rules and regulations from the offline work (which is, of course, difficult to police on company-run, closed-loop algorithmic platforms).

The result was a win-win for the community. Unemployment fell, jobs were filled, proper amounts of tax were collected, and wages actually went up. Minimum wages for childcare, for example, rose to around $22 an hour in the Long Beach area during the crisis, compared with a national average of $12.24. You might call that wage inflation, but you might also call it a fair-market wage no longer suppressed by the usual asymmetry of information that plagues so many markets, particularly in the digital space. Hours were tracked to make sure employers paid people who were working full-time as proper employees. Data on the platform was portable, meaning workers could share it with any employer they liked. "We are all about helping people leverage the value of their own personal data," says Schultz.[18]

Long Beach hopes to expand the nascent effort and move into construction, hospitality, long-haul trucking, and many other areas where there have been supply-and-demand mismatches. If successful, this would upend the notion of gig work as a race to the bottom. We need such markets wherever there's an asymmetry of power in the digital world—indeed, this type of decentralized sharing of profit and power is exactly what the internet was designed to do in the first place.

It need not stop with gig labor. Nearly any kind of digital market, from e-commerce to fintech to the various platforms of the sharing economy (Airbnb and sites that allow people to share bikes, cars, dresses, and so on), could be made better and fairer if an independent authority ensured that data transactions were completely transparent and that individuals retained the same rights to their own information that the companies ring-fencing it currently enjoy.

One might wonder why such markets don't yet exist at the national levels. (They do in many other places at the state and local levels, usually spearheaded by a coalition of public, private, and nonprofit interests.)[19] Schultz believes it is because city governments are simply nimbler and better able to effect quick change. Their focus on a more discrete set of local interests makes it easier for them to move the ball forward and creates multiple petri dishes of digital experimentation from which best practices for nations and regions can emerge.

This is exactly what the principle of federalism is all about. As Supreme Court justice Louis Brandeis once put it, "States are the laboratories of democracy." And decentralized technologies can exponentially increase the number of experiments taking place at a local level. They also have the potential to leverage monopoly power, political chaos, and social bifurcation, as we have seen all too well in the last couple of decades. This is not uncommon in periods of great technological change. In the 1430s, when the printing press was invented, there were decades of wars in Europe before the Peace of Westphalia and the creation of the modern nation-state.

There are some who believe the internet may eventually take us beyond the nation-state, to something far more decentralized and localized, a world in which individual communities can and will create their own digital currencies, data unions, and hyperlocalized economies. And yet, at the same time, the major problems of our day (things like inequality and climate change) are global phenomena that will require international cooperation to address. How to square that circle? One way will be by using decentralized technologies in the physical world, at a local level, to address global concerns. The next chapter will look at a disruptive entrepreneur doing just that.

——

CHAPTER 15

Think Global, Build Local

At first glance, Jason Ballard, the founder of the Austin-based 3D-printing company ICON, doesn't come across as a socially conscious eco-entrepreneur. He's a Stetson-wearing, East Texas–accented son and grandson of blue-collar workers for the region's thriving oil-refining and shipping industry. But like the area itself, he is a study in contrasts. Southeast Texas isn't just a hub for Gulf of Mexico oil production; it's also a heavily forested biosphere that has been nicknamed America's Ark because of the incredible diversity of plant and animal life there. The Big Thicket, as the area is also known, has ten different ecosystems boasting 186 species of birds and thousands of different grasses, herbs, and flowering plants.

It was exactly these contrasts that gave Ballard his mission in life: to disrupt the world's most environmentally hazardous business. Not oil, but housing. Home building is one of the most carbon-intensive industries in the world. The construction and maintenance of the buildings in which we live and work represent 36 percent of global energy usage and 39 percent of energy-related carbon emissions.[1] In the United States, homes account for some 40 percent of all energy usage.[2] That's why changing the entire model for construction and the related supply chains will be an essential part of meeting the goals of the Paris Climate Accords. In fact, if the world is to meet those goals of keeping global warming under 2 degrees Celsius by the end of the century (the level most scientists feel will be necessary to maintain life on earth in the longer term), housing-related carbon emissions need to decrease by 30 percent within the next eight years.[3] Meeting that goal will require more than just 5 percent increases in grid efficiency or more energy-efficient windows and doors. It's going to require an entirely different method of building—or, more accurately, a return to an older method of building, in which materials and labor were sourced closer to home.

The globalization of the construction industry has, over the last 150 years or so, followed roughly the path of globalization in general. As part of their empire building, the British and other colonial powers began to do mass contracting abroad in the nineteenth century. Later, in the twentieth century, as the United States grew as an economic power, it entered the fray and, predictably, began to financialize the business, introducing debt financing and bringing in U.S. financial institutions.[4] In the postwar era, this coincided with a building boom. Not only did the Baby Boomers need more houses, but they also needed more (and cheaper) things to put in them. As Europe began to rebuild and as the emerging markets began to emerge, this demand only grew.

The Financialization of Housing

The huge demand in growth ultimately led to major changes in the way homes were financed and crafted. Housing slowly but surely became not just shelter, but a tradable asset. This shift had many causes—from decades of easy monetary policy that drove up asset prices (including homes) while also enabling borrowers to take on more debt to purchase them; to the Republican politics of the "ownership society," which encouraged more and more people to buy homes from the nineties onward; to the securitization of mortgages, which led, of course, to the 2008 financial crisis.

But the bottom line is that, with so much of the market now driven by either global investors or rich second-home buyers whose salaries and asset wealth are pegged to global, not local, markets, housing prices have become decoupled from local economies. This trend was very much in evidence during the Covid-19 pandemic, which had little effect on the incomes of global knowledge workers, many of whom took the opportunity to buy up property outside large cities, thus raising local prices.

Consider, for example, Sullivan County, a beautiful place in the Catskill Mountains about two hours from New York City. According to the latest census figures, poverty levels there are about 25 percent higher than in the rest of the state, and per capita income is just under $31,000, roughly $5,000 below the national average. And yet, property prices in Sullivan County were up 32.8 percent year on year in July 2021. Modest wood cabins that might have gone for $200,000 or less prior to the pandemic were being dolled up and flipped for double that (or rented out at boutique hotel prices). All-cash offers and sight-unseen buys became common.

Part of it was Covid-19 madness, but the Borscht Belt boom was mirrored in many parts of the country and, indeed, the world. Just as investors drove the pre–financial crisis housing boom, they have also driven the postpandemic increase in home prices, which has, as of late 2021, reached levels of froth not seen since the subprime meltdown. According to the property site Redfin, investors purchased one out of every six homes in the United States in the second quarter of 2021. Global private equity firms picked up real estate on the cheap during the first part of the pandemic, just as they bought up foreclosed houses on courthouse steps in the wake of the financial crisis. Invitation Homes, which Blackstone founded and floated, became the country's largest single-family landlord after the crisis. At the time, its chairman and chief executive, Stephen Schwarzman, said the development was "good" for America. Many tenants disagree: private equity's moves into housing were followed by years of activist and tenant complaints about disproportionately high rents, absentee landlords, and increased evictions. More recently, these big investors have been snapping up multifamily rental units and even mobile home parks, backstopped by federal loans originally designed to benefit the poor.

Both institutional investors and cash-rich city dwellers who've bought second homes to rent or flip have benefited hugely from low interest rates and quantitative easing, not just since the pandemic began, but since the financial crisis. These central bank policies have bolstered both stocks and home prices, but they have also had an incredibly distorting effect on many local real estate markets, where locals are bidding against high-earning city dwellers to get access to shelter. This in turn adds fuel to the post-Covid-19 labor shortages plaguing U.S. businesses in areas such as travel, tourism, retail, and other parts of the service sector. Suddenly, the Catskills were becoming like Aspen—if you have to work there, you probably can't afford to live there.[5]

As we have already learned, easy monetary policy raises asset prices, but it can't create the income growth in local communities that allows people to keep up with the inflation in areas like health-care, education, and housing. Meanwhile, housing supply is constrained by everything from prices to limited land availability and zoning requirements in dense markets to Covid-19-related supply shortages. There are piecemeal solutions to the problem—housing co-operatives that allow residents to pool resources to buy land and even homes; new types of experimental loans that allow lenders to take some payment in equity or float based on the condition of the overall economy—but the bottom line is that the financialization of housing, the very thing that created the 2008 financial crisis, is still very much with us. Local housing markets have become a highly leveraged, highly risky business driven by global investors. The percentage of institutional investor portfolios in housing in America has gone up between three and five times in the last twenty years, as investors have looked for ways to diversify away from traditional assets like stocks and bonds.[6] According to the property company Redfin, the number of single-family homes purchased by corporations rather than individuals doubled over the last ten years, representing around 16 percent of all purchases in the second quarter of 2021.[7]

This has inflated prices not just in the United States but globally. One trade union leader in Germany—where there has been a push to seize corporate-owned rental units and put them in public ownership—called real estate prices the "bread prices" of today, a rallying point for revolution. Many Dutch cities want to ban investors from buying cheap homes to rent out. South Korea's ruling party took a beating in mayoral elections for failing to stop a 90 percent hike in the average price of a Seoul apartment.

The pressure was summed up well in a 2021 study by the McKinsey Global Institute that tallied up the balance sheets of ten countries representing 60 percent of global income (Australia, Canada, China, France, Germany, Japan, Mexico, Sweden, the United Kingdom, and the United States). It found that two-thirds of net worth are stored in residential, corporate, and government real estate as well as land. How did this happen? In three words: low interest rates. The McKinsey study found a strong inverse correlation between net worth relative to gross domestic product and five-year rolling averages of nominal long-term interest rates. The study's authors believe that declining interest rates have played a decisive role in lifting asset prices of all sorts, but particularly real estate prices, which subsequently became as much an investment as shelter. The result is that home prices have tripled on average across the ten countries over twenty years.[8]

The ramifications are troubling. For starters, asset values are now nearly 50 percent higher than the long-run average relative to income. Net worth and GDP have traditionally moved in sync with each other at the global level, with some country-specific deviations. Now wealth and growth are completely disconnected. This is, of course, behind much of the populist anger in politics today. Affordable housing has become a rallying cry for Millennials who can't afford to buy homes and start families as early as a previous generation did.[9]

The Globalization of Housing

Housing finance isn't the only dysfunctional aspect of the real estate market. While in the pre–World War II era many buildings were constructed with local materials and built onsite, in the decades from the fifties onward, "prefab" housing grew radically as a percentage of total construction. Suddenly, homes weren't so much built as manufactured in faraway places and shipped wholesale to wherever buyers were.[10] The nature of the companies involved in the building trades began to change as well. National construction firms grew into global behemoths that outsourced various parts of the supply chain and the construction process itself to myriad smaller firms around the world. This increased the carbon intensity of the industry because of the production and shipping costs inherent in the longer supply chains. It also made it more vulnerable to the sort of supply chain disruptions we've seen in recent years.[11]

Globalization made it easier to build bigger, cheaper, and faster, but it also contributed to massive housing inequality (thanks to the ability of international financial players to speculate in multiple markets), environmental degradation (as materials were sourced and produced en masse in multiple far-flung supply chains), increased risk during extreme weather (because of construction designed to be "efficient" rather than "resilient"), and a paradigm for housing that must be fundamentally changed, rather than simply tweaked at the edges, if we are to avoid climate catastrophe and even higher rates of housing inflation than we've already seen.

Home Repair

Fixing the building and construction industry starts with design,[12] and that's where ICON comes in as one of many companies looking to fundamentally reshape the way we make buildings from the ground up. In some ways, the idea for the company was born from this tragedy. Like many people in this portion of East Texas, Jason Ballard's family experienced more than their fair share of cancer survivors—something common in places that are home to industries like oil and mining. "There were several people in my high school that had cancer," he says. "One of them was quite close to me. Petrochemicals were what put a roof over my head and food on the table," he says, and yet he is well aware that it was also responsible, at least in part, for the degradation of the environment that produced that food. He was determined to find a way to make things better.

In 2001, when he was eighteen, Ballard left for Texas A&M, where he studied conservation biology with the aim of returning home to help protect the Big Thicket's biodiversity. But as he began to learn more about conservation, he discovered something startling. As easy as it was to blame Big Oil and mining companies for climate change, one of the most impactful industries in the world when it came to emissions throughout the supply chain was housing. "People love to point a finger at big business and say, 'They are the ones to blame,'" Ballard says, but he learned it wasn't as much "gas-guzzling SUVs or private jets" that were to blame for climate change and environmental degradation as the building industry. It was not only responsible for the most energy use, he says, but was number two behind agriculture as a consumer of water. What's more, 75 percent of construction materials end up in landfills.[13] And because humans spent more time indoors than out in most places, there was also a huge health impact from building materials (many of which were manufactured with toxins and scored low on sustainability indexes).

Following university, Ballard set out to learn as much as he could about sustainable housing. He moved to Boulder, Colorado, which was, at the time, the epicenter of green building. There, he worked across the business, jobbing for developers and eco-handymen, green carpenters and architects, and generally learning whatever he could. The process led him to see that access to green materials and clean tech–inspired engineering was in short supply. This led to the founding of his first start-up, TreeHouse, which helped people in the home building industry source such materials.

Ballard also worked at a homeless shelter, where he began to see that, all too often, affordability of housing and sustainability of housing went in different directions. "I hated that idea—that you had to be rich to live in a green home. I thought, 'There's no way that we're going to change the world if only two percent of the population can afford to live in sustainable housing.'" In a nod to his love of science fiction and fantasy, Ballard says, "I wanted to know, 'Where's Rivendell, or Wakanda, in green housing?'" For those who've never read Tolkien nor thumbed through a Marvel comic book, he's saying he wanted to create something not just incrementally disruptive, but completely revolutionary—an entirely new and better way of thinking about how to create a building. "I had this amazing catbird seat for all the innovation happening in almost any sector related to building products and services," he says. "But I also knew that playing around on the edges, making thermostats five percent more efficient or creating airtight windows" wasn't going to create the change he sought.

People who start tech businesses tend to throw around terms like *paradigm shift* and *phase change*. But what Ballard is doing with ICON, his second start-up, truly fits the bill. Realizing that he couldn't reduce emissions in housing unless he changed the entire model of how to build a house, Ballard came upon an idea: 3D printing. He'd heard about its uses in the industrial space and set out to see if it might be a solution to the problem of environmentally sustainable housing at scale. He began taking classes on additive manufacturing at his local trade school in Austin, where he and his wife were living by 2015. He read everything he could on the topic, listened to businesspeople lecture about the possibilities, and eventually came across a couple of other eager people with the same idea: to disrupt the entire slow, expensive, and bureaucratic model of housing by simply 3D printing an entire home to suit each client. "I had made a list of everything I wanted housing to be—resilient, affordable, scalable, beautifully designed, and with plenty of freedom—and the only thing that could accommodate all of those things was three-D printing."

He teamed up with another environmentalist, a mechanical engineer named Alex Le Roux who had been experimenting with 3D-printing techniques, and began to work on materials design, creating an entirely bespoke cement-based substance that was pliable enough to pour into precise shapes, but that could also dry quickly and harden into something as strong as steel, so as to provide a base on which a home could be created, layer by microscopic layer. "We thought a lot about volcanoes and how they spew molten, liquid rock that then hardens into something that lasts forever," he says. The resulting patented material, Lavacrete, has been used to print a Mars-simulated habitat at NASA's Johnson Space Center in Houston.

Indeed, resiliency rather than simplistic efficiency was Ballard's North Star. As he was starting ICON, he knew he needed to create homes that were just as beautiful and affordable as any others. But they also needed to be more sustainable than traditional homes when measured over an entire life cycle. In some ways, this was a relatively low bar. The housing industry works slowly, expensively, and bureaucratically. It involves dozens of separate industries and supply chains—one for paint, another for plastic or metal components, not to mention the building trade itself. Each one is run to its own specifications, with its own employees and regulations. Materials take a long time to ship, and the construction industry has been slow to digitalize. This was low-hanging fruit to be plucked. "You don't really need to three-D-print something like a spoon," Ballard says, "because those can already be made fast, cheaply, and easily." But home building, as anyone who's ever bought, built, or renovated a house knows, was ripe for disruption.

The first step was to reduce the number of supply chains and their length. An affordable and yet extremely resilient material was key to this, something that involved raw materials that could be sourced nearby wherever building might need to occur. Concrete (cement, gravel, and water) fit the bill—once it was tweaked by the company's materials scientists into a tougher bespoke product. The frames of ICON homes are built with Lavacrete, which is poured into a custom design that creates not only the frame and wall structure of a home, but space for other components, like insulation, plumbing, electricity, and drywall. "We are disrupting between five and seven different industries with each home," says Ballard, citing everything from exterior and interior finishing to the steel beams that might support a normal building. (Note: steel production is one of the most carbon-intensive activities in the supply chain.)

The result is that instead of a single home taking months to build and costing hundreds of thousands of dollars, an ICON home can be printed in eight days, with an industrial printer (designed for the task by the company itself) that costs a few hundred thousand dollars and yet can build multimillion dollars' worth of housing at a fraction of the time, dollar cost, and emissions cost of building a regular home. While ICON and the handful of other firms doing this type of work are still nascent, early data indicates that a 3D-printed home has about a third the carbon footprint of a traditional house. This figure will only get lower as the technology improves. What's more, the durability of the material means that one building will last far longer than a traditional stick frame house; moldable concrete has a life span of hundreds of years. Fewer houses made and bought over a lifetime means not only fewer emissions, but lower costs when amortized over a greater number of years.

This belies the argument that is often given about more localized production, which is that it will increase the costs of goods and services too dramatically for them to be affordable. Inflation will rise, and prosperity will decline. But the truth is that, for many key products, this simply isn't true. A 2021 BCG analysis of how to make the world's most-carbon-intensive supply chains more sustainable and local found that the process would add only a 2 percent markup on a $35,000 car, a dollar added to the price of a typical pair of jeans, 1 percent (or roughly a $4) increase in the price of a smartphone, and only 3 percent more for a $200,000 home. When you think of it this way—that sustainable construction adds only 3 percent to the cost of a $200,000 home—you have an entirely different calculus.[14]

Not only could this model transform the affordability of high-end sustainable design, but it could also provide resiliency to the increasing number of people living in places that will be subject to the hazards of climate change over the coming years. This subject is near and dear to Ballard's heart. While his work in a homeless shelter put affordability in the front of his mind, his own experience growing up on the Gulf Coast made him cognizant of how climate was making the current housing paradigm unsustainable. "My hometown has been destroyed by hurricanes repeatedly in my life," he says. In fact, with his childhood home almost completely gone, his family finally moved from the area a few years ago. "I've spent Christmas as a kid in FEMA trailers," with water having risen seven feet in a matter of hours. "I can't count how many times we've pulled the Sheetrock from my dad's house and put it right back in again." Talk about wasted energy and resources. It's no surprise that ICON homes were first tried at scale in disaster zones in Mexico. The company is now pushing ahead with a new spate of market-rate homes in prime locations in Texas.[15] In Austin, for example, the company is partnering with Lennar, one of the nation's leading homebuilders, and the Bjarke Ingels Group, a top architecture firm, to construct one hundred sleek new printed homes of up to three thousand square feet.

ICON's model is just one of many popping up globally that aim to change the nature of how we live and build, making both these more local and more sustainable. Additive manufacturing has gained traction in many countries, including the Netherlands, a leader in building technology (the legacy of living in a permanent flood zone). Recently, one of the world's top architectural firms, a Dutch company called UNStudio, founded UNSense, a firm that is partnering with a group of climate researchers, designers, landscape artists, and data scientists to work on a ten-year project called 100 Homes for Helmond. The company aims to blend localized building, energy conservation, and individual data ownership to create a new development in a town near Eindhoven, in the southern Netherlands. The idea is to help residents reduce their carbon footprint by organizing the necessities of life (work, school, healthcare, play) into a discrete area, but in doing so, to increase incomes, quality of life, and the amount of free time. The project takes many of the principles around sustainable design that motivated Jason Ballard (including additive manufacturing for buildings), but also incorporates the idea of individual data stewardship, the goal being to collect and study the data of people who live and work in the new development to create a "fifteen-minute city" in which both technology and design work together to minimize waste of all kinds.

Bas Menheere, the managing director of UNSense, says that the vision for the bespoke community has its intellectual roots not only in Jane Jacobs's vision of localization, but also in Glen Weyl's notion of data as labor. "We wanted to create a community in which residents themselves owned and controlled their own data," which could then be used to optimize life in the community. Example: Vertical farms on sustainably designed buildings connected by smart grids will help residents grow their own food, which will be sold at onsite markets. Excess energy will charge electric vehicles or help power residents' appliances. Data collected from schools, shops, clinics, banks, and homes within the community will be placed in a publicly accessible data bank and used to improve public services like traffic flows, determine where parks and open spaces should be placed, and locate opportunities for energy conservation and cost savings. Companies will work with public officials and community members to decide what the resulting tweaks in the community might be—and the community itself will share in the gains of any innovation drawn from their data, just as venture capital investors in new companies would.[16]

Climate as Commons

It sounds a bit utopian, and as we are all aware, utopias have been known to go awry. But the project leaders are approaching the 100 Homes effort with a reassuring degree of humility. They acknowledge that it's a "real-time experiment" in which some ideas may be discarded even as others are copied. The core goal is to trim the 80 percent of income that goes to basic necessities like housing, food, healthcare, and transit in the Netherlands—the average for rich countries is between 60 and 80 percent—by sharing and studying data generated by all the individuals, institutions, and businesses operating in the development. "Trust is our cement," says Menheere, who broke ground on the homes in September 2021. Everyone who takes part in the project must give explicit consent for the use of their data, and the community together decides exactly how it will be used. "We want to create more self-sufficiency for local communities by giving people control and ownership of the data they create and the value from it," Menheere says, not only to mitigate climate change, but also to bolster resiliency and help combat the populism he and many others believe will continue to surge if issues like housing security, inequality, and the stresses of city life aren't addressed.[17]

There is in this an implicit acknowledgment that the world simply isn't going to reset to the mid-nineties. We aren't going back to the golden era of neoliberalism and laissez-faire globalization. But neither do we need to return to the Hobbesian world of the thirties. The events of the last decade, from the 2008 financial crisis to the Covid-19 pandemic to the myriad challenges of climate change and its economic and political fallout, have shown us that we must find a place in between in which a just-in-time world gives way to a just-in-case world. If the last forty years were about unfettered commerce, economic "efficiency," and no-holds-barred globalization, the next forty years will be about bolstering community resilience and finding a new way to think about what economic success really means—and how it should be measured.

Climate issues will be ground zero for this shift. Never before has that old catchphrase "think global, act local" held truer. In the old economic paradigm, constant competition among individuals, states, and nations was encouraged. But as we've learned, market forces don't always allocate resources properly, particularly when it comes to the commons—our planet, of course, being the ultimate commons. American states, for example, have long competed with one another for everything from jobs and tax incentives to, amid Covid-19, vaccines and respirators. But as we saw amid the pandemic, this all too often became a race to the bottom in which risk was obscured. Just look at how Miami, a city beset by sinking land and rising seas, has lured billions of dollars of Wall Street and Silicon Valley money with promises of a more business-friendly environment. Or how southern states have courted jobs and investment from the North with deregulation, tax cuts, and lax labor laws. Florida and Texas, in particular, have benefited from this sort of arbitrage in recent years. But the problem with this approach is that it all too often ends up being a kind of zero-sum game in which investors benefit and public infrastructure and investment suffer.

Climate change takes the political stakes of this Hobbesian game to a new level. Consider just one of the many climate-related disasters of the last few years: a freak winter storm in Texas in 2021 that overwhelmed the power grid and left millions of people without food, water, or heat. Families froze, with some suffering from carbon-monoxide poisoning after trying to burn sticks and charcoal inside their homes to keep warm. This is the state that some economists believe was supposed to represent America's future—a cheap-housing, low-regulation sort of place. But when put under sudden stress, it looks more like Sudan.

Given the reality of climate change, there seems little doubt that states like Texas and Florida are going to be coping with such disasters again and again. And yet, as they cut taxes and public budgets in ways that seem "efficient" or "business-friendly" in the moment (but create costly vulnerabilities in the longer term), they also benefit from things such as federally underwritten flood insurance, something unheard of in many rich European countries, which tend to discourage building in vulnerable areas. It's not only in the United States, of course, that this kind of shortsighted thinking has led to disaster. Unfettered globalization and a focus on short-term growth have all sorts of international consequences, many of which we have explored in detail in the previous chapters.

We need to start tallying the real cost of the economic thinking that has brought us to this place. In fact, markets are finally beginning to do that themselves, as environmental issues are tallied into performance metrics and regulatory frameworks. So far, insurers and banks have borne most of the market risk of climate change.

But, more recently, individual companies are being held explicitly responsible for the risks of global warming. A court in The Hague has ordered Royal Dutch Shell to cut its emissions. The International Energy Agency says energy groups must stop new oil and gas projects in order to reach net-zero emissions by 2050. Indeed, market penalties for companies that make bad risk decisions around climate are broader than we might think. A 2021 report from Pentland Analytics, "Risk, Reputation and Accountability," looked at several episodes of extreme disaster, including the 2017 hurricane season, the most expensive in U.S. history. Dr. Deborah Pretty, the author, examined U.S.-listed companies with annual revenues exceeding $5 billion that disclosed financial damage from Hurricanes Harvey, Irma, and Maria. Modeling their share price reaction across the year, she found an average 5 percent discount to the S&P 500 index—the equivalent of $18 billion in lost shareholder value. Pretty also drilled down into companies that had more than 10 percent of their global insured property values in an affected area, to see what precautions such as flood or wind protection they had taken. Among companies that reported financial damage, fewer than half of recommended measures had been completed. Yet, among those that reported no material financial damage, almost two-thirds of the recommendations had been completed. Bottom line? Market perceptions of adverse outcomes from such natural disasters have "changed from bad luck to bad management," says Pretty.

This means that share prices, which we are all exposed to via our 401(k)s, now reflect whether the C-suite is taking climate change risk seriously. Indeed, Pretty's research shows that the top-performing companies are those that consider resilience more important than a balance sheet bargain. In other words, they take every possible action to mitigate such risk in all the communities in which they operate, even if the models show that the risk is slight. This might baffle economists, but as one engineer interviewed in the study put it, "Look, if you have four holes in your boat, and you plug three of them, you're still gonna sink!" It's part of the argument for resilience over economic "efficiency," which is influencing not only preparations for climate-related disasters but also supply chains, which so many companies are beginning to shorten.[18]

If regulators have their way, these risks will become more explicit, particularly with regard to climate. In June 2021, G7 leaders announced their commitment to mandatory climate-related financial disclosures modeled on those recommended by the G20's Task Force on Climate-Related Financial Disclosures. This provides a road map for how to integrate climate risk metrics in corporate governance and strategy. So far, Europe has made more progress than the United States in forcing companies to disclose such risks. But with the Biden administration push in areas like electric vehicles, America is taking action, too. In 2022, the Securities and Exchange Commission, headed by the ambitious regulator Gary Gensler, announced new proposed reporting rules for emissions. If adopted, companies will have to report not only how much carbon they emit in the course of their own business, but the emissions from their electricity purchases, and even parts of their supply chain.[19] The idea is that GDP alone—not to mention share prices—is a failed metric for economic success. In order to really understand the risks inherent in the neoliberal model of globalized capitalism, we need new and better metrics, fuller metrics. We need a more nuanced picture of the environmental, social, and real economic and political costs of living and working the way we have been.

Imagine, for example, if companies and countries alike had to show the true, planetary cost of doing business in the same way that food companies have to tally up calories, fat, sugar, protein, etc., on a label for any shopper to see. Imagine if voters were able to access such information just as clearly. This kind of change is coming. In the next few years, it's likely that companies will need to meet industry-specific standards for reporting to the public its emissions, the amount of waterfront property it holds, and prevention measures it has taken around flood zones. Some activists are pushing for extremely granular corporate disclosures around water insecurity, heat stress, and the extent to which businesses could be affected by disease, political unrest, and migration.

Should even a handful of such rules be adopted and actually enforced, it's hard to overstate what the market impact could be. The exposure of, say, an apparel maker to agricultural production (and to potential crop damage via drought, heat, or pestilence) could dramatically affect shareholder value. A price on carbon could change the calculus for some exporters, making activities such as long-distance shipping of heavy machinery much more costly. Asset managers holding too many investments in high-carbon sectors could find themselves in breach of their fiduciary duties. The ripple effects for individuals with retirement plans would have their own economic and political consequences. Chinese steel dumping, for example, would become impossible if there were a real price on carbon. Rather than engaging in contentious trade wars that never seem to reach their aim of getting everyone to play by the same rules, perhaps the United States, Europe, and other liberal democracies would do better simply to change the rules. After all, the rules of market capitalism aren't set in stone. They can be rebuilt. Indeed, they are being remade right now all over the world. There is no longer one global model for how the economy should function. We still have global challenges, climate change being first among them. And yet, we have left the era of laissez-faire globalization. The post-neoliberal world will be one characterized by pluralism. Countries and communities are already trialing all sorts of new ways of doing business. This experimentation at the local level is a wonderful thing, because if we want to make both market capitalism and liberal democracy work, we will have to find ways to serve the interests of individual communities even as we serve the planet.

Blueprint for a New World

Jason Ballard and his effort to disrupt the housing industry reflects all this, as do the efforts of all the entrepreneurs and policy leaders

I've profiled in this book. When I ask what his biggest challenge has been, Ballard says, "It's really hard to do something really, really differently. I wasn't trying to sell someone on materials that were fifteen percent cleaner. I was trying to shift the entire way they thought about shelter and how it could be created." Indeed, Ballard's ultimate mission, like those of many of the disruptors in this book, goes way beyond his own industry and region. In some ways, he's trying to 3D-print a new, post-neoliberal world. ICON doesn't aim to become the world's biggest sustainable housing construction company. Far from it. It simply started building homes to show people how a new technology, and a new paradigm, could change the way they live. "Think about Tesla," Ballard says. "They couldn't just put electric cars out there; they also had to build the charging network" and educate people about the possibilities of the smart grid and so on. ICON doesn't want to become the world's biggest home builder—it wants to show people what's possible when construction is more localized and sustainable.

Once additive manufacturing of homes takes off, Ballard hopes that his company will start exporting its printers to communities all over the world, which will in turn find entirely new problems to solve with them. "One of the problems with globalization is that it has a strong centralizing component," he says. With globalization, things that had traditionally been done in a far more decentralized, community-oriented way were suddenly taken out of the hands of individuals, hubbed in a factory far away, and sold back to them at a "cheaper" price—but only when that price is looked at in the context of short-term, efficiency-oriented thinking.

Ballard wants ICON to do the opposite—to build a tool in Texas that can be exported to any community to allow people in myriad places to build the homes, and futures, their local needs dictate. "I can't wait to see what architects in India or Africa are going to do when they have this kind of freedom, when they can design using their own local vernaculars." All they'll need is some concrete, a printer, and imagination.

CHAPTER 16

Where Do We Go from Here?

Ballard's company and many of the others featured in this book reflect a changing global economy, one that will never go back to the no-holds-barred globalism of the mid-nineties, but that won't be completely localized, either. That's as it should be. We live on a single planet, one where we must work together to address the most important challenges, like climate change. And yet, there's no getting around the fact that politics exists at the level of the nation-state, and likely will for a long time to come. As the last half century of globalization and more than a decade of backlash to it have shown us, we forget the needs of the citizens in those states at our peril.

The challenge of our time is how to craft a new international system that doesn't repeat the mistakes of the past, a system that better balances the needs of the local with the realities of the global. The neoliberals of the 1930s wanted to connect the world to buffer populism. And yet, the ability of global capitalists to control vastly more cross-border wealth and power than ever before in history has led us to a place in which neoliberal visions of globalization are collapsing. Populism and nationalism have been the result. The Washington Consensus has given way to a power struggle between Big Tech and the Big State. Individuals everywhere are left stranded in the middle.

As I've tried to outline in this book, if we want to find a happy place in between autocracy and oligopoly, we will need to find ways to retether wealth and place. Some of those changes are already being driven from the ground up, by business and civil society. Some are being pushed by policy. We are in a period of tremendous disruption, much of which can seem disorienting at best, terrifying at worst. There are new alliances and new conflicts; the reality of a bipolar, if not a tripolar, world; and worries about whether a Great Power conflict between the United States and China will result in a war.

But there are also so many positive counterexamples of individuals, businesses, and communities finding ways to reinvent themselves in a new, post-neoliberal world. While paradigm shifts can be scary, they also bring opportunity. New regional innovation hubs are emerging. Companies are moving away from assumptions of unfettered globalization toward more decentralization and system redundancy (namely, having extra resources to provide backup support) to avoid future shocks. The supply chain disruptions of the last few years have now lasted longer than the 1973–74 and 1979 oil embargoes combined. This isn't a blip but rather the new normal. Business is looking to produce more products and services locally as a way to smooth such disruptions and the inflationary pressures that result.

Meanwhile, the power of labor is rising. Antitrust efforts around the world are bringing attention to extreme concentrations of power. Digital technologies are allowing a greater number of small businesses and individuals to reach beyond their own borders and claim their share of wealth in the twenty-first-century economy. And increasingly, they can do it from their homes, wherever they might be.

Home matters. But acknowledging the importance of place isn't about thinking small or being provincial. It's about acknowledging that, over the last several decades of globalization, there have been losers as well as winners. And if we want to find ways to build a safer and more inclusive international system, we will have to start with building communities that make sense to people (wherever they live) and economies that balance the needs of labor and capital, consumption and production, and what's needed locally and globally.

The process is well under way. One of the only silver linings to Covid-19, in my mind, has been the way in which it reshaped the geography of work, allowing people far more freedom to choose where they live. Suddenly, opportunity can be had not just in a handful of global cities, but anywhere there is a broadband connection. Prepandemic, just 28 percent of all U.S. CEOs had 40 percent or more of their workers working remotely. In 2022, 53 percent will, and the CEOs plan to keep those figures even after the pandemic subsides as a way of keeping the talent. In the United States, more than anyplace else, remote work is here to stay.[1] Why pay New York or Boston or D.C. prices and deal with congestion and high taxes and more regulation when you don't have to? Suddenly, talent is pouring out of the biggest cities and into a far wider range of places. The states that have seen the biggest pandemic population influxes are Texas, Florida, Arizona, North Carolina, South Carolina, and Georgia.[2] Those adding the most jobs tend to be in the West, the South, or even the Midwest, off the usual coastal power grid.[3]

The changes in the geography of work will also change politics and culture across the land. In a state like Georgia, for example, Black voters are shifting the political landscape as cities become more liberal. You can see this in Atlanta and even elsewhere in the South, in places like Charlotte. Anecdotally, I can see it happening in some parts of the Midwest that I know well. My own hope is that, over time, as all the changes wrought by the pandemic settle out, these shifts will make the United States a better place, by reducing crowding in cities, increasing density in underpopulated parts of the country, and bridging some economic and political polarization. As everyone knows, we become more moderate when we are exposed to people of differing viewpoints. Maybe we will end up with a political map that looks more purple, rather than bright red and blue. I certainly think we'll end up with a more economically balanced country.

The Beauty of Localism

I can see the postpandemic changes happening outside my window in Brooklyn, where I have spent most of the last two years working in my home office. At many points during that time, it seemed unclear where the city was headed. When the pandemic hit New York, many people proclaimed that the city was headed back to the seventies. For those who don't remember, that's when David Berkowitz, aka the Son of Sam, dominated headlines; when the middle class fled to the suburbs amid rising crime; and when President Gerald Ford's refusal to offer a bailout during the 1975 fiscal crisis sparked the famous New York *Daily News* headline "Ford to City: Drop Dead."[4] With Covid-19, the city certainly seemed headed that way, at first. Nearly thirty thousand retail jobs there disappeared. Thousands of shops and restaurants were shuttered. Entire neighborhoods—often the priciest ones, like Tribeca, Soho, and the Upper East Side—suddenly seemed deserted. Many of the richest city residents fled to their second homes at the beach or in the mountains.[5]

But other areas began to thrive. While parts of the city that used to be known for luxury condos and free-spending foreigners were largely deserted between 2020 and 2021, once-unfashionable areas began booming. The highest price jump in the city over the course of the pandemic was in humble Windsor Terrace, a small Irish-Italian neighborhood just steps from my own, where nurses and firefighters living in small two-story brownstones were joined by cable talk show hosts and designers.

It could be that the lure of space will wear off and that people will migrate back to coastal cities. But I doubt it. I think we are witnessing a lasting change, one that could have big political consequences. Red states getting more people could, for example, belie the usual liberal argument about problems with the Electoral College, which has given big, sparsely populated places a disproportionate and, some say, unfair political advantage. It might also make the country more conservative: polls show that prospects for Democrats usually sink in rural areas.[6]

In my own city of New York, the neighborhoods that are newly thriving seem to have the common thread of being somewhat less economically bifurcated than many of the places being vacated. For the price of a one-bedroom apartment in a prime area of Manhattan, one could get a house in Brooklyn's Windsor Terrace in which a family of four could happily work from home and Zoom school. Rents in the neighborhood are affordable enough to support a variety of locally owned shops, bookstores, and restaurants. There's also a mix of industry in this part of South Brooklyn: industrial "makers" churning out manufactured goods, hospital complexes that employ thousands, and a variety of immigrant neighborhoods with their own local economic ecosystems. There's good transportation and decent public parks and playgrounds. This is a New York that isn't just for professionals and the people who serve them, but a broader section of society.

In a way, such places hearken back to a classic, Jane Jacobs view of the world, one in which the best neighborhoods are more local, sustainable, and mixed-use—communities in which people can afford to live and work in the same place, where there is something in between luxury high-rises that are investment vehicles for absentee global tenants, run-down company towns, swaths of empty space in flyover country, and urban jungles for the poor.

Jacobs, the urban activist and author of the classic 1961 book *The Death and Life of Great American Cities,* believed that cities, like their residents, were biological systems that could be understood only in the context of "organized complexity, like the life sciences." There were dozens of interrelated things happening in any one place at any given time. "The variables are many," she wrote in her most famous book, "but they are not helter-skelter; they are interrelated into an organic whole." As in the parable of butterfly wings creating a tsunami on the other side of the world, pushing slightly on one factor could shift the entire system.

Jacobs believed, for example, that citizens kept one another safe as much as, if not more than, police did—something worth thinking about in the context of today's debate around police reform.

Relationships and intimacy, cemented by a connection to place, were the secret to security—not external forces. "The first thing to understand is that the public peace—the sidewalk and street peace—of cities is not kept primarily by the police, necessary as police are. It is kept primarily by an intricate, almost unconscious, network of voluntary controls and standards among the people themselves, and enforced by the people themselves," Jacobs wrote. It was, however, a system that required trust. In some communities, trust came in the form of homogeneity and tribalism. But in large and diverse urban areas, it came from the casual contact with a diverse group of strangers that was the heart of the "intricate sidewalk ballet" of Jacobs's own neighborhood in Greenwich Village.

Her description of it shows the importance of localism, even within the context of a large urban area. On her little stretch of Hudson Street, she would make her appearance "a little after eight . . . when I put out the garbage can, surely a prosaic occupation, but I enjoy my part, my little clang, as the droves of junior high school students walk by the center of the stage dropping candy wrappers. . . ." Later, there were the other "rituals of morning," like Mr. Halpert unlocking the laundry handcart from its mooring to a cellar door, Joe Cornacchia's son-in-law stacking out the empty crates from the delicatessen, the barber bringing out his sidewalk folding chair, and Mr. Goldstein, who "arranges the coils of wire which proclaim the hardware store is open."[7]

I recognize this ballet from my own neighborhood. Like shopkeeper Joe Cornacchia, my local bodega owner keeps a set of our keys for acquaintances who want to use our place while we're away. He tells me when my fourteen-year-old son, who stops in for soda, has fallen in with the wrong group of friends. My hairdresser, two blocks away, lets me run home without paying if I've forgotten cash and I'm in a rush; he knows I'll get him next time. The old ladies in their curlers monitor the street from their lawn chairs as well as any cop. My next-door neighbor, a septuagenarian from the former Yugoslavia, who has lived in the house since she was a child, can tell me in which decade and exactly how the previous owners repaired the gutters. It's Pete Hamill's Brooklyn. In fact, Hamill spent some of his own childhood in a flat across the street.

Why does this level of trust still exist on my block? In part, because this neighborhood was, until recently, free from the socioeconomic extremes that plague many global cities. When I traded in a three-bedroom flat in London for my home in Park Slope, Brooklyn, in 2007, I did so in part because I knew I could send my children to public school; live near a green space; have easy access to libraries, hospitals, and shops; and use public transportation.

This "diversity of uses" still exists in many outer boroughs, but is harder to find in many neighborhoods in Manhattan, which, like prime London or the most expensive parts of any number of other global cities, has become extremely bifurcated in recent years. There are too many "landmark" buildings owned mainly by absentee investors from Russia or the Gulf, and oddly incoherent places like the newly developed Hudson Yards, which is hugely inconvenient for transporting normal working people and yet is filled with overpriced luxury condos and corporate tenants subsidized by the city. It's perhaps no surprise that these are the areas of the city that continue to struggle in the postpandemic era. They were built for the old world.

Former mayor Michael Bloomberg once called New York City a luxury product.[8] But for Jacobs, cities that were the biggest or best at anything were often sowing the seeds of their own demise. "Monopolistic shopping centers and monumental cultural centers cloak, under public relations hoohaw, the subtraction of commerce, and of culture too, from the intimate and casual life of cities." Iconic buildings need to be used like key chess pieces—sparingly. They take up too much air and reduce complexity—which, in Jacobs's view, is at the heart of successful neighborhoods, where each of the parts serves the whole.

Her own preference in architecture was for a mix of old and new, commercial and residential, with short blocks that allowed for close contact and enough people both living and working locally to offer both supply and demand. It's the fifteen-minute-city concept, really. Jacobs believed that it was "the smallness" within even large cities that made those cities desirable in the first place. "A metropolitan center comes across to people as a center largely by virtue of its enormous collection of small elements, where people can see them, at street level," she wrote.[9] More Brooklyn, less Manhattan. More Austin, less San Francisco. It's a trend that was emerging before the pandemic, but that is getting a tailwind now with what look to be permanently altered working, commuting, shopping, and living patterns.[10]

Pandemics always change things profoundly, reshaping cities, countries, and the world—and this time will be no different. Within five to ten years, New York and other big global cities may become less "luxury brands" than decentralized collections of local neighborhoods and economic regions that host not a handful of superstar tenants, but a greater variety of small, midsize, and large businesses. Already, Brooklyn and Queens, two outer boroughs of New York City, exist more in their own orbits, with a greater number of people living and working within them, rather than taking long, unproductive commutes to toil in skyscrapers.

It is an evolution that will continue for years and decades to come. Just as the neoliberal world wasn't shaped overnight, the new world will take shape over time, piece by piece, law by law, community by community. But it's coming. There will be new frictions and unexpected challenges as we move from a highly globalized economy to one in which production and consumption are more tightly geographically connected, and in which stakeholders, not just shareholders, have a voice. The world, as we've learned, isn't flat.

But there will also be huge opportunities. Around the country and, indeed, the world, you'll see a far greater number and variety of communities becoming economic hubs as both policy and business models push back against the existing trends of centralization and globalization. Panglossian ideas about the efficiency of unregulated markets will begin to fade. The needs of companies and consumers will be balanced with those of workers and citizens. Policy will slowly but surely shift to protecting our new data commons from being ring-fenced by a handful of public and private actors. Decentralized technologies in the hands of more people will allow for new kinds of bottom-up, locally driven growth.

If we're lucky, the result may be a world that is fairer, stabler, more varied, and a lot more interesting than what came before.

Acknowledgments

This book is in many ways the product of my entire three decades in global journalism. During that time, I have been lucky enough to live and work in many countries, where I have been influenced by hundreds if not thousands of people and stories—too many to list here. But it is also the product of having grown up in rural America as the child of immigrants, experiencing in my everyday life the delicate balancing act of local and global. For all that they have given me that led me to where I am, I thank my parents.

I also thank my colleagues at the *Financial Times,* which is surely the best place in the world to be a business and economics journalist. I have learned so much from all my brilliant colleagues, many of whom have challenged me and helped me sharpen my arguments in the pages of the *FT.* Thanks as well to CNN for giving me a global TV platform. And of course, thank you to both my book editors, Talia Krohn and Madhulika Sikka, and all the other great people at Crown for believing in me enough to buy not one, two, but *three* of my books. That process was of course made better and easier by my agent, Andrew Wylie, the smartest and savviest man in the business, who immediately embraced the promise of this book. It's a privilege to be represented by him.

Among the many, many individuals who contributed their thoughts, feedback, wisdom, and time to *Homecoming,* I want to particularly thank the following: Barry Lynn, Clyde Prestowitz, Glen Weyl, Heather Boushey, Robert Lighthizer, Mike Wessel, Lori Wallach, Garth Jensen, Bayard Winthrop, Molly Jahn, John Hoffman,

Dawn Thilmany, Matt Barnard, Nate Storey, Bob Hockett, Daron Acemoglu, Michael Pettis, Joseph Stiglitz, Raghuram Rajan, Rob Johnson, Henry Farrell, Gordon Hanson, Dan Alpert, Dan Breznitz, Bill Janeway, and Kiril Sokoloff.

On a very personal note, thank you to my researcher, Barbara Maddux, who fact-checked this book and made me feel just as secure as she always did in our years together at *Time* (any errors are solely my own). Thank you also to Gillian Tett and Anya Schiffrin, the best friends and journalists/critics that anyone could have. And finally, thank you to my husband, John Sedgwick, my children, Darya and Alex, and my entire extended family for all their love and patience. The very best homecoming is always the one that brings me to you.

Notes

Author's Note

1. Laura Silver et al., "In U.S. and UK, Globalization Leaves Some Feeling 'Left Behind' or 'Swept Up,' " Pew Research Center, Oct. 5, 2020.
2. Susan Lund et al., "The Future of Work in America," McKinsey Global Institute, July 2019.

Chapter 1: One World, Two Systems

1. Rana Foroohar, "What Chinese Cyber-Espionage Says About the Chinese (and U.S.) Economy," *Time*, May 20, 2014.
2. Jennifer Hillman and David Sacks, "China's Belt and Road: Implications for the United States," Council on Foreign Relations Independent Task Force Report No. 79, March 2021. Also see Rana Foroohar, "China Wants to Decouple from U.S. Tech, Too," *Financial Times,* Sept. 6, 2020.
3. Katherine Tai, "Biden Administration's 2022 Trade Policy Agenda," Ways & Means Committee, March 30, 2022.
4. Pew Research Center, "Americans, Like Many in Other Advanced Economies, Not Convinced of Trade's Benefits," Pew Research Center, Sept. 26, 2018.
5. Bob Davis and Jon Hilsenrath, "How the China Shock, Deep and Swift, Spurred the Rise of Trump," *The Wall Street Journal,* Aug. 11, 2016.
6. United Nations Conference on Trade and Development, "Trade and Development Report 2018: Power, Platforms and the Free Trade Delusion," UNCTAD, Sept. 26, 2018.
7. Drew DeSilver, "For Most U.S. Workers, Real Wages Have Barely Budged in Decades," Pew Research Center, Aug. 7, 2018. Also see John Schmitt, "America's Slow-Motion Wage Crisis," Economic Policy Institute, Sept. 13, 2018.

8. Author interview with Dani Rodrik, 2021.

9. Rana Foroohar, "Revamp Global Trade to Match Our New Reality," *Financial Times,* Sept. 30, 2018.

10. See my first book, *Makers and Takers: The Rise of Finance and the Fall of American Business* (New York: Crown Business, 2016), particularly chapter 1, page 45, in which I discuss the push by Walter Wriston and others to turn back Regulation Q. For an even deeper exploration of these topics, see Vincent Carosso's excellent history *Investment Banking in America: A History* (Cambridge, Mass.: Harvard University Press, 2013).

11. Quinn Slobodian, *Globalists: The End of Empire and the Birth of Neoliberalism* (Cambridge, Mass.: Harvard University Press, 2018), p. 5.

12. Ganesh Sitaraman, *The Great Democracy* (New York: Basic Books, 2019), p. 11.

13. Rana Foroohar, "Kiril Sokoloff: 'There Will Have to Be Massive Debt Relief,' " *Financial Times,* May 1, 2020.

14. Matthew C. Klein and Michael Pettis, *Trade Wars Are Class Wars: How Rising Inequality Distorts the Global Economy and Threatens International Peace* (New Haven, Conn.: Yale University Press, 2020), p. 20.

15. Slobodian, *Globalists,* p. 2.

16. Quinn Slobodian, "You Live in Robert Lighthizer's World Now," *Foreign Policy,* Aug. 6, 2018.

17. Barry C. Lynn, "Unmade in America," *Harper's Magazine,* June 2002.

18. Slobodian, *Globalists,* p. 7.

19. Jan-Werner Müller, *Contesting Democracy: Political Ideas in Twentieth-Century Europe* (New Haven, Conn.: Yale University Press, 2011), p. 5.

20. Slobodian, *Globalists,* p. 16.

21. Robert Skidelsky, "Keynes v. Hayek: The Four Buts . . . ," The Mont Pelerin Society, Jan. 16, 2020.

22. Sitaraman, *The Great Democracy,* p. 12.

23. For the detailed history on this, see Joseph E. Stiglitz, *Globalization and Its Discontents* (New York: W. W. Norton, 2002).

24. Stiglitz, *Globalization and Its Discontents,* p. 16.

25. Lynn, "Unmade in America," p. 37.

26. Author interview with Molly Jahn in 2021. Also see Rana Foroohar, "The U.S. Military Has a Plan to Make Food from Thin Air. No, Really," *Financial Times,* Dec. 11, 2021.

27. Knut Alicke et al., "How Covid-19 Is Reshaping Supply Chains," McKinsey and Company, Nov. 23, 2021.

28. Erik Lundh et al., "The Future of Global Supply Chains: Five Trends," The Conference Board, Dec. 10, 2021.

Chapter 2: The Problem with Big Food

1. John T. Hoffman, Testimony before the Senate Subcommittee on Oversight of Government Management, the Federal Workforce, and the District of Columbia for a hearing titled "Agro-Defense: Responding to Threats Against America's Agriculture and Food System," Sept. 13, 2011.

2. Mark Johnson, "The U.S. Was the World's Best Prepared Nation to Confront a Pandemic. How Did It Spiral to 'Almost Inconceivable' Failure?" *Milwaukee Journal Sentinel*, Oct. 14, 2020.

3. Ben Hewitt, *The Town That Food Saved* (Emmaus, Penn.: Rodale Books, 2010), p. 4.

4. Mark Hyman, *Food Fix* (New York: Little, Brown, 2020), p. 265.

5. Michael Pollan, "The Sickness in Our Food Supply," *The New York Review of Books*, June 11, 2020.

6. Sen. Cory Booker, "Booker Unveils Bill to Reform Farm System," press release, Dec. 16, 2019.

7. Author's own reporting for book.

8. Peter Atwater, "The Troubling Parallels Between Supply Chains and Securitisation," *Financial Times*, Aug. 31, 2021.

9. Nicole Pepperl, "Putting the 'Food' in Food Stamps: Food Eligibility in the Food Stamps Program from 1939 to 2012," Harvard Law School, April 2, 2012; U.S. Department of Agriculture, "A Short History of SNAP," Sept. 11, 2018.

10. Rana Foroohar, "The Problem with Big Food," *Financial Times*, June 21, 2020.

11. Ganesh Sitaraman et al., "Regulation and the Geography of Inequality," *Duke Law Journal* 70 (2021): 1763.

12. Mary K. Hendrickson et al., "The Food System: Concentration and Its Impacts," special report for the Family Farm Action Alliance, Nov. 19, 2020, p. 6.

13. Gracy Olmstead, "My Great-Grandfather Knew How to Fix America's Food System," *The New York Times,* March 19, 2021.

14. Rana Foroohar, "Antitrust Policy Is Ripe for a Rethink," *Financial Times*, June 24, 2018.

15. Hyman, *Food Fix,* p. 69.

16. Hyman, *Food Fix,* p. 68.

17. Open Secrets, Top Contributors to Political Campaigns by the Agribusiness Sector, 1990–2022.

18. Author interview with John Hoffman, 2021.

19. Anthony Janetos et al., "The Risks of Multiple Breadbasket Failures in the

21st Century," Boston University's Frederick S. Pardee Center for the Study of the Longer-Range Future, March 2017.

20. Jenny Schuetz et al., "Are Poor Neighborhoods 'Retail Deserts'?," *Regional Science and Urban Economics* 42, nos. 1–2 (January 2012): 269–85.

21. Hyman, *Food Fix,* pp. 34–35.

22. Hyman, *Food Fix,* pp. 22–25.

23. Jonathan Aguilar et al., "Crop Species Diversity Changes in the United States: 1978–2012," *PLoS One,* Aug. 26, 2015.

24. Rana Foroohar, "Democrats Take Aim at Big Agribusiness," *Financial Times,* May 12, 2019.

25. James M. MacDonald and Robert A. Hoppe, "Examining Consolidation in U.S. Agriculture," U.S. Department of Agriculture's Economic Research Service, March 14, 2018.

26. Hendrickson et al., "The Food System," p. 16.

27. Hendrickson et al., "The Food System," p. 18.

28. Caius Z. Willingham and Andy Green, "A Fair Deal for Farmers Raising Earnings and Rebalancing Power in Rural America," Center for American Progress, May 2019.

29. Foroohar, "Democrats Take Aim at Big Agribusiness."

30. Hyman, *Food Fix,* p. 277.

31. Foroohar, *Makers and Takers: The Rise of Finance and the Fall of American Business,* p. 182.

32. Foroohar, *Makers and Takers,* p. 180.

33. Izabella Kaminska, "Michael Masters on Speculation, Oil, and Investment," *Financial Times,* Feb. 3, 2015.

34. Rana Foroohar, "The Biggest Lesson of GameStop," *Financial Times,* Feb. 7, 2021.

35. Rana Foroohar, "U.S. Economy Is Dangerously Dependent on Wall Street Whims," *Financial Times,* March 8, 2020.

36. Rana Foroohar, "Small-Time Investing Fuels Real World Consequences," *Financial Times,* May 24, 2020.

37. Author interview with Dawn Thilmany, 2021.

Chapter 3: Systems Failure

1. Author interview with John Hoffman, 2021.

2. Katherine Blunt and Russell Gold, "PG&E Knew for Years Its Lines Could Spark Wildfires, and Didn't Fix Them," *The Wall Street Journal,* July 10, 2019.

3. Rana Foroohar, "We've All Got GM Problems," *Time,* June 12, 2014.

4. Author interviews with Molly Jahn, 2021. Also see Foroohar, "The U.S. Military Has a Plan to Make Food from Thin Air. No, Really."

5. Author interviews with Molly Jahn, 2021.

6. Adam Hochschild, *Bury the Chains: Prophets and Rebels in the Fight to Free an Empire's Slaves* (Boston: Houghton Mifflin, 2005).

7. Rana Foroohar, "Eat, Drink, and Go Slow," *Newsweek,* July 1, 2001.

8. Alice Waters, *We Are What We Eat* (New York: Penguin Press, 2021), p. 170.

9. Waters, *We Are What We Eat,* p. 139.

10. Waters, *We Are What We Eat,* p. 127.

11. Waters, *We Are What We Eat,* p. 78.

12. Author interview with Dawn Thilmany, 2021.

13. Hendrickson et al., "The Food System," p. 17.

14. Hendrickson et al., "The Food System," p. 18.

15. Alissa Quart, "Be Your Own Boss: More Co-op Businesses Are Returning Workers' Power," Economic Hardship Reporting Project, Sept. 6, 2021.

16. Pat Mooney et al., "Too Big to Feed: Exploring the Impacts of Mega-Mergers, Consolidation and Concentration of Power in the Agri-Food Sector," International Panel of Experts on Sustainable Food Systems, Oct. 2017.

17. Author interviews with Rushkoff and Sundararajan, June 2016.

18. Rana Foroohar, "Giving Back Is Good Business," *Time,* June 30, 2016.

19. Claire Kelloway, "Milking Profits: The Dairy Monopolies That Are Hurting Farmers," *Washington Monthly,* Sept. 14, 2020; and Leah Douglas, "How Rural America Got Milked," *Washington Monthly,* January/February/March 2018.

20. Timothy J. Bartik, "A New Panel Database on Business Incentives for Economic Development Offered by State and Local Governments in the United States," W. E. Upjohn Institute for Employment Research, Jan. 1, 2017.

21. Bartik, "A New Panel Database on Business Incentives for Economic Development Offered by State and Local Governments in the United States."

22. Arama Kukutai et al., "2020 Agrifood Tech Investment Review," Finistere Ventures, April 2021.

Chapter 4: Move Fast and Grow Things

1. Foroohar, "The Problem with Big Food."

2. Author interview with Matt Barnard, 2020.

3. M. Shahbandeh, "Projected Vertical Farming Market Worldwide in 2019 and 2025," Statista, July 20, 2020.

4. Willy C. Shih, "Global Supply Chains in a Post-Pandemic World," *Harvard Business Review,* September–October 2020.

5. Rana Foroohar, "The Economy's New Rules: Go Glocal," *Time,* Aug. 20, 2012.

6. Lundh et al., "The Future of Global Supply Chains: Five Trends."

7. Brooke Masters and Andrew Edgecliffe-Johnson, "Supply Chains: Companies Shift From 'Just in Time' to 'Just in Case,'" *Financial Times,* Dec. 20, 2021.

8. Rana Foroohar, "Columbus Shows Trump How to Thrive in the New World Order," *Financial Times,* April 1, 2018.

9. Foroohar, "The Problem with Big Food."

10. Author's reporting.

11. David Rodziewicz and Jacob Dice, "Drought Risk to the Agriculture Sector," Federal Reserve Bank of Kansas City, Dec. 3, 2020.

12. Author interview with Soren Bjorn, 2020.

13. Ashlee Vance, *Elon Musk: Tesla, SpaceX, and the Quest for a Fantastic Future* (New York: HarperCollins, 2015), pp. 167–68.

14. Jeanne Batalova, "Frequently Requested Statistics on Immigrants and Immigration in the United States," Migration Policy Institute, Feb. 11, 2021.

15. Andrés Villarreal, "Explaining the Decline in Mexico-U.S. Migration: The Effect of the Great Recession," *Demography,* December 2014.

16. Rana Foroohar, "Open the Door and Let 'Em In," *Time,* July 22, 2013.

17. Author interview with Steve Blitz, as well as references to TS Lombard's "The View" research report, June 23, 2020.

18. Author interview with Matt Barnard, 2020.

19. Author interview with Dawn Thilmany, 2021.

Chapter 5: Trade and Its Discontents

1. Slobodian, "You Live in Robert Lighthizer's World Now."

2. Robert E. Lighthizer, "How to Make Trade Work for Workers: Charting a Path Between Protectionism and Globalism," *Foreign Affairs,* July/August 2020.

3. Lighthizer, "How to Make Trade Work for Workers."

4. Thomas L. Friedman, *The World Is Flat: A Brief History of the Twenty-first Century* (New York: Farrar, Straus and Giroux, 2005).

5. Barry C. Lynn, *End of the Line: The Rise and Coming Fall of the Global Corporation* (New York: Doubleday, 2005), p. 67.

6. Lynn, *End of the Line,* p. 68.

7. David H. Autor, David Dorn, and Gordon H. Hanson, "The China Shock: Learning from Labor Market Adjustment to Large Changes in Trade," National Bureau of Economic Research, January 2016.

8. Yuqing Xing and Neal Detert, "How the iPhone Widens the United States Trade Deficit with the People's Republic of China," ADB Institute, May 2011.

9. Author interview with Kai-Fu Lee, 2017.

10. Author interview with Hockett in June 2019.

11. Rana Foroohar, "American Economic Policy Goes Back to Its Roots," *Financial Times,* June 10, 2019.

12. Rana Foroohar, "Plans for a Worker-Led Economy Straddle America's Political Divides," *Financial Times,* June 2019.

13. Rana Foroohar, "Liberals and Security Hawks Can Find Common Green Ground," *Financial Times,* Feb. 26, 2021.

14. Klein and Pettis, *Trade Wars Are Class Wars,* pp. 12–13.

15. Clyde Prestowitz, *The World Turned Upside Down* (New Haven, Conn.: Yale University Press, 2021), p. 148.

16. Klein and Pettis, *Trade Wars Are Class Wars,* p. 11.

17. David Ricardo, *On the Principles of Political Economy and Taxation* (London: John Murray, 1821), p. 148.

18. Prestowitz, *The World Turned Upside Down,* p. 151.

19. Klein and Pettis, *Trade Wars Are Class Wars,* p. 11.

20. Dan Breznitz, *Innovation in Real Places: Strategies for Prosperity in an Unforgiving World* (Oxford, U.K.: Oxford University Press, 2021), p. 41.

21. Lynn, "Unmade in America," pp. 34–39.

22. Jim Reid et al., "The Age of Disorder: The New Era for Economics, Politics and Our Way of Life," Deutsche Bank, September 2020.

23. Author interview with Clyde Prestowitz.

24. Brian Williams, "Clinton Sees Globalization as Key Issue," Institute for Agriculture and Trade Policy, Dec. 14, 2000.

25. Lynn, *End of the Line,* p. 68.

26. Foroohar, *Makers and Takers,* pp. 171–72.

27. I. M. Destler, "America's Uneasy History with Free Trade," *Harvard Business Review,* April 28, 2016.

28. Francis Fukuyama, *The End of History and the Last Man* (New York: Free Press, 1992).

29. Lynn, *End of the Line,* p. 65.

30. Author interview with Dani Rodrik, 2021.

31. Marc Levinson, *Outside the Box: How Globalization Changed from Moving Stuff to Spreading Ideas* (Princeton, N.J.: Princeton University Press, 2020). Also see Marc Levinson, "The Stuck Container Ship on the Suez Canal Was a Metaphor," *The New York Times,* March 31, 2021.

32. Foroohar, *Makers and Takers,* chap. 5.

33. Foroohar, *Makers and Takers,* pp. 167–68.

34. Peter Robison, "Boeing's 737 Max Software Outsourced to $9-an-Hour Engineers," *Bloomberg,* July 28, 2019.

35. Global Data, "Airbus Surpasses Boeing to Become the World's Leading Aircraft Manufacturer," Jan. 8, 2020.

36. Bill Saporito, "Rouge in Reverse," *Time,* Feb. 4, 2010.

37. Masters and Edgecliffe-Johnson, "Supply Chains."

38. Tonya Garcia, "Walmart, Target, Home Depot and Other Large Retailers Are Chartering Ships to Bypass Supply Chain Problems. Will the Strategy Save Christmas?" MarketWatch, Oct. 5, 2021.

39. Rana Foroohar, "Invest in Workers, Not Tax Cuts, to Boost U.S. Productivity," *Financial Times,* Dec. 10, 2017.

40. Rana Foroohar, "A Step Backward for Labor," *Time,* March 3, 2014.

41. Peter S. Goodman, "In Suez Canal, Stuck Ship Is a Warning About Excessive Globalization," *The New York Times,* March 26, 2021.

42. Nike's 10-K filing to the U.S. Securities and Exchange Commission for fiscal year ended May 31, 2021.

43. Larry Fink, "Larry Fink's 2022 Chairman's Letter," BlackRock, March 24, 2022.

44. Susan Lund et al., "Risk, Resilience, and Rebalancing in Global Value Chain," McKinsey and Company, Aug. 6, 2020.

Chapter 6: Exorbitant Privilege, Exorbitant Burden

1. Author interview with Robert Hockett, 2021.

2. Foroohar, *Makers and Takers.*

3. Foroohar, *Makers and Takers,* p. 7.

4. Jeffrey E. Garten, *Three Days at Camp David: How a Secret Meeting in 1971 Transformed the Global Economy* (New York: HarperCollins, 2021).

5. Klein and Pettis, *Trade Wars Are Class Wars,* pp. 174–221.

6. Foroohar, *Makers and Takers,* p. 53.

7. Foroohar, *Makers and Takers,* pp. 1–28.

8. Marc Lombard, "A Re-examination of the Reasons for the Failure of Keynesian Expansionary Policies in France, 1981–1983," *Cambridge Journal of Economics,* April 1995.

9. James K. Galbraith, "The Death of Neoliberalism Is Greatly Exaggerated," *Foreign Policy,* April 6, 2021.

10. Financial Stability Board, "Global Monitoring Report on Non-Bank Financial Intermediation 2018," Feb. 4, 2019.

11. Ruchir Sharma, "This Is How the Coronavirus Will Destroy the Economy," *The New York Times,* March 16, 2020.

12. Foroohar, *Makers and Takers,* pp. 55–56.

Chapter 7: The Post-Dollar World

1. Klein and Pettis, *Trade Wars Are Class Wars,* p. 211.
2. Autor, Dorn, and Hanson, "The China Shock."
3. Klein and Pettis, *Trade Wars Are Class Wars,* pp. 212–13.
4. Lighthizer, "How to Make Trade Work for Workers."
5. Raghuram G. Rajan, "Inclusive Localism: Communities' Place in a Globalized World," The Law Family Commission on Civil Society, 2019.
6. Rana Foroohar, "Sherry Turkle: 'Why Was I Asked to Make Steve Jobs Dinner?,'" *Financial Times,* March 26, 2021.
7. Hannah Arendt, *The Origins of Totalitarianism* (New York: Schocken Books, 1951).
8. Mark Muro et al., "Biden-Voting Counties Equal 70% of America's Economy. What Does This Mean for the Nation's Political-Economic Divide?," The Brookings Institution, Nov. 10, 2020.
9. Author interview with a Senate aide, 2021.
10. Raj Chetty et al., "Where Is the Land of Opportunity? The Geography of Intergenerational Mobility in the United States," National Bureau of Economic Research, January 2014.
11. Autor, Dorn, and Hanson, "The China Shock."
12. Gordon H. Hanson, "Can Trade Work for Workers?," *Foreign Affairs,* May/June 2021.
13. Klein and Pettis, *Trade Wars Are Class Wars,* p. 201.
14. William Lazonick, "Stock Buybacks: From Retain-and-Reinvest to Downsize-and-Distribute," Center for Effective Public Management at Brookings, April 2015.
15. John Asker et al., "Comparing the Investment Behavior of Public and Private Firms," National Bureau of Economic Research, Sept. 2011.
16. Paul Krugman, "How Crypto Became the New Subprime," *The New York Times,* Jan. 27, 2022.
17. Parag Khanna and Balaji S. Srinivasan, "Great Protocol Politics," *Foreign Policy,* Dec. 11, 2021.
18. Brendan Greeley, "MiamiCoin, a Currency Without Sovereignty," *Financial Times,* Nov. 20, 2021.
19. Dr. Jonathan Tiemann, "Historical Perspectives on Bitcoin," Investment Viewpoint, Tiemann Investment Advisors, Oct. 29, 2021.
20. Gillian Tett, "Central Bankers' Crypto Experiments Should Put Investors on Alert," *Financial Times,* March 25, 2021.
21. "2021 Report to Congress of the U.S.-China Economic and Security Review Commission," November 2021.

22. "2021 Annual Report to Congress of the U.S.-China Economic and Security Review Commission," November 2021.

23. Rana Foroohar, "Key U.S. Commission Heralds Coming Capital Wars," *Financial Times,* Nov. 21, 2021.

24. Farnaz Fassihi and Steven Lee Myers, "China, with $400 Billion Iran Deal, Could Deepen Influence in Mideast," *The New York Times,* March 27, 2021.

25. Rana Foroohar, "China, Russia and the Race to a Post-Dollar World," *Financial Times,* Feb. 27, 2022.

26. Author interview with Bill Janeway, 2020. Also see Rana Foroohar, "We May Be Heading Towards a Post-Dollar World," *Financial Times,* May 31, 2020.

27. Board of Governors of the Federal Reserve System, "Money and Payments: The U.S. Dollar in the Age of Digital Transformation," January 2022.

28. Robert C. Hockett, "Money's Past Is Fintech's Future: Wildcat Crypto, the Digital Dollar, and Citizen Central Banking," *Stanford Journal of Blockchain Law and Policy*, June 27, 2020.

29. Author interview with Robert Hockett in 2021.

30. Robert Hockett, "America's Digital Sputnik Moment," *The Hill,* May 12, 2020.

31. Dani Rodrik, "The Inescapable Trilemma of the World Economy," Dani Rodrik's blog, June 27, 2007.

32. Jessica E. Lessin, "Bitcoins, Unicorns, and Why All Bubbles Aren't Created Equal," *The Information,* Feb. 9, 2018. Also see Rana Foroohar, "A Productive Economic Bubble Is My Wish for 2020," *Financial Times,* Dec. 29, 2019.

33. Rana Foroohar, "Joe Biden's 'Buy American' Isn't Bad, It's Necessary," *Financial Times,* Jan. 31, 2021.

34. Garth Jensen et al., "A Strategy for National Resilience: Common Sense for the Common Good," working paper for the Naval Postgraduate School, Monterey, Calif., Feb. 25, 2021.

35. Rana Foroohar, "Liberals and Security Hawks Can Find Common Green Ground," *Financial Times,* Feb. 26, 2021.

Chapter 8: Not Your Grandfather's Factory

1. Chad P. Bown, "Covid-19: China's Exports of Medical Supplies Provide a Ray of Hope," Peterson Institute for International Economics, March 26, 2020.

2. Author interview with Clyde Prestowitz, 2021.

3. Author interview with Anderson Warlick, 2020. Also see Rana Foroohar,

"U.S. Factories Retool from Hoodies to Face Masks to Fight Coronavirus," *Financial Times,* March 24, 2020.

4. Rana Foroohar, "Weaponised Supply Chains," *Financial Times,* Oct. 11, 2021.

5. Katherine Tai, "Biden Administration's 2022 Trade Policy Agenda," Ways & Means Committee, March 30, 2022.

6. Rana Foroohar, "Cheap Masks Carry a High Cost for U.S. Manufacturing," *Financial Times,* Oct. 10, 2021.

7. Rana Foroohar, "The Great Uncoupling: One Supply Chain for China, One for Everywhere Else," *Financial Times,* Oct. 6, 2020.

8. Matt Leonard, "64% of Manufacturers Say Reshoring Is Likely Following Pandemic: Survey," Supply Chain Dive, May 14, 2020.

9. Lund et al., "Risk, Resilience, and Rebalancing in Global Value Chain."

10. Carol Ryan, "The Hidden Cost of Cheap Fashion Could Catch Up to Investors," *The Wall Street Journal,* May 21, 2021.

11. "First Insight Finds Expectations for Sustainable Retail Practices Growing with the Rise of Gen Z Shoppers," BusinessWire, Jan. 14, 2020.

12. Westfield, "How We Shop Now: What's Next?," industry report, February 2016.

13. Rana Foroohar, "How War Is Changing Business," *Financial Times,* March 21, 2022.

14. Choong, Y.Y.C., Tan, H. W., Patel, D. C. et al., "The Global Rise of 3D Printing During the COVID-19 Pandemic," *Nature Reviews Materials* 5, 637–639 (2020).

15. Rana Foroohar and Bill Saporito, "Made in the U.S.A.," *Time,* April 22, 2013.

16. Author interview with Eric Schmidt, 2021.

17. Debra Kamin, "How an 11-Foot-Tall 3-D Printer Is Helping to Create a Community," *The New York Times,* Sept. 29, 2021.

18. "What I Learned This Week," research note on 3D printing, 13D Global Strategy and Research, Feb. 27, 2020.

19. Author interview with Gerald Davis, 2021. Also see Gerald Davis, "Buying Furniture on iTunes: Creative Destruction in a World of 'Locavore' Production," Network for Business Sustainability, Nov. 7, 2012.

20. James Manyika et al., "Building a More Competitive U.S. Manufacturing Sector," McKinsey Global Institute, April 15, 2021.

21. Christopher Mims, "The Distributed Future of Manufacturing: Think Ikea, Minus the Furniture," *The Atlantic,* June 24, 2013.

22. Author interview with Garth Jensen, 2021.

23. Andrew T. Hill, "The First Bank of the United States: Alexander Hamilton's Grand Experiment in Central Banking Began in 1791 to Assist a

Post-Revolutionary War Economy and Ended 20 Years Later," Federal Reserve History, Dec. 4, 2015.

24. "FACT SHEET: Executive Order on Promoting Competition in the American Economy," The White House, July 9, 2021.

25. Rana Foroohar, "Old Economists Can Teach Us New Tricks," *Financial Times,* June 2, 2019.

26. Author interview with Bob Hockett, 2019.

27. Robert Irie et al., "Manufacturing Innovation Institutes Integral to U.S. Pandemic Response," U.S. Department of Defense, May 5, 2021.

28. Rana Foroohar, "U.S. Workforce: Paying Young Americans to Learn the Right Skills," *Financial Times,* June 15, 2017.

29. Author interview with Nils Schmid, 2013. Also see Rana Foroohar, "How Germany Can Save the Euro," *Time,* Aug. 19, 2013.

30. Sven Smit et al., "The Future of Work in Europe," McKinsey and Company, June 10, 2020.

31. Author interviews with Max Viessmann and Jeannette zu Fürstenberg, 2020. Also see Tobias Buck, "Germany's Mittelstand Gets to Grips with Digital Challenge," *Financial Times,* May 8, 2018.

Chapter 9: Why Making Things Matters

1. Foroohar and Saporito, "Made in the U.S.A."

2. Gary P. Pisano and Willy C. Shih, *Producing Prosperity: Why America Needs a Manufacturing Renaissance* (Cambridge, Mass.: Harvard Business Review Press, 2012).

3. Manyika et al., "Building a More Competitive U.S. Manufacturing Sector."

4. James Manyika et al., "A New Look at How Corporations Impact the Economy and Households," McKinsey Global Institute, May 31, 2021.

5. Manyika et al., "Building a More Competitive U.S. Manufacturing Sector."

6. Author interview with James Manyika, 2021.

7. Author interview with Catherine Novelli, 2021.

8. Justin Baer, "The Breakout Cities on the Forefront of America's Economic Recovery," *The Wall Street Journal,* May 9, 2021.

9. Manyika et al., "Building a More Competitive U.S. Manufacturing Sector."

10. Author interview with Kim Glas, 2021.

11. Joseph B. Fuller and Manjari Raman, "Dismissed by Degrees: How Degree Inflation Is Undermining U.S. Competitiveness and Hurting America's Middle Class," Harvard Business School, October 2017. Also see Rana Foroohar, "Young Americans Need to Be Taught Skills, Not Handed Credentials," *Financial Times,* Nov. 11, 2018.

12. Rana Foroohar, "U.S. Workforce: Paying Young Americans to Learn the Right Skills," *Financial Times,* June 15, 2017.

13. Judith Scott-Clayton, "The Looming Student Loan Default Crisis Is Worse Than We Thought," Brookings Institution's Evidence Speaks Reports, Jan. 10, 2018.

14. Robert Hiltonsmith, "At What Cost? How Student Debt Reduces Lifetime Wealth," Demos, Aug. 7, 2013. Also see Rana Foroohar, "The U.S. Student Debt Bubble Is a Study in Financial Dysfunction," *Financial Times,* July 29, 2016.

15. Anna N. Smith, "Student Debt Is a Racial Equity Issue. Here's How Mass Debt Relief Can Address It," Roosevelt Institute, Oct. 29, 2020. Also see Rana Foroohar, "A Student Debt Jubilee Could Kickstart U.S. Economic Recovery," *Financial Times,* Dec. 20, 2020.

16. Rana Foroohar, "Coronavirus Bursts the U.S. College Education Bubble," *Financial Times,* April 26, 2020. Also see Greg Ip, "Is Elite College Worth It? Maybe Not," *The Wall Street Journal,* March 20, 2019.

17. Rana Foroohar, "The School That Will Get You a Job," *Time,* Feb. 24, 2014.

Chapter 10: Two Americas

1. Jonathan D. Ostry et al., "Neoliberalism: Oversold?," International Monetary Fund's *Finance & Development,* June 2016.

2. Rana Foroohar, "Globalization's True Believers Are Having Second Thoughts," *Time,* June 3, 2016.

3. Karl Polanyi, *The Great Transformation* (New York: Farrar and Rinehart, 1944).

4. Heather Boushey, *Unbound: How Inequality Constricts Our Economy and What We Can Do About It* (Cambridge, Mass.: Harvard University Press, 2019).

5. Boushey, *Unbound,* p. 42.

6. Raj Chetty et al., "The Economic Impacts of Covid-19: Evidence from a New Public Database Built Using Private Sector Data," Opportunity Insights (Harvard University), November 2020.

7. Author interview with Gordon Hanson, 2021.

8. Autor, Dorn, and Hanson, "The China Shock," p. 37.

9. Autor, Dorn, and Hanson, "The China Shock," p. 24.

10. Autor, Dorn, and Hanson, "The China Shock," p. 3.

11. Author interview with Peter Orszag, 2021.

12. David Goodhart, *The Road to Somewhere: The Populist Revolt and the Future of Politics* (London: C. Hurst, 2017).

13. Muro et al., "Biden-Voting Counties Equal 70% of America's Economy."

Also see Joan C. Williams, "How Biden Won Back (Enough of) the White Working Class," *Harvard Business Review,* Nov. 10, 2020; and Rana Foroohar, "America's Other Identity Divide—Class," *Financial Times,* Nov. 15, 2020.

14. Manyika et al., "A New Look at How Corporations Impact the Economy and Households." Also see Rana Foroohar, "Five Lessons from 25 Years of Corporate Wealth Creation," *Financial Times,* May 30, 2020.

15. Jason Thomas, "When the Future Arrives Early," Carlyle Group, Sept. 16, 2020. Also see Rana Foroohar, "Covid Recovery Will Stem from Digital Business," *Financial Times,* Oct. 4, 2020.

16. Rana Foroohar, "U.S. Capital Expenditure Boom Fails to Live Up to Promises," *Financial Times,* Nov. 25, 2018.

17. "FACT SHEET: Biden-Harris Administration Announces Supply Chain Disruptions Task Force to Address Short-Term Supply Chain Discontinuities," Statements and Releases, The White House, June 8, 2021.

18. "The Biden White House Plan for a New U.S. Industrial Policy," Atlantic Council, June 23, 2021.

19. Jim Barrett and Josh Bivens, "The Stakes for Workers in How Policymakers Manage the Coming Shift to All-Electric Vehicles," Economic Policy Institute, Sept. 22, 2021.

Chapter 11: The Caring Economy

1. Advisory Board, "'There's Something Terribly Wrong': Why More Americans Are Dying in Middle Age," Advisory Board Daily Briefing, Dec. 2, 2019.

2. "The Cost of U.S. Healthcare," roundtable discussion, Renewing America series, Council on Foreign Relations, Nov. 21, 2013.

3. Steven H. Woolf and Laudan Aron, *U.S. Health in International Perspective: Shorter Lives, Poorer Health* (Washington, D.C.: The National Academies Press, 2013).

4. Author interview with Richard Jackson, May 2021. Also see Richard Jackson, "The Macro Challenges of Population Aging," The Concord Coalition and the Global Aging Institute, Spring 2021; and Rana Foroohar, "A Midlife Crisis Takes Shape in the U.S.," *Financial Times,* May 16, 2021.

5. Charles Goodhart and Manoj Pradhan, *The Great Demographic Reversal* (Cham, Switzerland: Palgrave Macmillan, 2020), p. 19.

6. Goodhart and Pradhan, *The Great Demographic Reversal,* p. 63.

7. Author interview with Daron Acemoglu, 2021.

8. Author interview with Boushey, 2021.

9. Jaana Remes et al., "Prioritizing Health: A Prescription for Prosperity," McKinsey Global Institute, July 8, 2020.

10. 13D Research, "Healthcare IT: The Coming Spending Boom," July 21, 2003.

11. Khalid Kark, "Reinventing Tech Finance," Deloitte Insights, Jan. 7, 2020.

12. David Goodhart, *Head, Hand, Heart* (New York: Free Press, 2020).

13. Janette Dill, "Is Healthcare the New Manufacturing?," *Public Health Post* (Boston University), Feb. 17, 2020.

14. "Fact Sheet: Obesity," Research America, November 2019.

15. Alice Park, "This Doctor Does Not Want to See You," *Time*, June 11, 2009.

16. Michael Porter and Elizabeth Teisburg, "Cleveland Clinic: Transformation and Growth 2015," Harvard Business School.

17. Porter and Teisburg, "Cleveland Clinic."

18. Gary Claxton et al., "Employer Health Benefits: 2019 Annual Survey," Kaiser Family Foundation, September 2019. Also see Rana Foroohar, "Healthcare Policy Is a Defining Issue for America," *Financial Times*, Nov. 10, 2019.

19. Melissa Thomasson interview on *All Things Considered*, "Accidents of History Created U.S. Health System," Oct. 22, 2009. Also see Mark J. Warshawsky, "Earnings Inequality: The Implications of the Rapidly Rising Cost of Employer-Provided Health Insurance," Mercatus Center (George Mason University), June 2016; and Rana Foroohar, "Employers Can Help Fix American Healthcare," *Financial Times*, March 19, 2017.

20. Rana Foroohar, "The American Way of Healthcare," *Financial Times*, Feb. 4, 2018.

21. Jeanna Smialek, "Powell Says Better Child Care Policies Might Lift Women in Work Force," *The New York Times*, Feb. 24, 2021.

22. Alissa Quart, *Squeezed: Why Our Families Can't Afford America* (New York: Ecco, 2018).

23. Quart, *Squeezed*. Also see Rana Foroohar, "The Decline of America's Middle Classes," *Financial Times*, June 22, 2018.

24. Author interview with Janet Yellen, 2014. Also see Rana Foroohar, "Janet Yellen: The Sixteen Trillion Dollar Woman," *Time*, Jan. 20, 2014; and Rana Foroohar, "Janet Yellen Is the Right Woman for the Times," *Financial Times*, Nov. 29, 2020.

25. Rana Foroohar, "A World Without Work—How AI Will Hit Employment," *Financial Times*, Jan. 3, 2020. Also see Daniel Susskind, *A World Without Work: Technology, Automation and How We Should Respond* (London: Allen Lane, 2020).

26. Michael J. Sandel, *The Tyranny of Merit: What's Become of the Common Good?* (New York: Farrar, Straus and Giroux, 2020). Also see Rana Foroohar, "Why Meritocracy Isn't Working," *Financial Times*, Sept. 3, 2020.

27. Hiltonsmith, "At What Cost?"

28. Bryan Caplan, "The World Might Be Better Off Without College for Everyone," *The Atlantic*, January/February 2018.

29. Hugh Son, "Jamie Dimon Says We've Split the U.S. Economy, Leaving the Poor Behind," CNBC, March 18, 2019.

30. Dominic Russel et al., "The Financialization of Higher Education," Roosevelt Institute, Sept. 19, 2016.

31. "Carnegie Mellon, Heinz Endowments Launch Initiative to Promote Economic Empowerment, Address Inequities in Pittsburgh Region," press release, Carnegie Mellon University and the Heinz Endowments, April 28, 2021.

32. Author interview with Illah Nourbakhsh, 2021.

Chapter 12: Chip Wars

1. James Manyika et al., "Digital Globalization: The New Era of Digital Flows," McKinsey Global Institute, March 2016.

2. "The Digital Acceleration," Wilson Center, Feb. 4, 2021.

3. Gillian Tett, "Reports of Globalisation's Death Are Greatly Exaggerated," *Financial Times,* Dec. 3, 2020.

4. Rory Green, "Superpower Chip Competition," TS Lombard, April 13, 2021.

5. Antonio Varas et al., "Strengthening the Global Semiconductor Supply Chain in an Uncertain Era," Boston Consulting Group, April 1, 2021.

6. The White House, "Building Resilient Supply Chains, Revitalizing American Manufacturing, and Fostering Broad-Based Growth," 100-Day Reviews Under Executive Order 14017, The White House, June 2021, p. 34.

7. The White House, "Building Resilient Supply Chains," p. 22.

8. The White House, "Building Resilient Supply Chains," p. 39.

9. The White House, "Building Resilient Supply Chains," p. 37.

10. The White House, "Building Resilient Supply Chains," p. 35.

11. The White House, "Building Resilient Supply Chains," p. 26.

12. Asa Fitch, "Chip Shortages Are Starting to Hit Consumers. Higher Prices Are Likely," *The Wall Street Journal,* June 21, 2021.

13. Blunt and Gold, "PG&E Knew for Years Its Lines Could Spark Wildfires, and Didn't Fix Them."

14. Deborah Pretty, "Respecting the Grey Swan: 40 Years of Reputation Crises," Aon and Pentland Analytics, April 15, 2021. Also see Rana Foroohar, "Wanted: A Resiliency Tsar for the U.S. Government," *Financial Times,* May 23, 2021.

15. The White House, "Building Resilient Supply Chains," p. 9.

16. The White House, "Building Resilient Supply Chains," p. 158.

17. Rana Foroohar, "Brian Deese on Biden's Vision for 'a Twenty-First-Century American Industrial Strategy,'" author interview with Deese for Atlantic Council event, June 23, 2021.

18. Foroohar, "Brian Deese on Biden's Vision."

19. Author interview with Don Rosenberg, 2021.

20. The White House, "Building Resilient Supply Chains."

21. Author interview with James Manyika, 2021. Also see Manyika et al., "Building a More Competitive U.S. Manufacturing Sector."

22. Michael Wayland, "General Motors Plans to Exclusively Offer Electric Vehicles by 2035," CNBC, Jan. 28, 2021.

23. Noam Scheiber, "The Biden Team Wants to Transform the Economy. Really," *The New York Times,* Feb. 11, 2021.

24. Emily Brooks, "Rubio Speech to House Conservatives Marks Free-Market Evangelism's Decline," *Washington Examiner,* May 12, 2021.

25. James Manyika et al., "Innovation and National Security: Keeping Our Edge," Council on Foreign Relations, September 2019.

26. Varas et al., "Strengthening the Global Semiconductor Supply Chain in an Uncertain Era." Also see Rana Foroohar, "Competition and Concentration," *Financial Times,* June 21, 2021.

27. Barry C. Lynn, *Liberty from All Masters* (New York: Macmillan, 2020).

28. Foroohar, "Brian Deese on Biden's Vision."

29. Author interview with Deborah Elms, 2021.

30. Madhumita Murgia and Anna Gross, "Inside China's Controversial Mission to Reinvent the Internet," *Financial Times,* March 27, 2020.

31. Adrian Shahbaz, "The Rise of Digital Authoritarianism," Freedom House, Oct. 18, 2018. Also see Rana Foroohar, "China's Xi Jinping Is No Davos Man," *Financial Times,* Jan. 20, 2019.

32. Office of the United States Trade Representative, "Economic and Trade Agreement Between the Government of the United States of America and the Government of the People's Republic of China: Phase One," USTR, Jan. 15, 2020. Also see Foroohar, "China Wants to Decouple from U.S. Tech, Too."

33. Tambiama Madiega, "E.U. Guidelines on Ethics in Artificial Intelligence," European Parliamentary Research Service, September 2019.

34. The White House, "U.S.-EU Trade and Technology Council Inaugural Joint Statement," Statements and Releases, The White House, Sept. 29, 2021.

35. President Joe Biden, "Remarks by President Biden on America's Place in the World," The White House, Feb. 4, 2021. Also see Rana Foroohar, "Wishful Thinking on China Will Not Serve American Interests," *Financial Times,* March 7, 2021.

36. China Power Project, "How Well-Off Is China's Middle Class?," Center for Strategic and International Studies, Sept. 30, 2021.

37. Martin Wolf, "China Is Wrong to Think the U.S. Faces Inevitable Decline," *Financial Times,* April 27, 2021.

38. Jose M. Plehn-Dujowich, "Product Innovations by Young and Small Firms," Plehn Analytical Economic Solutions, May 2013.

39. Organisation for Economic Co-operation and Development, "The Future of Corporate Governance in Capital Markets Following the COVID-19 Crisis," OECD report, June 30, 2021.

40. Jan Eeckhout, *The Profit Paradox* (Princeton, N.J.: Princeton University Press, 2021).

Chapter 13: Companies Versus Countries

1. Manyika et al., "A New Look at How Corporations Impact the Economy and Households." Also see Rana Foroohar, "Five Lessons from 25 Years of Corporate Wealth Creation," *Financial Times,* May 30, 2020.

2. Stephanie Segal, "Degrees of Separation: A Targeted Approach to U.S.-China Decoupling—Interim Report," Center for Strategic and International Studies, Feb. 3, 2021.

3. Yeling Tan, "How the WTO Changed China," *Foreign Affairs,* March/April 2021.

4. Giacomo Tognini, "The Countries with the Most Billionaires 2021," *Forbes,* April 6, 2021. Also see UBS's Billionaires Report 2020, "Riding the Storm."

5. David Barboza, "Billions in Hidden Riches for Family of Chinese Leader," *The New York Times,* Oct. 25, 2012.

6. Daron Acemoglu et al., "Import Competition and the Great Employment Sag of the 2000s," *Journal of Labor Economics,* January 2016.

7. David Dollar, "U.S.-China Trade War Has Its Seeds in the Financial Crisis," Brookings Institution, Sept. 14, 2018.

8. Author interview with George Soros, 2009.

9. Rana Foroohar, "Six Myths About China," *Newsweek,* Oct. 16, 2009.

10. Tan, "How the WTO Changed China."

11. Segal, "Degrees of Separation."

12. Rana Foroohar, *Don't Be Evil: How Big Tech Betrayed Its Founding Principles—and All of Us* (New York: Currency, 2019).

13. C. Miller et al., "People, Power and Technology: The 2020 Digital Attitudes Report," Doteveryone, May 2020. Also see Rana Foroohar, "Big Tech's Viral Boom Could Be Its Undoing," *Financial Times,* May 17, 2020.

14. Wilson Chow, "The Global Economic Impact of 5G," PricewaterhouseCoopers, June 2021.

15. Joel West, "Before Qualcomm: Linkabit and the Origins of San Diego's Telecom Industry," *The Journal of San Diego History,* Winter /Spring 2009. Also see "The Man Behind a Billion Connections," at Qualcomm.com.

16. Patrick Moorhead, "A Chat with Qualcomm's Licensing Business Leader, John Han," *Forbes*, Nov. 19, 2021. Also see Rana Foroohar, "How Big Tech Is Dragging Us Towards the Next Financial Crash," *The Guardian*, Nov. 8, 2019.

17. Will Croft and Joss Gillet, "Quarterly World Review: Q1 2009," GSMA Intelligence, June 2009. Also see Mark A. Lemley and Timothy Simcoe, "How Essential Are Standard-Essential Patents?," *Cornell Law Review*, March 2019.

18. Tripp Mickle and Asa Fitch, "Apple and Qualcomm's Billion-Dollar Staredown," *The Wall Street Journal*, April 13, 2019. Also see Shara Tibken, "Apple's 5G iPhone Shift Bogged Down by Qualcomm Chip Battle," CNET, Jan. 14, 2019; and Shara Tibken, "Apple and Qualcomm Settle: Here's What It Means for Your Next iPhone," CNET, April 16, 2019.

19. Christiaan Hetzner, "Intel's $5.4 Billion Foundry Acquisition Hopes to Catch Its Fabless Chip Rivals Flat-Footed," *Fortune*, Feb. 15, 2022.

20. Klint Finley, "The FTC Thinks You Pay Too Much for Smartphones. Here's Why," *Wired*, Jan. 12, 2019. Also see Mickle and Fitch, "Apple and Qualcomm's Billion-Dollar Staredown."

21. Federal Trade Commission, "FTC Charges Qualcomm with Monopolizing Key Semiconductor Device Used in Cell Phones," press release, FTC, Jan. 17, 2017.

22. Aaron Tilley, "Qualcomm's Profit Tanks 40% as Legal Fight with Apple Drags On," *Forbes*, July 19, 2017.

23. Ana Swanson and Alexandra Stevenson, "Qualcomm May Be Collateral Damage in a U.S.-China Trade War," April 18, 2018. Also see Rana Foroohar, "One World, Two Systems in the 5G Race," *Financial Times*, Feb. 17, 2020.

24. Tom Mitchell, "China Has the Upper Hand in Corporate Proxy Wars with U.S.," *Financial Times*, Sept. 22, 2020.

25. Jack Nicas et al., "Censorship, Surveillance and Profits: A Hard Bargain for Apple in China," *The New York Times*, May 17, 2021.

26. Richard Waters, "Chipmaker Broadcom Is Behaving Like a Private Equity Firm," *Financial Times*, July 4, 2019.

27. Jack Nicas et al., "Censorship, Surveillance and Profits: A Hard Bargain for Apple in China," *The New York Times*, May 17, 2021.

28. Kadhim Shubber, "U.S. Regulators Face Off in Court Tussle over Qualcomm," *Financial Times*, Feb. 9, 2020. Also see Kadhim Shubber, "Trump Administration Steps Up Push to Sway Antitrust Cases," *Financial Times*, Jan. 20, 2020.

29. Author interviews and translations of local media by the *Financial Times*'s Hong Kong bureau.

30. Jimmy O'Donnell et al., "The Startup Surge? Unpacking 2020 Trends in Business Formation," Economic Innovation Group blog, Feb. 8, 2021.

31. Office of Senator Mark Warner, "Warner and Daines Introduce Legislation to Establish an Emergency Portable Benefits Fund," press release, July 22, 2020.

32. Heather Kelly, "Companies Use Your Data to Make Money. California Thinks You Should Get Paid," CNN Business, Feb. 13, 2019.

33. See Jamie Dimon's JPMorgan shareholder letters for fiscal years 2019 and 2020.

34. Rana Foroohar, "Creative Destruction Is the Silver Lining of the Covid-19 Crisis," *Financial Times*, May 9, 2021.

35. Center for Strategic and International Studies, "Year-End Reflections on 2020 with Dr. Anthony Fauci," online event moderated by J. Stephen Morrison, senior vice president and director of the CSIS Global Health Policy Center, Dec. 14, 2020.

36. Leon S. Fuerth with Evan M. H. Faber, "Anticipatory Governance Practical Upgrades: Equipping the Executive Branch to Cope with Increasing Speed and Complexity of Major Challenges," National Defense University, October 2012.

37. Rana Foroohar, "Wanted: A Resiliency Tsar for the U.S. Government," *Financial Times*, May 23, 2021.

38. Mark Scott and Jacopo Barigazzi, "U.S. and Europe to Forge Tech Alliance amid China's Rise," Politico, June 9, 2021. Also see the transcript of the press briefing by Press Secretary Jen Psaki and National Security Advisor Jake Sullivan, June 7, 2021.

39. Javier Espinoza, "Brussels Looks to Impose Two-Tier Big Tech Regulation," *Financial Times*, Dec. 4, 2020.

Chapter 14: Digital Power to the People

1. Author interview with Audrey Tang, 2020.

2. Author interview with Audrey Tang.

3. Audrey Tang, "A Strong Democracy Is a Digital Democracy," *The New York Times*, Oct. 15, 2019.

4. Author interview with Audrey Tang.

5. Author interview with Audrey Tang.

6. Author interview with Glen Weyl, 2020.

7. Author interview with Chris Hansen, 2020. Also see Rana Foroohar, "Digital Tools Can Be a Useful Bolster to Democracy," *Financial Times*, Feb. 16, 2020.

8. David Furlonger et al., "Digital Disruption Profile: Blockchain's Radical Promise Spans Business and Society," Gartner Research, Feb. 13, 2018.

9. Brian K. Unwin and Paul E. Tatum, "House Calls," *American Family Physician*, April 15, 2011.

10. Robin Gelburd, "Telehealth Claim Lines Increased 4132% Nationally from June 2019 to June 2020," *American Journal of Managed Care*, Sept. 3, 2020.

11. Sara Nourazari et al., "Decreased Hospital Admissions Through Emergency Departments During the COVID-19 Pandemic," *The American Journal of Emergency Medicine*, April 2021.

12. Yibo Wang et al., "Smart Grids Innovation Challenge Country Report 2019," Mission Innovation, May 2019.

13. Brief on decentralized technology, 13D Global Strategy and Research, Oct. 8, 2020.

14. Author interview with Shiv Malik, 2020.

15. Eric Posner and Glen Weyl, *Radical Markets* (Princeton, N.J.: Princeton University Press, 2019).

16. Wingham Rowan, "Remaking the Modern Market," American Compass, June 2021.

17. Author interview with Wingham Rowan, 2021.

18. Author interview with Nick Schultz, 2021.

19. One of the most interesting efforts on this front was started by the Markle Foundation, which runs a skills-based jobs platform in Colorado.

Chapter 15: Think Global, Build Local

1. Global Alliance for Buildings and Construction, *Global Status Report 2017*, UN Environment Programme, December 2017.

2. U.S. Energy Information Administration, "Frequently Asked Questions," May 2021. Also see the EIA's "Monthly Energy Review."

3. Global Alliance for Buildings and Construction, *Global Status Report 2017*.

4. Goran Runeson and Gerard de Valence, "Globalisation in Construction," academic paper presented at the International Council for Research and Innovation in Building and Construction Joint International Symposium in 2009.

5. Rana Foroohar, "The U.S. Needs to Make Homes More Affordable—and Available," *Financial Times*, Sept. 12, 2021.

6. Coby Lefkowitz, "Why Everywhere Looks the Same," Medium, April 28, 2021.

7. Alex Viega, "Companies Step Up Buying Houses, Bet on Hot Housing Market," *U.S. News & World Report*, Sept. 9, 2021.

8. Jonathan Woetzel, "The Rise and Rise of the Global Balance Sheet: How Productively Are We Using Our Wealth?," McKinsey Global Institute, Nov. 15, 2021.

9. Woetzel, "The Rise and Rise of the Global Balance Sheet."

10. Joyce M. Rosenberg, "Changes Made in Way Houses Built: Construction Differs from the Post–World War II Era," *Los Angeles Times*, Oct. 4, 1987.

11. Xuefei Ren, *Building Globalization Transnational Architecture Production in Urban China* (Chicago: University of Chicago Press, 2011).

12. Jose Luis Blanco et al., "Call for Action: Seizing the Decarbonization Opportunity in Construction," McKinsey and Company, July 14, 2021.

13. Author interview with Jason Ballard, 2021.

14. Jens Burchardt, "Supply Chains as a Game-Changer in the Fight Against Climate Change," Boston Consulting Group, Jan. 26, 2021.

15. Kamin, "How an 11-Foot-Tall 3-D Printer Is Helping to Create a Community."

16. Author interview with Bas Menheere and other UNSense staff, 2020.

17. Author interview with Menheere and other UNSense staff. Also see Joann Plockova, "A 'Smart District' Takes Shape in the Netherlands," *The New York Times*, July 24, 2020.

18. Author interview with Deborah Pretty, 2021. Also see Rana Foroohar, "Storms Await Companies That Err on Climate," *Financial Times*, June 13, 2021.

19. U.S. Securities and Exchange Commission, "SEC Proposes Rules to Enhance and Standardize Climate-Related Disclosures for Investors," March 21, 2022.

Chapter 16: Where Do We Go from Here?

1. Charles Mitchell et al., "C-Suite Outlook 2022: Reset and Reimagine," The Conference Board, Jan. 13, 2022.

2. Camille Squires, "These Are the States Where Most Americans Moved in 2021," *Quartz*, Dec. 23, 2021.

3. World Population Review, "Job Growth by State 2021."

4. Frank Van Riper, "Ford to City: Drop Dead," *Daily News*, Oct. 30, 1975.

5. Ginia Bellafante, "Why SoHo Struggles and Indie Shops in Brooklyn Are Doing Fine," *The New York Times*, Feb. 12, 2021.

6. Astead W. Herndon and Shane Goldmacher, "Democrats Thought They Bottomed Out in Rural, White America. It Wasn't the Bottom," *The New York Times*, Nov. 6, 2021.

7. Jane Jacobs, *The Death and Life of Great American Cities* (New York: Ran-

dom House, 1961). Also see Jane Jacobs, "Downtown Is for People," *Fortune,* April 1958.

8. Diane Cardwell, "Mayor Says New York Is Worth the Cost," *The New York Times,* Jan. 8, 2003.

9. Jacobs, *The Death and Life of Great American Cities,* p. 148.

10. Rana Foroohar, "60 Years Ago Jane Jacobs Changed the Way We See Cities. She May Do It Again," *Financial Times,* July 9, 2021.

Bibliography

Boushey, Heather. *Unbound: How Inequality Constricts Our Economy and What We Can Do About It*. Cambridge, Mass.: Harvard University Press, 2019.

Breznitz, Dan. *Innovation in Real Places: Strategies for Prosperity in an Unforgiving World*. Oxford, U.K.: Oxford University Press, 2021.

Eeckhout, Jan. *The Profit Paradox: How Thriving Firms Threaten the Future of Work*. Princeton, N.J.: Princeton University Press, 2021.

Ferguson, Niall. *The Square and the Tower: Networks and Power, from the Freemasons to Facebook*. New York: Penguin Press, 2017.

Fletcher, Ian. *Free Trade Doesn't Work: What Should Replace It and Why*. Sheffield, Mass.: Coalition for a Prosperous America, 2011.

Foroohar, Rana. *Don't Be Evil: How Big Tech Betrayed Its Founding Principles—and All of Us*. New York: Currency, 2019.

———. *Makers and Takers: The Rise of Finance and the Fall of American Business*. New York: Crown Business, 2016.

Friedman, Thomas L. *The Lexus and the Olive Tree: Understanding Globalization*. New York: Farrar, Straus and Giroux, 1999.

———. *The World Is Flat: A Brief History of the Twenty-first Century*. New York: Farrar, Straus and Giroux, 2005.

Fukuyama, Francis. *The End of History and the Last Man*. New York: Free Press, 1992.

Garten, Jeffrey E. *Three Days at Camp David: How a Secret Meeting in 1971 Transformed the Global Economy*. New York: HarperCollins, 2021.

Goodhart, Charles, and Pradhan, Manoj. *The Great Demographic Reversal: Ageing Societies, Waning Inequality, and an Inflation Revival*. Cham, Switzerland: Palgrave Macmillan, 2020.

Goodhart, David. *Head, Hand, Heart: The Struggle for Dignity and Status in the 21st Century*. New York: Free Press, 2020.

———. *The Road to Somewhere: The Populist Revolt and the Future of Politics.* London: C. Hurst, 2017.

Gruber, Jonathan, and Simon Johnson. *Jump-Starting America: How Breakthrough Science Can Revive Economic Growth and the American Dream.* New York: PublicAffairs, 2019.

Hewitt, Ben. *The Town That Food Saved: How One Community Found Vitality in Local Food.* Emmaus, Penn.: Rodale Books, 2010.

Hochschild, Adam. *Bury the Chains: Prophets and Rebels in the Fight to Free an Empire's Slaves.* Boston: Houghton Mifflin, 2005.

Hyman, Mark. *Food Fix: How to Save Our Health, Our Economy, Our Communities, and Our Planet—One Bite at a Time.* New York: Little, Brown, 2020.

Inglis, David, and Debra Gimlin. *The Globalization of Food.* Oxford, U.K.: Berg, 2009.

Jacobs, Jane. *The Death and Life of Great American Cities.* New York: Random House, 1961.

Janeway, William. *Doing Capitalism in the Innovation Economy.* Cambridge, U.K.: Cambridge University Press, 2012.

Judis, John B. *The Nationalist Revival: Trade, Immigration, and the Revolt Against Globalization.* New York: Columbia Global Reports, 2018.

Katz, Bruce, and Jeremy Nowak. *The New Localism: How Cities Can Thrive in the Age of Populism.* Washington, D.C.: Brookings Institution Press, 2017.

Klein, Matthew C., and Michael Pettis. *Trade Wars Are Class Wars: How Rising Inequality Distorts the Global Economy and Threatens International Peace.* New Haven, Conn.: Yale University Press, 2020.

Lassus, Renaud. *The Revival of Democracy in America and the Better Angels of Your Nature: Letter from a European Friend.* Paris: Éditions Odile Jacob, 2021.

Levinson, Marc. *Outside the Box: How Globalization Changed from Moving Stuff to Spreading Ideas.* Princeton, N.J.: Princeton University Press, 2020.

Lind, Michael. *The New Class War: Saving Democracy from the Managerial Elite.* London: Portfolio/Penguin, 2020.

Lynn, Barry C. *End of the Line: The Rise and Coming Fall of the Global Corporation.* New York: Doubleday, 2005.

———. *Liberty from All Masters: The New American Autocracy vs. the Will of the People.* New York: St. Martin's Press, 2020.

Mandler, Peter. *The Crisis of the Meritocracy: Britain's Transition to Mass Education Since the Second World War.* Oxford, U.K.: Oxford University Press, 2020.

Markovits, Daniel. *The Meritocracy Trap: How America's Foundational Myth*

Feeds Inequality, Dismantles the Middle Class, and Devours the Elite. New York: Penguin Press, 2019.

Müller, Jan-Werner. *Contesting Democracy: Political Ideas in Twentieth-Century Europe.* New Haven, Conn.: Yale University Press, 2011.

Norberg-Hodge, Helena. *Local Is Our Future: Steps to an Economics of Happiness.* East Hardwick, Vt.: Local Futures, 2019.

Osman, Suleiman. *The Invention of Brownstone Brooklyn: Gentrification and the Search for Authenticity in Postwar New York.* Oxford, U.K.: Oxford University Press, 2011.

O'Sullivan, Michael. *The Levelling: What's Next After Globalization.* New York: PublicAffairs, 2019.

Petrou, Karen. *Engine of Inequality: The Fed and the Future of Wealth in America.* Hoboken, N.J.: John Wiley and Sons, 2021.

Philippon, Thomas. *The Great Reversal: How America Gave Up on Free Markets.* Cambridge, Mass.: Harvard University Press, 2019.

Piketty, Thomas. *Capital in the Twenty-First Century.* Cambridge, Mass.: Belknap Press, 2014.

Pisano, Gary P., and Willy C. Shih. *Producing Prosperity: Why America Needs a Manufacturing Renaissance.* Cambridge, Mass.: Harvard Business Review Press, 2012.

Polanyi, Karl. *The Great Transformation: The Political and Economic Origins of Our Time.* New York: Farrar and Rinehart, 1944.

Posner, Eric A., and E. Glen Weyl. *Radical Markets: Uprooting Capitalism and Democracy for a Just Society.* Princeton, N.J.: Princeton University Press, 2018.

Prestowitz, Clyde. *The World Turned Upside Down: America, China, and the Struggle for Global Leadership.* New Haven, Conn.: Yale University Press, 2021.

Quart, Alissa. *Squeezed: Why Our Families Can't Afford America.* New York: HarperCollins, 2019.

Rajan, Raghuram. *The Third Pillar: How Markets and the State Leave the Community Behind.* New York: Penguin Press, 2019.

Sandel, Michael J. *Democracy's Discontent: America in Search of a Public Philosophy.* Cambridge, Mass.: Belknap Press, 1996.

———. *The Tyranny of Merit: What's Become of the Common Good?* New York: Farrar, Straus and Giroux, 2020.

Sitaraman, Ganesh. *The Great Democracy: How to Fix Our Politics, Unrig the Economy, and Unite America.* New York: Basic Books, 2019.

Slobodian, Quinn. *Globalists: The End of Empire and the Birth of Neoliberalism.* Cambridge, Mass.: Harvard University Press, 2018.

Stiglitz, Joseph E. *Globalization and Its Discontents*. New York: W. W. Norton, 2002.

Susskind, Daniel. *A World Without Work: Technology, Automation and How We Should Respond*. London: Allen Lane, 2020.

Vance, Ashlee. *Elon Musk: Tesla, SpaceX, and the Quest for a Fantastic Future*. New York: HarperCollins, 2017.

Waters, Alice. *We Are What We Eat: A Slow Food Manifesto*. New York: Penguin Press, 2021.

Winant, Gabriel. *The Next Shift: The Fall of Industry and the Rise of Health Care in Rust Belt America*. Cambridge, Mass.: Harvard University Press, 2021.

Woolf, Steven H., and Laudan Aron. *U.S. Health in International Perspective: Shorter Lives, Poorer Health*. Washington, D.C.: National Academies Press, 2013.

Zuboff, Shoshana. *The Age of Surveillance Capitalism: The Fight for a Human Future at the New Frontier of Power*. New York: PublicAffairs, 2019.

Index

RANA FOROOHAR is the author of *Don't Be Evil,* winner of the 2019 Porchlight Business Book of the Year award, and of *Makers and Takers.* Currently CNN's global economic analyst and the global business columnist and associate editor for the *Financial Times,* she has served as the assistant managing editor and economics columnist at *Time* and as economics and foreign affairs editor and a foreign correspondent at *Newsweek.* She is a life member of the Council on Foreign Relations, and sits on the board of the Open Markets Institute.

ranaforoohar.com

Available from

RANA FOROOHAR

"Rana Foroohar
is a beacon
of insight in
the world of
financial
journalism."

—ROGER McNAMEE,
New York Times bestselling
author of *Zucked: Waking Up to
the Facebook Catastrophe*